MW01009380

Twentieth-Century Science | **Space and Astronomy**

Decade by Decade

Twentieth-Century Science | **Space and Astronomy**

Decade by Decade

Marianne J. Dyson

Set Editor: William J. Cannon

Facts On File

An imprint of Infobase Publishing

SPACE AND ASTRONOMY: Decade by Decade

Copyright © 2007 by Marianne J. Dyson

Facts On File, Inc.
An imprint of Infobase Publishing
132 West 31st Street
New York NY 10001

ISBN-10: 0–8160–5536–X
ISBN-13: 978-0–8160-5536-4

Library of Congress Cataloging-in-Publication Data

Dyson, Marianne J.
Space and astronomy : decade by decade / Marianne J. Dyson.
p. cm. — (Twentieth-century science)
Includes bibliographical references and index.
ISBN 0–8160–5536–X (acid-free paper)
1. Astronomy—History—20th century. 2. Space flight—History—20th century.
I. Title. II. Series.
QB32.D97 2007
520.9'04—dc22   2006012547

Facts On File books are available at special discounts when purchased in bulk quantities for businesses, associations, institutions, or sales promotions. Please call our Special Sales Department in New York at (212) 967-8800 or (800) 322-8755.

You can find Facts On File on the World Wide Web at http://www.factsonfile.com

Text design by Dorothy M. Preston and Kerry Casey
Cover design by Dorothy M. Preston and Salvatore Luongo
Illustrations by Bobbi McCutcheon
Photo research by Elizabeth H. Oakes

Printed in the United States of America

VB Hermitage 10 9 8 7 6 5 4 3 2 1

This book is printed on acid-free paper.

Contents

Preface xi

Acknowledgments xv

Introduction xvii

1. *1901–1910:*
   Development of a New Astronomy 1
   Milestones. 2
   The Canals of Mars 3
   The Equation for Space. 9
   The Rocket Equation *10*
   A New Astronomy 11
   Impacts and Omens 15
   Scientist of the Decade: Percival Lowell (1855–1916) *16*
   Further Reading 18

2. *1911–1920:*
   Giant Stars and General Relativity 20
   Milestones. 20
   The Size of Stars 23
   The Structure of Stars 28
   Changing View of the Universe 31
   Cosmology 35
   Scientist of the Decade: Henry Norris Russell (1877–1957). *38*
   Further Reading 41

3. *1921–1930:*
   The Expanding Universe **43**
   Milestones. 44
   Nebulae Become Galaxies 44
   The Hydrogen Question 51
   The Matter of Stars 54
   Planet X 56
   Rockets around the World. 58

     Tsiolkovsky's Plan of Space Exploration *60*

     Scientist of the Decade: Edwin Powell Hubble (1889–1953) *64*

  Further Reading 66

4. ***1931–1940:***
  Understanding What Makes Stars Shine and Rockets Fly **68**

  Milestones 68

  New "Eyes" on the Universe 70

  From Giants to Black Holes 73

  How Stars Shine 74

  The Development of Modern Rockets 78

     Flash Gordon *and* War of the Worlds *78*

     Scientist of the Decade: Robert Hutchings Goddard (1882–1945) *84*

  Further Reading 87

5. ***1941–1950:***
  From War to Space **89**

  Milestones 90

  The Pathway to Space Begins with Weapons 90

  Postwar Rocket Development 96

  Postwar Russian Rocket Development 97

  The First Science Rockets 99

  Wartime Astronomy 100

  Synthesis of the Elements 102

     Astronomical Peace Dividend *105*

     Scientist of the Decade: Wernher Magnus Maximilian Freiherr von

     Braun (1912–1977) *106*

  Radio and Solar System Discoveries 108

  Further Reading 109

6. ***1951–1960:***
  The Dawn of the Space Age **111**

  Milestones 112

  The Mystery of Radio Stars 112

The Elements of Life...116
Origin of the Solar System 118
Preparation for Manned Space Programs..........................120
New Improved Rockets..121
Satellites for Politics and Science 123
Flying to the Moon 128
Project Mercury..129
   Scientist of the Decade: Sergei Pavlovich Korolev (1907–1966)..........*132*
   Mercury Facts...*134*
Further Reading..134

7. *1961–1970*:
Putting Humans on the Moon..............................136
Milestones...136
The First People in Space 139
A Rendezvous with the Moon 142
Voskhod and Gemini 146
Probes and Satellites 148
Tragedy in 1967 150
Resumption of the Race..152
The Race Is Won 153
The Waning Moon 155
X-ray and Neutrino Astronomy 157
Quasars and Pulsars 158
Abundant Support for the Big Bang Theory 161
   Scientist of the Decade: Robert Rowe Gilruth (1913–2000)..............*162*
Further Reading..164

8. *1971–1980*:
From the Moon to Jupiter 167
Milestones...168
Roving around the Moon 168
The First Space Stations 171
From Apollo-Soyuz to Shuttles..................................174

Long-Duration Spaceflight 175
Deserted Mars 178
Picturing Venus 180
Exploring the Giants 181
Observing Space. 184
    Scientist of the Decade: Carl Edward Sagan (1934–1996) *186*
Further Reading. 188

9. 1981–1990:
Laboratories in Space **190**
Space Transportation System. 191
Milestones. 192
    Shuttle Flight Numbering System *197*
Challenger's Last Flight. 197
Return to Flight 199
Russian Space—From *Salyut* to *Mir* 200
The Moon, Venus, Mars, and Comets 203
Voyage to Uranus and Neptune 205
State of the Universe 207
    Scientist of the Decade: Vera Cooper Rubin (1928–) *210*
Further Reading. 213

10. 1991–2000:
Space Telescopes and Stations **215**
Milestones. 216
Research and Records 216
New Life in Moon/Mars Research 221
    Lunar Burial of Eugene Shoemaker *221*
No Little Green Men 222
Asteroids, Comets, and Extrasolar Planets 224
Space Observatories. 228
International Space 231
    Scientist of the Decade: Geoffrey Marcy (1954–) *236*
Further Reading. 239

Conclusion **241**
New Worlds 245
Further Reading 248

Bruce Medalists **249**
Glossary **262**
Further Resources **265**
Index **267**

Preface

The 20th century has witnessed an explosive growth in science and technology—more scientists are alive today than have lived during the entire course of earlier human history. New inventions including spaceships, computer chips, lasers, and recombinant DNA have opened pathways to new fields such as space science, biotechnology, and nanotechnology. Modern seismographs and submarines have given earth and ocean scientists insights into the planet's deepest and darkest secrets. Decades of weather science, aided by satellite observations and computer modeling, now produce long-term, global forecasts with high probabilities (not certainties) of being correct. At the start of the century, science and technology had little impact on the daily lives of most people. This had changed radically by the year 2000.

The purpose of Twentieth-Century Science, a new seven-volume set, is to provide students, teachers, and the general public with an accessible and highly readable source for understanding how science developed, decade-by-decade, during the century and hints about where it will go during the early decades of the 21st century. Just as an educated and well-informed person should have exposure to great literature, art, music, and an appreciation for history, business, and economics, so, too, should that person appreciate how science works and how it has become so much a part of our daily lives.

Students are usually taught science from the perspective of what is currently known. In one sense, this is quite understandable—there is a great deal of information to master. However, very often, a student (or teacher) may ask questions such as "How did they know that?" or "Why didn't they know that?" This is where some historical perspective makes for fascinating reading. It gives a feeling for the dynamic aspect of science. Some of what students are taught today will change in 20 years. It also provides a sense of humility as one sees how brilliantly scientists coped earlier in the century with less funding, cruder tools, and less sophisticated theories.

Science is distinguished from other equally worthy and challenging human endeavors by its means of investigation—the Scientific Method—typically described as:

a) observations

b) hypothesis

c) experimentation with controls

d) results, and

e) conclusions concerning whether or not the results and data from the experiments invalidate or support the hypothesis.

In practice, the scientific process is not quite so "linear." Many related experiments may also be explored to test the hypothesis. Once a body of scientific evidence has been collected and checked, the scientist submits a paper, reporting the new work to a peer-reviewed journal. An impartial editor will send the work to at least two reviewers ("referees") who are experts in that particular field, and they recommend to the editor whether the paper should be accepted, modified, or rejected. Since expert reviewers are sometimes the author's competitors, high ethical standards and confidentiality must be the rule during the review process.

If a hypothesis cannot be tested and potentially disproved by experiment or mathematical equations, it is not scientific. While, in principle, one experiment can invalidate a hypothesis, no number of validating experiments can absolutely prove a hypothesis to be "The Truth." However, if repeated testing using varied and challenging experiments by diverse scientists continues to validate a hypothesis, it starts to assume the status of a widely accepted theory. The best friend a theory can have is an outstanding scientist who doubts it and subjects it to rigorous and honest testing. If it survives these challenges and makes a convert of the skeptical scientist, then the theory is strengthened significantly. Such testing also weeds out hypotheses and theories that are weak. Continued validation of an important theory may give it the stature of a law, even though it is still called a theory. Some theories when developed can revolutionize a field's entire framework—these are considered to be "paradigms" (pronounced "paradimes"). Atomic theory is a paradigm. Advanced about 200 years ago, it is fundamental to understanding the nature of matter. Other such paradigms include evolution; the big bang theory; and the modern theory of plate tectonics, which explains the origin of mountains, volcanoes, and earthquakes; quantum theory; and relativity.

Science is a collective enterprise with the need for free exchange of information and cooperation. While it is true that scientists have strong competitive urges, the latter half of the 20th century has witnessed science becoming increasingly interdisciplinary. Ever more complex problems, with increasing uncertainty, are tackled and yet often elude precise solution.

During the 20th century, science found cures for tuberculosis and polio, and yet fears of the "dark side" of science (for example, atomic weapons) began to mount. Skepticism over the benefits of science and its applications started to emerge in the latter part of the 20th century even as its daily and positive impact upon our lives increased. Many scientists were sensitive to these issues as well. After atomic bombs devastated Hiroshima and Nagasaki, some distinguished physicists moved into the life sciences, and others started a magazine, now nearly 60 years old, *The*

Bulletin of the Atomic Scientists, dedicated to eliminating the nuclear threat and promoting peace. In 1975, shortly after molecular biologists developed recombinant DNA, they held a conference at Asilomar, California, and imposed voluntary limits on certain experiments. They encouraged adoption of regulations in this revolutionary new field. We are in an era where there are repeated and forceful attempts to blur the boundaries between religious faith and science. One argument is that fairness demands equal time for all "theories" (scientific or not). In all times, but especially in these times, scientists must strive to communicate to the public what science is and how it works, what is good science, what is bad science, and what is not science. Only then can we educate future generations of informed citizens and inspire the scientists of the future.

The seven volumes of Twentieth-Century Science deal with the following core areas of science: biology, chemistry, Earth science, marine science, physics, space and astronomy, and weather and climate. Each volume contains a glossary. The chapters within each volume contain the following elements:

- background and perspective for the science it develops, decade-by-decade, as well as insights about many of the major scientists contributing during each decade
- black-and-white line drawings and photographs
- a chronological time line of notable events during each decade
- brief biographical sketches of pioneering individuals, including discussion of their impacts on science and the society at large
- a list of accessible Further Resources

While all of the scientists profiled are distinguished, we do *not* mean to imply that they are necessarily "the greatest scientists of the decade." They have been chosen to represent the science of the decade because of their outstanding accomplishments. Some of these scientists were born to wealthy and distinguished families, while others were born to middle- and working-class families or into poverty. In a century marked by two world wars, the cold war, countless other wars large and small, and unimaginable genocide, many scientists were forced to flee their countries of birth. Fortunately, the century has also witnessed greater access to the scientific and engineering professions for women and people of color, and, hopefully, all barriers will disappear during the 21st century.

The authors of this set hope that readers appreciate the development of the sciences during the last century and the advancements occurring rapidly now in the 21st century. The history teaches new explorers of the world the benefits of making careful observations, of pursuing paths and ideas that others have neglected or have not ventured to tread, and of always questioning the world around them. Curiosity is one of our most fundamental human instincts. Science, whether done as a career or as a hobby, is, after all, an intensely human endeavor.

Acknowledgments

I will never forget where I was when *Apollo 11* landed on the Moon—at horseback-riding camp. After cleaning the stalls, I knelt in front of a black-and-white television at the ranch house to watch that "one small step." I fell in love with space even more than horses and was inspired to become the first woman in my family to graduate from college. I was fortunate enough to make my own "small step" in history and become one of the first women in Mission Control. I left NASA to raise my children and began to share my love of space through writing and speaking. When Fred Bortz (author of the *Physics* volume) approached me about taking on this book, I thought that with my background it would be relatively easy. The research for 100 years of history quickly made this former flight controller feel like that girl at camp who was surprised at how much work was involved in learning to ride and care for one small horse.

Thankfully, I had help. Fred Bortz supplied an initial time line and reviewed my early drafts. Agent Bill Cannon and editor Frank Darmstadt provided wise counsel and arranged to have the schedule extended to allow time for thorough research. Artist Bobbi McCutcheon was a genius at interpreting my sketches, and Beth Oakes professionally filled my photo requests. My fellow writers Carmen Bredeson and Christine Kohler provided advice and tips, along with members of the NFforKids Yahoo group. GoogleScholar.com saved me countless hours of searching for journal articles and biographical information. The members of the National Space Society (NSS) especially Jeffrey Liss, plus spacedaily.com and space.com, kept me up-to-date on happenings in space and astronomy.

My local library (Freeman Memorial) provided the books that were missing from my own collection, and librarian Marilyn Hopman graciously tracked down birth and death dates of dozens of people. Librarians, archivists, historians, engineers, and scientists kindly provided hard-to-find biographical and technical data and photos. Thanks to Daniel Tyson of the University of Wyoming, Dr. Katherine Collett of Hamilton College, Mott Linn of Clark University, Dr. David DeVorkin and Frank Winter of the National Air and Space Museum, Liesbeth van Iterson of the University of Amsterdam, Patrick Quinn of Northwestern

University, Shelly Kelly of the University of Houston, Dr. Rick Fisher of the National Radio Astronomy Observatory, Dr. Brent Tully of the Institute for Astronomy in Honolulu, Steve Vogt of the University of California, Walter Alvarez of the University of California-Berkeley, David S. McKay of Johnson Space Center, Kathie Thomas-Keprta of Johnson Space Center, Dr. John Huchra at the Harvard–Smithsonian Center for Astrophysics, Guy Thibodaux of the NASA Alumni League (NAL), John Lee of NAL, Norm Chaffee of NAL, Roger Weiss of SAIC, author Dr. Fred Ordway, Larry Wasserman of Lowell Observatory, Lonnie Jenkins of NAL, Stan Faber of NAL, Dr. Chris Kraft of NAL, Dr. Robert Wagoner of Stanford, Dr. Gil Levin of the Viking team, Dr. Geoffrey Marcy of the University of California–Berkeley, Dr. Adam Riess of STSCI, Dr. Saul Perlmutter of the University of California–Berkeley, Arthur Smith of NSS, Kyle Cudworth of Yerkes Observatory, Mike Gentry, Susan Erskin, and Gary Kitmacher of NASA.

I am ever grateful to my husband Thor, my mother, and other members of my family who put up with my lack of attention to their needs and patiently listened to me enthuse about gyroscopes and spectra. And finally, I wish to thank my Kuk Sool (martial art) instructors who showed me that I can do more than I think I can as long as I maintain a positive attitude and never give up. I hope to see them all stepping on the Moon someday.

Introduction

For thousands of years, humans have scanned the sky and charted the movement of celestial bodies. The daily and seasonal patterns of the Sun, the Moon, and the stars guided sailors home, dictated the timing of planting and harvesting, and became the focus of festivals, celebrations, and holidays. The appearance of *novae*, comets and storms of "shooting stars" lighting up the predawn hours, were interpreted as lucky signs, dire omens, or special messages from the gods. These practical and spiritual connections of astronomy with human activity motivated and inspired improvements in observations and technology that led to the understanding that ours is but one of billions of galaxies expanding through space and time and, yet, the only one we know of where life has risen up from the cradle of its world and walked on another.

Space and Astronomy is the decade-by-decade story of astronomers unraveling the mysteries of how the Sun shines, stars collapse into *black holes*, and the universe expands. It is the story of dreamers who designed rockets to reach space that were used for weapons of war, political tools, and finally to bring back knowledge of other worlds. This volume of the Twentieth Century Science set describes the progress of astronomy and the development of spaceflight decade by decade from 1901 to the year 2000.

There were no rocket scientists in 1901 and only about 300 practicing astronomers, most of them teachers. Six observatories were considered well equipped, and 12 had telescopes larger than 16 inches (40 cm). The largest telescope in the world was a 40-inch (1-m) refractor at Yerkes Observatory in Wisconsin. Reflecting telescopes had been invented in 1663 but were not in widespread use until after the 60-inch (1.5-m) telescope began to operate in 1908 on top of Mount Wilson in California. Radio communications, and thus radio telescopes, had not yet been invented. The first radio telescope was built in 1937. The performance of these telescopes were in turn surpassed throughout the century by larger telescopes that could detect all parts of the spectrum, with some operating in mines miles underground and others in arrays spread across interplanetary distances.

At the turn of the century, astronomers knew the basic orbital parameters, masses, and sizes of the planets out to Neptune (discovered in 1846). The rotation rates of these bodies were under investigation. The four largest moons of Jupiter had been discovered by Galileo Galilei

(1564–1642), and one other had been discovered since then (Amalthea in 1892). The two moons of Mars were found in 1877. Nine moons of Saturn were known (ninth found in 1893), four of Uranus, and one of Neptune. The big debate in astronomy focused on whether or not Mars harbored intelligent life that was capable of creating "canals," first mapped in 1877. This controversy and the improvements in astronomy that it motivated are the major topic of the first chapter.

The positions of the major stars were well known in 1901, having been cataloged by Tycho Brahe (1546–1601) hundreds of years earlier. The Greek Hipparchus (190–127 B.C.) had found that the stars move relative to one another, and in 1718, Edmund Halley (1656–1742) documented how much the stars had moved from the positions Hipparchus had recorded 2,000 years before. William Herschel (1738–1822) had measured the separations between 700 binary pairs and showed that some revolve around each other rather than just appearing close because of our look angle. But though their positions in the sky were known, only the distances to the very closest stars had been measured. Nova and supernova had been observed, but their connection to stellar evolution was not understood. The bright supernova (a term coined in 1885 to describe a nova in Andromeda that was 10,000 times brighter than any previously seen) was assumed to be bright because it was close to Earth. Improved telescopes and new ways of measuring distances revealed that stars come in different sizes and evolve over time. This is the major focus of chapter 2.

The "stretching" and "bunching" of light waves as they move away or toward an observer, called the Doppler effect, was discovered in 1842 and was applied to finding distances and rotations of objects in space in the early 20th century. The discovery that *variable stars* in star clusters (see photo below) had large Doppler shifts caused astronomers to revise their

Globular cluster Messier 15, about 40,000 light-years away in the Milky Way Halo, as seen by the Yerkes 40-inch (102-cm) refractor in a 200-minute exposure in 1900. The image covers a 9 × 9 arcminute area. (Original plate by G. Ritchey, Scan by Kyle Cudworth, Yerkes Observatory)

estimate of the size of the Milky Way from 10,000 light-years across to double that value (and later increase it 10 times). New telescopes permitted the discovery of variable stars in distant nebulae, showing that the Milky Way is not the only galaxy in the universe. Even more profound was the discovery, discussed in chapter 3, that the most distant nebulae are receding at the greatest speeds. This showed that the universe is expanding and provided major support for the new big bang theory of the origin of the universe.

The mystery of what makes the stars shine was perhaps the greatest astronomical breakthrough of the 20th century. It was generally accepted that the Sun was at least as old, or older, than the Earth. The discovery of radioactivity in 1896 led to a change in the estimated age of Earth from millions to billions of years. The most scientifically acceptable idea for the source of the Sun's energy was gravitational contraction, but this only provided energy for about 20 million years. How this problem was addressed and nuclear fusion discovered is covered in chapter 4. The answer to the energy question led to the investigation and understanding of how the elements are produced by stars and supernovae, a major topic in chapters 5 and 6.

Using rockets to fly into space was purely science fiction in 1901. Jules Verne had written *From the Earth to the Moon* in 1865, postulating that people would go to the Moon after being shot out of a giant cannon. Several key visionaries were inspired to turn that fiction into reality. Their work is described briefly in chapters 1 and 3 and in more detail beginning in chapter 4. The need for weapons in World War II drove the technological development of rockets described in chapter 5 that led directly to the launch of the first artificial satellite in 1957. The space race between the United States and the Soviet Union that culminated in the landing of *Apollo 11* on July 20, 1969, is the major topic of chapters 6 and 7.

The final chapters of the book describe advances in space technology, human achievements in space, and the use of space probes and observatories such as the *Hubble Space Telescope* to peer ever deeper into space (see photo at right). Chapter 8 focuses on the exploration of the outer planets and long-duration spaceflights aboard the first space stations. Chapter 9 describes the development and early flights of the space shuttle and the first missions to the Russian *Mir* space station. Chapter 10 details the first close-up looks at comets and asteroids and the discovery of the first planets around other stars.

The 20th century was a time of discovery and exploration in astronomy and space. The practical and spiritual connections of humans with the stars have taken on new and different meanings as a result. The finding that most of the universe is invisible dark matter and is expanding through the operation of a mysterious dark energy challenges the human mind, and the knowledge that the solar system and the Milky Way are full of planets and resources that humans may need to survive in the future, drives modern visionaries to design the starships of tomorrow.

Globular cluster Messier 15, as seen by the Hubble Space Telescope's *(HST)* Wide Field Planetary Camera *in 2000. The image covers less than two arcminutes and shows much fainter stars than the Yerkes image because of the HST's location above the atmosphere and a CCD detector that is much more sensitive than photographic plates available in 1900. The original image also captures the stars in their true colors along with one of only three known planetary nebulae found among stars that are 12 billion years old.* (NASA and The Hubble Heritage Team [STScI/AURA])

1901–1910:
Development of a New Astronomy

The decade opened with a very bright comet and closed with the return of perhaps the most famous of all comets, Halley's comet in 1910. These events punctuated a decade that tested astronomical superstitions and speculations with new and more-accurate observing tools and methods.

The wildest speculation at the dawn of the 20th century was one promoted by Percival Lowell, the featured scientist of the decade. He was convinced that features observed on the planet Mars were artificial canals that had been built by intelligent beings and that seasonal changes on Mars were the result of irrigated fields. He assumed that all planets began as wet worlds and dried over time, so Mars was much older and more evolved than Earth. He and others believed that a Martian race would be highly advanced and have much to teach humans. Contact with them offered a driving reason behind further study of Mars and the scientific exploration of space. Lowell dedicated his life and fortune to the task, building an observatory in Arizona, creating new spectral analysis techniques, and spurring the improvement of photographic and observational methods. The debate about Mars dominated the early part of the decade and reached a peak in 1907 when Mars made its closest approach to Earth. The controversy and how it was addressed and resolved are the major topic of this chapter.

The only way for humans to fly in 1901 was in a hot-air balloon. But one visionary, Russian teacher Konstantin Tsiolkovsky (1857–1935), knew that spaceflight was at least possible. He developed the rocket equation (see sidebar on page 10) the same year (1903) that the American Wright brothers made the first powered flight. Tsiolkovsky's achievement and influence on future scientists is briefly addressed in the chapter. Several decades pass before progress in aviation and engineering catch up with his designs.

The second major topic of the chapter is the transformation of astronomy from teaching and measuring to studying the physical nature of objects in space. The transformation was fueled by an explosion of data collected in sky surveys in the previous decade. As more spectra were taken with new telescopes and improved photographic techniques, differences among stars emerged. There were no professional female astronomers during this time period, but several women made major contributions to the new science. To organize the hundreds of spectra coming into Harvard, "computer" Williamina Fleming (1857–1911) invented a class system that divides the spectra by temperature, a system still in use today. Her system facilitated the discovery of the correlation between stellar temperature and brightness that is a building block of stellar evolution and the major topic of the next decade. Another Harvard "computer," Henrietta Leavitt (1868–1921), noticed that a certain type of *variable star*'s brightness was related to its period. This discovery provided a "yardstick" for measuring astronomical distances in the next decade.

University of Chicago astronomer George Ellery Hale (1868–1938) was one of the first scientists to embrace the "new astronomy" and contributed much of the new data on the Sun and the stars. Hale had successfully founded the Yerkes Observatory in 1897 and outfitted it with the biggest telescope in the world, a 40-inch (1-m) refractor. To see more detail in near objects and to observe more-distant faint objects, he needed a large reflecting telescope. Hale's construction of the 60-inch (1.5-m) reflecting telescope atop Mount Wilson in California in 1908 marked a change in astronomical observing. From then on, the largest and best telescopes were reflectors (see figure on page 13). These new telescopes let astronomers see farther into space than ever before and led

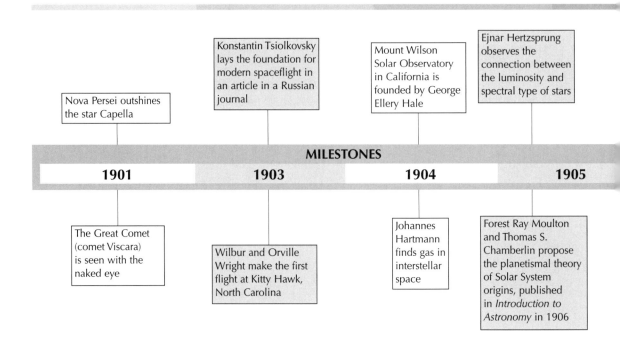

Konstantin Tsiolkovsky lays the foundation for modern spaceflight in an article in a Russian journal

Mount Wilson Solar Observatory in California is founded by George Ellery Hale

Ejnar Hertzsprung observes the connection between the luminosity and spectral type of stars

Nova Persei outshines the star Capella

MILESTONES

1901   **1903**   **1904**   **1905**

The Great Comet (comet Viscara) is seen with the naked eye

Wilbur and Orville Wright make the first flight at Kitty Hawk, North Carolina

Johannes Hartmann finds gas in interstellar space

Forest Ray Moulton and Thomas S. Chamberlin propose the planetismal theory of Solar System origins, published in *Introduction to Astronomy* in 1906 to many new discoveries, such as the true nature of sunspots. With his new telescope, Hale determined that there were no canals on Mars and, therefore, no intelligent Martians.

The Canals of Mars

Most of the progress in astronomy and space happened out of the public view, of interest mostly to scientists and academics. The exception was the sensational story of the decade—the possible discovery of intelligent life on Mars.

The Mars controversy had its roots in the 1877 map of Mars drawn by Italian astronomer Giovanni Schiaparelli (1835–1910). That year marked a favorable *opposition*, when the distance between the Earth and Mars is a minimum. Giovanni Schiaparelli's map included a network of lines labeled *canali*, the Italian word for channel that was inevitably translated as canals. In 1892, French astronomer Camille Flammarion (1842–1925) declared that the existence of such a complicated geometrical network on Mars implied the work of intelligence.

Another favorable Martian opposition in 1894 offered an opportunity to acquire better images that might resolve whether or not there were canals on Mars. Bostonian Percival Lowell, a wealthy businessman who greatly respected Giovanni Schiaparelli (who received a Bruce Medal in 1902—see page 249), built an observatory in Arizona in time for the event.

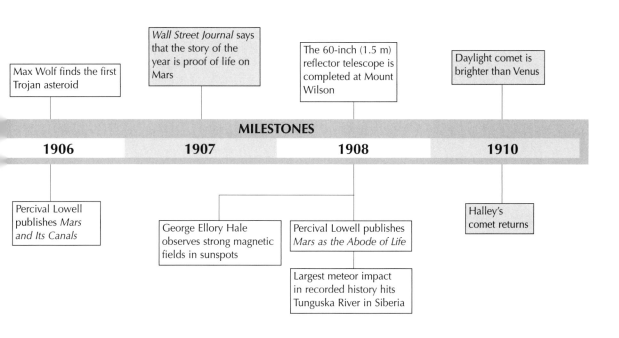

Max Wolf finds the first Trojan asteroid

Wall Street Journal says that the story of the year is proof of life on Mars

The 60-inch (1.5 m) reflector telescope is completed at Mount Wilson

Daylight comet is brighter than Venus

MILESTONES

1906   **1907**   **1908**   **1910**

Percival Lowell publishes *Mars and Its Canals*

George Ellory Hale observes strong magnetic fields in sunspots

Percival Lowell publishes *Mars as the Abode of Life*

Halley's comet returns

Largest meteor impact in recorded history hits Tunguska River in Siberia

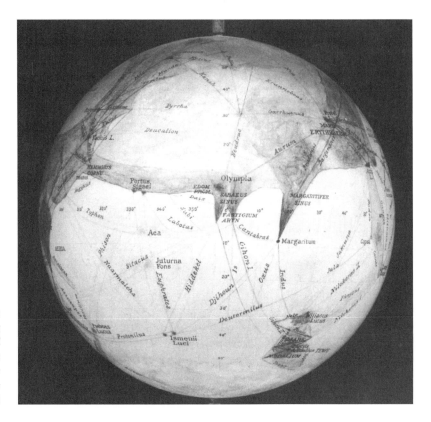

Percival Lowell created this globe of Mars in 1907 showing canals that he considered evidence of intelligent life on Mars. (Lowell Observatory Archives, Coleman-Kennedy Collection)

Lowell and two astronomers, William H. Pickering (1858–1938) and Andrew Douglass (1867–1962), made 917 drawings of Mars (photo above) during the opposition. Lowell sighted more than twice as many canals as Schiaparelli. Eventually, he would claim to see more than 700 canals.

After just a few months of observations, Lowell decided that the markings were the result of intelligent beings. He set forth this idea in a series of articles in *Popular Astronomy* from September 1894 through April 1895 and in the *Atlantic Monthly* in May 1895. He also gave lectures in Boston in February 1895 that drew capacity crowds and were reported in the press. A more complete statement of his theory appeared in his book, *Mars*, published in 1895. It began, "Are they worlds, or are they mere masses of matter? Are physical forces alone at work there or has evolution begotten something more complex, something not unakin to what we know on Earth as life? It is in this that lies the peculiar interest of Mars."

Initial reactions to Lowell's theory ranged from wonder to skeptical amusement. For many people of the day, if someone of Lowell's status declared something to be true, they were inclined to take his word for it. After all, he was a Harvard-educated world traveler, scholar, writer, and member of an old affluent New England family. His interpretation of markings as canals also seemed logical. The Suez Canal, considered a wonder of the modern world, had been completed in 1869. The Panama Canal was being planned (construction began in 1904), and Lowell's local Boston paper was debating a canal across Cape Cod.

Some of the most vehement attacks were launched by Edward Holden (1846–1914) and William W. Campbell (1862–1938) of the Lick Observatory in California. Their 36-inch (0.9-m) telescope was the best in the world prior to 1897 and failed to reveal any canals. They accused Lowell of biasing his data to prove himself right. Other astronomers took a more moderate position. Professor Charles A. Young (1834–1908) of Princeton wrote in *Cosmopolitan* magazine in October 1895 that "the observations of 1894 have made it practically certain that the so-called canals of Mars are real, whatever may be their explanation."

But science requires data, and Lowell intended to provide it. His plans to gather more observational support failed after an expedition to Mexico in 1897 when he became ill. He did not resume work again until late 1900.

Once recovered, Lowell ordered a spectrograph and hired Indiana University graduate Vesto Melvin Slipher (1875–1969) to operate it starting in 1901. A spectrograph is basically a prism attached to a telescope. When white light passes through the prism, the shorter wavelengths are bent more than the longer wavelengths so that the light is spread into the familiar rainbow pattern called a spectrum. Elements in the atmosphere absorb specific wavelengths of light, creating dark lines in the spectrum. Lowell hoped that the spectrum of Mars would show the substances needed for life, oxygen and water.

To show that the lines were not from Earth's atmosphere, Slipher had to observe Mars and the Moon at the same time and compare their spectra. The Moon and planets shine by reflecting sunlight. The Moon has no atmosphere, so any change to its spectrum as seen from Earth's surface is the result of atoms in Earth's atmosphere. Earth's spectrum is subtracted from the planetary spectrum, revealing what gases are present in the planet's atmosphere. The intensity of the line indicates the amount of the elements. Slipher used this method to find hydrogen in the atmosphere of Uranus. The lines of oxygen and water are in the faint red end of the spectrum. Therefore, the abundance of these gases in Earth's atmosphere overpowered any absorption lines from Mars.

To address this problem, Lowell invented the "velocity-shift" method (see figure on page 6) in 1902. He realized that because of a planet's rotation, its spectral lines would be wider than the same lines produced by the Earth's atmosphere. If a line is not only more intense but is broader, it shows that the element exists in the planet's atmosphere.

Photographic plates sensitive enough to the red part of the spectrum were not available until 1904 to test Lowell's velocity-shift method. Vesto Slipher's first results revealed very little water on Mars and none

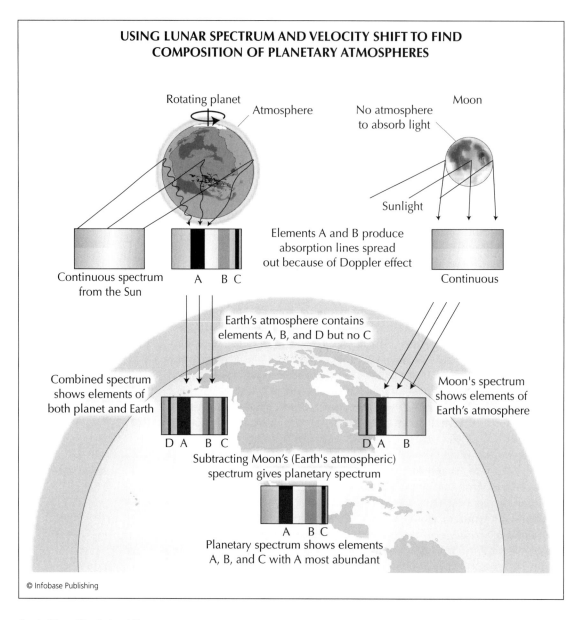

USING LUNAR SPECTRUM AND VELOCITY SHIFT TO FIND
COMPOSITION OF PLANETARY ATMOSPHERES

Rotating planet
Atmosphere

Moon
No atmosphere
to absorb light

Sunlight

Elements A and B produce
absorption lines spread
out because of Doppler effect

Continuous spectrum
from the Sun

A   B C

Continuous

Earth's atmosphere contains
elements A, B, and D but no C

Combined spectrum
shows elements of
both planet and Earth

D A   B C

Moon's spectrum
shows elements of
Earth's atmosphere

D A   B

Subtracting Moon's (Earth's atmospheric)
spectrum gives planetary spectrum

A   B C

Planetary spectrum shows elements
A, B, and C with A most abundant

© Infobase Publishing

Percival Lowell's velocity-shift method reveals the composition of planetary atmospheres. A planet's rotation spreads its spectral lines so elements can be identified after lines produced by Earth's atmosphere (found using the Moon's spectrum) are subtracted out.

on Venus. In 1908, Slipher obtained a clear spectrum that showed oxygen and water vapor in the atmosphere of Mars. But even those who accepted the data did not agree with Lowell that water inevitably meant that there was life on Mars. Some argued that the atmosphere was too thin to support life.

To confirm intelligent life, Lowell needed to prove the existence of the canals. Astronomical maps of the day consisted of hand-drawn sketches made while looking through telescopes. The accuracy thus depended on the eyesight and the drawing skill of the astronomer as well as the quality of the telescope and atmospheric conditions.

Lowell argued that the clear, calm skies and higher altitude of his observatory in Arizona accounted for why he and his assistants could see the canals while his critics at Lick Observatory in California could not. Photography offered a way to show the canals independently of his sketches.

Photography was rapidly advancing at the turn of the century. Astronomers were experimenting with new chemical mixtures at different temperatures to create coatings for glass plates that were sensitive to different colors and exposures of light. For example, the first photographs of Jupiter and Saturn were made in 1879–86.

To show the canals, an exposure needed to be long enough to pick up the details without being blurred by the movement of the Earth and its atmosphere. In 1902, Lowell hired another Indiana graduate, Carol Otto Lampland (1873–1951), to find a way around these difficulties.

On May 11, 1905, Lampland succeeded. Just after the opposition on May 8 when Mars was within 50 million miles (80 million km) of Earth, he developed photographic plates showing 38 canals. In his book, *Mars and Its Canals*, Lowell proclaimed, "Thus did the canals at last speak for their own reality themselves." Lampland's accomplishment was hailed in the press, and he received the 1907 medal of the Royal Photographic Society.

The photographs were less than a quarter inch (0.6 cm) in diameter and the shadings so delicate that it was impossible to reproduce them in a newspaper or journal. Enlargement distorted the images. Most astronomers who viewed the originals agreed that they provided proof of the linear markings.

The photographs did not convince Edward Pickering (1846–1919). He was William H. Pickering's brother and director of the Harvard College Observatory. He joined a chorus of astronomers saying that the markings were craters, cracks, or rills that only seemed linear because of the limits of observing so distant an object through Earth's atmosphere. Edward Pickering (who received a Bruce Medal in 1908, see page 249) would eventually be proven correct.

But Lowell never wavered in his belief in the canals. In 1906, he published his magnum opus entitled *Mars and Its Canals*. Appearing at a time when public interest was intense, it reached a large audience and was considered the best summary available of facts and theories about Mars. In this book, Lowell postulated that life was an inevitable result of evolution and could arise on any planet with the right physical conditions. Water was considered one of the essential requirements, and that implied a narrow temperature and pressure range. Mars appeared to be too cold and the air too thin for water. Yet, Lowell argued that high altitude plants survive under extreme conditions. "A short warm season in summer alone decides whether the species shall survive and flourish;

that it has afterwards to hibernate for six months at a time does not in the least negative the result."

He claimed the observed seasonal wave of darkening moved at a speed of 51 miles (82 km) per day and reversed directions with the seasons—requiring water to flow uphill at least one way. "Now the water which quickens the verdure of the canals moves from the neighborhood of the pole down to the equator as the season advances. This it does, then irrespective of gravity. No natural force propels it, and the inference is forthright and inevitable that it is artificially helped to its end."

The 1907 opposition of Mars (see figure on page 9) was the nearest of the decade and promised to settle the question once and for all. With much media fanfare, Lowell sent an expedition to South America to get photos from a high altitude. These photos were perhaps the most anticipated photos in the world.

Even these photos failed to convince the critics that the canals were the work of intelligent Martians. One critic was Alfred Russel Wallace (1823–1913), the co-originator of the Darwin theory of evolution, who was 84 in 1907. Wallace believed that life was unique to Earth. In a direct assault on Lowell's Martian theory, he published *Is Mars Habitable?* in late 1907. He stated that the canals were cracks caused by cooling of the planet; that there was not enough sunshine reaching the surface to support life; and that the polar caps were carbon dioxide, not water ice. He argued that any attempt to use open canals for irrigation was a sign of stupidity rather than intelligence.

Lowell responded to these arguments in *Mars as the Abode of Life*, published in 1908. The book included Vesto Slipher's new spectrographic evidence for water and oxygen and the 1907 photos of the canals. Lowell thought the existence of water proved that the temperature was warm enough for life on Mars. He never claimed that the canals were open channels, but he suggested that they were surrounded by vegetation fed through irrigation.

Bigger telescopes eventually proved that there were no canals. In 1909, George Hale observed Mars through the new Mount Wilson 60-inch (1.5-m) reflector, then the most powerful telescope in the world. He reported a lot of new detail but no trace of straight lines or geometrical structures. Andrew Douglass, Lowell's former assistant, did not see the canals through this new telescope either.

Though Lowell failed to convince his peers, the Mars debate provided a good distraction from the economic depression of 1907. The *Wall Street Journal* said on December 28, 1907, "What has been in your opinion the most extraordinary event of the twelve months? Not the financial panic which is occupying our minds to the exclusion of most other thoughts . . . but . . . the proof afforded by astronomical observations . . . that conscious, intelligent human life exists upon the planet Mars."

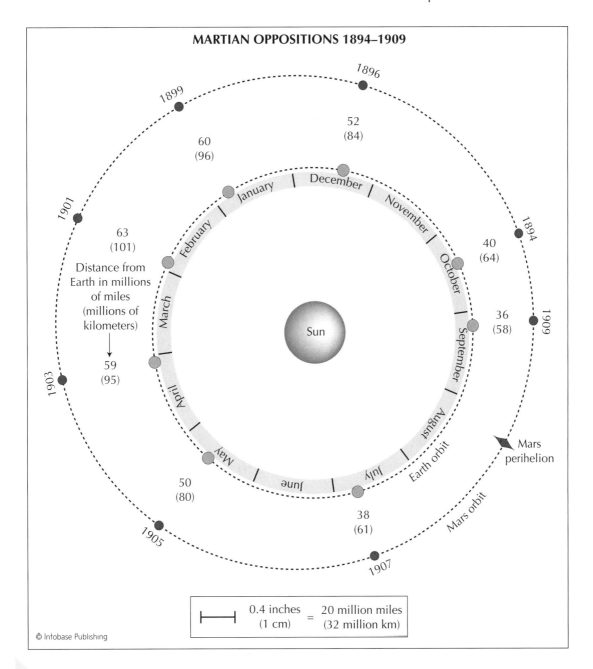

MARTIAN OPPOSITIONS 1894–1909

1896

52
(84)

1899

60
(96)

1894

1901

40
(64)

63
(101)

Distance from
Earth in millions
of miles
(millions of
kilometers)

36
(58)

1909

December
November
January
October
February
September
March
August
April
July
May
June

Sun

Earth orbit

Mars
perihelion

59
(95)

1903

50
(80)

Mars orbit

1905

38
(61)

1907

| 0.4 inches (1 cm) | = | 20 million miles (32 million km) |

© Infobase Publishing

The Equation for Space

While astronomers debated the existence of intelligent life on Mars, other scientists were working on how to lift intelligent life off of this planet. At the turn of the century, spaceflight was still the realm of science fiction. Though rockets in the form of missiles had been used in

Martian oppositions, when the Earth and Mars are on the same radial line to the Sun, happen every two years. The opposition of 1907 was the most favorable of the decade because Mars was near perihelion.

Russian mathematician Konstantin Eduardovich Tsiolkovsky is considered the father of human spaceflight. He published the rocket equation in 1903 and followed with hundreds of publications that paved the way for engineers to build practical rockets. His most famous quote (from a letter in 1911) is "the Earth is the cradle of humanity, but one cannot live in the cradle forever." (NASA–MSFC)

wars since the 1700s, they were small and slow. But when Jules Verne (1828–1905) suggested using a large gun for propulsion in his 1865 novel, *From the Earth to the Moon*, the idea captivated a young Russian named Konstantin Tsiolkovsky.

Deaf as a result of childhood illness, the self-educated genius first explored the problems of spacecraft design while working at a library in Moscow. Tsiolkovsky (photo at left) became a math teacher in the Kaluga Province and figured out the basic rocket equation (sidebar below) in May 1897. The equation was published in a monthly Russian magazine, *The Science Review*, in 1903—the same year as the Wright Brothers' first flight in America. In the article entitled "Research into Interplanetary Space by Means of Rocket Power," Konstantin Tsiolkovsky accurately described the state of weightlessness and the function of rockets in a vacuum. This was the first publication in the world on this subject, but it did not garner much attention outside Russia.

Tsiolkovsky anticipated and planned for a future when humans would no longer be confined to live on one world. At a museum in Russia, he is quoted as saying, "Men are weak now, and yet they transform the Earth's surface. In millions of years their might will increase to the extent that they will change the surface of the Earth, its oceans, the atmosphere, and themselves. They will control the climate and the Solar System just as they control the Earth. They will travel beyond the limits of our planetary system; they will reach other Suns, and use their fresh energy instead of the energy of their dying luminary."

To achieve this great vision, Tsiolkovsky contributed more than 500 scientific papers on topics including liquid-fueled rockets, double-walled pressurized cabins to protect crew members from meteorites, gyroscopes

The Rocket Equation

Konstantin Tsiolkovsky showed mathematically that a rocket moves at a rate that depends on the speed of its exhaust gas and its mass as follows:

The final velocity of a rocket,
$$v_2 = v_{ex} \times \ln(m_1 \div m_2) + v_1.$$

where v_2 = the final rocket velocity,
   v_{ex} = the velocity of the exhaust gases,
   m_1 = the starting mass of the rocket,
   m_2 = the ending mass of the rocket after the propellants are used as exhaust, and

v_1 = the initial rocket velocity (zero if it is at rest).

For the velocity of the rocket to equal that of the exhaust gas (that is, for $\ln(m_1 \div m_2) = 1$), nearly two-thirds of the mass must be exhausted. To minimize the mass of the exhaust, the exhaust velocity should be as large as possible. This requirement drives the need for efficient rocket engines and lightweight vehicles.

for attitude control, reclining seats to guard against high launch loads, and air locks for spacewalking cosmonauts. His 1903 paper even included a space station that spun to produce artificial gravity.

Tsiolkovsky's groundbreaking work and inspirational ideas influenced many young Russian scientists and engineers, including Sergei Korolev (1906–66), who would build the first rocket to fly a human into space.

A New Astronomy

On February 22, 1901, after racing through space for 1,500 years, the light from a nova burst into view in the constellation Perseus. Nova Persei reached a maximum brightness equal to that of Capella, the sixth-brightest star in the sky. Within a year, astronomers observed an expanding shell of gas, called the Firework Nebula, around the nova. This was the first nova to be studied using the new tool of spectroscopy. Yet, it would be decades before theories were developed to explain the meaning of this observational data.

In 1901, astronomers did not know how stars evolved or how long they "lived." Astronomy was mostly a mathematical science involved with measuring the positions, distances, movement, and brightness of stars. This emphasis began to change as astronomers examined spectra gathered in sky surveys of the 1890s. By comparing the spectra to those of hot gases in laboratories on Earth, astronomers discovered that stars were made of familiar elements. (Helium was first discovered on the Sun and then found in Earth's atmosphere in 1895.) Spectra offered another way (besides brightness, movement, and color) to distinguish one star from another. Some stars had many absorption lines, showing a range of elements in their atmospheres, while others had only a few. The brightness and spacing of the lines varied as well. Practitioners of what was called the new astronomy focused on the physical properties of stars that might explain these differences. The new astronomy became known as *astrophysics*.

Spectra were captured on glass photographic plates. To compare the spectra of one star with another and with itself over time, astronomers measured the location, width, intensity, and spacing between the often very faint lines. Much of this important work was done by Edward Pickering's "computers" at the Harvard College Observatory. These computers were not electronic but were actually a group of talented women headed by Williamina Fleming.

Fleming was originally hired as Edward Pickering's maid. When Pickering became frustrated with his male assistants' work classifying spectra at the observatory, he famously declared that his maid could do a better job. So in 1881, he hired Williamina Fleming. She devised and helped implement a system to classify stars by the amount of hydrogen in their spectra. The stars with the most were given the letter A, and the next-most a B, and so on. Later, Annie Jump Cannon (1863–1941) rearranged the spectra by temperature but kept the letter designations. In nine years at Harvard, Fleming catalogued the glass plates of more than 10,000 stars. In 1907, she published a list of 222 variable stars that she had discovered through changes in their spectra.

One of the most famous "new astronomers" was George Hale of the University of Chicago, who was honored with a Bruce Medal in 1916 (see page 249). He founded the *Astrophysical Journal* in 1895 and played a key role in forming the American Astronomical Society in 1899. Many new theories, techniques, observations, and methods to analyze them were published in the pages of the *Journal* or debated at society meetings. Hale was also pivotal in providing the community with world-class observing facilities to provide more accurate data. He founded the Yerkes Observatory in Wisconsin in 1897 and equipped it with the world's largest telescope. As the observatory's first director, he invented the spectroheliograph, a device to take photos of the light of a single element in the Sun. (The sunspot cycle had been shown to be 11.1 years in 1851, but the cause of sunspots was not yet known.) The famous astronomer William Herschel had speculated much earlier that they were holes in the Sun and that the surface underneath was lush with vegetation. In 1905, Hale took the first photographs of a sunspot's spectrum. His observations proved that sunspots were cooler areas on the Sun and not the "holes" that Herschel had suggested.

To spread the spectrum out and observe finer details, Hale needed a larger telescope. The Yerkes 40-inch (1-m) telescope remains the biggest refractor ever built. Hale realized that a lens any larger would sag from its own weight or be so thick that it would block the light. What he needed was a reflecting telescope (see figure on page 13) that used a mirror instead of a lens.

Hale's father paid $25,000 to have a 60-inch (1.5-m) mirror made for his son. Yerkes Observatory could not afford to build the mounting and dome for this telescope, so the mirror was kept in storage for 12 years. In pursuit of better seeing conditions, Hale moved to sunny Pasadena, California, where he founded the Mount Wilson Solar Observatory in 1904. He moved the 40-inch (1-m) refractor there and obtained a $300,000 grant from the Carnegie Foundation to finish and install the 60-inch (1.5-m) reflector on Mount Wilson. When it went into operation in 1908, it was the largest telescope in the world. With it, Hale helped settle the Mars debate and provided the data for a coming revolution in astrophysics.

One of Hale's first discoveries in 1908 was that spectral lines from sunspots showed the Zeeman effect. This effect is named for a Dutch physicist, Pieter Zeeman (1865–1943), who discovered in 1896 that spectral lines split in the presence of a strong magnetic field. Hale found solar magnetic fields hundreds of miles across that persist long after the sunspot associated with them disappeared.

Binary and variable stars were also of special interest to astrophysicists. In the early 1800s, John William Herschel discovered that stars did

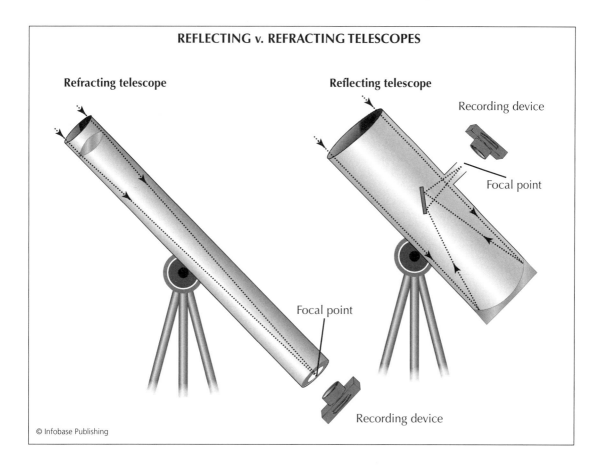

REFLECTING v. REFRACTING TELESCOPES

Refracting telescope

Reflecting telescope

Recording device

Focal point

Focal point

Recording device

© Infobase Publishing

not just appear double because of their direction relative to Earth but because some orbited each other. In 1827, Mizar, the middle star in the handle of the Big Dipper and the first star identified as a double in 1650, was found to be two stars: Mizar A and Mizar B that orbit each other every 60 years. In 1889, Edward Pickering discovered that the absorption lines in the spectra of the atmospheres of binary stars double as one star moves away from Earth and the other moves toward Earth. Edward Pickering observed that Mizar A's spectrum had double lines, and thus was two stars, the first discovered spectroscopic binary. In 1908, E. B. Frost (1866–1935) found that Mizar B is also a spectroscopic binary. So Mizar is actually four stars revolving around each other.

Some spectroscopic binaries were found to eclipse one another and thus brighten and fade periodically. But other variable stars changed in brightness and had no companion to block their light. Delta Cephei, first identified as a variable star in 1784, did not have a companion. Yet, studies of its spectra showed that it went from bright to dim and back to the same brightness level every five days. Stars whose brightness

Refracting telescopes use lenses and reflecting telescopes use mirrors to gather and focus light. Refractors are limited in size because of the weight of the lens.

varies in a periodic way like Delta Cephei are called *Cepheid variables*. The North Star, Polaris, is a Cepheid variable with a period of just under four days.

In 1908, Henrietta Leavitt, another of Edward Pickering's "computers," published "1777 variables in the Magellanic Clouds" in the *Annals of Harvard College Observatory*. The list included 16 Cepheid variables with periods between 1.25 to 127 days. She reported on page 107, "it is worthy of notice that . . . the brighter variables have the longer periods." Although her report of this relationship between brightness and period went unnoticed for many years, Henrietta Leavitt had made a discovery that would provide astronomers with a new way to measure distances in space.

The amount of accumulating data on stars led astrophysicists to see relationships between properties of stars that would lead to theories of stellar evolution. In 1905, Danish astronomer Ejnar Hertzsprung (1873–1967) observed that the brightness and spectral type (the letters A, B, and so forth that Williamina Fleming assigned) were correlated. All "O" stars were brighter than "A" stars, for example. At the same time, American Henry Norris Russell (1877–1957) used orbital data from binary stars to determine their densities. Being able to correlate density with brightness and spectral lines led directly to breakthroughs in understanding of stellar evolution in the next decade.

The collection of spectra of binary systems also led to a serendipitous discovery by German Johannes Hartmann (1865–1936) in 1904. In addition to the usual two sets of spectral lines that shifted back and forth as two stars orbited each other, he found a narrow line of *ionized* calcium that did not move. The line did not shift because it was not associated with the stars. Hartmann had discovered that the space between stars was not an empty void but contained a thin veil of gas.

Vesto Slipher at Lowell Observatory confirmed Hartmann's discovery in 1908 when he also found lines of calcium in the spectra of double stars. Slipher provided evidence for interstellar gas in three widely spaced regions of the Milky Way. In 1910, Slipher showed that the Pleiades in Taurus are bright because light from nearby stars reflects off a cloud of interstellar gas.

In 1906, Joel Stebbins (1878–1966), director of the University of Illinois Observatory, added to the tools that astrophysicists could use to study stars. He began to measure the brightness of astronomical objects using a photometer. In photometry, the light collected by the telescope is focused on a metal surface or container of gas called a photoelectric cell. This cell produces an electric current when struck by particles of light. The current can be amplified and measured to determine the brightness of the source. Before this, the only way to measure brightness was to compare an image of a new star with a known one.

Joel Stebbins used a selenium photometer to observe a lunar eclipse on July 24, 1907. In 1908, he measured the change in brightness of the eclipsing binary star Algol. In 1910, he studied Halley's comet. From 1909 to 1925, Stebbins and Mount Wilson astronomer Albert Whitford (1905–2002) continued to improve the photoelectric cell. Both men received Bruce Medals for their work (see page 249). As the sensitivity of the photometer increased, they were able to use it to measure the light of the solar corona during a total eclipse. Photometry would eventually become a more accurate method of measuring brightness than photography.

Impacts and Omens

Way back in 1577, Tycho Brahe had determined that comets were not in the Earth's atmosphere and, therefore, were celestial objects. The first decade of the 20th century was punctuated by bright comets. On April 12, 1901, the Great Comet, also known as comet Viscara, was observed in the Southern Hemisphere. It became as bright as the brightest star in the sky and grew two tails, one 45 degrees and the other 15 degrees long. At the end of the decade, from January 12 to mid-February 1910, the Daylight comet was visible with the unaided eye. It was brighter than Venus.

Though scientists made great strides in understanding planets and stars throughout the decade between these two astronomical events, people clung to their superstitious ideas about comets. This was especially true of Halley's comet that arrived soon after the Daylight comet in the spring of 1910. This comet was named for Edmund Halley who had determined its approximately 76-year period in 1682. Although most people knew that comets were small, icy bodies in orbit around the Sun, many still saw Halley's comet as a sign that the world was about to end. After all, when the comet appeared in 1066, England fell to the Norman invaders. Maybe Lowell's Martians would attack!

People became nervous when Halley's comet became visible to the unaided eye in April, and the author Mark Twain (1835–1910), who had been born under the comet, died under it as he had predicted. It did not grow as bright as the Daylight comet, but its tail was more than twice as long. It stretched up to 120 degrees, from the constellation Taurus all the way to Aquila. The Earth passed through this tail on May 18 with no ill effects. The fading comet remained visible to the naked eye until mid July, destined to return in 1986.

If people had been aware of an event on June 30, 1908, they may have feared Halley's comet even more. On that date in a remote area near Tunguska River in central Siberia, the largest known cosmic impact in recorded history occurred. The mass of the object has been estimated at about 100,000 tons. If it had hit a few hours earlier, it would have struck the Russian city of St. Petersburg, and as many as 500,000 people might have been killed. The only known casualties were a herd of about 700 reindeer that were incinerated in the blast and two people who died of fright.

The impact felled trees in a radial pattern over an area more than half the size of Rhode Island. A column of flame was visible more than 100

Scientist of the Decade: Percival Lowell (1855–1916)

Percival Lowell was certain that given a chance, life could evolve on any world. When he saw straight lines on Mars, it was easy for him to accept that they were canals built by intelligent Martians. He built an observatory and dedicated the last 22 years of his life to proving this was true. His charming and humorous lectures, articles, and books made him into one of the most recognized and respected celebrities of his time.

Lowell was born in Boston on March 13, 1855, into a family so distinguished that there were two cities, one for his father's family and one for his mother's, named after them in Massachusetts. Lowell was not only wealthy but also brilliant. He graduated Phi Beta Kappa with a degree in math from Harvard in 1876. His commencement talk, "The Nebular Hypothesis," focused on the origin of the solar system.

Lowell did not pursue astronomy until he was 39; instead, he worked in the family business and became rich in his own right. He learned to speak Japanese, served as a diplomat to Korea, and traveled around the world twice. He discussed Eastern culture in *The Atlantic Monthly* and in four books published between 1886 and 1894. With a clear and colorful writing style, Lowell claimed that Western superiority in inventions and technology was the result of its emphasis on individualism versus the Eastern emphasis on conformity. He bluntly stated, "No man ever cooperated with another in the idea that made him great."

Lowell's great idea was to study Mars to discover if life existed elsewhere in the solar system. In 1894, he sent Andrew Douglass to the Arizona Territory to choose the best location for an observatory. This was the first time anyone had selected a site based on the clarity of the air, what astronomers call seeing. The seeing was so good in Flagstaff that Lowell observed faint objects as well as observatories elsewhere with larger telescopes.

Lowell, Andrew Douglass, and Harvard astronomer William Pickering settled in on "Mars Hill"

Percival Lowell created a sensation when he claimed that intelligent beings had built canals on Mars. He built an observatory in Flagstaff, Arizona, to gather data and published his evidence in best-selling books. (Lowell Observatory Archives)

in Flagstaff to observe Mars during its opposition in 1894. Within a few months, Lowell's theory that the canals were the result of intelligent life on Mars appeared in popular magazines. He elaborated further on his ideas in his books: *Mars* in 1895, *Mars and Its Canals* in 1906, and *Mars as the Abode of Life* in 1908. These books were best sellers of their time, translated even into Chinese. Lowell summed up his arguments in four points in *Mars*:

1. the physical conditions on Mars were "not antagonistic to some form of life";
2. there is not much water, and, therefore, "if beings of sufficient intelligence inhabited it, they would have to resort to irrigation to support life";
3. there "turns out to be a network of markings . . . precisely counterparting what a system of irrigation would look like"; and
4. there are "spots placed where we should expect to find the lands thus artificially fertilized and behaving as such constructed oases should."

With Mars having one-third of Earth's gravity, Lowell speculated that Martians would be three times larger than earthlings, an idea adopted by popular novelist Edgar Rice Burroughs (1875–1950). Lowell also thought Martians would be superior to earthlings. He said that, in *Mars,* because "Mars shows unmistakable signs of being old . . . and evolution on its surface must be similarly advanced."

Though Lowell's connection to Mars was legend, he also studied the other planets. In 1896, he reported that Venus had a day equal to its year, a result suggested by his friend Giovanni Schiaparelli in 1890. Though some scientists argued that Venus had a 23-hour day, they questioned Lowell's method more than his result. Instead of using cloud patterns as Giovanni Schiaparelli had done, Lowell claimed that he saw dark surface markings through the clouds! Unlike the "canals" on Mars, no one else ever claimed to see the surface of Venus. It would take radar in the 1950s to penetrate the clouds and show that a "day" on Venus is actually longer than a Venusian year.

As the Mars debate subsided, Lowell turned to other pursuits. On June 10, 1908, at the age of 53, he married Constance Savage Keith. They honeymooned in Europe and took a hot-air balloon ride to 5,500 feet (1,700 m) above London.

Lowell's last book was published in 1909. *The Evolution of Worlds* proposed that planets evolved in stages. When the book was blasted for unfounded assumptions in geology, biology, and paleontology, Lowell attacked one of the critics, University of Chicago astronomer Forest Ray Moulton (1872–1952). Lowell cited math errors in Forest Ray Moulton's book (*Introduction to Astronomy* published in 1906) as a way to discredit the Planetismal or "Encounter theory." The theory, proposed by Forest Ray Moulton with fellow astronomer Thomas C. Chamberlin (1843–1928), claimed the planets formed from debris pulled from the Sun by a passing dark star. Lowell preferred the nebular hypothesis that the Sun and planets formed together, a theory generally accepted today. Lowell's attempt to discredit Forest Ray Moulton failed because his own book contained so many flaws. Eventually though, others would emulate Lowell's multidisciplinary approach to the study of planets.

Lowell predicted the existence of a "Planet X" beyond Neptune. He searched for it from 1905 until his death, not knowing that if his camera's field of view had been just a bit wider, he would have found it. His calculations did however lead to Pluto's discovery in 1930. The name was chosen so that the first two letters are his initials.

Never relenting in his study of the solar system, in Lowell's last journal article ("The Genesis of Planets"), before his death he claimed to have seen new divisions in the rings of Saturn and repeated his assertion that there were canals on Mars. A massive stroke ended Lowell's life on November 12, 1916, after a night spent observing the inner satellites of Jupiter. The death of the man who ignited the debate about life on Mars was mourned around the world.

Recent missions indicate that water once flowed on Mars. Some scientists believe that Martian meteorites contain evidence of ancient life. Others hypothesize that bacteria are producing methane on Mars today. Was Lowell right? Does life automatically evolve when conditions allow? The systematic study of Mars and other worlds that began with Percival Lowell still might lead to the discovery of alien life.

miles away. The impact caused disturbances in Earth's magnetic field, tremors, and a cloud of ash that was recorded halfway around the world at Mount Wilson Observatory. Yet, people did not know how close they had come to catastrophe. Scientists assumed that an earthquake caused the effects they had measured. It was not until 19 years later that a Russian scientist organized the first expedition to the site.

Astronomers still do not know what hit Tunguska River in 1908, other than that it was not one of the asteroids or comets already discovered by that time. The first and largest asteroid, Ceres, had been found in 1801. By 1900, more than 450 asteroids were known.

In 1906, German astronomer Max Wolf (1863–1932) discovered the first of the Trojan asteroids. These asteroids are 60 degrees ahead and behind Jupiter in its orbit around the Sun. Their discovery proved a mathematical prediction by Comte Joseph-Louis Lagrange (1736–1813) in 1772 that there are five gravitationally neutral points (designated L1–L5) around any two large bodies in space. Smaller bodies can orbit at these points without being drawn toward either of the large bodies. Wolf received a Bruce Medal in 1930 for his work.

By the end of the decade, improvements in photography, spectrography, photometry and telescopes had given astronomers the tools to map and catalog and classify the bodies of the solar system and its neighbors in space. This knowledge would soon lead to an understanding of how those bodies formed and evolved.

Further Reading

Books and Periodicals

Florenskiy, K. P. "Preliminary Results of the 1961 Combined Tunguska Meteorite Expedition." *Meteoritica* 23 (1963). Translated by Spectrum Translation and Research, Inc. Taurus Press, 1965. Available online. URL: http://abob.libs.uga.edu/bobk/tungmet.html. A detailed report of the largest impact event in recorded history, including tables, graphs, maps, and charts of scientific measurements.

Hoyt, William Graves. *Lowell and Mars.* Tucson: The University of Arizona Press, 1976. A detailed scholarly biography and history of Percival Lowell, his observatory, and his quest for knowledge about Mars.

H. S. Leavitt. "1777 variables in the Magellanic Clouds." *Annals of Harvard College Observatory* 60 (1908): 87–108. Available online. URL: http://articles.adsabs.harvard.edu/cgi-bin/nph-iarticle_query?1908AnHar..60...87L. The original publication of Henrietta Leavitt's discovery of the relationship between the brightness and period of Cepheid variables.

Levy, David H., and Wendee Wallach. *Cosmic Discoveries.* Amherst, N.Y.: Prometheus Books, 2001. This collection of essays on astronomical discoveries includes Henrietta Leavitt's discovery of the period relation of Cepheid variables and Harlow Shapley's work that built upon it.

Lowell, Percival. "The Genesis of Planets." *The Journal of the Royal Astronomical Society of Canada* 10 (August 1916): 281–293. Available online. URL: http://adsabs.harvard.edu/cgi-bin/nph-bib_query?bibcode =1916JRASC..10..281L&db_key=AST. Percival Lowell's last journal article where he discusses his ideas of planet formation.

———. *Mars.* London: Longmans, Green and Co., 1895. Available online. URL: http://www.wanderer.org/references/lowell/Mars/.

———. *Mars and Its Canals.* New York: The Macmillan Co., 1906.

Web Sites

Jay Bitterman. "Joel Stebbins." Lake County Astronomical Society. URL: http://www.bpccs.com/lcas/Articles/stebbins.htm. Accessed on February 7, 2006. This is a brief biography of Joel Stebbins who pioneered the use of photometry in astronomy.

Harvard-Smithsonian Center for Astrophysics. "What's New at the CfA." John G. Wolbach Library Exhibit. URL: http://cfa-www.harvard.edu/ newtop/previous/011700.html. Accessed on February 7, 2006. This is a brief profile that includes two photos of Harvard "computer" Williamina Fleming.

Florence M. Kelleher. "George Ellery Hale: The Yerkes Years, 1892–1904." Yerkes Observatory Virtual Museum. URL: http://astro.uchicago.edu/ yerkes. Accessed on August 28, 2006. Site contains a short history of the founding of Yerkes Observatory by George Hale.

Evgeny N. Kusin, Director. "The Life of Konstantin Eduardovitch Tsiolkovsky." Konstantin E. Tsiolkovsky State Museum of the History of Cosmonautics. URL: http://www.informatics.org/museum/. Accessed on February 7, 2006. A good illustrated overview of Konstantin Tsiolkovsky's life and contributions, with a bibliography for further reading.

Alison F. Schirmer and Steven R. Majewski. "History of Photography in Astronomical Measurements." Virtual Museum of Measuring Engines. URL: http://www.astro.virginia.edu/~afs5z/photography.html. Accessed on February 7, 2006. Provides a brief overview of the history of photographic techniques used in astronomy at the turn of the 20th century.

Mike Simmons. "The History of Mount Wilson Observatory." Mount Wilson Observatory. URL: http://www.mtwilson.edu. Accessed on August 28, 2006. This site contains articles about the building of the observatory and the installation of the 60 and 100-inch telescopes and a short biography of George Hale who founded the observatory in 1904.

2

1911–1920:
Giant Stars and General Relativity

During the first year of this decade, a unique celestial event occurred: two comets, Brooks and Beljawsky, were visible to the naked eye in the sky at the same time during October 1911. Perhaps these comets signaled the new dual nature of astronomy in this decade as observations and theory together tackled the problems of stellar evolution with new methods to measure, and theories to explain—the distance, movements, sizes, and energy source of stars.

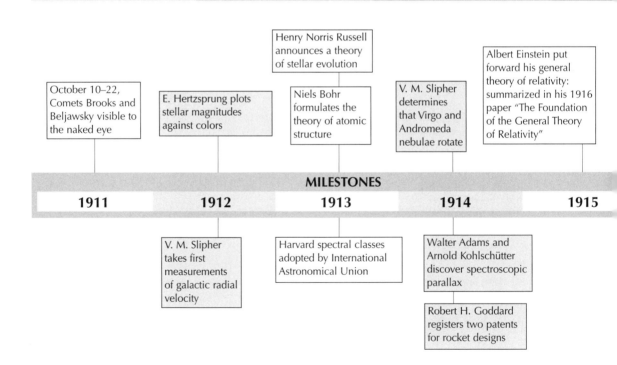

Henry Norris Russell announces a theory of stellar evolution

Albert Einstein put forward his general theory of relativity: summarized in his 1916 paper "The Foundation of the General Theory of Relativity"

October 10–22, Comets Brooks and Beljawsky visible to the naked eye

E. Hertzsprung plots stellar magnitudes against colors

Niels Bohr formulates the theory of atomic structure

V. M. Slipher determines that Virgo and Andromeda nebulae rotate

MILESTONES

| 1911 | 1912 | 1913 | 1914 | 1915 |

V. M. Slipher takes first measurements of galactic radial velocity

Harvard spectral classes adopted by International Astronomical Union

Walter Adams and Arnold Kohlschütter discover spectroscopic parallax

Robert H. Goddard registers two patents for rocket designs

The fact that stars come in both giant and dwarf sizes was proven during this decade, mostly through the stellar parallax (see figure on page 24) work of Princeton astrophysicist Henry Norris Russell, the pioneer of the decade. (See sidebar and photo on page 38.) He and German astronomer Ejnar Hertzsprung (see photo on page 23) discovered a relationship between a star's size, brightness, color, temperature, and spectrum. Russell compiled the data for more than 300 stars and plotted their brightness versus their temperature on what became known as the Hertzsprung-Russell diagram (see figure on page 29), which was first released in 1913. (Both men received Bruce Medals [see page 249] for their work.) This diagram revealed that most stars fall along a band called the main sequence, with blue giants at one end and *red dwarfs* at the other. Red giants and *white dwarfs* did not fit the pattern, and Russell proposed a theory of stellar evolution to explain them. His theory was that blue giants contracted and cooled into red giants. Throughout the decade, Russell gathered data on the density of blue and red giant stars in binary systems, proving his theory wrong but providing the data that would lead to an understanding of stellar structure and energy.

Mount Wilson astronomer Harlow Shapley (1885–1972) (see photo on page 35) rediscovered a relationship between the period and

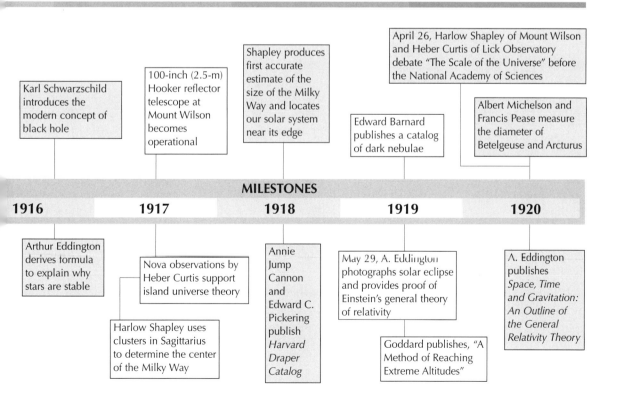

brightness of giant Cepheid variable stars that originally had been found by Henrietta Leavitt in the previous decade (see figure on page 32). Shapley used the relationship to find the distance to globular clusters and to redefine the size of the Milky Way and the Sun's position away from the center. (He received a Bruce Medal in 1939 [see page 249] partly for this work.) Not knowing about interstellar dust, he overestimated the size and thought that the galaxy was big enough to include spiral nebulae. Vesto Slipher of Lowell Observatory and Heber Curtis of Lick Observatory used different methods to determine that the spiral nebulae were distant galaxies of their own. In 1920, Shapley and Curtis were paired in a debate on the size of the universe that revolved around the nature of spiral nebulae. Curtis won, using what turned out to be an incorrect argument.

Cambridge astrophysicist Arthur Eddington (1882–1924) (see the photo on page 30) searched for an explanation to what made the giant Cepheid variable stars pulsate. He worked out a set of equations called the radiative theory that showed that stars are stable when the force of gravitational contraction balances internal radiation pressure. He noted that contraction alone could not provide the energy necessary for stars to radiate energy for billions of years. The question of a star's source of energy would be the focus of much debate in the following years.

During the course of the decade, stellar spectra grew from being a tool to determine the elements and eclipsing properties of stars to a way to discover a star's temperature, brightness, size, and distance. A Harvard "computer" Annie Jump Cannon rearranged the spectral classes that had been created by her predecessor Williamina Fleming into order by stellar temperature. Using the H-R diagram, astronomers could now tell the brightness of a star and hence its distance, from its spectra alone. This technique is called spectral parallax.

Throughout the decade, astrophysicists searched for explanations to physical correlations between properties of astronomical objects. Indian physicist Meghnad Saha (1893–1956) discovered an answer to why the spectra of hot blue stars had fewer lines than spectra of cooler red stars. He found that as temperature increased, electrons had fewer energy states from which to choose and thus would emit light at fewer frequencies. This work would lead to a deeper understanding of the differences between stars and how they produce energy.

Understanding of the universe on the largest scale was also under way. Albert Einstein's general theory of relativity (GTR), published in 1915, described gravity as the curvature of space (see figure on page 37). The GTR accounted for small changes in the orbit of Mercury and predicted that light would not travel in a straight line past massive objects. This latter prediction was tested by Eddington during a solar eclipse in 1919. Further implications of GTR to astronomical problems would come to light in later decades.

The first steps toward building vehicles to reach space were made during this decade by American physicist Robert Goddard, whose contributions are highlighted in later chapters. Destined to become the father of American rocketry, he earned his first patents in 1914, got his first grant to build a rocket in 1916, and published a landmark paper, "A Method of Reaching Extreme Altitudes," in 1919.

The Size of Stars

Since ancient times, people have known that not all stars are alike. But it was not until the 20th century that they began to discover why. In 1905, Ejnar Hertzsprung showed that the hottest stars are also the brightest stars. Differences in the brightness of stars of the same color or temperature were a result of distance. Using the parallax of stars (see figure on page 24), Hertzsprung found that both the brightest and faintest red stars had small parallaxes, meaning that they were equally distant.

Ejnar Hertzsprung studied the connection between stellar color and magnitude that led to the Hertzsprung-Russell diagram that shows the correlation between stellar luminosity and spectral class. (Yerkes Observatory Photographs)

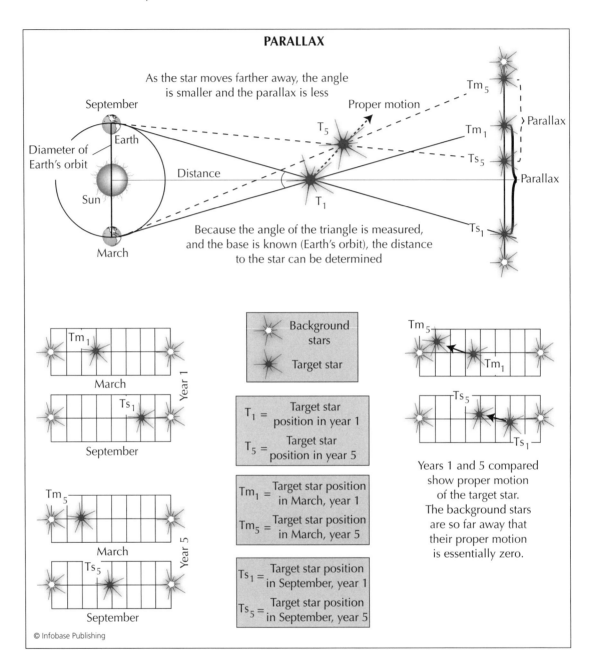

PARALLAX

As the star moves farther away, the angle is smaller and the parallax is less

September

Earth

Diameter of Earth's orbit

Sun

March

Distance

Because the angle of the triangle is measured, and the base is known (Earth's orbit), the distance to the star can be determined

Proper motion

T_5

T_1

Tm_5

Tm_1

Ts_5

Ts_1

Parallax

Parallax

Tm_1

March

September

Year 1

Background stars

Target star

$T_1 =$ Target star position in year 1

$T_5 =$ Target star position in year 5

$Tm_1 =$ Target star position in March, year 1

$Tm_5 =$ Target star position in March, year 5

$Ts_1 =$ Target star position in September, year 1

$Ts_5 =$ Target star position in September, year 5

Tm_5

Tm_1

Ts_5

Ts_1

Years 1 and 5 compared show proper motion of the target star. The background stars are so far away that their proper motion is essentially zero.

Tm_5

March

September

Year 5

Ts_5

© Infobase Publishing

Trigometric parallax is the most accurate way to find the distance to a star.

He correctly decided that the difference in brightness was because of physical size. Hertzsprung's mentor, Karl Schwarzschild (1873–1916), coined the term *giant* for these stars. The revolutionary idea that stars come in different sizes would lead to an understanding of how stars form and evolve.

Ejnar Hertzsprung discovered that red giant stars had different spectra from other red stars—a difference noted by Antonia Maury (1866–1952), the only woman trained in science who was working on E. C. Pickering's staff at Harvard. She had dubbed them "c-stars" and suggested that a subclass be created for them.

In 1906, Hertzsprung wrote to Pickering saying that he supported adding the "c" subclass. Pickering thought that Antonia Maury's sample was too small to warrant adding a subclass. He had only agreed to let Maury publish her paper on c-stars because she was the niece of Henry Draper (1837–82), Harvard's major patron.

Hertzsprung explained in *Astronomishche Nachrichten* in January 1909 that a new radiation formula developed by Max Planck (1858–1947) could be used to estimate the diameter of stars from their temperature. He proved mathematically that Arcturus, one of Maury's c-stars, had a diameter more than 100 times that of the Sun. Hertzsprung again urged Pickering to adopt the subclass, but again he refused. (Maury's subclass was finally adopted in 1922, three years after Pickering's death.)

Henry Norris Russell of Princeton was aware of Hertzsprung's work and quickly focused on discovering why only a rare few red stars were giants. He believed, as most astronomers do today, that stars form when gravity draws gas clouds together. The contraction of the cloud heats the gas until it glows hot enough to become a star.

Nuclear fusion was not yet understood, so most astronomers (incorrectly) assumed that starlight was produced by gravitational contraction. The resulting loss of energy through starlight caused the stars to cool and become fainter as they aged, so red stars were considered the oldest and smallest of stars. The idea of giant red stars contradicted this theory.

As a student, Henry Norris Russell had studied under George Darwin (1845–1912, son of Charles) at Cambridge in England. He had come to favor Darwin's fission theory that stated that at a certain spin rate, a condensing body would fly apart and form two or more bodies in orbit around each other. (The competing encounter theory said that closely passing stars pulled mass away to form binary stars and solar systems.) The fission theory predicted that as binary stars aged, they would continue to move apart. To test this theory, Russell examined 74 multiple-star systems. His analysis, "On the Origin of Binary Stars," appeared in the January 1910 issue of the *Astrophysical Journal*. It showed that binary systems with periods less than two days had blue and white stars. Long-period binaries contained yellow, orange, and red stars. Russell's work supported the fission theory and also the (incorrect) idea that blue stars were young and red stars old. (The real explanation is that blue stars have short lifetimes compared to red stars.)

In 1910, Dutch astronomer Jacobus Kapteyn (1851–1922) and Lick Observatory Director William Campbell (who both received Bruce

Medals—see page 249) announced that the hottest (blue) stars had the smallest *proper motion*, and that the coolest (red) stars had the largest proper motion. They speculated that space somehow resisted larger (blue) stars more than small dense (red) ones like objects moving through a fluid (though they knew that space was a vacuum). Because red stars were believed (incorrectly) to be the oldest and most contracted stars, the proper motion data seemed to prove that red stars could not be giants. (They found large proper motions because dim red stars must be close to Earth to be seen, whereas hotter stars are brighter and visible from great distances.)

Henry Norris Russell began to question the assumption that stars cool as they age. He was not alone. In 1902, English astronomer Norman Lockyer (1836–1920) published the meteoritic hypothesis that suggested that stars heated to a peak temperature before beginning to cool down. His theory was based on Lane's law that stated that temperature increased when radius decreased. Russell speculated (incorrectly) that stars began life as red giants. As the pressure of the gas resisted contraction, the stars would heat up and become orange, then yellow, white, and—if they had enough mass—blue. This would continue until the stars reached a critical density. After that, the stars could not contract further and would enter their cooling phase—slowly going from white to yellow to red again.

Henry Norris Russell believed (correctly) that the contraction phase was fairly quick and that not many stars had enough mass to heat up to blue. This explained the observation that both red giants and blue stars were rare. Russell then tested this theory of stellar evolution by measuring the density of binary stars. If the contraction/cooling theory were right, then blue stars would have the lowest densities, and both giant and dwarf red stars would have high densities.

Measuring stellar density was tricky and time consuming. The time it took one binary star to eclipse another was used to estimate the volume of stars. Then the total mass of a binary system was derived, using Kepler's third law that relates the sum of the masses to their separation and period of revolution about each other. Careful measurements of how much each star moved relative to the center of the system yielded how much mass belonged to each star in the system. The mass was then distributed among the stars and divided by the estimated volume to get the density. Because some binaries have periods of years, it takes a long time to gather the data to determine the density of stars.

Russell presented his initial density findings at a symposium in April 1912. He found that blue stars had higher densities than red stars and that red giants were less dense than red dwarfs. So red giants were not bigger because they had more mass. Blue giants could not evolve into red giants because the densities were the reverse of what the contraction theory predicted. "This is a revolutionary conclusion," Russell said, "but, so far as I can see, we are simply shut up to it with no reasonable escape."

Russell misinterpreted this data as support for his theory that red giants were the first stage of a star's life and that they evolved into red dwarfs. William Campbell objected to Russell's theory of stellar evolution because it did not explain the large proper motion of red stars. Russell needed more data to make his case and turned to his graduate student, Harlow Shapley, and his friend Pickering at Harvard for help.

Harvard had completed a sky survey in conjunction with other observatories. The enormous job of sorting all the spectra into classes fell to Annie Jump Cannon, who was appointed curator of the astronomical photographs there in 1911. Pickering asked her to sort all stars down to the ninth *magnitude:* a quarter million objects. Between 1911 and 1915, Cannon classified 5,000 stars per month.

Annie Jump Cannon's predecessor, Willamina Fleming, had created a classification system based on 15 categories named alphabetically from A to Q. Cannon dropped some empty categories and rearranged the rest from hottest to coolest stars rather than alphabetically. The new sequence became OBAFGKM, memorized by astronomy students ever since as "Oh Be A Fine Girl, Kiss Me." This classification system, called the Harvard Spectral Sequence, was adopted by the International Astronomical Union in December 1913.

Using the data provided by Harvard, Henry Norris Russell stunned the astronomical community in December 1913 with a plot of magnitude versus spectral type for more than 300 stars. He used radiation theory and lab tests to show the temperature sequence was reflected in the spectral classes. Hertzsprung had previously shown that temperature determined brightness (with the exception of the red giants). Russell showed with overwhelming observational data that spectral class (OBAFGKM) determined both temperature and brightness.

Russell's diagram was the first "family tree" of stars and was later called the Hertzsprung-Russell, or simply H-R, diagram (see figure on page 29). It clearly showed that 90 percent of stars fall into a band that was defined by brightness and class, later called the main sequence. Though the reasons would not be understood for another decade, it was clear that there were rules to how stars formed and evolved.

The diagram also provided astronomers with a powerful new way to find the distance to stars. Because Russell had correlated spectral class with brightness, just having a spectrum of a star was enough to determine its intrinsic or *absolute brightness*. By comparing this brightness with the observed or *apparent brightness*, the distance was found.

In December 1920, giant stars were proven to exist beyond doubt by the spectacular measurement of the angular diameter of Betelgeuse. Albert A. Michelson (1852–1931) and Francis Pease (1881–1938) mounted an *interferometer* on the new 100-inch (2.5-m) Hooker telescope that had gone into operation on Mount Wilson in November 1917. The diameter of Betelgeuse was found to be 240 million miles (386 million km), compared to the Sun's 870,000 miles (1.4 million km).

The Structure of Stars

In 1913, Henry Norris Russell determined that Cepheid variables were giant stars, and he ruled out that their variability in brightness was a result of being eclipsed by companions. Harlow Shapley, Russell's student, was convinced that Cepheids actually changed size, almost like they were breathing. Shapley earned his Ph.D. in astronomy and left Princeton for Mount Wilson in 1914, taking his interest in Cepheids with him. He found that their surface temperature changed along with brightness. The stars also pulsed in radial velocity, meaning that they moved slightly closer and then farther away from Earth. Shapley measured the velocity using the Doppler effect. When a light source moves toward and then away from an observer, the wavelength of light shifts to shorter and then longer wavelengths, similar to the way waves bunch up in front of a speed boat as it approaches and then spread out behind it as it moves away. The temperature and velocity data were consistent with a star whose surface expanded and became cooler and then contracted and grew hotter.

Arthur Eddington (see photo on page 30), Darwin's successor as director of the Cambridge University Observatory, was intrigued by Shapley's work. In 1916, Eddington derived a formula for a process called radiative equilibrium. In a stable star, he found that gravitational contraction is balanced by internal pressure. Eddington calculated that for a star the size of the Sun, the pressure only had to be about 10 percent of the gravitational force to keep the star together. For a huge star like a Cepheid, radiation pressure must be as high as 80 percent that of the star's gravity. In the June 1917 *Monthly Notices of the Royal Astronomical Society* (MNRAS) Eddington wrote, "A gas sphere under the influence of two opposed and nearly balanced forces would probably be on the verge of instability. . . . The suggestion is that though the radiation-pressure does not actually break up the mass, it produces a state in which the mass will, under ordinary circumstances, be broken up by rotation or other causes. Occasional large masses with exceptionally low angular momentum may survive, as in the case of Canopus."

Eddington found that the total radiation of a giant star was independent of its density and was dependent on its mass. As a giant contracted, it would not change much in luminosity because as its surface area diminished, it heated up and its energy efficiency increased. The more mass a star had, the hotter and brighter it would be.

Eddington noted that the brightest stars would not last long. Gravitational contraction would provide energy for only about 100,000 years. "We can only avoid a short time scale by supposing that the star has some unknown supply of energy," Eddington stated in the publication of his stellar theory "On the Radiative Equilibrium of the Stars" in the June 1917 issue of MNRAS. Eddington already had a theory that atomic radiation was at the heart of stellar energy. German physicist

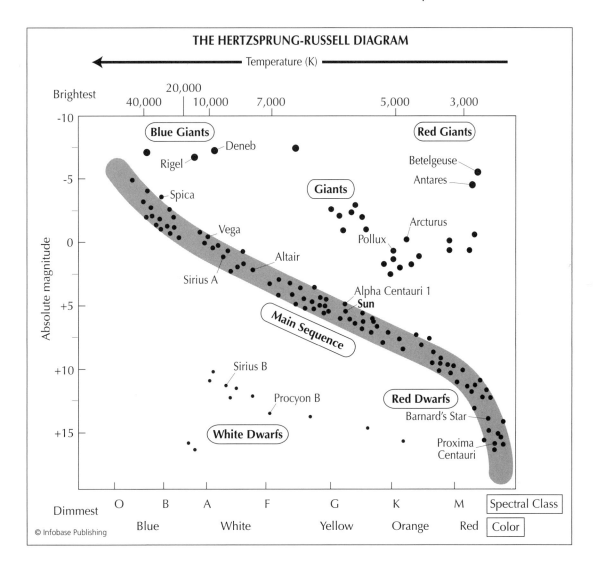

THE HERTZSPRUNG-RUSSELL DIAGRAM

Albert Einstein (1879–1955) articulated his famous equivalency equation, $E = mc^2$, where E stands for energy, m stands for mass, and c is the speed of light, in his 1905 paper "On the Electrodynamics of Moving Bodies." Energy can therefore be converted into matter and matter into energy. Because the speed of light is such an enormous number (186,000 miles [300,000 km] per second), even a tiny mass is equal to a huge amount of energy. Though no one knew how stars could convert mass to energy, Eddington concluded that they must. He also correctly concluded that the energy source was in the center of the star because otherwise the center would collapse under the weight of the overlying layers.

The Hertzsprung-Russell diagram is a graph of the brightness of stars versus their temperature and spectral class. Once absolute brightness and spectral type are known, apparent brightness is used to find a star's distance. The majority of stars lie along a band called the main sequence. Astronomers used this diagram to unravel the mysteries of stellar structure and evolution.

Sir Arthur Eddington successfully modeled the interior of stars and was a leading expert on general relativity. (AIP Emilio Segrè Archives)

Eddington's chief critic was James Jeans (1877–1946) who had written the standard text on gases and still favored the contraction theory because of the proper motion issue. He attacked Eddington's radiative equilibrium theory by disparaging the equations used to derive it. Eddington responded in kind, with the two royal astronomers dueling in Greek symbols in the scientific journals. Eddington eventually "won" (and received the Bruce Medal [see page 249] in 1924) because his theory was supported by observational evidence that mostly was provided by Henry Russell. He and Russell determined that the proper motion data was an artifact of a disproportionate number of high-mass bright stars being visible from great distances.

The answer to what makes a star shine was still a mystery at the end of the decade, but the foundation for understanding had been laid. In Albert Einstein's 1905 explanation of the photoelectric effect (that won him a Nobel Prize in physics), he stated that light was absorbed by atoms in bundles that corresponded to their wavelength times a constant named after its inventor, Max Planck. No matter how bright the light, if it were not the right wavelength, like a burner on low that will never make water boil, it would not make the gas atoms glow. Each element had a different-threshold wavelength that "excited" it to emit light. After that, more energy just added to the speed of the gas atoms. So light came in discrete bundles, later dubbed photons.

In 1913, Niels Bohr (1885–1962) formulated the "planetary" model of the atom with tiny electrons orbiting the much larger nucleus. In the Bohr model, electrons made transitions between allowed energy levels by emitting or absorbing a photon that has energy equal to the difference between the levels. The Bohr model predicted a set of frequencies of light that matched the hydrogen spectrum precisely.

The next breakthrough came in October 1920 when Indian astrophysicist Meghnad Saha (1893–1956) published an article that explained that the strength of spectral lines changed in sequence, according to what energy state that electrons occupied in atoms. As temperature increased, more electrons "jumped" to higher energy states defined by Bohr's model, increasing the intensity of lines in the spectra of hot stars. Some atoms would become so hot that they would be ionized—losing all their electrons. Thus, the lines for those states would disappear from the spectra. Only cooler stars had lines that represented lower energy states. There was now an explanation for why bright stars had fewer, but more intense lines than cool stars.

Even before Saha explained the connection between stellar temperature and spectral lines, Mount Wilson astronomers Walter Sydney Adams (1876–1956) and Arnold Kohlschütter (1883–1969) had discovered and used the relationship to find the distance to stars. In 1913, they had compared distant clusters of stars with close clusters to look for interstellar absorption in their spectra. All the stars in a cluster are at the same distance, so differences in brightness are caused by size. Adams found that the spectral lines intensified with stellar brightness. So just using the spectra gave him the absolute brightness that he could compare to apparent brightness to find distance. This method is called spectroscopic parallax. Adams received the Bruce Medal (see page 249) in 1928 partly for this work.

During the course of the decade, stellar spectra grew from being a tool to determine the elements and eclipsing properties of stars to a way to discover a star's temperature, brightness, size, and distance. Spectra also provided clues to the nature of stellar constitution and evolution. Astronomers depended on accurately classified spectra, and Annie Jump Cannon continued to provide what they needed. Between 1918 and 1924, Harvard published nine volumes of the *Henry Draper Catalog*. The catalog listed the spectral classification of 225,300 stars, each star's position in the sky, and its visual brightness. This catalog remains as an international standard that is valuable to astronomers because of its consistency as the work of one person.

Changing View of the Universe

At the turn of the century, the accepted model of the Milky Way was one developed by Jacobus Kapteyn that put the Sun about 6,500 light years from the center of a flattened galaxy with the stars thinning out in all directions. The modern view of the Milky Way with the Sun far from the center was a result of Harlow Shapley's work on globular clusters.

Shapley used the 60-inch (1.5-m) telescope at Mount Wilson to confirm Henrietta Leavitt's discovery that the period of pulsation of a Cepheid was related to its brightness (see figure on page 32). He discovered another type of variable stars, called RR Lyrae, that are similar to Cepheid variables except that they are average-sized stars instead of giants. The RR Lyrae stars pulsate with periods between 1.5 hours and one day. Cepheid stars were too far away to use parallax to determine their distance, so Shapley used the new H–R diagram spectra/brightness relation to determine their absolute brightness and hence the distance to globular clusters containing Cepheids. For clusters that lacked variable stars, Shapley estimated the distances based on an assumption (not a very good one) that the globular clusters were all about the same size.

A globular cluster is a tight spherical collection of as many as several hundred thousand stars. Globular clusters are not distributed uniformly in the sky. All but a few are in the thickest part of the Milky Way in the constellation Sagittarius.

In 1917, Harlow Shapley mapped out the 3D distribution in space of the 93 globular clusters then known. He found that the clusters formed a spherical system with a center point about 50,000 light-years from the Sun in the direction of the constellation Sagittarius. (Not knowing about dust effects, he overestimated the distance by a factor of two.) Shapley

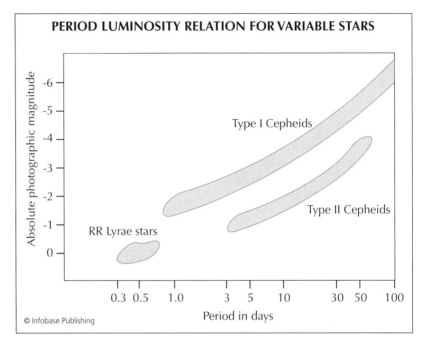

PERIOD LUMINOSITY RELATION FOR VARIABLE STARS

By measuring the period during which stars vary in brightness, their absolute brightness can be found and, from this, their distance. Until 1944, RR Lyrae and Cepheids of Type I and II were grouped together, leading to an underestimate of the distance to the brighter Type I Cepheid variables.

© Infobase Publishing

correctly decided that the center of these massive clusters was also the center of the galaxy. This led him to conclude that the Sun is far from that center.

Heber Curtis (1872–1942) of Lick Observatory proposed in 1917 that novae could be used in the same way as Cepheids to determine the distance to *nebulae*, mysterious fuzzy patches in the sky whose nature was not yet known. Christopher Wren (1632–1723) had suggested in the 17th century that nebulae might be star systems that were so distant that the light of the individual stars blurred into a milky, continuous glow. He called them *island universes*. Over the years, nebulae had been divided into two basic types: irregular ones that were concentrated near the Milky Way, and symmetrical (elliptical or spiral) ones that were the most numerous in the sky away from the Milky Way.

By 1917, several novae had been discovered in the spiral nebulae. If those novae were as luminous as the 26 novae then known to have occurred in our galaxy, then these nebulae would have to be about a million light-years away—they would be island universes. Heber Curtis studied how novae brighten and dim, what is called their light curve. He found that the light curves were the same shape for all novae but were much fainter for the ones in the nebulae. He interpreted this (correctly) to mean that the nebulae were island universes. Within a year, the island universe was again a popular theory, and Curtis was one of its primary proponents.

Curtis also noted that some of the nebulae, seen edge-on, had dark lanes that bisect them. He correctly suggested that if such a structure existed in our galaxy, it would block our view through the middle and explain why we do not see spiral nebulae in the Milky Way.

Yerkes Observatory director Edward Barnard's 1919 catalog of dark nebulae supported Curtis's idea of an obscuring plane of dust in the Milky Way. Commenting on the blackness of the dark nebulae in his catalog, Barnard (1857–1923) wrote that he had "proven" them to be "obscuring masses of matter in space." He pioneered the technique known as star counting, comparing an expected to an observed density of stars in the sky and attributing the difference to interstellar dust. By associating this dust with gas that absorbed background starlight and produced emission-line nebulae near hot young stars, researchers correctly concluded that large clouds of interstellar material collapse to form new stars. Barnard received a Bruce Medal (see page 249) in 1917 for this work.

Vesto Slipher produced data that gradually convinced him that the nebulae were island universes. By December 1910, Slipher had obtained a spectral plate of the Great Nebula in Andromeda using a 30-hour exposure of the Lowell 24-inch (0.6-m) refractor. During the last four months of 1912, Slipher obtained spectrograms of Andromeda that revealed a considerable Doppler displacement of lines toward the violet, indicating an unusual velocity of approach. The final plate required exposures for three consecutive nights. He advised Percival Lowell, "I feel it safe to say here, that the velocity bids fair to come out unusually high." A month later after careful measurements, Slipher reported that Andromeda was approaching the solar system at the then unheard of speed of 186 miles per second (300 km/sec). Slipher then found a velocity of recession of about 620 miles per second (1,000 km/sec) for NGC 4594. During the next three years, his observations of 22 other spirals turned up similar velocities. If these objects were part of the Milky Way, how could they be moving toward or away from it so fast? This was a question that would be answered years later by Edwin Hubble (1889–1953), then a graduate student who attended one of Slipher's lectures.

In 1913, Vesto Slipher noted that the spectral lines of the Virgo nebula were tilted as well as Doppler shifted. A tilt in a spectrum revealed rotation, and so he assumed (correctly) that the Virgo nebula was rotating. The faintness of the nebula made it terribly difficult to study. Slipher required exposure of the same plate for several nights, all of which had to be clear nights with good seeing conditions. It was a full year before he got another plate to confirm the tilt. On May 24, 1914, he wired Percival Lowell that "Spectrograms show Virgo nebula rotating." A few months later, he found evidence that the Andromeda nebula also rotated. In April 1917, Slipher told a meeting of the American Philosophical Society that his work supported the island universe theory.

Not everyone agreed that nebulae were island universes. Astronomers refuted Heber Curtis by pointing out that one nova (now recognized as a supernova) in Andromeda had increased in brilliance in 1885 until it was one-tenth as bright as the entire nebulae. Astronomers were reluctant to believe that a nebula composed of many stars could have one star as bright as millions of others. They thought this meant that Andromeda was only a few thousand light-years away.

Astronomer Adriann van Maanen (1884–1946) used the new 100-inch (2.5-m) telescope on Mount Wilson to provide data that seemed to prove that the nebulae were part of the Milky Way. He compared photos of spirals taken years apart and calculated their period of rotation to be about 100,000 years. If these spirals were distant island universes, then they would have to be so large that the outer parts would move at or near the speed of light—impossible! The high rotation rates were later shown to be measurement errors, but at the time, this data convinced two very influential astronomers, Henry Norris Russell and Harlow Shapley, that the island universe theory was wrong.

On April 26, 1920, Harlow Shapley (see photo on page 35) and Heber Curtis formally debated the "The Scale of the Universe" before the National Academy of Sciences in Washington, D.C. Curtis supported the island universe theory, and Shapley opposed it.

From his studies of the Cepheids, Harlow Shapley had established that the Milky Way was 10 times bigger than previously thought. Not understanding the effects of dust, Shapley had underestimated (by a factor of two) the distance to the Small Magellanic Cloud (SMC) to be about 75,000 light-years. He had overestimated (by a factor of two) the size of the Milky Way to be 300,000 light-years. This convinced him that the gigantic Milky Way included the SMC. He thought that it was big enough to include the spiral nebulae, too, and used the data from van Maanen to argue that they were gas clouds within the Milky Way. In Shapley's model, the Sun was far from the center of this universe/galaxy. His former professor and good friend, Henry Russell, supported him in this argument.

Heber Curtis thought that the galaxy was far smaller than Shapley's measurements indicated. Because the galaxy was small, the nebulae were comparable in size to our own galaxy and far away from it. He placed the Sun near the center of our relatively small galaxy. Curtis had strong support from Arthur Eddington, who thought that nebulae were galaxies like our own.

History records that Curtis "won" the debate using the wrong argument. Shapley was right about the Milky Way being huge and the Sun not being at the center, but he was wrong about the position of the SMC and the nebulae. Curtis was right about the relative positions of the nebulae, but he was wrong about the size of the Milky Way and the Sun's location in it. The "great debate" served the purpose of stimulating a lot of research that in a few years would lead to a breakthrough in understanding of humanity's place in the universe.

Harlow Shapley discovered that the Milky Way was much larger than previously thought. A protégé of Henry Russell, he lost a debate on the size of the universe in 1920 by claiming that the Andromeda "nebula" was part of the Milky Way. He headed the Harvard Observatory. (AIP Emilio Segrè Visual Archives. Shapley Collection)

Cosmology

While astronomers debated our place in the universe, physicists tried to define what *place* actually meant. Does the universe have a center? Is there a place that is not moving relative to all other places, a fixed background? The search for answers to these questions led to the development of *cosmology*, the scientific (as opposed to theological) study of the origin and the evolution of the universe.

Albert Einstein's special theory of relativity explained that two observers moving at a constant rate relative to one another would each think that the other was moving while they held still. Both would measure the same speed for light. For the speed (distance versus time) of light to be constant for all "places," time and distance must be adjustable, or relative. Special relativity is a set of equations that show observers in one place, or frame of reference, how to convert their time and distance measures to that of another place, moving at a constant velocity relative to them.

The effects of relativity are tiny unless one observer is moving at a great speed compared to the other. For example, if one twin stays home while the other jets around the world, even after 20 years, there will be no perceptible difference in their ages. But if one twin stays home and the other boards a spaceship moving at 90 percent the speed of light, after 20 Earth years, in what is called the twin paradox, the one who rode the ship will return only about nine years older. The twin on Earth will measure the spaceship's time units as stretched. The twin on the spaceship would measure the Earth-bound twin's time units as shortened. They would both measure the same speed of light.

The fact that space and time vary did not have much impact on astronomy until Albert Einstein published his general theory of relativity (GTR) in 1915. The GTR is much more mathematically difficult than the special theory of relativity because it applies to accelerated frames of reference versus ones that are moving at constant speeds. Physicists still argue over the physical interpretations of the solutions to the equations. Yet, GTR immediately explained one astronomical mystery.

Astronomers had known for decades that Mercury's perihelion, its closest point to the Sun, shifts by 43 seconds of arc per century beyond what *Newton's law of gravity* predicts. In the mid-1800s, French astronomer Urbain-Jean-Joseph Leverrier (1811–77) tried to explain the shift or precession by perturbations from another planet closer to the Sun, called Vulcan. The GTR accounted for the precession of Mercury without the need of Vulcan. GTR predicted that a body in close orbit around a large mass has its movement altered by the curvature of space. Albert Einstein's friend Abraham Pais (1918–2000) wrote, "This discovery was, I believe, by far the strongest emotional experience in Einstein's scientific life, perhaps in all his life. Nature had spoken to him." He said that Einstein was beside himself "with joyous excitement."

GTR explained that gravity was the result of the curvature of space. As an object falls toward Earth, it accelerates as it approaches the ground. One gravity or *g* is an acceleration of 32 feet (9.8 m) per second per second. In other words, an object falls 32 feet (9.8) the first second, then 64 feet (19.6 m) the next second, and so on until impact. GTR says that this acceleration is the result of the Earth's mass curving space around it, like a ball on a bed.

Light has no mass to accelerate, so it cannot speed up. It can change direction toward "down." In "empty" space, light moves in a straight line. In a highly curved space, the GTR predicts that light dips into the "well" caused by the mass and then continues in a different direction.

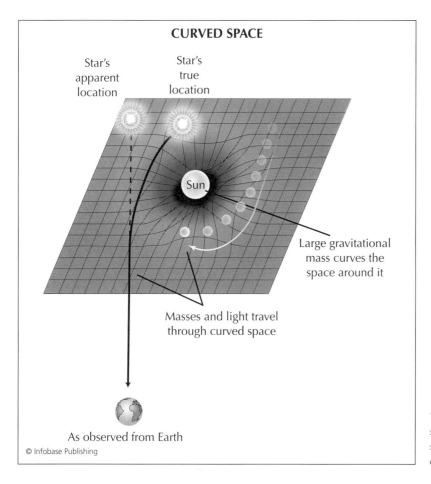

CURVED SPACE

Star's apparent location

Star's true location

Sun

Large gravitational mass curves the space around it

Masses and light travel through curved space

As observed from Earth

© Infobase Publishing

The general theory of relativity states that matter curves space so that light follows a bent path around stars.

Astrophysicists needed a solar eclipse to test whether or not light bent as it passed around the Sun because otherwise the Sun's glare would wash out the starlight. Also, the star must be near the line of sight to the Sun and part of a cluster of bright stars to use for comparison. In some periods of history, it would have been necessary to wait a thousand years for a total eclipse to meet these conditions. May 29, 1919 offered a perfect opportunity: an eclipse with the Hyades star cluster in the background.

Arthur Eddington took advantage of this historical opportunity. He photographed the Hyades while they were opposite the Sun. He calculated that if the target star was deflected 0.87 arc seconds during the eclipse, it would agree with Newton's law of gravity. If it were deflected 1.75 arc seconds, then the data would agree with Einstein's GTR prediction. Planning an expedition near the end of World War I was a challenge. The British Royal Astronomer, Sir Frank Dyson (1868–1939) (see Bruce Medalists, page 249), smoothed the way for Eddington. He obtained

Scientist of the Decade: Henry Norris Russell (1877–1957)

Henry Norris Russell was best known for his work on stellar evolution that is embodied in the Hertzsprung-Russell diagram and for 43 years of monthly columns in *Scientific American*. Called the dean of American astronomers, the Princeton Observatory director from 1912 until his retirement in 1946 had the power to decide career appointments, advise on research programs, control juried publication, and direct much of the national money that was earmarked for astronomy.

The son of a Presbyterian minister, Russell was born in Oyster Bay, New York, on October 25, 1877. Sent to Princeton Prep School at age 12, he entered Princeton University at 15. Russell's senior thesis was "Visual Observations of Star Spectra." He graduated with the appellation insigni cum laude, a standing above summa and magna. The *New York Tribune* called him "one of the most remarkable scholars educated at Princeton in many years." The head of the math department said Russell was "by far the best mathematician who has ever come under his instruction."

While a Princeton graduate student, Russell found a new graphical way to measure mass in binary star systems and used it to derive the density of stars. This early work on density would later open a window into stellar evolution.

On May 9, 1900, Russell received his Ph.D. in astronomy. His thesis was "General Perturbations of the Major Axis of Eros by the Action of Mars." Russell was very embarrassed when the asteroid on which he worked was named Eros. A deeply religious Puritan who did not drink coffee or smoke, Russell's classmates teased him about being a world-renowned expert on Eros, the god of love.

In 1902, Russell went to Cambridge, England, to work under George Darwin who was known for his fission theory. This theory, combined with work on binary systems with Arthur Hinks (1873–1945), would lead to Russell's ideas on how stars aged. Russell found a technique to reduce the time it took to derive stellar parallaxes that helped

Henry Norris Russell was called the dean of American astronomy. (Yerkes Observatory Photographs)

observatories reduce their backlog of unprocessed photographic plates.

Russell returned home in 1904 and contracted typhoid. His Cambridge fellowship was not renewed, so he returned to Princeton in 1905 with a pile of unfinished parallax work. He was hired as an instructor and was promoted to assistant professor in 1908. Secure at Princeton, Russell married Lucy May Cole on November 24, 1908. His father led the ceremony. He and Lucy had twin daughters in 1911, a son in 1912, and another daughter in 1914.

By 1910, Russell finished his stellar parallax analysis. He discovered a relationship between the absolute magnitudes and spectral types of stars, similar to the magnitude and color relationship that Ejnar Hertzsprung had found in 1905. Russell published his ideas in "Some Hints on the Order of Stellar Evolution" in the June 1910 issue of *Science*.

In 1911, Russell became a full professor, and his first graduate student, Harlow Shapley, arrived, beginning a long professional and personal friendship. The two men worked on binary systems that presented difficult mathematical problems. Russell applied his genius to the data and declared that exact solutions were not possible or necessary. He created the Russell method to simplify the computations to a set of standardized tables. When some people resisted his "shortcut" methods in 1914, he said, "I am always trying to best Father Time with the aid of what mathematical weapons I can bring to bear on things."

In 1913, Russell first used his famous diagram relating stellar magnitude to spectral class. His proposed path for the evolution of stars from giants to dwarfs was subsequently shown to be wrong. His data showed that there are both giant and dwarf stars and that spectral class could be used to determine absolute brightness and, thus, distance. He received the Royal Astronomical Society's Gold medal in 1921 and the Bruce Medal in 1925 for this work. A former student of Hertzsprung, Gerard (Gerrit) Kuiper (1905–73), got the name of the diagram changed from Russell to Hertzsprung-Russell, or just H-R in 1940.

Russell was considered the most intelligent astronomer around in the 1920s and was offered the directorship of both the Yerkes and the Harvard Observatories. He decided to stay at Princeton where he avoided administrative work and focused on research of stellar spectra. He also wrote many essays on religion from the perspective of a scientist, promoting the view that theory and theology both benefited from observations of nature.

In 1925, Russell reviewed the thesis of Cecilia Payne (1900–80) that revealed stars are mostly hydrogen and helium. He thought that the proportion of these elements to others such as iron should be the same in the Sun as found on Earth. Such was his influence that Payne changed her conclusion to say, "The stellar abundance deduced for these elements is improbably high, and is almost certainly not real." Working with his assistant, Charlotte Moore Sitterly (1898–1990) who received a Bruce Medal (see page 249) in 1990, Russell derived the relative abundance of some 50 different elements in the Sun. He eventually accepted and proved Payne (then Gaposchkin) was right.

With physicist Frederick A. Saunders (1875–1963), Russell discovered an additional quantum requirement, the Russell-Saunders coupling that explained lines in stellar spectra. Russell and Heinrich Vogt (1890–1968) independently discovered the Vogt-Russell theorem that the physical properties of stars depend solely on mass and chemical composition.

Russell retired from Princeton in 1947, passing control of Princeton's Observatory and Astrophysics Department to one of his former graduate students, Lyman Spitzer, Jr. (1914–97). Russell worked on stellar composition tables until his death by heart failure on February 18, 1957, at the age of 79.

Perhaps Henry Norris Russell's greatest achievement was not the Hertzsprung-Russell diagram but the example he set of insisting that theory be tested by a program of observations. His idea that giant stars cool into dwarfs was proven wrong by his own careful calculations. The testing of that theory led directly to his discovery that the properties of a star depend on its mass and chemical composition. He later derived the relative abundance of more than 50 elements in the Sun and other stars, proving himself wrong in assuming that stars have the same proportion of hydrogen and helium as found on Earth. As head of national committees that determined what projects were funded, and as associate editor and columnist for *Scientific American* where he shaped public opinion of astronomy and astronomers, Henry Norris Russell promoted the testing of theory with observations that resulted in breakthroughs in understanding of stars and established the framework for all future work on stellar composition and evolution.

the official blessings and funding for two expeditions, one to Brazil and one to an island off the coast of Africa.

Eddington's first attempt to witness a solar eclipse in Brazil in 1912 had been rained out. Hoping for good weather this time, he went to Africa. But on the morning of May 29, there was a tremendous rainstorm at Eddington's site. The rain stopped just before the eclipse, but the sky remained cloudy. Eddington wrote in his journal, "We had to carry out our programme of photographs in faith." He took 16 photographs. Only one plate was clear of clouds, but the measurements agreed with Einstein. Back in England he found one other that confirmed the result.

The group that went to Brazil, headed by Andrew Crommelin (1865–1939), had perfect weather, or so they thought. Their photo results agreed with Newton! Eddington suspected that the bright sun in Brazil had warped the telescope's mirror. Luckily, the Brazilian team had also taken photos with a small refractor that had not been affected by the heat. The results from the refractor agreed with Einstein. The announcement put Albert Einstein and his theory of general relativity onto the front pages of newspapers around the world. An urban legend arose that when asked by a reporter who suggested that only three people in the world understood relativity, Eddington jokingly replied, "Oh, who's the third?"

In 1920, Arthur Eddington published *Space, Time and Gravitation: An Outline of the General Relativity Theory*, which quickly became a classic. In this book, Eddington predicted an effect called gravitational lensing. In the same way that starlight is bent around the Sun, Eddington predicted that light from a distant object would be focused by a large mass situated between an emitter and an observer. This effect is now used as a sort of natural telescope to view the most distant objects in the universe.

A third prediction of GTR was the effect of curved space on light leaving the surface of a large mass. Light cannot slow down, but it can lose energy by reducing its frequency like a stretched spring. The highest frequency waves, those in the blue end of the visible spectrum, are stretched into low frequency waves in the red end of the spectrum. The amount of stretching of the wavelength is called its gravitational redshift, not to be confused with Doppler redshift that is caused by movement away from an observer.

It was not until 1960 that this effect was measured. Robert V. Pound (1919–   ) and Glen A. Rebka, Jr. (1931–   ) demonstrated that a beam of high energy gamma rays was slightly redshifted as it fought against gravity to go up an elevator shaft in the physics building at Harvard. The redshift predicted by the GTR for the 74-foot tower was only two parts in a thousand trillion. The gravitational redshift detected came within 10 percent of the computed value.

A strange consequence of gravitational redshift was discovered in 1916 by German physicist Karl Schwarzschild. He calculated the radius of an object so dense that its gravity would prevent light from escaping at all. A mass contracted to what is called the Schwarzschild radius is now called a *black hole*. The idea of a black hole was first suggested by French astronomer Pierre-Simon de Laplace (1749–1827) in 1796, but Schwarzschild was the first to explain them as a consequence of the GTR. At a time when the source of energy of stars was still a mystery, no one imagined that such dense objects really existed.

In 1917, Einstein realized that a curved universe was not stable—the matter and energy in it must be either accelerating "out" or falling "in" so that it was expanding or contracting. The observable universe appeared stable, so he added a *cosmological constant* to the formula. The cosmological constant, represented by the Greek symbol lambda, corresponds to a sort of tension in the cosmic "substrate" so that work has to be done on the universe for it to expand. When Edwin Hubble later showed that the universe was expanding, Einstein called this addition to the formula a mistake. In the 1990s, when the expansion was discovered to be accelerating, it appeared that lambda might belong in the equations after all.

The interaction between astronomy and physics would continue to grow in the next decade and be reinforced by the influx of theorists from Germany after World War I.

Further Reading

Books and Periodicals

Chaisson, Eric, and Steve McMillan. *Astronomy Today: Fifth Edition.* Upper Saddle River, N.J.: Prentice Hall, 2004. A comprehensive astronomy text for nonscience majors that covers the history, the planets, stellar evolution, galaxies and cosmology, and space-based astronomy with many helpful diagrams and appendices for references.

C. A. Chant. "Betelgeuse: How Its Diameter Was Measured." *Journal of the Royal Astronomical Society of Canada* 15 (1921): 133–136. Available online. URL: http://adsabs.harvard.edu//full/seri/JRASC/0015//0000133.000. html. The original technical journal article describes how astronomers measured the diameter of the first star other than the Sun.

DeVorkin, David H. *Henry Norris Russell: Dean of American Astronomers.* Princeton, N.J.: Princeton University Press, 2000. A scholarly biography that covers the astronomer's life and the major topics of astronomy during the early 20th century.

A. S. Eddington. "On the Radiative Equilibrium of the Stars." *Monthly Notices of the Royal Astronomical Society* 77 (November 1916): 16–35. Available online. URL: http://articles.adsabs.harvard.edu/cgi-bin/nph-iarticle_query ?1916MNRAS..77...16E. The original, highly technical journal article that proposes the radiative theory that stars balance their contraction by radiation. James Jeans's article refuting the theory and Eddington's response are in Vol. 78, November 1917, of the same periodical.

Sandage, Allan. *Centennial History of the Carnegie Institution of Washington: Volume 1, The Mount Wilson Observatory: Breaking the Code of Cosmic Evolution.* Cambridge: Cambridge University Press, 2005. This book covers the science and personal stories of those involved in theories of stellar evolution and cosmology at the Mount Wilson Observatory.

Web Sites

Walter Adams. "Adams Reminiscences." Mount Wilson Observatory Association. URL: http://www.mwoa.org/adams.html. Accessed on February 4, 2006. A personal history of Mount Wilson Observatory including the installation of the 100-inch (2.5-m) telescope in 1917, written by Walter Adams in 1947. Adams was a close associate of George Hale who founded the Observatory and became its director when Hale retired.

Robert Nemiroff and Jerry Bonnell. "The Shapley-Curtis Debate in 1920." URL: http://antwrp.gsfc.nasa.gov/debate/debate20.html. Accessed on February 4, 2006. This site includes a transcript of the debate "The Scale of the Universe" and a discussion of the importance and issues involved in the debate.

Nick Strobel. "Einstein's Relativity." URL: http://www.astronomynotes.com/relativity/s1.htm. Accessed on January 4, 2007. An astronomy professor discusses concepts of spacetime and gravity and proofs of Einstein's special and general relativity theories.

University of Illinois. "Spacetime Wrinkles Map." NCSA Mulitmedia Online Exp. URL: http://archive.ncsa.uiuc.edu/Cyberia/Expo/numrel_nav.html. Accessed on February 4, 2006. A good series of explanations of relativity in layman's terms.

Yerkes Observatory. "Edward Emerson Barnard (1857–1923)." Yerkes Observatory Virtual Museum. URL: http://www.phys-astro.sonoma.edu/BruceMedalists/Barnard/index/html. Accessed on August 28, 2006. An illustrated biography of the astronomer and his work at the Yerkes Observatory.

3

1921–1930:
The Expanding Universe

Breakthroughs in astronomy and rocket science played out against a background of social upheaval and cultural change in the 1920s. It was the decade of the Model T, the transatlantic flight of Charles Lindbergh (1902–74), prohibition, gangsters and the first movie stars. Telephones and radios sold in huge numbers, and the first television station was created. Concerned that people needlessly feared new technology, American immigrant and inventor Hugo Gernsback (1884–1967) published the first issue of *Science and Invention* magazine in August 1920. This was the first magazine to include science fiction, a term that Gernsback coined. Science-fiction stories from his magazines became the basis for popular movies, comic strips, and radio and television shows. Science fiction helped the public accept the many discoveries in astronomy and inspired a generation of scientists to invent the new technologies that would lead to human exploration of space in future decades.

The study of the physical properties of astronomical objects, the great debate of 1920 about the size of the universe, and the completion of the 100-inch (2.5-m) telescope set the stage for one of the most significant discoveries of the century: that the universe is expanding. The man who made this discovery in 1929 was Edwin Hubble, the featured scientist of the decade. The expansion of the universe was the second of Hubble's major discoveries: the first was proof that the Milky Way is not the only galaxy in the universe. The circumstances of these momentous discoveries are a major topic of this chapter.

Throughout this decade, astrophysicists continued to explore the mystery of how stars produce energy and remain stable for billions of years. Arthur Eddington produced a landmark book called *The Internal Constitution of Stars* in 1926 that included a complete mathematical treatment of stellar thermodynamics. Subrahmanyan Chandrasekhar (1910–95) adjusted the equations that describe stellar structures to account for relativity, deriving limits to the mass of collapsing stars. Applying a new understanding that the intensity of spectral lines provides information on the abundance of elements in stars, Cecilia Payne showed that the Sun and other stars are mostly made of hydrogen. Her influential adviser, Henry Russell, forced her to change her conclusions before publication but eventually proved that she was right. The work of the theorists and astronomers described in this chapter will combine in future decades to answer the fundamental question of how stars live and die. Also described in this chapter is the historical discovery of Pluto by Clyde Tombaugh (1906–97) in 1930.

Hermann Oberth (1894–1989) in Germany and Robert Goddard in the United States devoted themselves to making science fiction into reality. While Oberth worked on theory, Goddard designed and tested the first liquid-fueled rocket in 1926. Publicity over his work attracted the patronage of Charles Lindbergh and the Guggenheim Foundation. The stock-market crash of 1929 and the worldwide Depression that followed dried up funding in both Germany and the United States, stalling the development of space-capable rockets. Rocket scientists would be forced to pursue their dreams under the military banners of their countries in future decades.

Nebulae Become Galaxies

In the 1920s, everything was being electrified and motorized, and on October 21, 1923, the public first saw an artificial night sky. In Munich,

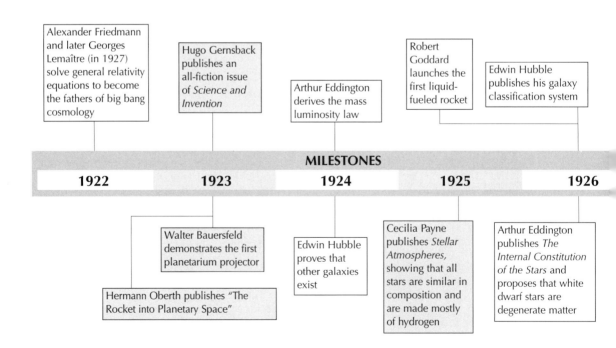

Alexander Friedmann and later Georges Lemaître (in 1927) solve general relativity equations to become the fathers of big bang cosmology

Hugo Gernsback publishes an all-fiction issue of *Science and Invention*

Arthur Eddington derives the mass luminosity law

Robert Goddard launches the first liquid-fueled rocket

Edwin Hubble publishes his galaxy classification system

MILESTONES

| 1922 | 1923 | 1924 | 1925 | 1926 |

Walter Bauersfeld demonstrates the first planetarium projector

Hermann Oberth publishes "The Rocket into Planetary Space"

Edwin Hubble proves that other galaxies exist

Cecilia Payne publishes *Stellar Atmospheres,* showing that all stars are similar in composition and are made mostly of hydrogen

Arthur Eddington publishes *The Internal Constitution of the Stars* and proposes that white dwarf stars are degenerate matter

Germany, Professor Walter Bauersfeld (1879–1959) demonstrated the first (Zeiss) planetarium projector at the Deutsches museum, where it was permanently installed in 1925. The projector produced, on the inside of a dome, dots of light that represented stars in the night sky. But thanks to Einstein's general theory of relativity and Edwin Hubble's observations through the new 100-inch (2.5-m) telescope on Mount Wilson, the public's view of the universe would soon change in even more dramatic ways.

After serving in World War I, Major Hubble arrived at Mount Wilson to begin his investigations of nebulae. The question of whether or not they were part of the Milky Way galaxy or island universes was destined to be his to answer.

On the night of October 4, 1923, despite very poor seeing conditions, Hubble took a long exposure of the spiral nebula in Andromeda. He thought that he saw a nova on the plate, so he took another exposure the next night under better conditions. That plate confirmed the existence of two novae, but more importantly, it showed the first Cepheid variable star seen in a nebula. Harvard "computer" Henrietta Leavitt had discovered in 1908 that the period of Cepheids can be used to find their distance. Harlow Shapley had used this relationship to "resize" the Milky Way galaxy in the previous decade. The ability to resolve these bright stars in a nebula was new. Only the 100-inch (2.5-m) telescope was

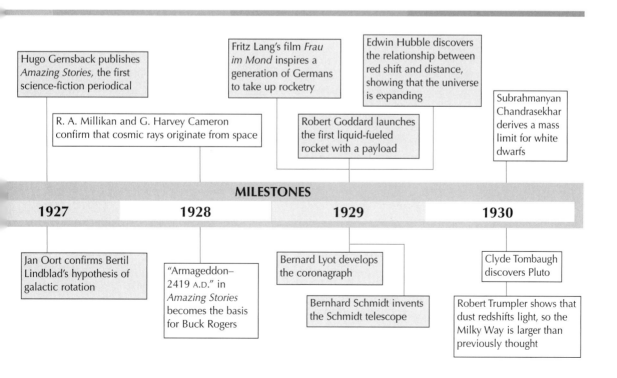

Hugo Gernsback publishes *Amazing Stories*, the first science-fiction periodical

Fritz Lang's film *Frau im Mond* inspires a generation of Germans to take up rocketry

Edwin Hubble discovers the relationship between red shift and distance, showing that the universe is expanding

Subrahmanyan Chandrasekhar derives a mass limit for white dwarfs

R. A. Millikan and G. Harvey Cameron confirm that cosmic rays originate from space

Robert Goddard launches the first liquid-fueled rocket with a payload

MILESTONES

1927   **1928**   **1929**   **1930**

Jan Oort confirms Bertil Lindblad's hypothesis of galactic rotation

"Armageddon–2419 A.D." in *Amazing Stories* becomes the basis for Buck Rogers

Bernard Lyot develops the coronagraph

Bernhard Schmidt invents the Schmidt telescope

Clyde Tombaugh discovers Pluto

Robert Trumpler shows that dust redshifts light, so the Milky Way is larger than previously thought powerful enough to do it. Hubble found that the Cepheid in Andromeda had an apparent brightness of only one ten-thousandth of those in the Small Magellanic Cloud (SMC) that Henrietta Leavitt had cataloged in 1908. Because the apparent brightness of an object decreases by the square of its distance, Hubble concluded that the Andromeda nebula was 100 times farther than the SMC, or about 1 million (now estimated at 2 million) light-years away. Though some astronomers, such as Heber Curtis in the 1920 debate with Harlow Shapley, had argued that nebulae were galaxies, Hubble now had proof. No other telescope was powerful enough to confirm his results, so Hubble searched for other examples of Cepheids during the next year before announcing his discovery at an American Astronomical Society meeting on December 30, 1924.

The astronomical community found Hubble's data thoroughly convincing. Copernicus had proven that Earth was not the center of the universe, Shapley had shown that the solar system was not the center of the Milky Way. And now Hubble had proven that the Milky Way was only one of many galaxies in the universe.

With the existence of galaxies established, the astronomical community turned its attention to the evolution and distribution of galaxies in space. British astronomer James Jeans had already proposed that nebulae evolve from spheres to ellipses to spirals. This theory was not seriously challenged until decades later when ellipticals were shown to contain mostly old stars.

Hubble favored Jeans's galactic evolution idea and developed a system of classifying nebulae (see figure on page 47) that reflected it. Hubble submitted this system to the International Astronomical Union, hoping for a speedy endorsement. While they debated, Hubble published a preliminary version in 1922. The committee felt that the evolutionary sequence needed to be established before formally adopting a system. In 1926, Swedish astronomer Knut Lundmark (1889–1958) proposed a classification system that was nearly identical to Hubble's. Hubble criticized Lundmark for not giving him due credit and published his own revised system that same year in the *Astrophysical Journal*. The Hubble classification system was easy to use and widely adopted. The familiar "tuning fork" diagram first appeared in his 1936 book, *The Realm of the Nebulae*.

While Hubble photographed more nebulae, others studied their properties. Adrian van Maanen had calculated fast rotation rates for nebulae. He believed that these calculations (cited by Harlow Shapley in the 1920 debate) supported the theory that nebulae were nearby and part of the Milky Way galaxy. Hubble's Cepheid data proved that the nebulae were distant and that van Maanen was wrong. Therefore, Shapley's position in the debate with Heber Curtis, that the Milky Way was the only galaxy, was also wrong. Swedish astronomer Bertil Lindblad (1895–1965) found an explanation for the fast rotation rates that van Maanen had measured. He suggested that galaxies do not rotate as solid objects but that the speed of rotation of stars about the galactic center depends on their

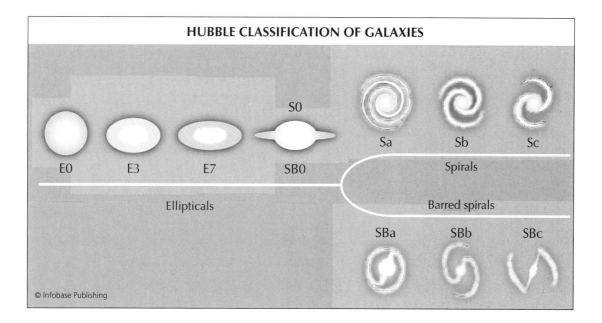

HUBBLE CLASSIFICATION OF GALAXIES

SO

E0 E3 E7 SB0

Sa Sb Sc

Spirals

Ellipticals

Barred spirals

SBa SBb SBc

© Infobase Publishing

distance from it, what is called differential rotation. In 1927, Swedish astronomer Jan H. Oort (1900–92) confirmed this hypothesis by analyzing motions of distant stars. Both Lindblad and Oort received the Bruce Medal (see page 249) partly for this work.

Most astronomers assumed that galaxies would be distributed evenly in space, and Hubble planned to prove it with observational data. Hubble estimated how many galaxies of each magnitude he should see as distance increased. The 100-inch (2.5-m) telescope has a very deep, narrow field of view, so it would take thousands of years to photograph the entire sky with it. So Hubble chose 1,283 sample regions and counted the galaxies on each photograph, finding more than 44,000 in all.

Hubble found most galaxies near the galactic poles and found hardly any in what he called the zone of avoidance that corresponds to the light-blocking dust of the Milky Way. He concluded that galaxies are distributed evenly in all directions and that the density of galaxies is the same at all distances. This conclusion was challenged in the 1930s after wide sky surveys showed that galaxies clump into clusters.

Hubble and his assistant, former Mount Wilson janitor Milton Humason (1891–1972) continued to find Cepheids in more nebulae. Using them as distance markers, Hubble plotted the distance of nebulae against their speeds that Slipher had measured years before. He found that the speed of a galaxy increased linearly with its distance from the Sun, a relationship now called Hubble's law (see figure on page 48). This was such a surprise that Hubble and Humason checked many more nebulae before they published their discovery in 1929.

Edwin Hubble devised a simple way of classifying galaxies by their shape.

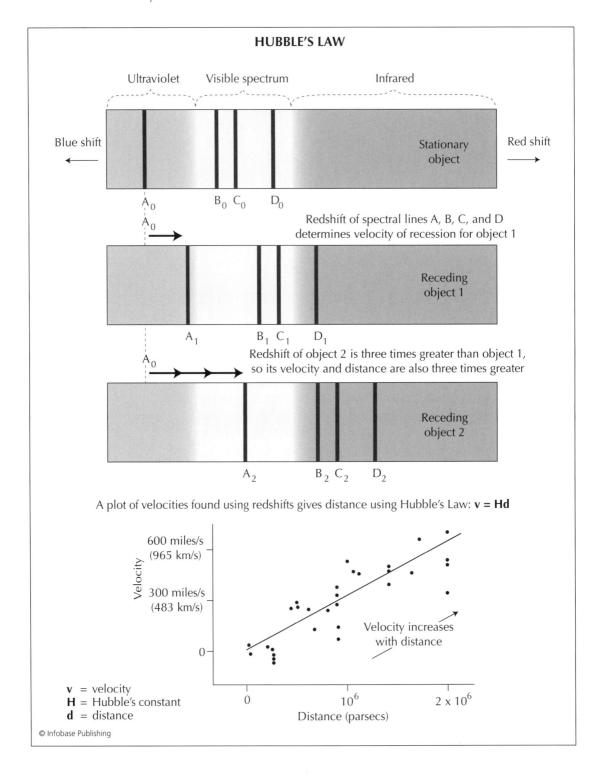

HUBBLE'S LAW

Ultraviolet   Visible spectrum   Infrared

Blue shift   Stationary object   Red shift

A_0 B_0 C_0 D_0

A_0 Redshift of spectral lines A, B, C, and D
determines velocity of recession for object 1

Receding object 1

A_1 B_1 C_1 D_1

A_0 Redshift of object 2 is three times greater than object 1,
so its velocity and distance are also three times greater

Receding object 2

A_2 B_2 C_2 D_2

A plot of velocities found using redshifts gives distance using Hubble's Law: **v = Hd**

600 miles/s
(965 km/s)

Velocity

300 miles/s
(483 km/s)

Velocity increases
with distance

0

0   10^6 2×10^6

Distance (parsecs)

v = velocity
H = Hubble's constant
d = distance

© Infobase Publishing

Hubble's law allowed redshift alone to be used to measure distance to nebulae. But even more importantly, the new law solved the puzzle of fast-moving galaxies. Their motion was the result of the universe expanding and "carrying" them away like dots on the surface of a balloon (see figure on page 50). Not only did the Milky Way share the universe with other galaxies, but the universe was not even stable. It was in a constant state of expansion.

Astronomers soon realized that the rate of expansion, called the Hubble constant, could be used to find the time elapsed since all galaxies were clumped together in the past, a beginning now called the *big bang*. Hubble first calculated this "Hubble time" at 2 billion years, off by at least 10 billion. The estimate was off because he had underestimated the distances to galaxies. Among other things, the reddening, or extinction effect, of interstellar dust was not yet understood. In 1930, Robert Trumpler (1886–1956) found that stars in distant clusters were redder than stars of the same spectral type in nearby clusters. He concluded that interstellar space is filled with dust that scatters blue light, making stars appear dim. Walter Baade would also later find that Cepheids in Andromeda were brighter and more distant than Hubble thought.

Unknown to Hubble until after his discovery, theoreticians had predicted the expansion of the universe. The prediction came from Russian mathematician Alexander Friedmann (1888–1925) in 1922 and independently in 1927 from Belgian priest and physicist Georges Lemaître (1894–1966). The work of these men was published in obscure journals and therefore were not generally known. Einstein had originally determined that the general theory of relativity predicted an expanding universe. Ironically, he had rejected this prediction because astronomers assured him that the universe was static. His solution to the resulting equations described a flat, static universe called simply Solution A. Dutch astronomer Willem de Sitter (1872–1934) who received a Bruce Medal (see page 249) in 1931, had proposed "Solution B." It was a changing universe that was devoid of matter. He justified the lack of matter by pointing out that the universe is mostly empty space. When two objects were introduced into the de Sitter universe, the light traveling between them was redshifted. This redshift was not a result of expansion, but it was a way to account for a faraway clock to appear to run slowly. Hubble was familiar with this de Sitter effect and wrote at the end of his 1929 paper "A Relation between Distance and Radial Velocity among Extra Galactic Nebulae" that "The outstanding feature is the possibility that the velocity–distance relation may represent the de Sitter effect, and hence that numerical data may be introduced into discussions of the general curvature of space."

As word spread about Hubble's discovery, Lemaître realized that Eddington had not read his 1927 paper (*Annales de la Société Scientifique de Bruxelles*, 47A, 49) and sent it to him. Eddington promoted the work

(Opposite page) *Hubble's law states that the faster an object is moving away, the farther away it is. The velocity is measured using the redshift of spectral lines.*

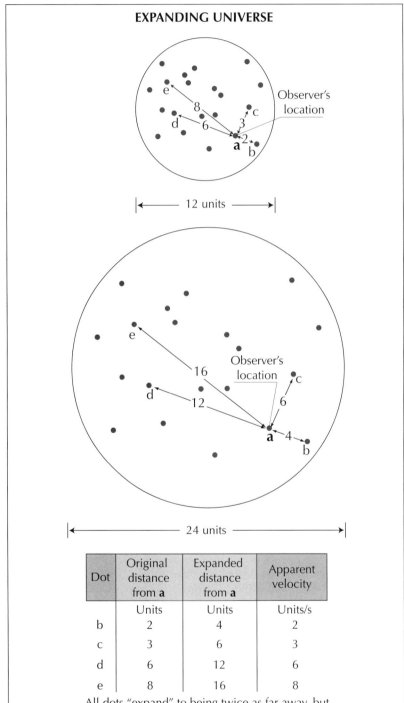

EXPANDING UNIVERSE

Dot	Original distance from **a**	Expanded distance from **a**	Apparent velocity
	Units	Units	Units/s
b	2	4	2
c	3	6	3
d	6	12	6
e	8	16	8

All dots "expand" to being twice as far away, but the farthest dots appear to be moving faster.

© Infobase Publishing

As the universe expands, galaxies that are far away appear to speed away faster than ones that are nearer.

in a popular article "On the Instability of Einstein's Spherical World" in the *Monthly Notices of the Royal Astronomical Society* (vol. 90, p. 668) in 1930. Friedmann and Lemaître, later designated the fathers of big bang cosmology, had followed Einstein in assuming that the universe was homogeneous and isotropic, in other words that it was the same in all directions as seen from all locations. But contrary to Einstein, they assumed that the universe could expand. Allowing for expansion simplified the equations and led to three solutions: one in which parallel lines diverged (open universe expands forever); one in which they converged (closed universe ends in "big crunch"); and one in which they remained parallel (space is flat and expands forever). The amount of matter in the universe, that Hubble set out to measure by counting the density of galaxies, would determine the curvature of space and thus which one of the three solutions best described reality.

To map the sky and measure the curvature of space, a telescope that could both see deeply into space and also photograph large sections of the sky was needed to choose targets for the large reflectors. In 1929, a Swedish-born German optician named Bernhard Schmidt (1879–1936) invented just such a telescope. The Schmidt telescope uses a spherically curved main mirror with a corrector plate lens at the front. The refracting lens makes up for the *spherical aberration* of the mirror and also allows wide-angle photography. After a trip to view the solar eclipse of 1929, Schmidt showed a prototype to his countryman Walter Baade. Baade joined the Mount Wilson staff in 1931 and shared the idea with George Hale. In the next decade, Hale would build several Schmidt telescopes that would map the sky and change the view of the universe once again.

The Hydrogen Question

The assumption that the planets and the Sun formed from the same basic material was verified as spectroscopic technique improved during the early 20th century, and more terrestrial elements were found in the solar spectrum. British astronomer Alfred Fowler (1868–1940) (see Bruce Medalists, page 249) wrote in 1918 that, "as work proceeds, it becomes less and less probably [*sic*] that the Sun contains any elements which do not also enter into the composition of the Earth. It seems natural to infer that the composition of the Sun may be practically identical with that of the Earth." Even the relative abundance of these elements matched closely, with the very notable exception of hydrogen.

In 1921 and early 1922, Meghnad Saha and Henry Russell exchanged personal and editorial letters in various publications asking why hydrogen was so persistent in stellar spectra. When British astronomers Edward Arthur Milne (1896–1950) and Ralph Howard Fowler (1889–1944) showed that the pressure in stellar atmospheres was much lower than everyone had assumed, Russell and others thought that might explain the hydrogen abundance. Another idea proposed by Norwegian Svein

Rosseland (1894–1985) was that hydrogen was electrostatically repelled from the star's interior and then concentrated in the outer layers. Neither explanation held up under further analysis.

Russell sent his graduate student Donald Menzel (1901–76) to Harlow Shapley at Harvard to use the plate vaults for his thesis on the *ionization potential* for titanium. Cecilia H. Payne (see photo below) arrived at Harvard in 1923 from Cambridge where she had studied with R. H. Fowler, Milne, and Eddington also on ionization potential. Shapley let Menzel finish his work and limited Payne to working on giant stars that would help explain Antonia Maury's spectral c-class. Menzel completed his thesis "A Study of Line Intensities in Stellar Spectra" in 1924. To make her thesis stand out, Payne did a detailed analysis of neutral and ionized silicon using 200 spectra. She recalibrated the temperature

Cecilia Payne (later Payne-Gaposchkin) was a graduate student whose thesis was correct about the Sun being composed of mostly hydrogen and helium. Her adviser, Henry Norris Russell, made her say that her results were incorrect. (Yerkes Observatory Photographs)

sequences and refined the values for ionization potentials. Russell called it a first-class piece of work. However, he thought that the lines of hydrogen were too strong in low-temperature giants where theory called for them to be the weakest. Russell had Payne determine the relative abundances of elements using a method developed by Saha to obtain the fraction of atoms available to contribute to the intensity of a given line as a function of temperature. The hydrogen numbers in Payne's resulting analysis were orders of magnitude greater than the rest of the elements. Russell could not accept this: "It is clearly impossible that hydrogen should be a million times more abundant than the metals" he wrote in January 1925.

Payne changed her thesis as Russell dictated. "His word was law. If a piece of work received his imprimatur, it could be published; if not, it must be set aside and its author had a hard row to hoe," she said. She added a sentence to her paper about the hydrogen and helium results, saying, "The stellar abundance deduced for these elements is improbably high, and is almost certainly not real." Her thesis, *Stellar Atmospheres*, was published as a Harvard Observatory monograph in 1925 and was called one of the most brilliant doctoral theses ever written in astronomy. Payne had proven that the differences in stellar spectra were the result of physical conditions such as temperature and not the result of abundance variations.

The evidence for the abundance of hydrogen in stars continued to build. Russell hired John Quincy Stewart (1894–1972) in 1922 as an assistant professor. Stewart provided the first theoretical evidence that the spreading out of spectral lines, called line broadening, was a result of abundance. Russell and his "computer," Charlotte E. Moore, examined the intensities of lines in the solar spectrum and showed that the widest lines were from the lowest-lying levels; that meant that they reflected abundance. Russell then reaffirmed that the abundance of solar elements and Earth's crust were alike. He still sought some other explanation for hydrogen.

Moore calculated the relative number of atoms that were involved in production of each line, using Russell's predictions from quantum theory. She compared these with the observed intensity that had been determined with a photoelectric densitometer used at Mount Wilson. The data continued to show that hydrogen was the most abundant element in stars, but Russell still refused to believe it. Eddington established that thermodynamic equilibrium could not account for the strength of the hydrogen lines.

In 1926, Donald Menzel, then at Lick Observatory, determined from eclipse data that hydrogen was the dominant element in the chromosphere of the Sun. In late 1927, Stewart announced his finding that the number of neutral hydrogen atoms in the solar atmosphere was enormous. German Albrecht Unsöld (1905–95) completed his thesis on the solar spectrum in 1927. He also confirmed Payne's abundances and said that hydrogen was on the order of 5 million times more abundant than calcium. He attributed this abundance to the electrostatic repulsion mechanism.

The data finally convinced Russell that stars were made mostly of hydrogen. He published "On the Composition of the Sun's Atmosphere" in the July 1929 *Astrophysical Journal* (vol. 70, p. 11). (See Further Reading.) He stated, "The conclusion from the 'face of returns' is that . . . the great abundance of H [hydrogen] can hardly be doubted." At the end of his paper, Russell gave full credit to Payne's 1925 conclusions.

Further investigations of the Sun firmly established that hydrogen was its main ingredient. In 1929, Bernard-Ferdinand Lyot (1897–1952) developed an optical system that eliminated scattered light to create the *coronagraph*, a device that allows observation of the solar corona without an eclipse. By 1931, he was obtaining photographs of the corona and its spectrum. He found new spectral lines in the corona, and he made the first motion pictures of solar prominences. He received a Bruce Medal (see page 249) in 1947 partly for this work.

The Matter of Stars

Throughout this decade, astronomers and physicists continued to find connections between tiny atoms and giant stars. Niels Bohr's work on the hydrogen atom had led to an understanding of spectra that finally exposed the abundance of hydrogen in stars. In 1920, Francis W. Aston (1877–1945) had precisely measured the mass of various atoms and found that four hydrogen nuclei (that is, protons) had more mass than a helium nucleus (two protons and two neutrons). Using Aston's mass difference and Einstein's equivalency of energy and matter equation ($E = mc^2$), Eddington calculated that fusion of hydrogen to helium would allow the Sun to shine for about a hundred billion years. The lifetime was an overestimate, but he was right about the Sun being fusion powered.

However, the connection between the source of energy and the evolution of stars had not yet been made. Most astronomers assumed that as stars aged, they cooled and contracted, ending their lives as dwarfs. The relationship between mass and stellar evolution would only gradually emerge. Eddington had already shown that the more mass a star had, the hotter and brighter it would be. Then, in 1924, using data for main sequence stars, he derived the mass-luminosity law which stated that stellar luminosities are roughly equal to their masses raised to the fourth power. If large stars evolved to dwarfs as scientists (incorrectly) thought, then stars had to lose a lot of mass along the way. Eddington suggested matter annihilation as a possible source of mass loss, but Hubble's expanding universe restricted the timetable for stars to billions versus the trillions of years needed for that model. Eddington summarized his work in a book published in 1926, *The Internal Constitution of the Stars.*

This book included detailed mathematical discussions of the balancing act between gravitational contraction and outward pressure that goes on inside stars. In 1924, Eddington had discovered that the usual gas-law equations broke down under high density conditions such as those predicted for stars called *white dwarfs*. White dwarfs, such as Sirius B, have about the same mass as the Sun but are about the size of Earth. Eddington found that compressed atoms form a substance called a *degenerate gas*. In this state, the star cannot contract further. Eddington puzzled over how such a star could cool and become a *black dwarf*.

Cambridge physicist R. H. Fowler used statistical methods and quantum mechanics to resolve this dilemma in 1926. Somewhat like a compressed spring, degenerate matter could only exist under very high external pressure. If it were removed from the interior of the star, it would expand to a gas of extremely high temperature. Most astronomers then accepted that stars aged to a degenerate state with their lifetimes and all their other properties, determined by their mass and chemical abundance. This idea was formally stated in the Vogt-Russell theorem that was published in 1926 by Heinrich Vogt and independently by Henry Russell in 1927.

While on a boat to England in 1930, Indian graduate student Subrahmanyan Chandrasekhar realized that at the pressures involved in degenerate stars, electrons would move so fast that special relativity would give them a higher mass. When he included relativity values in the equations, he found that there was a limit, later called Chandrasekhar's limit, to the size of a white dwarf of about 1.2 (later revised to 1.4) times the mass of the Sun. (He received a Bruce Medal [see page 249] in 1952 for this work.) A mass of more than this amount would have so much gravity that it would overcome the pressure produced by degeneracy. Chandrasekhar did not yet know what would happen physically at that point. The connection between degeneracy and what Walter Baade called "hauptnovae" (chief novae, later called supernovae) would be made in the next decade, thanks in part to Nova Pictoris, which was discovered in 1925.

Edward Milne (who received a Bruce Medal [see page 249] in 1945) had developed a model of a star with a collapsed core that was surrounded by a thin envelope of gas. This model helped to circumvent the degeneracy problem for higher mass stars, and it also seemed to explain the abundance of hydrogen in the atmospheres of stars. As Nova Pictoris turned into a *planetary nebula*, Milne speculated that a nova outburst was a star driving off its outer layers to reveal the collapsed inner portion that looked like a white dwarf. "The collapse theory of novae accounts for the facts of observation," Milne told Henry Russell.

The collapse theory would soon also lead to an explanation for ionization that was first discovered in Earth's atmosphere in 1900. It was first assumed to be a result of Earth's natural radioactivity. In 1912, Victor Hess (1883–1964) used a balloon launch to discover that ionization increased with altitude, showing that Earth was not the source. He then showed that the radiation was similar both day and night, so the source was not the Sun. In 1927, Dutch physicist Jacob Clay (1882–1955) showed that the intensity of radiation varies with latitude and was less at the equator. This meant that the source was affected by Earth's magnetic field and therefore could not be photons that have no electric charge. In 1928, Nobel Laureate Robert A. Millikan (1868–1953) and G. Harvey Cameron (1902–77) found that radiation decreases under water in lakes, proving that it originated in space. Millikan coined the term *cosmic rays* for this radiation. In 1934, Baade and Fritz Zwicky (1898–1974) would correctly suggest that these charged particles come from distant supernovae.

Planet X

Clyde Tombaugh (see photo on page 57) grew up on farms in Illinois and Kansas, occupying his mind with mathematical puzzles such as how many cubic inches (1 duodecillion, 1 followed by 39 zeroes) were in Betelgeuse. In 1927, he purchased the optics for a nine-inch (23-cm) reflector and used parts from his father's 1910 Buick and a cream separator for the mounting. When a hailstorm destroyed the Tombaughes' entire crop in the summer of 1928, Tombaugh decided to trade agriculture for astronomy. He wrote to Lowell Observatory about a job. His drawings of Jupiter and Saturn, carefully dated for comparison with photos at Lowell, impressed Vesto Slipher enough to hire him. Tombaugh arrived in Arizona in January 1929 and began the search for what Percival Lowell had called Planet X.

Lowell had searched for a planet beyond Neptune starting in 1905. In 1909, William Pickering of Harvard predicted seven new planets, using a graphical method based on comets. He called the closest one "Planet O." Lowell wrote on his copy of the paper, "this planet is very properly designated 'O' [and] is nothing at all." Lowell constructed a general planetary law based on the idea of *commensurability*, simple ratios such as 1:2 or 2:3, between orbital periods of bodies revolving around the Sun. He published his predictions in April 1913. In January 1915, Lowell still had not found the planet, so he published his detailed calculations. After Lowell died in 1916, his brother donated $10,000 to build a wide-angle telescope for future searches.

Tombaugh took about 100 one-hour exposures before the break for summer storms in 1929. He found nothing. Working the farm that summer, he realized that the outer planets all show *retrograde* motion as Earth moves around the Sun, with the farthest planet having the smallest motion. This movement could be found by comparing photographic plates of the same field of sky that were taken on different dates, a process called *blinking*.

Tombaugh was confident that if the planet were brighter than the 17-magnitude limit of the telescope, he should find it. On January 21, 1930, he began a long exposure of Delta Geminorum, an area that Lowell had most favored for his search. A biting wind sprang up, and Tombaugh struggled with the telescope. He took another exposure two nights later, and on January 29, he took a third.

Clyde Tombaugh was 24 and did not have a college degree when he discovered Pluto in 1930. This photo shows him at the telescope in 1931. (New Mexico State University)

On February 18, Tombaugh placed the second and third Delta Geminorum plates in the comparator, the device used for blinking. Tombaugh reported that his eyes grew tired from blinking the plates. In the late afternoon, he finally "saw a little image popping in and out." The shift was right for a trans-Neptunian planet. "The image on the earlier plate was to the east, the one on the later was to the west; it was retro-grading!" Tombaugh ruled out that the images were variable stars. He then checked the plate that he had taken during the storm on January 21. With trembling hands, Tombaugh aligned the plate and looked through the eyepiece. The object was east, right where it belonged. "I was walking on the ceiling," Tombaugh recalled. "I can hardly describe to you how intense was the thrill I felt." He exclaimed to the director, "Dr. Slipher—I have found your Planet X."

By March, they had confirmed that the movement was consistent with a planet beyond Neptune. They made the announcement on March 13, the anniversary of Herschel's discovery of Uranus. The news of the farmer-turned-astronomer who found a new planet splashed across the front pages of newspapers around the world. His father wrote and said, "The old town feels that you have put them on the map, and although the discovery of new planets is something over the heads of most people in country towns, they are proud of you in a quiet way, and glad that you have made good." Tombaugh, who had no college degree at the time of the discovery, later earned his bachelors and masters degrees from the University of Kansas. He remained at Lowell Observatory until 1945 and then moved to work on the first missile-tracking systems at White Sands.

Henry Norris Russell wrote in *Scientific American*, "the initial credit for the discovery of Pluto justly belongs to Percival Lowell. His analytical methods were sound, his profound enthusiasm stimulated the search; and, even after his death, was the inspiration of the campaign which resulted in its discovery at the Observatory which he had founded." In late spring 1930, the planet (reclassified as a dwarf planet in 2006) was named Pluto with the first two letters Percival Lowell's initials. Disney's cartoon dog acquired the name just a few months later.

Pluto was found at 39.5 *astronomical units* (AU) versus the 43 Lowell had predicted, and at an inclination of about 17 degrees, only six degrees higher than he had expected. His prediction for mass was way off. Pluto's mass is only about one five hundredth that of Earth. Lowell thought that a giant world of 6.6 Earth masses was needed to explain the motions of Uranus and Neptune. Once their positions were known more precisely, no new world was needed. Pluto's orbit is in a 3:1 ratio with Uranus and 3:2 with Neptune. Lowell would have found Pluto in 1907 if the camera's field of view had been wider—the high inclination placed it just off the plate.

Rockets around the World

In 1921, Robert Goddard obtained funding from the U.S. Navy to work on liquid-fueled propulsion. His work during the previous decade convinced him that solid fuels would never obtain the thrust required to reach space. The switch to liquid fuel, however, required a much more complicated combustion system. The fuel had to be under pressure, and that required pumps. The pumps blew out, seized up, or simply failed. The chamber itself had to receive, mix, and burn the fuel and the oxidizer and then exhaust the combustion gases. Goddard tried

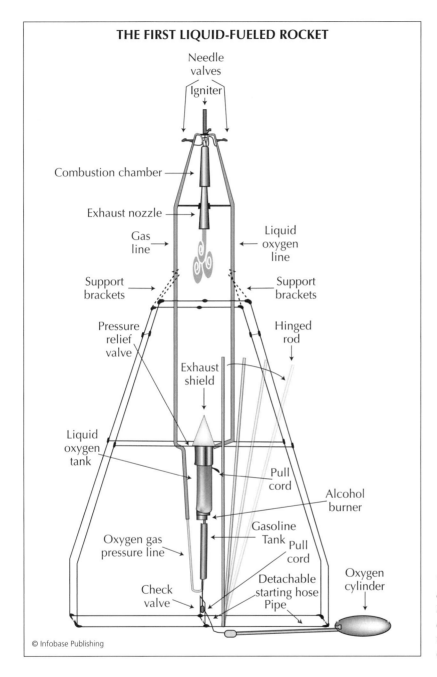

THE FIRST LIQUID-FUELED ROCKET

Needle valves

Igniter

Combustion chamber

Exhaust nozzle

Gas line

Liquid oxygen line

Support brackets

Support brackets

Pressure relief valve

Hinged rod

Exhaust shield

Liquid oxygen tank

Pull cord

Alcohol burner

Oxygen gas pressure line

Gasoline Tank

Pull cord

Oxygen cylinder

Check valve

Detachable starting hose Pipe

© Infobase Publishing

The first liquid-fueled rocket, designed by Robert Goddard, had the combustion chamber and the exhaust in the center, unlike later rockets that put the exhaust nozzle on the bottom.

various ways of igniting the mix, including cotton soaked in kerosene. His technical assistant, Swedish immigrant Nils Riffolt (1888–1957), said, "Most of our tests ended with something jamming, or sticking, or the chamber burning through. Yet I never saw [Goddard] discouraged.

These were not failures, he usually said, but what he called valuable negative information."

Goddard's biggest technical challenge was to increase the exhaust velocity. To reach high altitude, the rocket had to be big enough to carry its own supply of fuel and liquid oxygen (LOX). He built an 11-pound (5-kg) rocket out of aluminum and magnesium alloy. The exhaust nozzle was above the fuel tank, unlike modern rockets that exhaust out the bottom. Goddard designed the rocket to pull its own weight rather than push it up (see figure on page 59).

Goddard launched the world's first liquid-fueled rocket on March 16, 1926, from his Aunt Effie's farm in Auburn, Massachusetts (see photo on page 61). Powered by gasoline and LOX, the rocket flew a mere 41 feet (12.5 m) and then crashed 184 feet (56 m) from the launch site. The flight that heralded the start of modern rocketry lasted only two and a half seconds. The fact that it flew at all was enough to satisfy Goddard. He reported the successful flight to his benefactors at the Smithsonian, but he asked that they not announce it publicly. Goddard had been ridiculed in the press after the publication of his 1920 paper on rocketry and preferred ever after to work out of the public eye.

While Goddard was busy finding a practical way to get into space, others worked on the theory and vision. In 1926, Russian father of cosmonautics Konstantin Tsiolkovsky published a grand "Plan of Space Exploration." It outlined 16 steps for human expansion into space (see sidebar below) starting with the creation of rocket airplanes and ending with humans spread throughout the Milky Way.

Tsiolkovsky's Plan of Space Exploration

1. Creation of rocket airplanes with wings
2. Progressively increasing the speed and altitude of these airplanes
3. Production of real rockets—without wings
4. Ability to land on the surface of the sea
5. Reaching escape velocity and the first flight into Earth orbit
6. Lengthening rocket flight times in space
7. Experimental use of plants to make an artificial atmosphere in spaceships
8. Using pressurized space suits for activity outside of spaceships
9. Making orbiting greenhouses for plants
10. Constructing large orbital habitats around the Earth
11. Using solar radiation to grow food, to heat space quarters, and for transport throughout the solar system
12. Colonization of the asteroid belt
13. Colonization of the entire solar system and beyond
14. Achievement of individual and social perfection
15. Overcrowding of the solar system and the colonization of the Milky Way (the galaxy)
16. The Sun begins to die and the people remaining in the solar system's population go to other suns.

Robert Goddard is the father of American rocketry. He is shown here with a rocket chamber that he tested in the 1920s. (NASA; AIP Emilio Segrè Visual Archives)

German Hermann Julius Oberth (see photo below) wrote a dissertation on spaceflight in 1922, but it was rejected by the faculty at the University of Munich as too "fanciful." He published it privately in 1923 as *The Rocket into Planetary Space*. He had designed a rocket that he believed could reach the upper atmosphere by using alcohol and hydrogen. Goddard's work was cited in the appendix, but Oberth claimed that the only influence on his early work had been science-fiction author Jules Verne. Oberth's book reached the United States in 1924 and angered Goddard. When the press asked him about the book, he said that Oberth had stolen his ideas and was only a theorist, whereas he was experiment-

Hermann Oberth was a German rocket pioneer who published The Rocket into Planetary Space *in 1923. He was one of the founders of the German Rocket Society and inspired Wernher von Braun to build the first space-capable rockets.* (NASA)

ing and would work out getting to the Moon in due course. Many pictures and articles appeared showing Goddard with his inventions. The public expected his rocket to reach the Moon any day.

Oberth's book inspired Willy Ley (1906–69) to write his own book, *Travel in Outer Space* in 1926. In 1927, Ley and Oberth founded the Society for Space Travel. By 1929, they had 870 members, including a new high school graduate, Wernher von Braun (1912–77) who would build the first Moon rockets. Oberth was tapped as a technical adviser to German producer Fritz Lang (1890–1976) during the making of the 1929 movie *Die Frau im Mond* (Woman in the Moon). This movie, the first to include a countdown sequence, was destined to inspire many young Germans to pursue careers in science and engineering. Oberth was supposed to create a rocket to launch as a publicity stunt at the film's opening. However, Oberth was a theoretician, not an engineer. One of his colleagues said, "If Oberth wants to drill a hole, first he invents the drill press." Oberth hired some young engineers to help, but they could not build a rocket in time for the movie's release. Oberth's liquid rocket motor was eventually built and had a successful test firing on July 23, 1930. Additional work halted when the rocket blew up during a test in September. The society then rented a facility in Berlin to continue their research.

By 1929, Goddard was back at the farm with a new liquid rocket; it weighed 57 pounds (26 kg) and had a payload consisting of a camera, a thermometer, and a barometer. The camera was operated through a trip lever that was connected to the recovery parachute. Goddard launched it on July 12. Emitting a tremendous roar from a 20-foot (6-m) exhaust flame, the rocket rose out of the tower. It climbed 20 feet (6 m), then tipped and made it to 80 feet (24 m), then dove to the ground. The gasoline tank exploded on impact and started a grass fire. The blast was heard for miles. Goddard's wife Esther recorded the flight with a movie camera. The parachute had not deployed, and the instruments were smashed. Still, it had worked, and the Goddards toasted their triumph with ginger ale. Then a dozen automobiles and two ambulances came, looking for what the locals assumed from the noise and the smoke was a crashed airplane. The newspaper headlines read: "Rocket Starts for the Moon but Blows up on the Way." Shortly afterward, the local fire marshal banned Goddard from further testing in the state of Massachusetts.

Though the press coverage of Goddard's 1929 launch was all negative, it drew the attention of world-renowned U.S. aviator Charles Lindbergh. Two years earlier, Lindbergh had become famous for the first nonstop transatlantic solo flight between New York City and Paris. Lindbergh was an advocate for new aviation technology. He arranged for the Daniel Guggenheim Foundation to pledge $100,000 toward Goddard's research.

In 1930, Goddard took leave from Clark University and moved to a secluded ranch in Roswell, New Mexico. On December 30, 1930, Goddard launched his first rocket from Roswell. It attained an altitude of 2,000 feet (610 m) in seven seconds, his highest yet.

Scientist of the Decade: Edwin Powell Hubble (1889–1953)

A man called the greatest astronomer since Galileo, Edwin Hubble proved the existence of other galaxies and that the universe is expanding.

Hubble was born November 20, 1889, in Marshfield, Missouri. His father was an insurance agent and moved the family to Chicago when Edwin was nine. He graduated from the University of Chicago in 1910 at age 20 with a degree in math and astronomy. A gifted athlete as well as a top student, Hubble won a Rhodes scholarship and headed to Oxford in England.

Hubble felt obligated to heed his father's wishes to study law instead of astronomy. After his father died in 1913, Hubble returned with a degree, that he would never use. He pretended to some to have passed the Kentucky bar, perhaps one reason why he later shunned discussions of his past. Hubble taught high school Spanish and physics in Indiana. Legend has it that girls took these difficult classes just to have the handsome Oxford-sophisticated Professor Hubble for a teacher. By 1914, Hubble returned to his true calling and pursued his doctorate in astronomy at the University of Chicago's Yerkes Observatory.

While at Yerkes, Hubble attended a lecture on redshift of nebulae by Vesto Slipher of Lowell Observatory, who received a Bruce Medal (see page 249) in 1935. Slipher had determined that nebulae such as Andromeda were moving faster than anything ever observed before. Hubble was so intrigued by the puzzle of these speeds that he chose photographic investigations of faint nebulae for his thesis topic.

George Hale, the director of the Mount Wilson Observatory, was impressed with Hubble's work. He offered Hubble the opportunity to use the world's largest telescope to study nebulae as soon as he graduated. But the world was at war in 1917, and Hubble was eager to serve his country. So Hubble taught his fellow soldiers night marching using the stars, and he com-

Edwin Hubble proved that the Milky Way was not the only galaxy and showed that the universe is expanding. (Yerkes Observatory Photographs)

manded a battalion in France. Major Hubble arrived at Mount Wilson in 1919 and began to study nebulae with the new 100-inch (2.5-m) telescope.

Hubble married Grace Burke (1889–1981) on February 26, 1924. Grace's family was extremely wealthy and included Hubble in their celebrity-filled social life. They gave the couple an elegant house for a wedding gift that Hubble used to entertain and meet with the scientific elite of the time. He and Grace never had children.

During the fall of 1923, Hubble made his finding of Cepheid variables in Andromeda.

Their distance proved that the Milky Way was not the only galaxy. For his discovery, Hubble was awarded the American Association for the Advancement of Science prize and received $500, a large sum in 1925. Not everyone was pleased with Hubble's success. Harlow Shapley had argued against "island universes" in the 1920 debate. He had met Hubble and found him pretentious in part because of his fake British accent. When he learned of Hubble's discovery, Shapley's graduate student remembered him saying, "Here is the letter that has destroyed my universe." The two men became famously bitter rivals, verbally sparring in the pages of astronomical journals.

Hubble photographed hundreds of nebulae and developed a way to classify them by shape. He submitted his classification proposal to the International Astronomical Union in 1923, and it was eventually adopted and is still in use today. Hubble and his assistant Milton Humason photographed more nebulae, calculated their distances, and plotted these against the speeds that Slipher had reported years before. Hubble discovered that the speed of a nebula increased linearly with its distance, a relationship now called Hubble's law. The stunning results were published in 1929 (see Further Reading).

Although many astronomers hailed Hubble's discovery of the velocity–distance relation, it was not until 1931 that Hubble became famous. Prior to that, scientists simply did not yet accept that galaxies were speeding apart because the universe expanded like some giant balloon. Even as late as 1937, Hubble was quoted saying, "Well, perhaps the nebulae are all receding in this peculiar manner. But the notion is rather startling."

Then, the "smartest man in the world," Albert Einstein, visited Mount Wilson in 1931. During his visit, Einstein made a startling announcement: he was abandoning his static-universe theory as a direct result of Hubble's work (and that of theoretician Richard Tolman [1881–1948]). Headlines characterized Hubble as the young man who caused Einstein to change his mind. Photos of the two men at the telescope adorned newspapers around the globe. Hubble, the new celebrity, was invited to dinner by movie stars and gave lectures to packed auditoriums. Perhaps Hubble's favorite accolade was an honorary doctorate of science that was bestowed on him from Oxford in 1934, though he also received the Bruce Medal (see page 249) in 1938.

Hubble summarized his work in *The Realm of the Nebulae* in 1936. This book contained his famous "tuning fork" diagram showing galactic evolution and was wildly popular with the public. But not with Harlow Shapley. He criticized Hubble's assertion that galaxies were evenly distributed in space. Their rivalry may explain why Hubble was unable to admit that Shapley was right even after astronomers Bart Bok (1906–83) (see Bruce Medalists, page 249) and Clyde Tombaugh provided data showing that galaxies grouped into clusters.

Hubble set aside astronomy to do ballistic research during World War II. He returned by June 1948 for the debut of the 200-inch (5-m) telescope on Mount Palomar. Hubble pointed the instrument at NGC 2261 for its first photo. This nebula, also known as Hubble's variable nebula, was Hubble's first discovery as a student in 1916.

In July 1949, Hubble suffered two heart attacks just four days apart. His doctor barred him from high altitudes, and thus observing, until he recovered in 1950. Then he and Humason confirmed that the velocity-distance relation held out to a billion light-years. On September 28, 1953, he talked with Humason about future plans to study the redshift and died that afternoon in Pasadena, California, at age 63.

Hubble's achievements live on in the many astronomical terms named after him, plus the *Hubble Space Telescope*, an asteroid, a crater on the Moon, and even a comet he discovered in 1937.

Further Reading

Books and Periodicals

Christianson, Gale E. *Edwin Hubble: Mariner of the Nebulae.* New York: Farrar, Straus and Giroux, 1995. This is a biography of Hubble.

Edwin Hubble. "A Relation between Distance and Radial Velocity among Extra-Galactic Nebulae." *Proceedings of the National Academy of Sciences* 15, no. 3 (March 15, 1929): 168–173. This is Hubble's original paper showing that the more distant the galaxy, the faster it is moving away. This result is interpreted to mean that the universe is expanding.

Ordway, Frederick I., III. *Visions of Spaceflight.* New York: Four Walls Eight Windows, 2000. This is an annotated historical collection of space and science-fiction illustrations.

———, and Mitchell R. Sharpe. *The Rocket Team.* Foreword by Wernher von Braun. Ontario, Canada: Apogee Books, 2003. This book offers a detailed history of the German rocket program.

H. N. Russell. "On the Composition of the Sun's Atmosphere." *Astrophysical Journal* 70 (1929): 11–82. Available online. URL: http://articles.adsabs.harvard.edu//full/seri/ApJ../0070//0000011.000.html. Accessed on August 12, 2006. This is Russell's paper concluding that Payne was correct in finding that hydrogen is the most abundant element in the Sun.

Allen Sandage. "Edwin Hubble." *The Journal of the Royal Astronomical Society of Canada* 83, no. 6 (December 1989). Available online. URL: http://antwrp.gsfc.nasa.gov/diamond_jubilee/1996/sandage_hubble.html. The essay discusses Hubble's many discoveries and their historical context.

Silk, Joseph. *The Big Bang.* New York: W. H. Freeman and Company, 2001. This is the story of the development of the big bang theory.

Web Sites

Owen Gingerich and Heather Miller. "Cecilia Payne-Gaposchkin: Astronomer and Astrophysicist." Harvard Smithsonian Center for Astrophysics. Available online. URL: http://www.harvardsquarelibrary.org/unitarians/payne2.html. Accessed on January 5, 2007. Site contains an in-depth profile of Payne by one of her students at Harvard.

Hidden Knowledge. "Publishers: Hugo Gernsback." Hidden Knowledge. Available online. URL: http://www.magazineart.org/publishers/gernsback.html. Accessed on February 22, 2006. This site provides a good summary of the magazines and influence of Hugo Gernsback. Links provide more information on science and invention topics that were important in the 1920s.

History Learning. "America 1918–1939." History Learning. Available online. URL: http://www.historylearningsite.co.uk/america_1918.htm. Accessed on May 2005. The site contains links to major historical events that provide context for the scientific progress during the 1920s.

Lowell Observatory. "Discovery of Pluto Reaches 75th Anniversary." Lowell Observatory. Available online. URL: http://www.lowell.edu/press_room/releases/recent_releases/PL_75_rls.html. Accessed on August 29, 2006. A good summary on the 75th anniversary on the discovery of Pluto.

NASA Goddard Spaceflight Center. "History of Robert Goddard." NASA Goddard Spaceflight Center. Available online. URL: http://www.nasa.gov/centers/goddard/about/dr_goddard.html. Accessed on August 29, 2006. Good overview on the career of this rocket pioneer.

Christian Stange. "Herman Oberth: Father of Space Travel." Kiosek Web Design. Available online. URL: http://www.kiosek.com/oberth/. Accessed on February 22, 2006. Site includes a short biography of Oberth with photos and a list of books about the German rocket program.

4

1931–1940:
Understanding What Makes Stars Shine and Rockets Fly

Though the world economy was in the midst of the Great Depression in 1931, astronomy and rocket science experienced a boom of progress. The decade opened with the serendipitous discovery that the Milky Way produces radio waves. This discovery led to the development of the first radio telescope (see photo on page 71) and eventually opened a whole new field

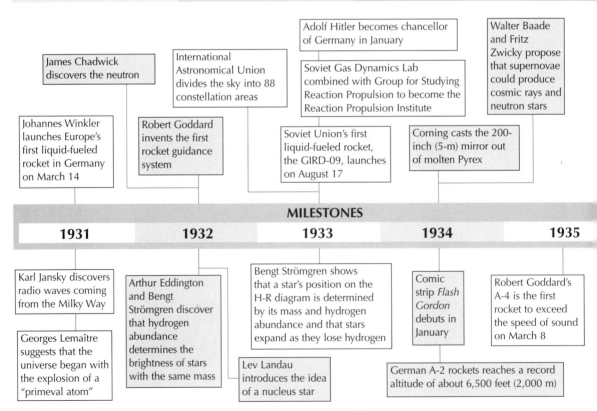

James Chadwick discovers the neutron

International Astronomical Union divides the sky into 88 constellation areas

Adolf Hitler becomes chancellor of Germany in January

Soviet Gas Dynamics Lab combined with Group for Studying Reaction Propulsion to become the Reaction Propulsion Institute

Walter Baade and Fritz Zwicky propose that supernovae could produce cosmic rays and neutron stars

Johannes Winkler launches Europe's first liquid-fueled rocket in Germany on March 14

Robert Goddard invents the first rocket guidance system

Soviet Union's first liquid-fueled rocket, the GIRD-09, launches on August 17

Corning casts the 200-inch (5-m) mirror out of molten Pyrex

MILESTONES

1931	1932	1933	1934	1935

Karl Jansky discovers radio waves coming from the Milky Way

Arthur Eddington and Bengt Strömgren discover that hydrogen abundance determines the brightness of stars with the same mass

Bengt Strömgren shows that a star's position on the H-R diagram is determined by its mass and hydrogen abundance and that stars expand as they lose hydrogen

Comic strip *Flash Gordon* debuts in January

Robert Goddard's A-4 is the first rocket to exceed the speed of sound on March 8

Georges Lemaître suggests that the universe began with the explosion of a "primeval atom"

Lev Landau introduces the idea of a nucleus star

German A-2 rockets reaches a record altitude of about 6,500 feet (2,000 m)

of astronomy. This development and the building of the 200-inch (5-m) telescope (see photo on page 72) are both described in this chapter.

The most significant discovery of the decade, and perhaps the century, was made by physicist Hans Bethe (1906–2005) who fled Germany in 1933. Bethe figured out the chain of nuclear reactions (see figures on pages 75 and 77) that allow the Sun and other stars to produce energy. With this mystery solved in 1938, other aspects of stellar composition and brightness that were observed earlier in the decade were also explained. Astronomers realized that as stars use up their nuclear fuel, they expand and become red giants. What happened as massive stars aged remained a mystery, but mathematical theories were constructed to show that stellar cores might collapse into "nucleus" stars, and astronomer Fritz Zwicky (see photo on page 73) proposed correctly that this causes supernovae events. The idea that the universe itself may have had a beginning in an explosion was first seriously discussed during this decade.

The worldwide economic depression that began in 1929 made it difficult for individuals to raise enough private funds to develop rockets that were capable of reaching high altitudes and remaining under control.

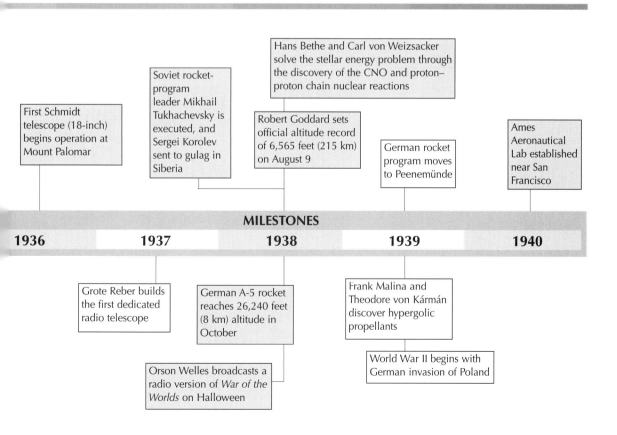

Robert Goddard (see photo on page 85), the featured scientist of the decade, supported himself by teaching until money was again available to continue his rocket development full time. By 1932, he had developed the first guidance system (see figure on page 80), and by 1935, his A-series rocket (see figure on page 81) went faster than the speed of sound. But his private efforts were destined to be surpassed by the military-supported rocket programs in Germany and Russia. The Nazi Party, led by Adolf Hitler (1889–1945), came to power in Germany in 1933 and began a major military buildup. With funding from the German army, Wernher von Braun went to work developing the first rocket that would reach space early in the next decade. In Russia, Sergei Korolev was likewise employed to build military rockets, though his work was interrupted and almost ended by a wave of political assassinations ordered by Soviet leader Joseph Stalin (1879–1953). All three rocket men, Goddard, von Braun, and Korolev, dreamed of using their rockets to explore space, but first they would be used for World War II, which began in Europe in 1939.

The discovery of nuclear reactions as the Sun's source of power and the invention of the first guided and controlled rockets in this decade led directly to the development of nuclear bombs and ballistic missiles in the next decade that would forever scar the history of the 20th century.

New "Eyes" on the Universe

In 1931, observational astronomy was limited to what was visible to the human eye or able to be captured on film. New observations of comets or asteroids were reported to be "in" the direction of this or that constellation. In 1933, the International Astronomical Union officially divided the sky into 88 constellations with nonoverlapping boundaries. Thus, the center of the Milky Way is "in" Sagittarius. This area of the sky was the first to be observed, not with human eyes or with a camera but by the noise it makes in the radio part of the spectrum.

In 1932, radio engineer Karl Guthe Jansky (1905–50) was investigating the sources of noise in transoceanic radio circuits for Bell Laboratories in New Jersey. Using a directional antenna that he had built in 1929, he had determined that local and distant thunderstorms contributed to noise in the radio circuits. He realized that there was a third source of static. This source varied, not every 24 hours but every 23 hours and 56 minutes: the length of Earth's sidereal day defined by its rotation relative to the stars, not the Sun. Therefore, Jansky correctly concluded that the source was outside the solar system. He located the source near the center of the Milky Way and published his findings in 1933. The *New York Times* covered this discovery on the front page on May 5, 1933, assuring the public that the waves were low intensity and not signals from aliens.

Another radio engineer, Grote Reber (1911–2002), was intrigued by Jansky's discovery. He later wrote "In my estimation it was obvious that Jansky had made a fundamental and very important discovery.

Furthermore, he had exploited it to the limit of his equipment facilities. If greater progress were to be made it would be necessary to construct new and different equipment especially designed to measure the cosmic static." Reber decided to build a parabolic reflector in his backyard. He used sheet metal for the 31-foot (9-m) diameter dish and screwed it to 72 wooden rafters cut to shape. He cut, drilled, and painted the whole thing and completed the work in four months at a cost of $4,000 of his own money. The world's first radio telescope (see photo below) opened its metallic eye in September 1937. By 1940, Reber had confirmed that Jansky's radio source was in Sagittarius, the center of the Milky Way. From 1937 until the end of World War II, Reber (who received a Bruce Medal [see page 249] in 1962) was the world's only active radio astronomer.

In 1929, George Hale had secured what was at the time the biggest grant to a scientific project, $6 million, to build a 200-inch (5-m) telescope. In the optimism of the roaring twenties, it seemed that with this telescope, astronomers would finally answer the big questions of the size, structure, and origin of the universe. In the changed economy of the Depression, Hale realized that this would be the last large telescope for a long time. So he refined the design to include automatic controls and features. In 1934, he chose Mount Palomar in California as the site for the telescope.

During the first few years of the decade, General Electric had tried unsuccessfully to create a mirror out of fused quartz. By 1934, their failed effort had cost a fourth of the project's entire budget. Hale then assigned the project to Corning Glass to make a mirror out of their new "wonder glass"— Pyrex. Changes in temperature make Pyrex expand and contract much less than ordinary glass, so a Pyrex mirror would be much less prone to the focus and distortion problems that plagued the 100-inch (2.5-m) telescope. Physicist George McCauley (1882–1976) worked out the procedure for casting the giant mirror.

The host of a popular radio show heard about the upcoming casting of the mirror and featured it on his show. During the Depression, news of grand achievements such as the Empire State Building (tallest in the world) and the Golden Gate Bridge (longest suspension bridge) gave people needed hope that life was improving. So after the radio broadcast, the story of the world's

Grote Reber built the first radio telescope in 1937. (National Radio Astronomy Observatory/ Associated Universities, Inc.)

Corning Glassware of New York cast the 200-inch (508-cm) mirror out of molten Pyrex in 1934. The image shows two people standing on the original unpolished surface. The disk cooled for a year in a special oven, was transported to California in 1936, and was stored during World War II. Final polishing was not completed until 1947. (Palomar Observatory, Caltech)

most expensive, biggest, most daring telescope attracted thousands of people to wait in line and buy tickets to see the casting of the mirror. Thousands more followed the story in papers and on the radio, especially the "heroic" efforts of McCauley, who had to move transformers to higher ground during a flood to keep power to the annealing oven and save the precious disk from a rare earthquake. Unfortunately, the first disk had to be discarded because of technical problems. The second casting was successful (see photo above).

In 1936, the mirror blank was shipped across the country on a special train from New York to Pasadena, California. Thousands of people lined the tracks to see the historic 17-foot (5-m) disk. Guards were posted around the mirror at night, and police controlled crowds in Buffalo, Cleveland, and Kansas City. Schools closed so that children could see the "giant eye."

Though the telescope dome, weighing 1,000 tons, was finished by the end of the decade, it took years for the glass to be polished to perfection within a few millionths of an inch (centimeter). The technicians at the California Institute of Technology (Caltech) had to painstakingly remove about 10,000 pounds (4,500 kg) of glass. In 1936, as work on the "giant eye" progressed, an 18-inch Schmidt telescope went into operation on Mount Palomar. This new, wide-angle eye was immediately put to use searching for supernovae. Work on the giant mirror was interrupted for World War II. The grand achievements of the new "eyes" on the universe had to wait until scientists and engineers could again focus their attention on research instead of making war.

From Giants to Black Holes

At the end of the previous decade, astrophysicists had determined that the main ingredient of stars is hydrogen, and they were closing in on an explanation for stars' source of energy. Arthur Eddington had shown that the more mass a star has, the brighter it is. Then in 1932, he found that among stars with the same mass, the ones with less hydrogen were brighter. Swedish astrophysicist Bengt Georg Daniel Strömgren (1908–87) independently reached the same conclusion.

In 1933, Strömgren (who received a Bruce Medal [see page 249] in 1959) showed that the position on the H-R diagram of any star was determined solely by its mass and hydrogen abundance. He discovered that as hydrogen became less abundant, stars moved toward the region of the giants. He was the first to suggest that as hydrogen was consumed, stars expand. In 1935, Gerard Kuiper (1905–73), then at Harvard and later at Yerkes Observatory, linked Strömgren's model of stars moving on the diagram to the observations of star clusters by Robert Trumpler at Lick Observatory. Kuiper found that clusters with differing hydrogen content diverged from the main sequence toward the giant region. The main sequence on the H-R diagram was then understood to be states of stars in equilibrium (their energy production balancing their gravitational contraction).

However, the fate of the most massive stars was still debated. The Chandrasekhar limit for degenerate stars was gradually accepted by everyone except Eddington. What happened beyond this mass would soon be revealed. In 1932, Soviet physicist Lev Davidovich Landau (1908–68) demonstrated independently of Chandrasekhar that there is an upper-mass limit for dense stellar objects of about 1.5 solar masses. He then conceived of the idea for a "nucleus star," a collapsed star with the density of a nucleus. Later that year, British physicist Sir James Chadwick (1891–74) discovered the neutron, and this gave astronomer Fritz Zwicky (see photo at right) an idea. At the December 1933 meeting of the American Physical Society (proceedings published in 1934), Zwicky and Walter Baade proposed "with all reserve … the view that supernovae represent the transitions from ordinary stars to neutron stars, which in their final stages consist of extremely closely packed neutrons." They also suggested that supernovae were the source of cosmic rays.

J. Robert Oppenheimer (1904–67) did not take Zwicky's theories seriously because Zwicky had a reputation of being "flaky." When he discovered Landau's work, Oppenheimer reconsidered Zwicky's proposal that supernovae created *neutron stars*. Together with Canadian physicist George M. Volkoff (1914–2000), he calculated in 1939 that above a certain mass, even the degeneracy pressure of neutrons could not support the star, and it would contract indefinitely. Later that year, he showed, with Hartland S. Snyder (1913–62), that as a massive star exhausted its source of energy and contracted, its light would be reddened and then no

Mount Wilson astronomer Fritz Zwicky made several important discoveries (including dark matter) in the 1930s but was mostly ignored by the astronomical community because of his eccentric personality and bad temper. (NASA)

longer be able to escape; in other words, it would become what is now called a black hole. Prior to this time, black holes were not considered something that could actually exist in Nature. Oppenheimer predicted that a neutron star of 0.7 solar masses would have a radius of only six miles (10 km). So even if the surface were extremely hot, its small size would make it a million times fainter than the Sun. Because they were predicted to be so dim, neutron stars were of little interest to astronomers for almost 30 years.

Another of Zwicky's discoveries that was more or less ignored for 30 years was his research on missing mass, later called *dark matter*. In 1933, he measured the velocities of individual galaxies that are members of the Coma cluster. He then used a formula that Eddington had derived to estimate the total mass of the cluster and their gravitational attraction to one another. He discovered that the gravity was not nearly enough to bind the galaxies together. Because the galaxies were obviously bound to each other, Zwicky correctly concluded that the amount of matter in the cluster was much greater than what he could see. He estimated that about 90 percent of the mass was "missing."

Zwicky's research on supernovae was not nearly as "flaky" as the idea of neutron stars or missing mass. Using the new Schmidt telescope on Mount Palomar, he began a systematic search for supernovae in 1936, and between 1937 and 1941, he found 18 new ones outside the Milky Way. Until then, only about 12 of these spectacular events had been recorded in the entire history of astronomy. There were no supernovae in the Milky Way during the entire 20th century. While Zwicky searched the skies for supernovae, Baade derived their brightness versus time, or light curves. Using this data, Baade confirmed that Tycho's "nova" of 1572 in the Crab nebula had been a supernova in our galaxy.

Baade worked with Rudolph Minkowski (1895–1976), a fellow German whom he helped to flee to the United States when Adolf Hitler came to power. Minkowski did the spectroscopic observations of super-novae beginning in 1937. Within a few years, they had accumulated enough observational data to separate the class of less energetic novae from supernovae.

How Stars Shine

As astronomers considered that stars evolved into giants and that giants collapsed into neutron stars, Ukrainian physicist George Gamow (1904–68) was wondering what made them shine. He had arrived in the United States from the Soviet Union in 1934 and hosted meetings of physicists each spring at Georgetown University in Washington, D.C. He chose the topic of stellar energy for the meeting of March 1938. The meeting was not open to the public so that the participants could freely exchange ideas without fear of losing face. That year, German physicist Carl F. von Weizsacker (1912–   ) had discovered a nuclear cycle, now known

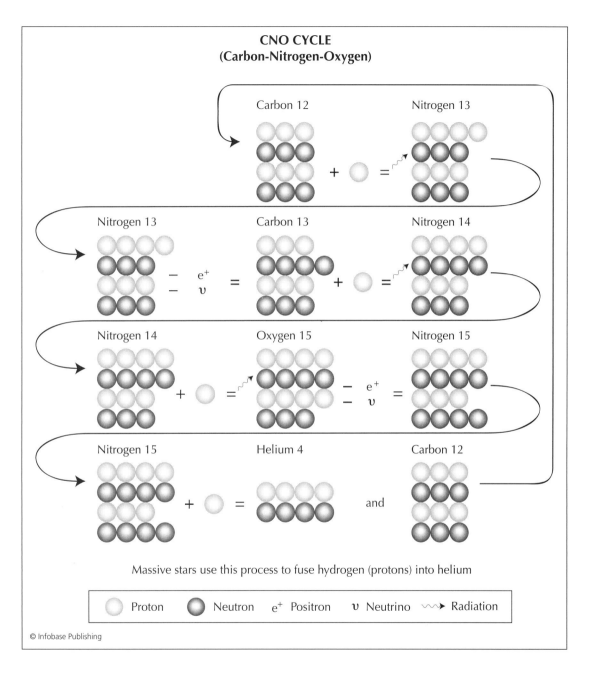

CNO CYCLE
(Carbon-Nitrogen-Oxygen)

Carbon 12   Nitrogen 13

Nitrogen 13   Carbon 13   Nitrogen 14

Nitrogen 14   Oxygen 15   Nitrogen 15

Nitrogen 15   Helium 4   and   Carbon 12

Massive stars use this process to fuse hydrogen (protons) into helium

○ Proton   ● Neutron e^+ Positron υ Neutrino   ⤳ Radiation

© Infobase Publishing

as the carbon–nitrogen–oxygen or CNO, cycle (see figure above) in which hydrogen nuclei fused to make helium using carbon as a catalyst. However, von Weizsacker did not investigate the rate at which energy would be produced in a star by the CNO cycle or its dependence on stellar temperature. That problem would be solved by German physicist

Massive stars fuse hydrogen into helium using the carbon–nitrogen cycle that was discovered by Hans Bethe and Carl von Weizacker in 1938.

Hans Bethe (1906–2005) who had fled to the United States in 1933. Bethe was at Cornell University and had just completed a set of three papers known as "Bethe's bible" (see Further Reading) in which he reviewed and analyzed all that was then known about nuclear physics.

As a result of the conference, Bethe took a closer look at von Weizsacker's work. Bethe pondered which nuclear reactions were most likely to occur at temperatures of 20 to 30 million degrees that Eddington had calculated for the centers of stars. He knew from spectroscopic studies that stars were mostly hydrogen and helium, followed by carbon, nitrogen, and oxygen. Because none of the common forms of these elements are subject to radioactive decay, Bethe ruled out nuclear fission. He analyzed the different possibilities for reactions and selected two processes that physicists now believe are responsible for sunshine. One process is the proton-proton chain (see figure on page 77) that builds helium out of hydrogen and was later found to be the primary energy source in stars like the Sun. The other was the one that Weizsacker had studied, the CNO cycle that was later shown to operate only in stars that were more massive than the Sun. Bethe's calculations led to a relation between stellar mass and stellar luminosity that agreed with the available observations. Bethe is reported to have said, "I went through the periodic table step by step and looked at the various nuclei that could react with protons. Nothing seemed to work, and I was almost ready to give up. But when I tried carbon, it worked. So, you see, this was a discovery by persistence, not by brains."

Bethe submitted the paper, "Energy Production in Stars," to the *Physical Review* but then found out there was a $500 prize being offered for the best unpublished paper about energy production in stars. He asked *Physical Review* to return his paper and proceeded to win the prize. Bethe recounts, "I used part of the prize to help my mother emigrate. The Nazis were quite willing to let her out, but they wanted $250, in dollars, to release her furniture. Part of the prize money went to liberate my mother's furniture." The paper was then published in the March 1939 issue of the *Physical Review* (see Further Reading). The solution to the mystery of how stars shine earned Bethe the Nobel Prize in physics in 1967.

George Gamow wrote to Henry Russell in the fall of 1938 that, "[T]he question about nuclear reaction which gives rise to stellar energy seems to be finally settled." Russell was not as sure as Gamow, pointing out that nitrogen was not that abundant in stellar atmospheres. He suggested that the heavy elements may have formed in an early phase of the expanding universe and thus were older than stars. Gamow had similar thoughts that were inspired by Georges Lemaître, whose 1927 paper describing the beginning of the universe had been reprinted in the *Monthly Notices of the Royal Astronomical Society* in March 1931. Lemaître proposed that the universe began with the explosion of a single particle that he called the primaeval [*sic*] atom at a single point in time, later called the big bang.

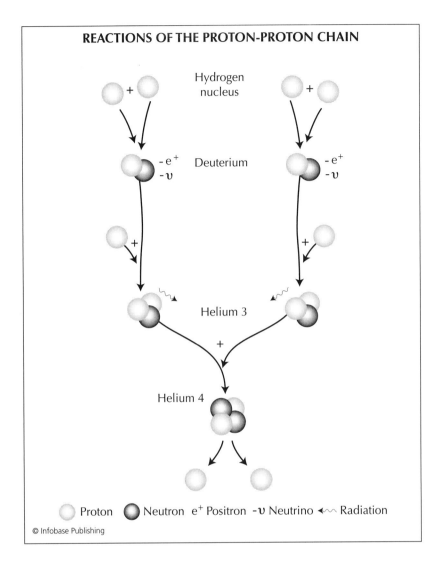

REACTIONS OF THE PROTON-PROTON CHAIN

Hydrogen nucleus

+   -e⁺ Deuterium -e⁺
    -υ   -υ

+   +

Helium 3

+

Helium 4

Proton   Neutron e⁺ Positron -υ Neutrino Radiation

© Infobase Publishing

The ancient question of what makes stars shine was answered in the 1930s with the discovery of the proton-proton chain reaction. Stars use this reaction to fuse hydrogen to helium and to release energy as starlight for millions to billions of years.

Many scientists resisted Lemaître's theory that the universe had a beginning. Arthur Eddington wrote in a letter to *Nature* in 1931 that the idea was "repugnant." After the discovery of the neutron in 1932, Lemaître's "atom" was modeled as a sea of neutrons that were closely packed together. The primaeval [*sic*] neutrons were supposed to decay into protons and the chemical elements, as well as cosmic rays. Because it appeared that the interiors of stars were not hot enough for synthesis of heavier elements, many astrophysicists began to wonder if the big bang was responsible for their creation. Working out the details of nuclear synthesis of the elements would be the work of the next two decades.

The Development of Modern Rockets

The men responsible for reaching space and landing on the Moon took their first steps toward that goal during the 1930s. Parallel developments in the United States, Germany, and Russia would challenge their best scientists and engineers to be the first to solve the problems of rocket-propelled flight. Though these men dreamed of using rockets to explore space that were similar to the flights of fancy depicted in science fiction (see sidebar below), their respective governments directed their work at providing new weapons for war.

The Russian rocket program was greatly influenced and inspired by Konstantin Tsiolkovsky who published a series of books on advanced airplanes and jet engines in the late 1920s. His final book was *Space Rocket Trains*, published in 1929. This mathematically dense work included the design of multistage rockets. In 1934, Tsiolkovsky told a group of students, "I am not sure, of course, that my 'space rocket train' will be appreciated and accepted readily, at this time. For this is a new conception reaching far beyond the present ability of man to make such things. However, time ripens everything; therefore I am hopeful that some of you will see a space rocket train in action." Sergei Korolev would make that hope a reality.

At the beginning of the decade, there were two groups that were conducting rocket-related research in Russia. One was in Leningrad, and the other in Moscow. The group in Leningrad was under the leadership of Nikolai Tikhomirov (1859–1930). They test-fired the first smokeless powder rocket in 1928. Tikhomirov's lab was expanded and renamed the Gas Dynamics Laboratory (GDL) in 1930. This group included a young engineer named Valentin Glushko (1908–89), who would later work in

Flash Gordon *and* War of the Worlds

Reflecting the public's need to escape the harsh economic and social reality of the Great Depression and to imagine a positive future, Alex Raymond (1909–56) created a new science-fiction comic strip called *Flash Gordon* in 1934. As the comic reached its peak popularity in 1936, Universal Studios bought the rights. With a $350,000 budget and the talented Larry "Buster" Crabbe (1908–83) and Jean Rogers (1916–91) to play the main characters of Flash Gordon and Dale Arden, the new moving picture serial was a huge success. *Flash Gordon* and its sequels, *Flash Gordon's Trip to Mars* (1938) and *Flash Gordon Conquers the Universe* (1940), captured the public's imagination with spark-spewing spaceships engaged in dogfights and attacks on alien monsters. With men such as Robert Goddard and his very real rockets that were featured in the newspapers and promoted by famous aviator Charles Lindbergh, such a future seemed very believable and very near. Thus, the public was fooled into thinking that Martians were invading on Halloween in 1938 when Orson Welles (1915–85) broadcast a radio version of H. G. Wells's (1886–1946) *War of the Worlds*. Less than a year later, a real invasion, of humans against humans, would start a world war that would kill millions and include real rockets and nuclear bombs.

the Soviet space program. They built the ORM–1 and –2 experimental rocket engines that had electrical ignition systems, had expandable nozzles, and used various liquid fuels.

The smaller Moscow group was formed in 1930 and called the Group for Studying Reaction Propulsion (GIRD). It was led by Fridrikh Arturovich Tsander (1887–1933), a man with an idea for a vehicle like a space shuttle that combined aircraft and rocket capabilities. Inspired by Tsiolkovsky, Tsander had begun work on rocket-propulsion theory in 1908. He wrote *Flights to Other Planets* in 1934. Working for Tsander in his spare time was the future chief designer of the Soviet space program, Sergei Pavlovich Korolev.

A Russian military man, Marshal Mikhail Tukhachevsky (1893–1937), already involved with GDL, saw the potential value of rockets to military applications and wanted to expand research in this area. To increase funding, he had GDL combined with GIRD in 1933 to become the Reaction Propulsion Institute (RNII), whose focus was weapons development. Korolev became deputy chief engineer.

The Soviet Union's first liquid-fueled rocket, the *GIRD-09*, was launched on August 17, 1933. It weighed 40 pounds (18 kg) and had a fuel of solid gasoline and liquid oxygen. The flight lasted 18 seconds and reached an altitude of about 1,300 feet (400 m). Korolev wrote, "It is necessary also to master and release into the air other types of rockets as soon as possible in order to thoroughly study and attain adequate mastery of reactive techniques. Soviet rockets must conquer space!"

The GIRD–09 was far less advanced than Goddard's rockets of the same time period. Goddard's rocket weighed less than half the 09 rocket—only 16 pounds (7.27 kg), including the fuel and oxygen. Goddard had reduced weight (and added stability) by moving the exhaust nozzle to the tail, thus eliminating the insulated supply lines of his earlier designs. Focusing on control, in 1932, he added a *gyroscope* that operated four vanes at the mouth of the nozzle (see figure on page 80). If the rocket deviated from vertical, the blast vanes would dip into the exhaust and correct for the error. In this way, the rocket would proceed on course. His work was interrupted because the Depression had dried up his source of funds. He went back to teaching at Clark University until the money resumed in 1934.

In Germany, development of liquid-fueled rockets moved from private civilian efforts into government-funded weapons research. The first president of the German Society for Space Travel, Johannes Winkler (1897–1947), launched Europe's first liquid-fueled rocket in Germany on March 14, 1931. It was a tiny methane and liquid-oxygen engine, generating only 14 pounds of thrust. Although their rockets were small, the society succeeded in getting media coverage for their efforts. This caught the attention of German army general Walter Dornberger (1895–1980) who shared their dream of space travel and also saw potential military applications. The society arranged a special demonstration for him, but the rocket failed. However, Dornberger was impressed with the men

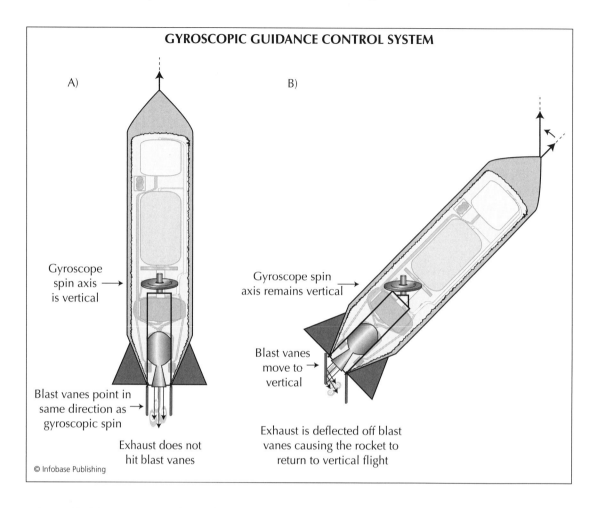

GYROSCOPIC GUIDANCE CONTROL SYSTEM

A)

Gyroscope spin axis is vertical →

Blast vanes point in same direction as → gyroscopic spin

Exhaust does not hit blast vanes

© Infobase Publishing

B)

Gyroscope spin axis remains vertical →

Blast vanes move to → vertical

Exhaust is deflected off blast vanes causing the rocket to return to vertical flight

Robert Goddard designed a gyroscopic control system in 1932. If the rocket deviated from vertical (A), the blast vanes would dip into the exhaust and correct for the error (B).

themselves and hired Wernher von Braun in 1932. The army work was done at Kummersdorf, about 15 miles (25 km) south of Berlin.

Von Braun's first rocket for Dornberger was designated A1 (assembly 1). It weighed 330 pounds (150 kg) and had a 660-pound (300-kg) thrust motor. It was 4.5 feet (1.4 m) long and 12 inches (30.4 cm) in diameter. The propellants were liquid oxygen and ethyl alcohol. The concept was sophisticated, but A1 never flew. A spinning payload in the nose that was supposed to make it stable made it too top-heavy. In 1934, A1 was redesigned and became A2. The gyroscopic payload was shifted to the middle of the rocket. In December 1934, von Braun took two of these rockets to an island to launch. They were nicknamed Max and Moritz, after two troublemaking lads in a popular comic strip. Each flew perfectly, reaching an altitude of about 6,500 feet (2,000 m). These tests proved the design and showed that gyroscopic control was possible.

Back in Roswell, New Mexico, in 1934, Robert Goddard continued his pursuit of a rocket that could reach high altitudes and remain under control. His "A" series rockets (see figure on page 81) were 13–15 feet

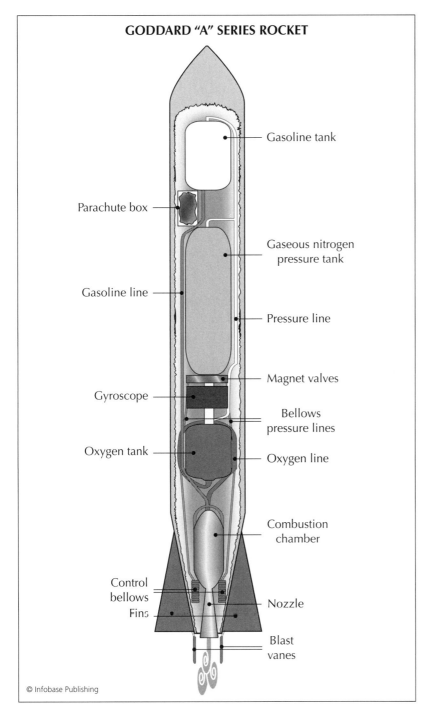

GODDARD "A" SERIES ROCKET

- Gasoline tank
- Parachute box
- Gaseous nitrogen pressure tank
- Gasoline line
- Pressure line
- Magnet valves
- Gyroscope
- Bellows pressure lines
- Oxygen tank
- Oxygen line
- Combustion chamber
- Control bellows
- Fins
- Nozzle
- Blast vanes

© Infobase Publishing

In 1935, Goddard's "A" series rocket was the first to go faster than the speed of sound. It was about 13 feet (4 m) tall and nine inches (23 cm) in diameter.

(3.9–4.5 m) tall and about nine inches (23 cm) in diameter. A third of the length went to a gaseous nitrogen tank that forced propellants into the motor and powered the gyroscope blast vanes. The first few A rockets failed. But on March 8, 1935, the A-4 went up about 1,000 feet (304 m), tilted, and then roared across the prairie, becoming the first rocket to exceed the speed of sound. An A-5 on March 28 rose more than a mile (0.6 km) high, and its speed exceeded 700 miles (1,100 km) per hour before it crashed into the scrub two miles (3.2 km) away. The A-6 and A-7 were failures, but the A-8 and A-10 rose higher than a mile (0.6 km) in May and July of 1935. Goddard had successfully solved the problem of the motor design, gyroscopic control, and steering vanes. The A-11 and A-12 failed while Goddard's patrons Harry Guggenheim (1890–1971) and Charles Lindbergh were there to watch in September. The final rocket in the A series was A-14. It reached a disappointing 2,000 feet (609 m).

Goddard then designed shorter, but fatter (about 18 inches [45 cm] in diameter) rockets in his quest to achieve higher altitudes. He increased the combustion chamber size and got rid of the large nitrogen tank by using liquid nitrogen. The "K" series were tested from November 1935 to February 1936. The combustion chambers became too hot and habitually blew holes in the sides. The burnout problem was a result of the high combustion temperatures of liquid fuels. Goddard used a kind of "curtain cooling" that injected the fuel so that it swirled around the chamber walls, but it was not enough.

Goddard launched a total of 30 "L" series rockets. The L-13 achieved the highest altitude of all his rockets, reaching almost 9,000 feet (2,744 m) in 1937, though the parachute failed. L-14 failed. L-15 went up about a half mile (0.3 km) and floated down beautifully. L-16 and -17 had swiveling tail sections and climbed higher than 2,000 feet (609 m). But the design was too complex, and Goddard set it aside. Goddard obtained a *barograph* for his L-28 rocket to measure and officially establish an altitude record. It reached 4,215 feet (1,285 m) on April 20, 1938, but the barograph was smashed on impact with the prairie. Another attempt crashed on May 26. In June, a tornado took out the launch tower and rocket. It was rebuilt, and the final flight of the L series occurred on August 9. The flight was perfectly vertical, and the parachute deployed as designed. The official record was set at 6,565 feet (21.5 km), but after correcting for elevation, it was only 3,294 feet (1,004 m). Unknown to Goddard, the Germans were reaching altitudes four times higher.

By 1935, the team at Kummersdorf had grown to about 80 people. They needed a bigger place, and joint funding was arranged between the German army and the Luftwaffe, the new German air force in 1936. A remote coastal area, designated Peenemünde, was selected as the site.

While the new site was under construction, the German A3 was launched in December 1937. It had a sophisticated guidance system with three gyroscopes and two *accelerometers*. These instruments sensed deviations from the established path and fed corrective signals to actuators that turned platinum vanes within the exhaust gases of the motor. The system eventually failed because it was too advanced for the engineering of the day.

The A5 was the next to launch in October 1938. It reached 26,240 feet (8 km) and was recovered by parachute. The recovery system was so reliable that many of the A5s were recovered and launched several times during the next three years. The A5 was soon capable of reaching altitudes of 42,640 feet (13 km). In 1939, the team, with von Braun as the lead designer, moved to the sprawling Peenemünde site.

Meanwhile, the Russian rocket program came to a standstill in 1938 as a result of political assassinations, exiles, and imprisonments. The Soviet leader Joseph Stalin had decided to rid the Communist Party of anyone whose loyalty to him was in doubt. One victim of the "Stalin purges" was Marshal Tukhachevsky who had established the RNII where Korolev worked. Tukhachevsky was shot, along with his wife, sister, two brothers, and his staff. The 31-year-old Korolev barely escaped the same fate. Instead, he was dragged from his bed in June 1938 and sent to one of the Soviet Union's most infamous prisons, Kolyma gulag in far eastern Siberia. Fortunately for the future Russian space program, its chief designer survived long enough for a former teacher to get him moved to a low-security prison in Moscow in 1940. There, he was put to work, not on rockets but on bombers for the war with Germany.

War had started in 1939 when Germany invaded Poland. Funding for the rocket program at Peenemünde experienced its first of many interruptions that year as Hitler decided first that the new missiles would not be needed and then decided that they were vital to the war effort. The up-and-down funding delayed production of an operational rocket (the A4 that became the V-2) by about two years. The rockets were very expensive, and a lack of telemetry required one test flight after another to check changes made in designs. Just perfecting the propellant shutoff valves for the A4 required 20 launches. Because of the war, metals for the rockets were in short supply as was the ethyl alcohol that was used for fuel. A somewhat humorous addition to the problem was that many of the workers were pilfering the alcohol to make "instant schnapps" to drink. (One rocket used alcohol equivalent to about 66,000 dry martinis.) A purgative was then added to the propellant to discourage this practice, and the resulting absenteeism almost brought the test program to a halt. By the beginning of 1940, about $14 million dollars had been spent on Peenemünde's construction and operations, making the German rocket program the most sophisticated in the world.

The U.S. government had little interest in rockets. The National Advisory Committee on Aeronautics (NACA), established in 1915, had recommended that the government focus on aircraft capabilities. The first NACA facility, named Langley after an aeronautical pioneer, was completed on June 11, 1920, in Virginia. This facility would later form the core of the American space program. A large wind tunnel was added in 1931, built by young engineers who were eager for jobs during the Depression. By 1939, the staff had grown to 523. As the war drove a need for more research into fighter planes, NACA expanded and built what would become the Ames Aeronautical Lab near San Francisco,

Scientist of the Decade: Robert Hutchings Goddard (1882–1945)

Considered the father of modern rocketry, American physicist Robert Goddard was born on October 5, 1882, in Worcester, Massachusetts. From 1883 to 1898, the family lived in Boston but returned to Worcester when Goddard's mother fell ill with tuberculosis.

An avid reader whose favorite books included H. G. Wells's *War of the Worlds,* Goddard also enjoyed experimenting. On October 19, 1899, while up in a cherry tree, he saw a vision of what his experiments might accomplish. In an autobiographical sketch, he wrote, "I imagined how wonderful it would be to make some device which had even the possibility of ascending to Mars." He had found his purpose in life.

Goddard enrolled in Becker's Business College, but bookkeeping was not for him. So he went to high school and graduated as class valedictorian in 1904. His graduation speech included the famous phrase, "it has often proved true that the dream of yesterday is the hope of today, and the reality of tomorrow."

Goddard entered Worcester Polytechnic Institute in 1904. In 1907, he was featured in the news after exploding a rocket in the school's basement. Goddard earned his degree in physics in 1908. He then earned his masters and doctorate in physics from Clark University, also in Worcester, in 1910 and 1912.

While on a fellowship at Princeton in August 1912, Goddard received his first patent, on an early radio tube called an oscillator. He spent 1913 bedridden with tuberculosis. But by July 1914, he had patents for a multistage rocket and a "liquid-fuel gun" pumping system.

In 1914, Goddard became a physics instructor at Clark. He used the school's shop for experiments that he funded from his own pocket. He discovered in 1915 that rockets needed to increase exhaust velocity if they were to ever reach space. Goddard then used a tapered nozzle that had been invented by Swedish engineer Carl Gustaf de Laval (1845–1913) to increase exhaust speed.

Goddard understood that rockets move by throwing mass (as hot exhaust) in the opposite direction. He did not worry that rockets would not have anything to push against in space. However, the effects of vacuum on combustion were unknown. He used a vacuum chamber in 1915 to prove that rockets work better in vacuum than in air. In 1916, he sent his results to the Smithsonian Institution. They granted him $5,000 to build rockets to fly to high altitudes.

WWI interrupted Goddard's work in 1917. By 1918, Goddard demonstrated a prototype of the bazooka for the army, though it was never used.

In 1919, Goddard published "A Method of Reaching Extreme Altitudes" in the Smithsonian Miscellaneous Collections. He reviewed his experiments and derived formulas for rocket propulsion. On January 13, 1920, the *New York Times* editorial stated, "That professor Goddard . . . does not know the relation of action to reaction; and of the need to have something better than a vacuum against which to react—to say that would be absurd. Of course, he only seems to lack the knowledge ladled out daily in high schools."

The *Times* did not know their physics, but the ridicule caused Goddard to shun future publicity and become secretive about his work. He told reporters that "every vision is a joke until the first man accomplishes it; once realized, it becomes commonplace." He debunked the "there is nothing to push against" objection in a 1921 issue of *Scientific American.*

Goddard worked as a navy consultant from 1920 to 1923 to develop rockets to use against submarines. Then he returned to Clark, and in 1924 he married Esther Christine Kisk.

At Clark on December 6, 1925, Goddard was the first to prove that a liquid rocket could lift its own weight. Then on March 16, 1926, Goddard launched the historic first liquid-fueled rocket. Goddard reported this milestone to his financiers, but he also insisted on no press coverage.

Robert Hutchings Goddard tested and observed his rockets in Roswell, New Mexico, from a control shack while standing by the firing control panel. He flew the first liquid-fueled rocket faster than the speed of sound in 1935 from this test site. (NASA)

On July 12, 1929, Goddard launched the first rocket with a payload. Though the flight was a success, the parachute failed, and the rocket loudly exploded on impact and caused a fire. Once again, Goddard "the moon man" was made fun of in the press. The authorities banned him from further launches in Massachusetts. A student working for Goddard remarked that the press "ain't done right by our Nell" referring to a Broadway melodrama, *Salvation Nell,* about a downtrodden girl. The Goddards, who had no children, decided to name all their rocket "children" Nell.

The press coverage attracted the attention of famous aviator Charles Lindbergh. He arranged for the Guggenheim Foundation to fund Goddard's research. In 1930, the Goddards moved to Roswell, New Mexico. They awed their neighbors by entertaining the celebrity Lindberghs.

In 1932, Goddard developed the first guidance system for a rocket. On March 8, 1935, he launched the first liquid-fueled rocket to travel faster than the speed of sound. On March 26, 1937, *Nell L-13* reached the highest altitude of Goddard's career, almost 9,000 feet (2,700 m). However, the official record was set via barograph at 6,565 feet (21.5 km) on August 9, 1938. That year, *Scientific American* declared him the Number One Rocket Man.

(continued on next page)

(continued from previous page)

One of Goddards's most embarrassing moments came on February 9, 1940. Lindbergh, photographers from *National Geographic,* the Guggenheims, and government officials gathered to watch the first launch of his newest rocket and instead witnessed a spectacular failure as the oxygen pump blew apart in a thunderous blast.

Goddard's final launch occurred on October 10, 1941. The engine ignited, but the rocket jammed in the launch tower. As the flames died, so did Goddard's vision of reaching space. His paranoia of spies stealing his work prevented him from contributing to the efforts at NACA or Caltech.

The Goddards left Roswell for Annapolis, Maryland, in 1942. Goddard resigned from Clark and worked on rocket-assisted takeoff programs for the navy and then for Curtiss-Wright. The cigar-smoking rocket man died of throat cancer on August 10, 1945.

Goddard was awarded 214 patents. Young rocket engineers found it nearly impossible to work without his designs. In 1960, Mrs. Goddard and the Guggenheim Foundation received a million-dollar settlement for patent infringement by the U.S. government. Goddard would have been pleased to know his work was so valuable. He would also likely have enjoyed the "Correction" to the *Times* editorial of 1920, printed on July 17, 1969, while Apollo 11 sped to the Moon. It read, "it is now definitely established that a rocket can function in a vacuum as well as in an atmosphere. The *Times* regrets the error."

California, in 1939. In June 1940, Congress approved a third research facility, this one in Cleveland, Ohio. It was named Lewis in 1948, and now is the Glenn Research Center. All of these labs worked on aircraft and jet improvements.

To exceed his previous altitudes, in 1938, Goddard focused his attention on new propellant pumps. The 24-foot (7.3-m) "P" series rocket was Goddard's most advanced design. The new series included a pump–turbine engine, a gyroscopic stabilizer, a high-pressure combustion chamber, lighter-weight fuel tanks, and a parachute deployment system. None of the "P" rockets was successful. The turbo pump worked, but bad luck, weather, and other problems caused one failure after another. The last launch attempt occurred in October 1941 when the rocket jammed in the launch tower.

Charles Lindbergh urged Goddard to work with engineers at NACA and the California Institute of Technology, but Goddard refused. The new Guggenheim Aeronautical Lab at Caltech (GALCIT) under the direction of Theodore von Kármán (1881–1963) then took the lead in advancing rocketry in the United States. Between the fall of 1936 and early 1937, von Kármán's student Frank Malina (1912–81) worked on liquid-rocket designs. This work led to a contract in August 1939 from the U.S. Army Air Corps to work on jet-assisted takeoff (JATO). JATO capability was desired to address a concern that long runways would not be available in combat zones.

To meet the military's needs for reliable and storable rockets, Malina and von Kármán successfully solved many of the problems that had caused Goddard's rockets to fail. In 1939, they switched from liquid oxygen (LOX) and gasoline to aniline that spontaneously ignites in the presence of nitric acid. Malina found out after the war that the Germans had also discovered what are referred to as *hypergolic* propellants that do not require an ignition system and, unlike LOX, will not build up in pockets in the engine and cause explosions. They also realized that solid propellants, though they cannot be switched off once ignited, are simpler and lighter to use for JATO applications, while liquid rockets, that can be switched on and off, are better for adding speed during long flights.

As World War II spread, the Russian, the American, and the German governments increased the pressure on their engineers to provide new weapons. In the next decade, the Germans would surpass all the others in this deadly task with the creation of the highly accurate and destructive V-2 ballistic missile.

Further Reading

Books and Periodicals

Hans Bethe. "Energy Production in Stars." *Physical Review* 55 (March 1939): 434–456. Abstract available online. URL: http://prola.aps.org/ abstract/PR/v55/i5/p434_1. Accessed on March 4, 2006. This technical paper, that earned a Nobel prize in physics for the author, details the fusion reactions that power the Sun and other stars.

———. "Nuclear Physics A: Stationary States of Nuclei." *Reviews of Modern Physics* 8 (April 1936): 82–229. "Nuclear Physics B: Nuclear Dynamics, Theoretical." *Reviews of Modern Physics* 9 (April 1937): 69– 244. "Nuclear Physics C: Nuclear Dynamics, Experimental." *Reviews of Modern Physics* 9 (July 1937): 245–390. These three scholarly papers were called "Bethe's Bible" and provided the foundation and conditions that Bethe used to determine how stars produce energy.

Clary, David A. *Rocket Man: Robert H. Goddard and the Birth of the Space Age.* New York: Hyperion Press, 2003. This is a biography of Robert Goddard.

Florence, Ronald. *The Perfect Machine: Building of the Palomar Telescope.* New York: Harper Collins, 1994. Read about the design, financing, construction and operation of the 200-inch telescope.

Goddard, Robert H. *Rockets.* New York: Dover Publications, 2002. This book includes *A Method of Reaching Extreme Altitudes* and *Liquid-Propellant Rocket Development*, originally published in 1919 and 1936, respectively.

Ella, Ryndina, translated by Arthur Gill. "Portrait of Lev Landau." *Physics Today* 57 (February 2004): 53. The article is a brief biography of Soviet physicist Landau who first described neutron stars.

Web Sites

John N. Bahcall. "How the Sun Shines." The Nobel Foundation. Available online. URL: http://nobelprize.org/physics/articles/fusion/index.html.

Posted on June 29, 2000. Accessed on August 29, 2006. The article discussing proton–proton chain and CNO cycle is included.

Clark University. "Robert Hutchings Goddard Home Page." Available online. URL: http://www.clarku.edu/offices/library/archives/Goddard.htm. Accessed on March 4, 2006. The site has a brief biography, drawings, photos, and copies of Goddard's papers.

Mark Midbon. "A Day without Yesterday: Georges Lemaître & the Big Bang." *Commonweal*, 2000 March 24, 18–19. Available online through the Catholic Educator's Resource Center. URL: http://www.catholiceducation.org/articles/science/sc0022.html. Accessed on March 4, 2006. Provides a brief history, and photo, of Belgian priest and mathematician Georges Lemaître who is the father of the big bang theory.

ParkNet. "Reber Radio Telescope." ParkNet, National Park Service. Available online. URL: http://www.cr.nps.gov/history/online_books/butowsky5/astro4o.htm. Accessed on November 5, 2001. The site provides an overview of the history of radio astronomy, photographs of the first telescopes, and a bibliography.

Trueman. "America 1918–1939." Trueman. Available online. URL: http://www.historylearningsite.co.uk/america_1918.htm. Accessed on August 29, 2006. The site provides an overview of the economic and political events that influenced American scientists in the 1930s.

5

1941–1950:
From War to Space

The world was at war from 1941 until 1945, and scientists were hard at work to win it. Astronomical questions were set aside while astronomers taught navigation, computed ballistics, and worked on weapons programs. Rocket scientists in Germany, the United States, and the Soviet Union made great advances because of wartime funding. Progress in electronics, photography, communications, and computers during the war years had tremendous impacts on astronomy and space science.

The main topic of this chapter is the development of rockets for war that led directly to the "space race" in the next decade. The first rocket to reach space above the Earth's atmosphere, loosely defined as 50 miles (80 km) in altitude, occurred during this decade. It was a German rocket called the A4 (see figure on page 93) that was renamed the V-2, the second "vengeance" weapon. This rocket was designed by Wernher von Braun (see sidebar and photo on page 106), who is the featured scientist of the decade. The chapter describes how von Braun and his team of rocket scientists developed and tested the A4 at a secret base called Peenemünde (see figure on page 94) in northern Germany (see figure on page 95) and how these Germans were absorbed into the Russian and American space programs. The end of the war gave rise to the dominance of two world superpowers, the United States and the Soviet Union. The competition between them to build intercontinental nuclear missiles became a driving force in the development of space-capable rockets.

Though the war interrupted most of the scientific work being done by astronomers, the chapter describes some very important discoveries, theoretical breakthroughs, and new technologies that were developed for war (see sidebar on page 105) and proved to be of significant benefit to astronomical studies. German immigrant Walter Baade (see photo on page 101) doubled the size of the known universe when he discovered that Cepheid variables (used to calculate distance) came in two different types. British astronomer Fred Hoyle (1915–2001; see photo on page 103) realized that the implosion mechanism that created the high temperatures required for a nuclear bomb to explode could also explain how elements were synthesized during a supernova. Hoyle formulated a detailed mathematical description of the reactions and abundance of elements produced in supernovae that matched cosmic abundance data very well. With an explanation of how elements were formed, he developed the steady-state theory (see figure on page 104) as an alternative to what he called the big bang hypothesis of universal origin. Wartime technology such as improvements to computing and radio astronomy would provide data to distinguish between the two major theories in the next decade.

The Pathway to Space Begins with Weapons

During the war, development of rockets in the United States focused on improving the performance of fighter jets. Early experiments indicated that solid propellants, favored for jet-assisted takeoff (JATO) applications, generated an ever-rising pressure in the combustion chamber

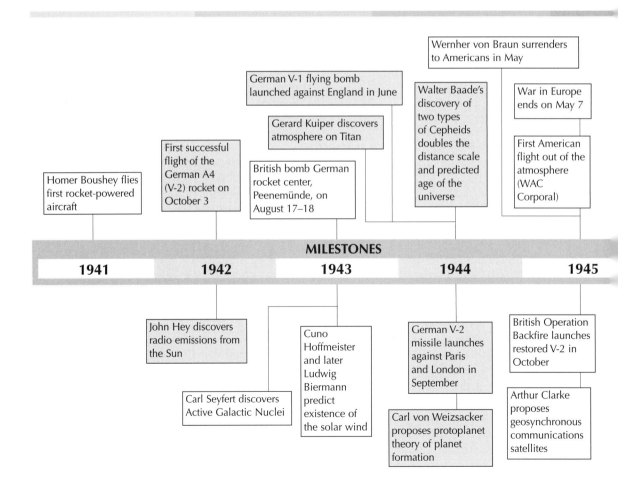

Wernher von Braun surrenders to Americans in May

German V-1 flying bomb launched against England in June

Gerard Kuiper discovers atmosphere on Titan

Walter Baade's discovery of two types of Cepheids doubles the distance scale and predicted age of the universe

War in Europe ends on May 7

First successful flight of the German A4 (V-2) rocket on October 3

British bomb German rocket center, Peenemünde, on August 17–18

First American flight out of the atmosphere (WAC Corporal)

Homer Boushey flies first rocket-powered aircraft

MILESTONES

1941	1942	1943	1944	1945

John Hey discovers radio emissions from the Sun

Cuno Hoffmeister and later Ludwig Biermann predict existence of the solar wind

German V-2 missile launches against Paris and London in September

British Operation Backfire launches restored V-2 in October

Carl Seyfert discovers Active Galactic Nuclei

Carl von Weizsacker proposes protoplanet theory of planet formation

Arthur Clarke proposes geosynchronous communications satellites that quickly caused an explosion. Some scientists questioned whether or not it was theoretically possible to build a long-burning solid-rocket engine. In 1940, Theodore von Kármán, head of the GALCIT project at Caltech, and Frank Malina, who became the first director of the Jet Propulsion Laboratory (JPL), proved mathematically that stable burning was possible as long as the ratio of the throat of the exhaust nozzle to the burning area of the propellant charge was constant. With this knowledge, the team successfully built the first rocket-powered aircraft flown by Captain Homer A. Boushey, Jr. (1910–2001) on August 12, 1941.

John W. Parsons (1913–52), a self-trained chemist who worked with Malina, discovered a new material to use as a solid fuel, asphalt–potassium perchlorate composite. This discovery eventually led to development of other castable solid propellants such as the material called Thiokol used in the space-shuttle solid rocket boosters.

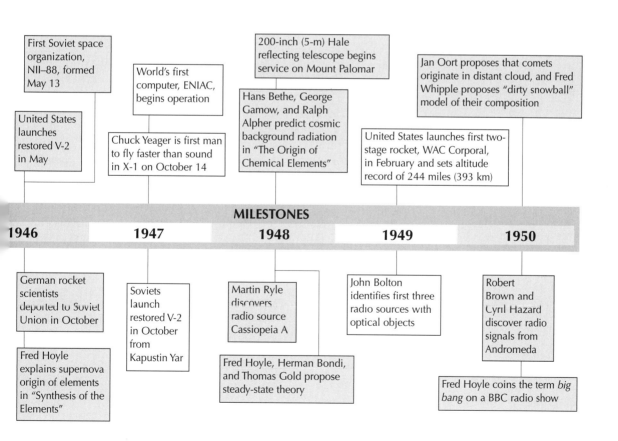

MILESTONES

First Soviet space organization, NII–88, formed May 13

United States launches restored V-2 in May

World's first computer, ENIAC, begins operation

Chuck Yeager is first man to fly faster than sound in X-1 on October 14

200-inch (5-m) Hale reflecting telescope begins service on Mount Palomar

Hans Bethe, George Gamow, and Ralph Alpher predict cosmic background radiation in "The Origin of Chemical Elements"

Jan Oort proposes that comets originate in distant cloud, and Fred Whipple proposes "dirty snowball" model of their composition

United States launches first two-stage rocket, WAC Corporal, in February and sets altitude record of 244 miles (393 km)

| 1946 | 1947 | 1948 | 1949 | 1950 |

German rocket scientists deported to Soviet Union in October

Fred Hoyle explains supernova origin of elements in "Synthesis of the Elements"

Soviets launch restored V-2 in October from Kapustin Yar

Martin Ryle discovers radio source Cassiopeia A

Fred Hoyle, Herman Bondi, and Thomas Gold propose steady-state theory

John Bolton identifies first three radio sources with optical objects

Robert Brown and Cyril Hazard discover radio signals from Andromeda

Fred Hoyle coins the term *big bang* on a BBC radio show

Malina and his team at JPL also worked on liquid rockets. They developed and launched America's first rocket to escape the atmosphere. Called the WAC (Without Attitude Control) Corporal, it reached a height of 250,000 feet (76,219 m) in October 1945. Their better-funded counterparts in Germany had reached space three years earlier.

Progress on the A4 at Peenemünde was threatened in 1941 by a labor shortage. General Dornberger and Marshal Walther von Brauchitsch (1881–1948), then commander of the army, authorized formation of a special battalion of scientists and engineers. The men were civilians who were called to active duty at their same jobs at less pay, or soldiers who were pulled from the infantry or released from hospitals. Women were hired as *Messfrauen* (measurement girls) to do drafting, illustrating, and mathematical calculations. Prisoners of war were also assigned to Peenemünde despite this practice being strictly forbidden by the Geneva Convention. At the Nuremberg trails after the war, Minister of Armaments and Munitions Albert Speer (1905–81) admitted that by 1944, 40 percent of all prisoners in Germany were employed in the production of weapons. Russian prisoners made graphite jet vanes for the A4 control systems. Hitler's personal bodyguards called the *Schutzstaffel*, or SS, maintained tight control over the prisoners, and attempts at sabotage were few.

By 1941, Walter Thiel (1910–43) had scaled up the 1.5-ton engine of the German A4 to 25 tons while reducing size. He solved the problems of fuel injection and burn-through of the walls of the combustion chamber. The A4 had a gross weight of 12.52 tons. The powerful rocket could carry a one-metric ton payload 124 miles (200 km). It was 46.5 feet (14.3 m) long and had a diameter of 5.36 feet (1.65 m).

The first flight of the A4 was June 13, 1942. It crashed into the Baltic and sent up a tremendous fountain of water. The second attempt in August also failed. The guidance system was the biggest challenge. One solution was to use radio control and keep the expensive and large precision radar antenna on the ground. This provided extreme accuracy but was vulnerable to jamming and required complicated ground support. This method was chosen for the Fi103. The A4 (see figure on page 93) was outfitted with an inertial system with gyroscopes, accelerometers, and an analog computer to furnish data to position the jet vanes.

The third A4 test, on October 3, hit its target 119 miles (192 km) down range. Dornberger said, "We have invaded space with our rocket for the first time—mark this well—have used space as a bridge between two points on earth; we have proved rocket propulsion practicable [*sic*] for space travel." Hitler had more immediate uses for rockets. In July 1943, he told Speer, "The A4 is a measure that can decide the war. And what encouragement to the home front when we attack England with it!"

But first, the British would attack Peenemünde (see figure on page 94). Because of its distance, they could not use ground-based radar to guide

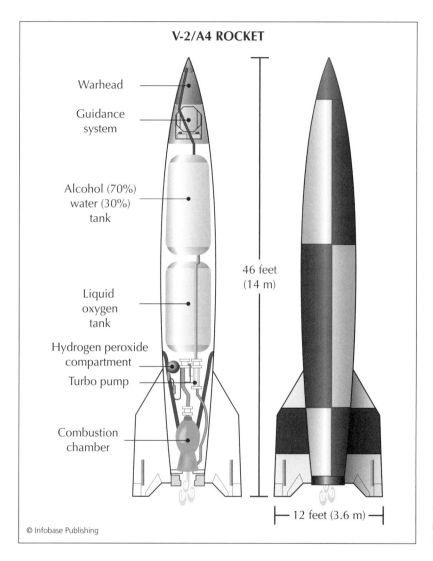

V-2/A4 ROCKET

Warhead

Guidance
system

Alcohol (70%)
water (30%)
tank

Liquid
oxygen
tank

Hydrogen peroxide
compartment

Turbo pump

Combustion
chamber

46 feet
(14 m)

12 feet (3.6 m)

© Infobase Publishing

The V-2/A4 rocket designed by Wernher von Braun was the first to reach space and also the first long-range missile.

the bombers. So they waited until August 17–18, 1943, when the night was long enough and a full Moon was available to help with navigation. Six hundred bombers set out, with the priority target being the housing units of the scientists. Target-marking flares were dropped at the wrong location, so the Trassenheide labor camp was hit hard, killing about 500 prisoners. Only two key scientists died: propulsion expert Walter Thiel (?–1943) and Erich Walther, chief of maintenance. With the propulsion system already in production, the bombing delayed deployment of the A4 by only about two months.

In the attack 735 people died, but the rocket facilities were barely damaged. The Germans decided to disperse the facilities anyway. The valve factory and the wind tunnels were moved. The A4 was put into

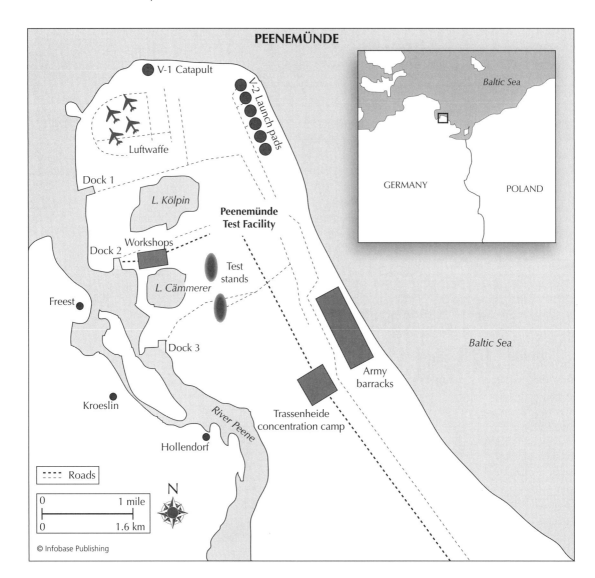

PEENEMÜNDE

V-1 Catapult

V-2 Launch pads

Luftwaffe

Dock 1

L. Kölpin

Peenemünde
Test Facility

Dock 2   Workshops

L. Cämmerer   Test
stands

Freest

Dock 3

Army
barracks

Kroeslin

River Peene

Trassenheide
concentration camp

Hollendorf

Baltic Sea

GERMANY   POLAND

Baltic Sea

---- Roads

0   1 mile
0   1.6 km

N

© Infobase Publishing

The German rocket program that developed the V-2 was based at Peenemünde from 1939 to 1945. The British bombed the facility in August 1943, intending to target the barracks housing the rocket scientists, but instead destroyed the Trassenheide labor camp.

production at Mittelwerk near Nordhausen, Germany (see figure opposite). The remaining team at Peenemünde, including von Braun, worked on improvements to the A4 and antiaircraft rockets.

A special committee was established for the missile program under the control of *Obergruppenführer* (Major General in the SS) Hans Kammler (1901–45?). A ruthless and ambitious man, he used forced labor from concentration camps to meet a production goal of 600 missiles a month at Mittelwerk. The former underground supply depot contained about 1.2 million square feet (111,600 sq. m) of tunnels extending more than a mile under about 140–200 feet (43–61.5 m) of rock. The plant required enormous amounts of heat, water, compressed air, and propane gas. A total workforce of about 8,000 worked there. The equipment cost more than $8 million. Working conditions were barbarous. A secretary reported, "Because of the dampness, many died of pneumonia."

The first 25 missiles produced at Mittelwerk were tested at Peenemünde. Fearing another attack there, rocket testing activities were moved to Blizna in southern Poland in early 1944. Only 10 to 20 percent of the test missiles hit their targets. Most accidents were the result of leaky oxygen pipes.

One group of Germans under Ludwig Roth (1909–67) worked on a modified A4 with wings called the A4b (b for bastard). Two were launched in January 1944 and reached three times the speed of sound, demonstrating the feasibility of supersonic winged rockets.

The first engineering plans for a multistage rocket were the combination of the A-9 and A-10 rockets called an A-11. The upper-stage A-9

The A-4/V-2 rockets were designed and tested at the secret Peenemünde facility and assembled for use by forced labor at Mittelwerk near Nordhausen. The V-2 rockets were the first long-range missiles and were used against Paris and London. Lead rocket scientist Wernher von Braun was born in Wyrzysk (or Wirsitz), Poland, which was under German rule at the time. Oberjoch is near where he and his rocket team surrendered to the Americans in 1945.

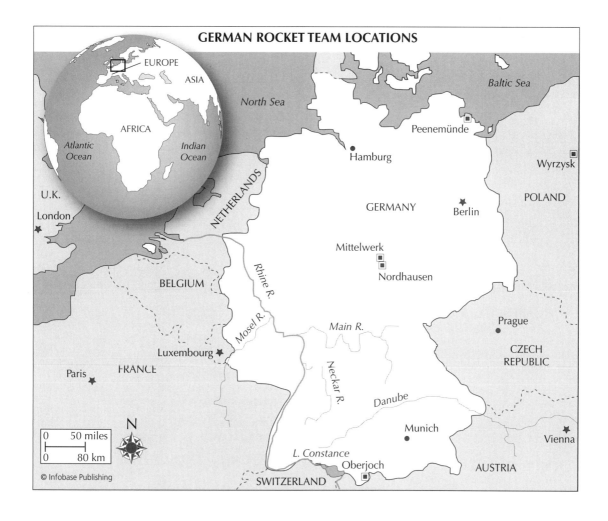

GERMAN ROCKET TEAM LOCATIONS

© Infobase Publishing

was modified to become the A4b. Work on the A-10 was discontinued in 1944 because development was expected to take two years. One version of the A-9 was a "shuttle" with a pressurized cabin for the pilot who would take off vertically and glide to a landing.

In June 1944, the Fi103, renamed the V-1, the first vengeance weapon, was launched against England. The V-1s were air-breathing cruise missiles that had a relatively short range. The Germans could launch a missile every 90 minutes and averaged 102 V-1s every day until the beginning of September. Allied attacks on the launch sites were pretty ineffective. The Germans could build a new site in 10 days or less, and only 15 men were required for firing. The V-1 were relatively slow, at less than 400 mph (640 kmph), so Allied pilots shot down many of them. The V-1 assault ended on September 1 when the French launch sites were overrun by Allied troops. V-1 casualties were 24,165 killed or badly injured, compared to conventional bombing casualties of 112,932 for the same period.

General Kammler took over the operation of the A4 from Dornberger in 1944 and ordered the first attack from Holland on September 6, 1944. Renamed the V-2, the rocket was 46 feet (14 m) long and weighed 27,000 pounds (12,300 kg). It flew at speeds faster than 3,500 mph (5,600 kmph) and delivered a 2,200-pound (1,000-kg) warhead. The first long-range missiles used in combat hit Paris, then England on September 8. Between October 13 and March 29, 1945, more than 1,000 V-2s were fired on London. Antwerp (a port for Allied supplies) endured nearly 1,500 missiles. Casualty figures were 9,277 killed or seriously injured. Each V-2 cost about $13,330. About 6,000 were produced during the war with a 25 percent failure rate. An analysis showed that it cost the Allies four times more to defend against the V-2 than it cost the Germans to produce the weapons.

In early 1945, von Braun orchestrated the exodus of about 4,000 people from Peenemünde, heading toward American lines to avoid being killed by the SS or being taken captive by the Russians. (Key personnel were assassinated rather than allowed to fall into enemy hands. General Kammler was presumably assassinated.) The last group left Peenemünde on March 7, 1945. Peenemünde fell to the Russians on March 9. Magnus von Braun (1919–2003), Wernher's brother who was a chemist and spoke English, surrendered the team to the Americans on May 2, 1945, near Oberjoch on the Austrian border.

Postwar Rocket Development

After the war, with much of Europe and Asia in shambles, the United States and the Soviet Union emerged as the world's two superpowers. The two nations, with very different political philosophies, competed for technological dominance. The atomic bomb was the most threatening invention of the war, and both superpowers sought ways to deliver it across the intercontinental distances that separated them. Both superpowers immediately moved to capture and interrogate the German rocket scientists to learn the secrets of the V-2. Though the British were the first to reconstruct a V-2 and fire it during Operation Backfire in October 1945, they were too consumed with postwar reconstruction to develop it further.

The American effort to get this new technology began in May 1945. Colonel Holger N. Toftoy (1903–67), the chief of U.S. Army Ordnance Technical Intelligence in Europe, organized Special Mission V-2 to gather and ship the parts to build 100 V-2s in the United States. Mittelwerk was captured in April and was to be turned over to the Russians by June 1, 1945. With little time, Toftoy had his men pick up 100 of everything in sight and had it shipped to the United States.

Another secret mission was under way to identify and use German scientists in the war against Japan. The task was given to Major Robert Staver (1917–2003) who worked for Toftoy in London. Staver got approval from General Dwight D. Eisenhower (1890–1969) to bring some of the Germans to the United States. In July 1945, Operation Overcast (later Project Paperclip) was established for this purpose. Staver got 100 Peenemünde workers out just hours before the Russians took over.

The German workers were offered six-month contracts. Wernher von Braun was given the top salary of $750/month. Some Germans were sent to Aberdeen Proving Ground to translate recovered documents. These were used by those developing rockets at Fort Bliss near El Paso, Texas, and the White Sands Proving Ground in New Mexico.

With the help of the Germans, the navy designed and built the Viking research rockets. On May 3, 1949, the first Viking (initially called Neptune) sounding rocket was launched from White Sands. It was built by Glenn L. Martin Co. for the Naval Research Lab. These rockets pioneered gimbaled engines and integral fuel tanks and evolved into the first stage of the *Vanguard* satellite program.

The speeds of jets increased dramatically during the war. NACA's wind tunnels could not provide accurate data for transonic speeds (over mach 1), so they used rockets to drop payloads from high altitudes. The Langley facility in Virginia was expanded to include a surplus naval station that became the Wallops Flight Center. Sounding rockets were launched from this facility. NACA also established a high-speed research station at Edwards, California, where, on October 14, 1947, Air Force Captain Charles E. Yeager (1923–   ) flew the *X-1* aircraft faster than the speed of sound.

Postwar Russian Rocket Development

Red Army Major Boris Chertok (1912–   ) arrived in Germany in April 1945 to recruit German specialists. He headed the Institut Rabe (rocket manufacturing and development) based near Nordhausen, Germany. The Institut's job was to restore the documentation for the V-2 that von Braun had taken to the United States. The most senior of the German recruits was Helmut Gröttrup (1916–81). He was given a generous salary of $1,250/month and was put in charge of Zentralwerke with responsibility for guided-missile development. By September 1946, the Germans had redone all the drawings, and a pilot production line was turning out flight-worthy V-2s. The V-2s were not launched from Zentralwerke but were test fired at Lehesten under the direction of Valentin Glushko.

The Germans did what their Soviet captors had asked but were kidnapped and shipped, with their families, by train and truck, to workplaces outside Moscow in October 1946. They worked for the newly created Scientific Research Institute–88 (NII-88) headed by General Lev Mikhailovich Gaidukov (1911–   ). The creation of this institute was signed by Joseph Stalin himself on May 13, 1946, and is considered the birth of the rocket industry in the Soviet Union.

The Ministry of Armament, under the leadership of Dmitri Fedorovich Ustinov (1908–84), rather than the Ministry of Aviation was given the responsibility for rocket research. The result of this decision kept the rocket and aviation industries separate in the USSR while in the United States, the two combined into the aerospace industry. Sergei Korolev who had been working on a "stretched" version of the V-2 for Gaidukov in Germany, was appointed to head Department 3, devoted to long-range ballistic-missile design. The chief engineer of NII–88 was Yuri Pobedonostsev (1907–73). His deputy was Boris Chertok. Valentin Glushko was chief designer of the OKB-456 rocket-engine plant in Khimki near Moscow.

The first goal of NII-88 was to set up a pilot production line of V-2s in Russia. For an unknown reason, the documentation from Zentralwerke was not delivered for a year. By May 1948, about 150 Germans were confined to the island of Gorodomliya, surrounded by barbed wire and guarded by women gunners. They restored 30 German V-2s and then worked on a new rocket called the R-10. It used a film of alcohol emitted through small holes in the chamber walls to cool it. The pressurized propellant tanks became load-bearing parts of the rocket, saving a lot of weight. This improvement was also used in the Atlas in America and on the British missile called the Blue Streak. The tanks were made of aluminum instead of steel, also to reduce weight. Gases from the combustion chamber were piped back for use in the turbopumps, saving more weight by eliminating the generator that had been used to provide steam to the pumps. The warhead was separated from the rocket with no loss of momentum by using small retro-rockets fired at engine cutoff. Guidance was "beam riding," using four antennas on the ground to establish a path. The range was considered to be about 570 miles (917 km).

In August 1947, Gröttrup was spirited away by train again, this time to a test site near the village of Kapustin Yar (later Baikonur space center), about 75 miles (120 km) from Stalingrad. Gröttrup's wife joined him in October and wrote about the countdown of the first V-2/R-1 launch on October 30, 1947, ". . . zero minus 5 . . . Suddenly the launching platform collapses sideways and with it the fully loaded rocket. One leg of the platform has given way. . . . We make a dash for the bunker, while workmen run toward the rocket and, with absolutely no sign of fear, winch the whole thing back into position, platform, rocket and all, and prop it up with girders. There's Russia for you!" The countdown resumed, and the rocket launched successfully. Sergei Korolev hugged Gröttrup. About 20 V-2s were launched from Kapustin Yar by December 1947. The launchings were done by alternating German and Russian teams. The Russian team was headed by L. A. Voskresensky (1913–65), who became Korolev's deputy as space-vehicle-systems designer.

In 1948, the Germans worked on the R-12 multistage rocket, but problems with stage separation were too much to overcome. In April 1949, they designed the R-14 to send a 6,600-pound (3,000-kg) warhead 1,800 miles (2,900 km). The design was far advanced from what von Braun came up with in the United States. The R-14 was 77.6 feet (23.9 m) long and nine feet (2.7 m) in diameter. It had no fins or control surfaces. The exhaust gases from the turbopump were vented through a nozzle that could be swiveled to counteract rolling. The warhead was separated by explosive bolts instead of rockets, saving weight. The design was reviewed in October 1949, but other than redesigning the body to aluminum versus steel, the Germans were not asked to work on it. They were given no meaningful work, and conditions at their camp deteriorated. There were several suicides. The Germans were not allowed to return to Germany until 1953.

The First Science Rockets

The Germans in America similarly assisted industry and research institutions with assembly, checkout, and launching of V-2s, and they studied new guided-missile projects. The first U.S. V-2 was launched on April 16, 1946, and failed. May 10 was the first success, reaching 71 miles (114 km). On May 29, 1947, one was accidentally sent toward Juárez, Mexico, during a fiesta. It blasted a huge crater, but fortunately no one was injured. (Supposedly, the enterprising Mexicans sold 10 to 15 tons of souvenir material from a rocket weighing only four tons.) One V-2 was launched from an aircraft carrier, and two were fired from the Long Range Proving Ground that eventually became the Kennedy Space Center in Florida. Through September 1952, more than 60 V-2s were launched from White Sands as part of Project Hermes.

The V-2s gave American scientists access to the upper atmosphere. In 1946, they set an altitude record of 116 miles (186 km) with a V-2 launched from White Sands. In 1947, they launched seeds and fruit flies to high altitudes to expose them to cosmic rays. The curvature of the

Earth was photographed in 1948. They also used the V-2 to make the first observation of the Sun's ultraviolet and X-ray spectrum. In 1949, a V-2 that had been mated with a WAC Corporal (produced at JPL as part of Project Bumpers), reached a record altitude of 244 miles (393 km) and velocity of 5,150 mph (8,290 kmph). It provided data on the density of ions in the atmosphere.

From June 1948 through the end of 1949, Project Albert used V-2s to determine the effects of high acceleration and freefall on primates. The first monkey died of suffocation, and the second was killed on impact. The data showed that primates could survive a liftoff of 5.5 g's. Two more monkeys were flown and died, one during an in-flight explosion and the other on impact.

The army estimated that having American engineers and scientists confer with the Germans gained 10 years in research and saved the nation at least $750 million. The Germans and their families, who joined them in late 1946, were moved to Huntsville, Alabama, in the fall of 1950. They began work at the Redstone Arsenal of the U.S. Army Ordnance Department that had opened in 1941 and had been used to build small rockets during the war. The former German weapons experts would form the nucleus of the NASA Marshall Spaceflight Center that would build rockets to take men to the Moon.

Wartime Astronomy

The war interrupted and changed the lives of millions, and astronomers were no exception. The patriotic Edwin Hubble who had served in WWI was anxious to serve again. He finished a paper on nebular rotation in 1941, showing that spiral arms trail the more rapidly rotating nucleus. His paper appeared while he was designing bullets and bomb trajectories at Aberdeen Proving Ground. Fritz Zwicky turned from supernova studies to rocket development and interrogated Wernher von Braun at the end of the war. Walter Baade (see photo on page 101) was left with the 100-inch (2.5-m) telescope practically to himself. After the attack on Pearl Harbor, Mount Wilson was considered a target and made part of a military district. Baade then became a victim of his own procrastination. After arriving from Germany in 1931, he had filed for United States citizenship but lost the papers and never completed the process. So in December 1941, Baade was officially an enemy alien and therefore required to remain in his home between 8 P.M. and 6 A.M. He was thus barred from astronomical work in early 1942 until his case was reviewed.

Once free of the curfew, Baade took advantage of dark conditions during blackouts in Los Angeles (to prevent Japanese attacks) and new red-sensitive plates to photograph individual stars in Andromeda and its satellite galaxies. He discovered that old red and yellow giants were found mostly in the center of nebulae and in globular clusters, while young metal-rich stars congregated in the disks or along spiral arms of nebulae.

Walter (Wilhelm H.) Baade made a discovery that doubled the size of the universe: the Cepheid variable stars whose brightness was used to find distances were four times brighter than previously thought. This discovery meant that the universe was bigger and older. (National Optical Astronomy Observatory/ Association of Universities for Research in Astronomy/ National Science Foundation)

He called the young stars population I or type I stars and the old giants population II or type II stars.

Baade realized that the Cepheid variables used to calculate distances to galaxies also came in different types. He determined that type I Cepheids were four times brighter than type II Cepheids (see figure on page 32). This meant that Andromeda and other galaxies whose distances were calculated using Cepheids were twice as far away as previously thought. The universe had just doubled in size.

Baade's discovery announced in 1944 rocked the astronomical community (and helped earn him a Bruce Medal [see page 249] in 1955). He had addressed one of Hubble's doubts about the theory of the expansion of the universe. When the expansion rate was run backward, it provided an age for the universe of only about 2 billion years, younger than the Earth's estimated age. With Baade's revised calculations, the distance, and thus the time required for the expansion, doubled from what Hubble had assumed. In the next decade, Fred Hoyle would use the relative abundances of the elements to increase the age of the universe to 10 billion.

Another astronomer at Mount Wilson during the war was Carl Keenan Seyfert (1911–60). He found that the center, or nucleus, of some galaxies were unusually bright. In a paper published in 1943 (while in Cleveland teaching navigation to the troops), he showed that this brightness was not the result of stars but of highly ionized atoms. The astronomical community quickly dubbed galaxies with the characteristic *active galactic nuclei* (AGNs) to be Seyfert galaxies. The identification of Seyfert galaxies led to the discovery of other objects with AGNs, including radio galaxies and eventually quasars. Decades later, it would be determined that AGNs are produced by massive black holes.

After six years of grinding and polishing and within a few wavelengths of being done, the precious disk of the 200-inch (5-m) telescope was crated and leaned against a wall of the optical lab at Caltech for the duration of the war. The lab was converted to making periscope mirrors and lenses for aerial cameras. Work resumed after the war; it was dedicated on June 3, 1948, and officially named after George Hale. Hubble oversaw the taking of the first photograph in September. The "Big Eye" could see twice as far as the 100 inch (2.5 m)—out to one billion light-years.

Hubble and Milton Humason used the new instrument to add hundreds of nebulae to the original clusters that defined the velocity–distance relation. By 1950–51, the greatest velocity Humanson found was about one-fifth the speed of light in the constellation Hydra. He hoped to find nebulae receding up to one-fourth the speed of light, but sky brightness swamped the spectra. Humason remarked, "Well, there is apparently no horizon, at least as far as the 200-inch goes—it just continues—the number of stars continues to build up and the nebulae go on, they get fainter and fainter. . . ."

Synthesis of the Elements

As part of a British war committee on radar in 1944, Fred Hoyle (see photo opposite) went to Washington, D.C., to confer with his American colleagues. After the meeting in D.C., Hoyle went to Mount Wilson where Baade provided him with his latest information on supernovae. While waiting in Montreal, Canada, to catch a plane back to England, Hoyle met with men working on the British nuclear-bomb project. "Combining what I learned with my speculations about implosion being relevant to the plutonium bomb, I wondered if a supernova might not be like a nuclear weapon, with implosion as the cause of instability, leading eventually to an enormously violent outburst," Hoyle wrote in his auto-biography (see Further Reading).

After the war Hoyle returned to Cambridge, England, and began calculations to test his idea of the origin of the elements. Synthesis of the elements required tremendous temperatures. This requirement led George Gamow to suggest that the elements were formed in the explosion that created the universe. Hoyle discovered that "heavier nuclei would come apart to yield mostly neutrons, protons, and helium nuclei." Hoyle realized that the latter "would be energy-absorbing rather than energy-yielding, inevitably causing the core of a highly evolved star to implode. . . . Implosion would lead to the release of more than sufficient energy from gravitation to explain the eventual outburst of a supernova." It would also provide the high temperatures required to make the heavier elements.

To finalize his theory, Hoyle used knowledge of nuclear masses to plot the relative abundances of elements on Earth. The simplest elements were 10 times more abundant than the ones with masses higher than silicon. Except for the elements with masses between 45 and 60, the abundances then dropped to 100 times less up to the metals copper and zinc. After that abundances dropped by a million times compared to silicon.

For elements between atomic masses of 45 and 60, the most abundant was iron. These results "implied that the physical conditions I used in the calculations, which were consistent with statistical equilibrium, really occurred in nature," Hoyle wrote. The temperatures required to create these elements were staggering: 2 to 5 billion degrees, more than 100 times the temperatures of main sequence stars. If such temperatures occurred in supernovae, then all temperatures in between could also. Hoyle published his ideas in 1946 in "The Synthesis of the Elements from Hydrogen." The paper was not widely read.

Hoyle's paper "Note on the Origin of Cosmic Rays" received more attention. Baade and Zwicky had suggested that supernovae might be the source of cosmic rays but with the rays appearing as part of the main outburst. Hoyle suggested that the cosmic rays emerged from the rotation of a neutron star and that therefore heavy elements would be found in cosmic rays. This prediction was confirmed in 1947.

George Gamow also spent the war years exploring the origin of the elements. He speculated that elements were forged when the universe exploded in the big bang. Gamow, his former student Ralph A. Alpher (1921–) and Robert C. Herman (1914–97) were the first to systematically develop the physical and observable aspects of the big bang theory. With Hans Bethe, Gamow and Alpher published "The Origin of Chemical Elements" in 1948. This paper predicted the existence of radiation, later called *cosmic background radiation*, left over from the initial big bang explosion. This prediction was confirmed in 1965. Gamow, Alpher, and Herman first suggested that all the elements were created in the big bang, but it was soon shown that another mechanism (nuclear synthesis in stars suggested by Hoyle) was required for elements heavier than beryllium.

British astronomer Sir Fred Hoyle showed how elements were synthesized in stars and supernovae. He also coined the term big bang *for the theory of the universe that competed with his own steady-state theory. He is shown here on the Caltech campus in 1967 when he was 51.* (Clemson University and Donald D. Clayton)

Not everyone accepted the big bang explanation for the expansion of the universe. In 1948, Hoyle began work with Herman Bondi (1919–2005) and Thomas Gold (1920–2004) on a competing model called the steady-state theory (see figure below). Instead of the universe having a beginning, the steady-state theory proposed that matter was continuously

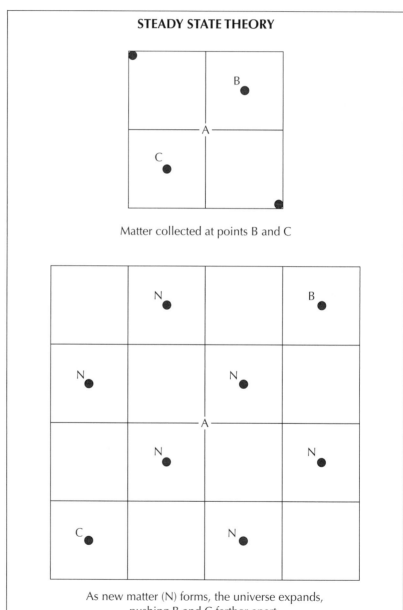

STEADY STATE THEORY

Matter collected at points B and C

As new matter (N) forms, the universe expands, pushing B and C farther apart.

© Infobase Publishing

In the steady-state theory, new matter forms and causes the universe to expand, but the density of matter remains constant.

created, and this creation caused the universe to expand. Hoyle provided a mathematical theory of the model that was consistent with the general theory of relativity.

In 1950, Hoyle popularized astronomy via a series of lectures for a BBC radio program. The show had a prime listening spot on Saturdays and hit the top of the annual national ratings. In the last lecture, Hoyle coined the famous term *big bang* for the theory that competed with his own steady-state theory. Ironically, his work on the synthesis of the elements would provide some of the data that supported the big bang theory.

Astronomical Peace Dividend

The president of the Carnegie Institute, Vannevar Bush (1890–1974), met with President Roosevelt in June 1940 and convinced him to create a new organization called the National Defense Research Committee (NDRC). The NDRC brought together government, military, business, and scientific leaders to coordinate military research. This committee and the Office of Science and Research Development, of which Bush was made director, proved that technology was key to winning the war. It also institutionalized the relationship between government and the scientific community and generated a new respect for scientists.

New technology that had been developed for the war was quickly adapted for civilian use after the war. The development of the first computers had an enormous impact on astronomy. Prior to the war, "computers" in the astronomical community were generally women who analyzed and cataloged spectra and performed other repetitive mathematical tasks. After the war, mechanical and digital computers became available and were employed by a new generation of astronomers who had utilized and improved them during the war. Czech-born British astronomer Zdenek Kopal (1914–93) was typical of many young astronomers who worked at military labs during the war. He led a team at MIT's Center of Analysis using an analog device called a differential analyzer, invented by Vannevar Bush, to compute firing tables. Though time consuming, Kopal preferred the precision given by the new mechanical meth-

ods to the approximate ones used by older astronomers such as Henry Russell. Kopal predicted that the new methods "should render the solutions of many problems, shirked so far because of their laboriousness, both practicable [sic] and easy."

The army also used Bush differential analyzers to solve equations, but their mechanical nature caused frequent breakdowns. To obtain a faster and more reliable computer, they hired the Moore School of Electrical Engineering at the University of Pennsylvania to create an electronic numerical integrator and computer (ENIAC). Considered the world's first computer, ENIAC weighed 30 tons and used 200 kilowatts of electricity. It was officially accepted in 1946 and began operation at Aberdeen Proving Ground in 1947. A skilled person with a desk calculator could compute a 60-second trajectory in about 20 hours. The Bush differential analyzers took about 15 minutes. The ENIAC took 30 seconds. ENIAC was retired in 1955, surpassed by newer and faster computers.

In addition to computers, the photoelectric photometer with the RCA 931 photomultiplier was added to telescopes to measure the intensity of stars accurately. Military photographic processes, including new chemicals for film development and fixing, were adapted for use in observations. The perfection of electronic computers greatly facilitated the solution of mathematical problems involved in lens design, and many new lenses became available for astronomical use.

Scientist of the Decade: Wernher Magnus Maximilian Freiherr von Braun (1912–1977)

Wernher von Braun led the German rocket team who developed the deadly V-2 long-range missile during World War II. After the war, he became a champion of the U.S. space program, the first director of the NASA Marshall Spaceflight Center, and the genius behind the Saturn rocket that first took men to the Moon.

He was born the second of three sons in what is now Wirsitz (or Wyrzysk, see map on page 95), Poland, on March 23, 1912. His father was Baron Magnus von Braun, minister for Agriculture. His mother was Baroness Emmy von Quistorp. She taught him to play piano and gave him a telescope at age 13. After they moved to Berlin in 1920, he read Herman Oberth's book *The Rocket into Planetary Space* and decided to become a rocket engineer. He later joined the Society for Space Travel and built rockets with Oberth.

Von Braun finished his degree in mechanical engineering in 1932 while working on rockets for the German army under Walter Dornberger. He earned his pilot's license in 1933. He received his doctorate in 1934 from the University of Berlin and in December had his first successful launch. In 1939, von Braun moved to Peenemünde as lead designer on the A4. One of von Braun's greatest achievements came on October 3, 1942, when the A4 became the first rocket to reach space.

Adolf Hitler bestowed the honorific title of "Professor" on von Braun after he and Dornberger briefed him on the "wonder weapon" (V-2) in 1943. He was later given honorary officer ranks by SS General Heinrich Himmler (1900–45) in an attempt to get von Braun to work for him instead of Dornberger. Von Braun refused to wear the uniforms. After Himmler gained control over rocket production, von Braun's rebuff of Himmler's offers almost cost him his life.

On March 5, 1944, von Braun attended a party with his brother Magnus. Their conversation about

Wernher von Braun (shown in this undated photo) built the first rocket to reach space, though it was used as a weapon in World War II. He immigrated to the United States and built the Saturn V that took the first men to the Moon. (U.S. Army Aviation and Missile Command)

rockets for space travel with Helmut Gröttrup and Klaus Riedel (1907–44) was monitored by a gestapo agent. At 2:00 A.M. on March 15, von Braun was taken by gestapo agents. Magnus, Reidel, and Gröttrup were also arrested.

Dornberger was told that the men could lose their lives for planning sabotage—using the rockets for space instead of as weapons. Dornberger knew that Himmler was behind the arrests and drove to Berlin to see him. He met with the top gestapo general who told

Dornberger that he had a thick dossier on him as well. Dornberger bravely asked to be arrested right then, but the general backed down because of publicity about Dornberger's "mystery weapon." After spending his birthday in prison, von Braun and the others were released "provisionally" and lived under constant threat.

Despite protests from Dornberger and von Braun, Himmler pressed the unfinished rocket into production. Von Braun called the first use of the A4/V-2 his darkest hour. "We wanted our rockets to travel to the Moon and Mars, not to hit our own planet." Critics contend that von Braun put his ambition ahead of the suffering of thousands and should have quit work on the V-2. Considering that all the V-2s together delivered a third less explosives than one bomber attack, Sir Winston Churchill (1874–1965) said, "It was fortunate that the Germans devoted many of their efforts to rockets and not to bombers. . . ."

In late 1944, von Braun faced a history-changing decision at Peenemünde. "I had ten orders on my desk. Five promised death by firing squad if we moved, and five said I'd be shot if we didn't move." His team voted unanimously to move toward U.S. territory, a decision that would allow the Americans to beat the Russians to the Moon in the 1960s. While moving in March, von Braun's driver plunged off the road. Von Braun's injuries were not properly treated. Near total collapse, he finally sought a hospital in April. He underwent surgery without anesthetic and, at risk of having his arm amputated, was not moved even when the town was attacked. Dornberger sent an ambulance to rescue him. Von Braun's torso and arm were in a cast when he surrendered on May 2, 1945.

Von Braun was sent to Fort Bliss, Texas, where he lived in an isolated military barracks with his fellow "prisoners of peace." He worked on rocket designs, and he wrote his first book, *Das Marsprojekt* [The Mars Project] (see Further Reading), published first in Germany in 1952.

Von Braun returned to Germany to marry his 18-year-old second cousin, Maria von Quistorp, in a Lutheran church on March 1, 1947. They had two daughters and a son. The family lived in Huntsville, Alabama, from 1950 to 1970.

Von Braun was as well known for his advocacy of space as for his rockets. He published about 500 essays. The special 1952 issue of *Collier's* magazine included his space-station plans, and in 1954, *Collier's* published his eight-part series on Mars. He was one of the authors of *Conquest of the Moon* in 1953. His starring role in Disney's "Man in Space" in 1955, followed by Moon and Mars shows, raised him to celebrity status.

In 1958, von Braun's Jupiter C rocket carried the first U.S. satellite into orbit. "That success made me particularly happy," he said, "because it allowed me to show my deep gratitude to the American people. . . ." He had become a citizen in 1955.

When his rocket team joined NASA in 1960, he became director of Marshall Space Flight Center and manager of the complex Saturn program. The first Saturn launched in 1961 and the first Saturn V in 1967. When the *Apollo 11* crew returned from the Moon in 1969, von Braun said, "That was an hour of exuberant joy, and I admit, also of tremendous relief!"

After Apollo, von Braun moved to Washington, D.C., as NASA associate administrator. He retired in 1972 and worked for Fairchild Industries in Maryland on satellite programs. His last Saturn rockets boosted *Skylab* in 1973 and the Apollo-Soyuz mission in 1975.

In 1974, von Braun was elected the first president of the National Space Institute (later National Space Society), which was formed to promote space. He told the members, "It is man's nature that he always wants to explore—to move on, to develop, and to advance." Cancer put an end to his personal quest. He died on June 16, 1977.

Radio and Solar System Discoveries

In 1942, John (James) Stanley Hey (1909–2000) made an important discovery while analyzing the jamming of British radar by the Germans. Hey discovered that the Sun emits radiation at radio wavelengths as well as optical wavelengths. Other discoveries in the radio spectrum would soon follow.

Hendrik Christoffel van de Hulst (1918–2000) was a Dutch graduate student under Jan Oort during the war. As part of his thesis in 1943, van de Hulst (see Bruce Medalists, page 249) proposed that a photon of 21 centimeter (8.2 inches) wavelength excites hydrogen so that the proton and electron spin line up, called a spin-flip transition. With so much hydrogen in the galaxy, he expected the resulting spectral line to be observable. Following the war, Oort led the Dutch group that built a 25-meter radio telescope, but it did not find the line. It was first detected by Edward Mills Purcell (1912–97) and Harold Irving Ewen (1922–   ) on March 25, 1951, at Harvard, ironically, while van de Hurst was doing a sabbatical there. Oort and van de Hurst then used the technique Ewen had invented to map hydrogen gas in the galaxy to reveal its spiral structure.

Scientist and science-fiction author Sir Arthur C. Clarke (1917–   ) proposed another practical way to use radio in space. In 1945, he proposed that three satellites placed in geosynchronous orbit (22,240 miles/35,790 km) above the equator would be able to bounce radio waves around the globe. While this had to wait for rockets that could lift the satellites to space, other applications of radio were made soon after the war.

In 1948, Martin Ryle (1918–84), who worked on radar for the British during the war, discovered the brightest radio source in the sky other than the Sun, supernova remnant Cassiopeia A. Beginning in the last few years of this decade and resulting in a Nobel Prize in physics and a Bruce Medal (see page 249) in 1974, Ryle developed the aperture-synthesis technique of radio astronomy. By adjusting the positions of a group of small telescopes, he found that he could achieve a precision equal to that obtained by one giant telescope covering the same area. Using this method, radio astronomers eventually exceeded the resolution capabilities of their optical colleagues. In 1949, British astronomer John Bolton (1922–93) (see Bruce Medalists, page 249) and his team in Australia achieved sufficient angular resolution to identify the first-known radio sources with optical objects. Their interferometer identified Taurus A as the Crab Nebula, Virgo A as the galaxy M87, and Centaurus A as the galaxy NGC 5128.

Working at Jodrell Bank Observatory in Australia in 1950, Robert Hanbury Brown (1916–2002) and his student Cyril Hazard (1928–   ) discovered radio emissions from the Andromeda galaxy. The emissions were very similar to those in the Milky Way. In the next decade, these radio astronomers discovered much more distant radio sources and began to probe the mystery of what produces this energy.

Despite the war, a few astronomers continued their studies of the solar system. One question addressed was why comet tails point away from the Sun. Light pressure alone cannot explain it. In 1943, Cuno Hoffmeister (1892–1968) in Germany, and after the war, Ludwig Biermann (1907–86) (see Bruce Medalists, page 249), proposed that the Sun emits a steady stream of particles, now called the solar wind, in addition to sunlight. Tail particles move at about the same velocity as the comet. So solar wind particles could easily "push" the tail outward. The ions in the tail respond to the charged particles in the wind, explaining why some comets have split tails.

The proposal of solar wind fed into theories of the formation of the solar system. In 1944 Carl von Weizsacker proposed that protoplanets formed as a result of condensations in the rotating nebular disk. Their moons formed from smaller subcondensations. Much of the material in the nebula was "blown away" by the solar wind, explaining why the inner planets lacked the abundant gases of the outer planets.

In 1944, Gerard Kuiper passed sunlight reflected off Titan through a spectrometer and found methane. He concluded correctly that this meant that Titan has an atmosphere.

In 1950, Jan Oort proposed that comets originate in a cloud of material, now called the Oort cloud, about 100,000 times Earth's distance from the Sun. In the still generally accepted theory, he said, "Through the action of the stars fresh comets are continually being carried from this cloud into the vicinity of the sun." That same year, Fred Whipple (1906–2004) proposed the "dirty snowball" model that comets have a rocky core covered by ice. This model was confirmed when spacecraft flew by Halley's comet in 1986, earning Whipple a Bruce Medal (see page 249).

Further Reading

Books

Von Braun, Wernher. *The Mars Project.* Translated by Henry J. White. Urbana: University of Illinois Press, 1953. Originally published as *Das Marsprojekt* (Germany: Weltraumfahrt magazine, 1952). Wernher von Braun's classic work about the technical challenges of space travel to Mars.

———, F. L. Whipple, and W. Ley. Edited by C. Ryan. *The Conquest of the Moon.* New York: Viking Press, 1953. This is one of von Braun's most popular and influential books.

Stuhlinger, Ernst, and Frederick I. Ordway III. *Wernher von Braun: A Biographical Memoir.* Malabar: Krieger, 1994. A detailed history of the man and the early German and the American rocket programs.

Web Sites

R. M. Clarke. "Radio Telescopes." The Salopian Web. Available online. URL: http://www.r-clarke.org.uk/astrolinks_radio.htm. Accessed on

March 6, 2006. The site lists the world's major radio telescopes with links to their home pages.

Tracy Dungan. "The A–4/V–2 Resource Site." V2rocket.com. Available online. URL: http://www.v2rocket.com/start/start.html. Accessed on March 6, 2006. This site covers the development, operations, timeline of attacks, and diagrams of the V–2 rocket with links to related international Web sites.

Eugene M. Emme. "NASA Aeronautics and Astronautics Chronology, 1945–1949." NASA. Available online. URL: http://www.hq.nasa.gov/office/pao/History/Timeline/1945-49.html. Accessed on August 30, 2006. This site provides a list and brief description of key events in space development.

Eamon Harper. "Getting a Bang out of Gamow." *George Washington Magazine*, Spring 2000. Available online. URL: http://www.gwu.edu/~physics/gwmageh.htm. Accessed on March 6, 2006. This site includes a brief biography of George Gamow, who played a major role in promoting the big bang theory.

Lt. Col. William L. Howard. "History of the U.S. Army's Technical Intelligence in European Theater of Operations." Available online. URL: http://www.wlhoward.com/id574.htm. Accessed on March 6, 2006. The article describes intelligence gathered on the German weapons programs during WWII, including the V–2 rocket.

Lt. Col. William L. Howard. "Operation Overcast/Paperclip, how the German scientists were brought to the United States." NewsMine. Available online. URL: http://www.newsmine.org/archive/coldwar-imperialism/operation-paperclip.txt. Posted October 7, 1998. Accessed on August 29, 2006. An article about how the German rocket scientists were brought to the United States after World War II.

Marshall Space Flight Center. "Wernher von Braun." MSFC History Office. Available online. URL: http://history.msfc.nasa.gov/vonbraun/index.html. Accessed on March 6, 2006. This site contains interviews, a biography, notes about the V–2 rocket, a photo gallery, and a complete bibliography of von Braun's publications.

6

1951–1960:
The Dawn of the Space Age

Astronomers and space scientists of the 1950s continued to reap the benefits of technology that was developed during World War II. As science-fiction readers imagined exploring space through books such as Ray Bradbury's (1920–) *Martian Chronicles* (1950) and Robert Heinlein's (1907–88) *Starship Troopers* (1959), the Soviet Union and the United States developed intercontinental ballistic missiles (ICBMs) and used them to send the first satellites and animals into space. The beginning of the space age is the major topic of this chapter, from the development of the rockets to the first scientific investigations of the effects of space on materials and biology.

The competition between the two superpowers turned into a space race with the launch of the first artificial satellite, *Sputnik 1* (see photo on page 124), on October 4, 1957. The development of the Russian R-7 by Sergei Korolev, scientist of the decade (see sidebar and photo on page 132), and the American Jupiter rocket (see figure on page 126) and Vanguard are discussed. Also covered is the American response to the Soviet successes including the first U.S. satellite, *Explorer 1* (see photo on page 125) that discovered the Van Allen radiation belts (see figure on page 127), and the creation of NASA. Progress in rocket technology was rapid during this decade. The launches of the first satellites were followed by the first flights of mammals and the first satellites to reach the Moon. The chapter describes how the first astronauts (see photo on page 130) and cosmonauts were selected and trained, as well as the challenges, such as reentry heating, that were addressed and overcome by the Russian Vostok (see figure on page 129) and the American Mercury spacecraft (see sidebar on page 134).

As color television became the new way to communicate across America, radio astronomy provided a new tool to probe the universe. The first maps of the Milky Way's spiral arms (see figure on page 113) were made in this decade. The major issue raised by radio astronomy that is discussed in the chapter is the origin, identification, and interpretation of astronomical radio sources. Martin Ryle, who mapped and catalogued more sources than anyone else, proposed that stars were the source of the radio radiation, but his rival British astronomer Fred Hoyle argued that the sources came from outside the Milky Way. Hoyle was proven correct but at the expense of damage to his steady-state theory that failed to explain why the sources were not evenly distributed with distance.

Another major topic discussed in this chapter is Hoyle's discovery of how all the elements in nature are forged and recycled by stars in a cosmological framework (see figure on page 117). He found that interstellar gas (mostly hydrogen and helium) collect into stars that use slow and rapid (supernova) processes of nuclear fusion to generate elements in abundance consistent with observations. Thus, astrophysicists learned in this decade that stars provide not only the energy but also the basic elements necessary for life. Also described in the chapter is the work of Gerard Kuiper, who created a model that explained how these elements combined to form the solar system.

The Mystery of Radio Stars

Radio astronomy matured in this decade and offered a new way to map the galaxy and test theories of the origin of the universe. In 1951, Harold Ewen and Edward Purcell confirmed van de Hulst's predicted radio emissions from interstellar hydrogen at 8.3-inch (21.2-cm) wavelength. This detection marked the beginning of spectral-line radio astronomy that was used to reveal the Perseus, Orion, and Sagittarius spiral arms of the Milky Way (see figure opposite).

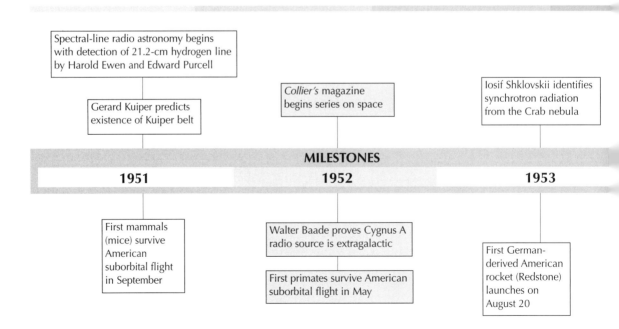

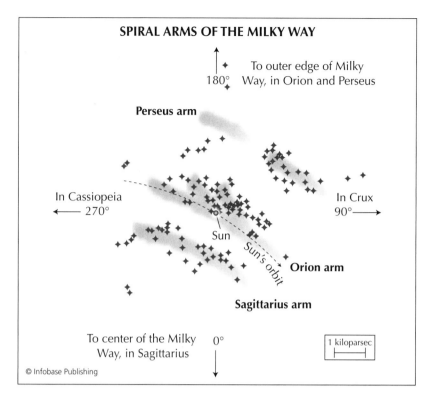

SPIRAL ARMS OF THE MILKY WAY

180° To outer edge of Milky Way, in Orion and Perseus

Perseus arm

In Cassiopeia ← 270°

In Crux 90° →

Sun

Sun's orbit

Orion arm

Sagittarius arm

To center of the Milky Way, in Sagittarius 0°

1 kiloparsec

© Infobase Publishing

Radio astronomy provided a new way to map the Milky Way and revealed the first detailed images of the three nearest spiral arms. The Sun is located on the inner edge of the Orion arm.

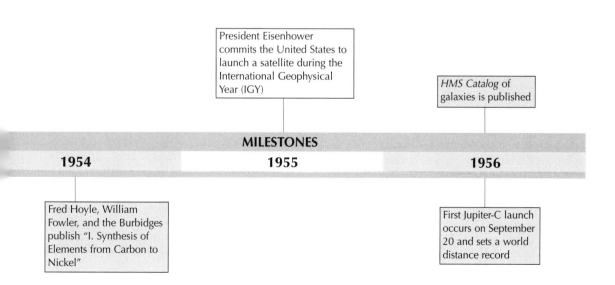

President Eisenhower commits the United States to launch a satellite during the International Geophysical Year (IGY)

HMS Catalog of galaxies is published

MILESTONES

| 1954 | 1955 | 1956 |

Fred Hoyle, William Fowler, and the Burbidges publish "I. Synthesis of Elements from Carbon to Nickel"

First Jupiter-C launch occurs on September 20 and sets a world distance record

While some radio astronomers mapped hydrogen clouds, others puzzled over energetic radio sources such as *Cygnus A* that did not correlate with visible objects. Knowing that the Sun was a proven radio source, Martin Ryle proposed that these sources were radio stars that were just not visible in the optical spectrum. By 1950, observations proved that these radio sources "twinkle" similar to optical stars. Unlike planets that have a disk, stars twinkle because they are point sources of light. This information supported Ryle's theory that the radio sources were stars.

In 1951, Thomas Gold and Fred Hoyle proposed (see Further Reading) that radio stars were objects outside of the Milky Way. They argued that the radio sources were not concentrated like stars in the Milky Way but were scattered around the sky. Ryle disagreed, beginning a long-standing rivalry with Hoyle. To settle the question, Francis Graham Smith (1923–   ) collected more accurate positions using an improved radio telescope at Cambridge, England. Walter Baade then pointed the new 200-inch (5-m) telescope at those positions. In 1952, Baade found that a source in Cassiopeia was an unusual nebula in the Milky Way and that Cygnus A had a redshift corresponding to a distance of about 500 million light-years, clearly outside the Milky Way.

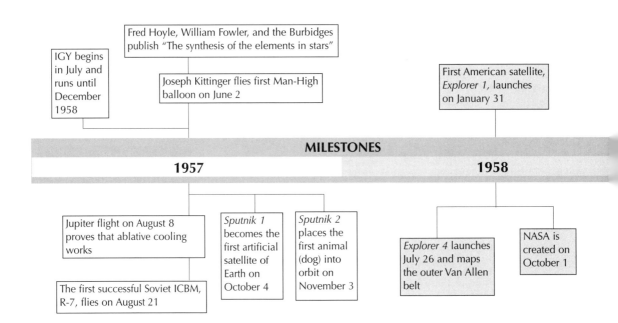

IGY begins in July and runs until December 1958

Fred Hoyle, William Fowler, and the Burbidges publish "The synthesis of the elements in stars"

Joseph Kittinger flies first Man-High balloon on June 2

First American satellite, *Explorer 1*, launches on January 31

MILESTONES

1957

1958

Jupiter flight on August 8 proves that ablative cooling works

The first successful Soviet ICBM, R-7, flies on August 21

Sputnik 1 becomes the first artificial satellite of Earth on October 4

Sputnik 2 places the first animal (dog) into orbit on November 3

Explorer 4 launches July 26 and maps the outer Van Allen belt

NASA is created on October 1

Two other intense sources were identified by Australians as the Crab Nebula supernova remnant and M87, a peculiar nebula in Virgo. Thus, the first four identified sources were so different that no general conclusion could be made about radio sources. Ryle combined the data from several telescopes by radio *interferometry* to identify 1,936 sources by 1955 (and later received a Nobel Prize in physics for his work). Baade again looked for optical counterparts. He proposed that Cygnus A and another source were the result of galaxies in collision. Baade and Lyman Spitzer, Jr., (1914–97) (see Bruce Medalists, page 249) had just published a paper on galactic collisions. This prompted 1961 Bruce Medalist Rudolph Minkowski to quip, "Baade and Spitzer invented the collision theory, and now Baade finds evidence for it in Cygnus A." Angry, Baade bet Minkowski a bottle of whiskey that he was right. A collision's hot gas would produce emission lines in the spectra, whereas stars produce mostly absorption lines. So Minkowski took spectra of the radio sources. He found emission lines. Baade won the bet, but his collision theory was incorrect.

Grote Reber had found in the late 1940s that astronomical radio power was weaker at higher frequencies, meaning that the source was not caused by heat. So a nonthermal process was sought to explain

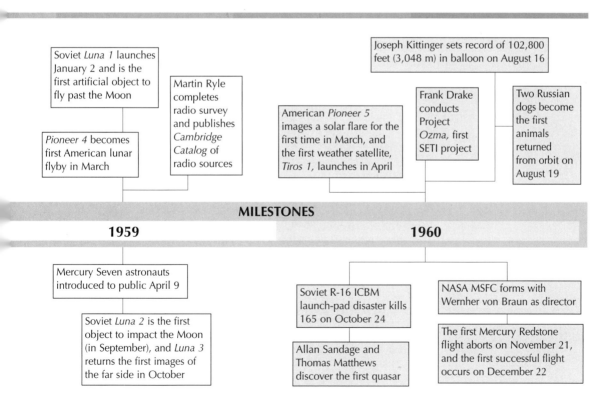

radio stars. The correct answer, synchrotron radiation, was proposed by Swedish physicist Hannes Alfvén (1908–95) and Norwegian Nicolai Herlofson (1916–2004) in 1950. Synchrotron radiation results from electrons moving at close to the speed of light in magnetic fields. In 1953, Russian Iosif Samuilovich Shklovskii (1916–85) confirmed that the Crab-nebula supernova remnant produced synchrotron radiation. In 1958, Geoffrey R. Burbidge (1925–   ) showed that synchrotron radiation from Cygnus A was not caused by a galactic collision. New measurements revealed that Cygnus A has the shape of a giant dumb-bell with the galaxy in the center. This shape could not be the result of a collision but of some sort of explosion. The mystery of the physical phenomena that could produce the enormous amount of synchrotron radiation of Cygnus A would not be solved until the discovery of *quasars* and black holes.

Ryle completed an extensive survey of radio sources by 1959. He was forced to admit that Hoyle had been right that most sources were outside the galaxy. However, Hoyle's suggestion to plot the number of sources versus distance dealt a severe blow to his steady-state theory. Ryle discovered that the number of intense sources increased with distance. This implied that galaxies produced more radio waves in the past, and it supported the big bang theory. In Hoyle's theory, the universe is the same at all times. Measurements by Australian observers disagreed with Ryle's, leading to heated debates between Ryle and Hoyle.

To test the theories, radio astronomers sought more accurate data and new radio sources. Several pivotal publications helped the search for optical counterparts and distance measurements. One was the *HMS Catalog*, named after its authors, Milton Humason, Nicholas U. Mayall (1906–93), and Allan Rex Sandage (1926–   ). Published in 1956, this catalog contained redshift and magnitude data for all known galaxies. The second was the first catalog of clusters of galaxies, called the *Abell Catalog* after its author, George O. Abell (1927–83). Published in 1958, this catalog was based on the Palomar Sky Survey (completed in 1954) that covered the entire Northern Hemisphere using the Schmidt telescope. In 1959, Ryle published the third *Cambridge Catalog* listing radio sources. In the next decade, astronomers used these catalogs to discover the most powerful objects in the universe, quasars. In 1960, Allan Sandage and Thomas A. Matthews matched an intense radio source, 3C–48, with an optical object. A few years later, this object was identified as a quasar.

The Elements of Life

Fred Hoyle believed that stars, and not some original big bang, created all the elements found in Nature (see figure opposite). During this decade, he would prove his case, but at the same time, he would provide evidence supporting the big bang theory.

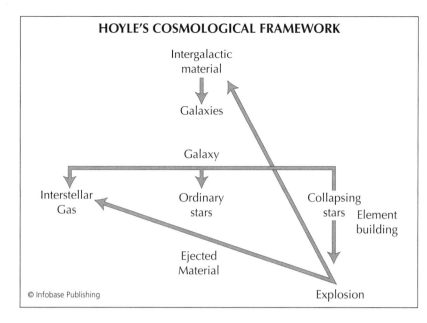

HOYLE'S COSMOLOGICAL FRAMEWORK

Intergalactic material

Galaxies

Galaxy

Interstellar Gas

Ordinary stars

Collapsing stars Element building

Ejected Material

Explosion

© Infobase Publishing

This diagram appeared in Fred Hoyle's 1954 paper on the synthesis of the elements. He argued that the elements between carbon and neon are the product of collapsing stars that eject these elements.

In 1953, Hoyle discovered the triple-alpha process, when one beryllium 8 joins with one helium atom to become carbon. He realized that this process required carbon and oxygen to have certain stable energy states to be able to accumulate in stars. Hoyle calculated these energy levels and William "Willy" A. Fowler (1911–95) and Geoffrey and Eleanor Margaret Burbidge (1919–   ) confirmed them experimentally. The results, "I. Synthesis of the Elements from Carbon to Nickel," were published in 1954 (see Further Reading).

In 1953, Martin Schwarzschild (1912–97) provided further proof that stars synthesize elements by showing that the ratio of hydrogen to iron varied among stars. Iron produced in a big bang would be distributed evenly. But Hoyle still needed a process for stars to make iron. He joined forces with Schwarzschild's Princeton group to build computer simulations of main-sequence stars as they used up the hydrogen in their cores. The results, published in 1955 (see Further Reading), detailed how stars evolve and expand into red giants as they age. Schwarzschild showed in 1958 that the youngest stars formed from the leftovers of older stars and therefore have the most metals. The metal ratio could be used to date clusters of stars. Schwarzschild received a Bruce Medal (see page 249) in 1965 partly for this work.

Canadian Alastair G. W. Cameron (1925–2005) showed in 1955 that neutrons are produced by a carbon 13 reaction with helium. Hoyle realized that a similar process would provide the neutrons necessary to build the higher elements in stars. He found that when growth to the next element required a slow process (taking millions of years), the original element would accumulate and be more abundant than the next one in the sequence. The Burbidges confirmed that Hoyle's estimated abundances matched what was found in stars. Hoyle also determined that the rarest elements form by what he called a rapid process taking only a few seconds during supernovae. Hoyle, Fowler, and the Burbidges published "The synthesis of the elements in stars" in 1957 (see Further Reading). This landmark paper explained that stars produce all the elements, and it correctly predicted the behavior of supernova 1987A observed 30 years later. All members of the team received Bruce Medals (see page 249) and other awards for their work in solving the basic question of the origin of the elements.

An understanding of the times that were required to produce elements provided another way to fix the ages of stars. Hoyle estimated that the oldest stars in the Milky Way were 12 billion years old. In 1959–60, Hoyle and Fowler calculated the primeval abundance ratios of thorium, uranium, and other elements using terrestrial rocks. They estimated that the galaxy was 10 to 15 billion years old.

By the end of the decade, George Gamow's suggestion that elements were made during a big bang was replaced with the overwhelming evidence that elements were made in stars. However, Hoyle found that stars did not produce enough helium to account for the amounts observed in galaxies. Galaxies were about 30 percent helium, and calculations suggested that stars would produce only about 2 percent. Hoyle's helium data would be used to support the big bang theory in the 1960s.

Origin of the Solar System

In 1950–51, Gerard Kuiper provided the first modern mathematical model for how planets form. Working backward, Kuiper used the current composition of the planets to determine that the mass of the original nebular disk was about six-tenths of the mass of the Sun. He spread this mass in a ring out to the orbit of Pluto and then worked out the dynamics of condensation, including gravitational and temperature effects. The resulting model was the first to predict the masses of the planets accurately. He showed mathematically that a large planet could not form in the asteroid belt because of Jupiter's gravity. He estimated that five to 10 small worlds formed there instead, and then two of these collided to produce the fragments in the belt. "It is assumed that Ceres and a few other asteroids are true planetary condensations," he told a meeting of the National Academy of Sciences (see Further Reading).

The effect of collisions on the final structure of the solar system was just beginning to be appreciated. Eugene Merle Shoemaker (1928–97) proved in 1960 that the crater near Flagstaff, Arizona, was caused by an asteroid impact. He then proposed that the Moon's craters formed in a similar way. This proposal was confirmed as satellites and people ventured outward to explore the solar system in the coming space age.

Kuiper calculated the temperature and the density of the nebula outside the orbit of Neptune and predicted that icy comets would condense in a region between 30 and 50 AU, now called the Kuiper belt. The Oort cloud is more distant than the Kuiper belt and accounts for the origin of long-period comets, whereas the Kuiper belt is the home of short-period comets that orbit the Sun in less than 200 years. The Kuiper belt was confirmed in 1992 when several objects were found at the predicted distance. Pluto is considered the largest member of the Kuiper belt, leading to its reclassification as a dwarf planet in 2006. Neptune's satellites, Triton and Nereid (discovered by Kuiper in 1949), and Saturn's satellite, Phoebe may be captured Kuiper belt objects.

Kuiper believed that "the process of formation of a planetary system is a special case of the almost universal process of binary-star formation." He speculated that if the solar nebula had been three times more or less dense, instead of planets, a companion star or a flurry of comets would have formed. Kuiper estimated that the probability of planets forming around a star is between one in a hundred and one in a thousand. He expected that with the number of stars in the galaxy, there should be at least a billion planetary systems. "One can only speculate on the possible forms of life which may have developed on these many unknown worlds," he said.

Percival Lowell's old idea of life arising as long as conditions allowed gained support in 1953 as a result of experiments by Harold C. Urey (1893–1981) and Stanley L. Miller (1930–). In a laboratory experiment, they successfully created complex amino acids, the building blocks of proteins, by sparking the proposed ingredients of Earth's primordial atmosphere: water vapor, methane, ammonia, and hydrogen.

In 1959, physicists Philip Morrison (1915–2005) and Giuseppe Cocconi (1914–) calculated that military radar transmissions could be detected from light-years away. They suggested that galactic civilizations might be discovered by eavesdropping on their radio traffic. Astronomer Frank Drake (1930–) independently came up with the same idea and began the first search for extraterrestrial intelligence (SETI) using a radio telescope at Green Bank, West Virginia. In 1960, his Project Ozma looked for patterns in radio waves from Tau Ceti and Epsilon Eridani. None were found. (See Further Reading.)

Radio also contributed to studies of the Sun. In 1946, Martin Ryle developed the technique of aperture synthesis interferometry and showed that the Sun's radio emissions come from Sun spots. Building on this work, Horace Babcock (1912–2003) and his father Harold Babcock (1882–1968) were the first to measure distribution of magnetic fields over the surface of the Sun. Horace Babcock proposed the idea of *adaptive optics* to correct for atmospheric turbulence and get a sharper image. His idea was implemented after fast computers were available to deform the mirrors. Between 1952 and 1955, the Babcocks first established the presence of a small polar field in the Sun and reported a reversal of the polarity in 1957. In 1960, Robert B. Leighton (1919–97) of Caltech devised a camera to map the complicated patterns of the Sun's magnetic field. He found that the Sun's surface vibrates up and down at a variety of frequencies. By studying these oscillations, astronomers plotted the temperature and chemical composition of the Sun's interior. This new field is called *helioseismology*. Both Babcocks received Bruce Medals (see page 249) partly for this work.

Preparation for Manned Space Programs

A group of visionary scientists helped pave the way for the space age. In 1951, Wernher von Braun, Harvard astronomer Fred L. Whipple, and geophysicist Joe Kaplan (1902–91) persuaded Cornelius Ryan (1920–74) of *Collier's* magazine to do a series of stories on space. *Man Will Conquer Space Soon* was published between March 1952 and April 1954. The series included von Braun's plan for a space station and Willy Ley's description of living on it. Whipple covered astronomy from space, and Kaplan described studies of Earth's atmosphere. Three books based on this series were illustrated by "the father of space art" Chesley Bonestell (1888–1986) and two others. More articles followed, plus three Disney space films that aired on television between 1955 and 1957. The scientists became celebrities and successfully built public and political support for investing in the technologies that would transform the arms race with the Soviets into a space race.

Other scientists prepared for the exploration of space by founding the field of space biology in 1946. They oversaw rocket flights that carried fruit flies, fungus spores, and small mammals to high altitudes. In 1951, air force Lt. Col. James P. Henry (1914–96), M.D., worked with NACA scientists to send aloft anesthetized monkeys and mice. On September 20, 1951, 11 mice became the first living creatures to survive space-flight. That same year, the Soviets sent two dogs, Dezik and Tsygan, to 62 miles (100 km) in a capsule later used for the dog Laika on *Sputnik 2*. In May 1952, two American monkeys named Pat and Mike became the first primates to survive space and return safely. Both nations' scientists concluded that weightlessness and high acceleration would not stop humans from exploring space.

Balloon flights offered longer exposure to low pressure and weightlessness than rockets. Animal experiments in 1950 and 1951 led to Project Man-High in 1955. Using a 2-million-cubic-foot (56,634-cubic-m), 172.6-foot (52.6-m) diameter balloon and a cramped aluminum-alloy capsule/gondola, Joseph Kittinger (1928–   ) made the first Man-High ascent on June 2, 1957. He remained aloft for almost seven hours and climbed to 96,000 feet (29,261 m). Two other Man-High flights followed in 1957 and in 1958.

To study humans' ability to escape from a space capsule, on November 16, 1959, Kittinger piloted *Excelsior* to 76,000 feet (23,165 m) and jumped. His small parachute opened too early and caught him around the neck.

Unconscious, he spiraled out of control at 120 revolutions per minute while freefalling toward the New Mexico desert. His life was spared when his emergency parachute opened automatically at 10,000 feet (3,048 m). Despite this close call, Kittinger went on to set an altitude record of 102,800 feet (31,333 m) in *Excelsior III*, an open gondola with a license plate made from a cereal box by his five-year-old son. He floated at peak altitude for about 12 minutes on August 16, 1960, with only a thick pressure suit to protect him against temperatures of –90°F (–70°C). He then fell for 13 seconds and reached speeds of more than 600 miles (900 km) per hour before opening his parachute. He proved that it was possible to exit a spacecraft at high altitude and survive a return to Earth.

New Improved Rockets

While scientists proved that human spaceflight was survivable, ballistic missiles were being developed that would make it possible. Von Braun's team in Huntsville completed design of a guided missile called Redstone in 1952. It launched from a movable platform like the V-2 but had several new features. Welded aluminum tanks served as the outer skin so that the external steel shell was not needed. The nose cone separated from the rest of the rocket. The new technology of transistors replaced glass electron tubes in the guidance system. These transistors were fast enough to work problems such as propellant sloshing and shear forces. Transistors also had lower power usage than mechanical systems, and their use improved simulators and telemetry. The V-2 telemeter at Peenemünde had six channels and was the size of a bookcase. The Redstone telemeters had hundreds of channels and fit in small boxes.

Kurt Debus (1908–83), who had been in charge of V-2 static testing at Peenemünde, became director of the Missile Firing Laboratory (later Kennedy Space Center) in Florida. Rocco Petrone (1926–2006) joined Debus in September 1952. They developed launch pads and blockhouses in time for the first Redstone launch on August 20, 1953. Through 1958, 36 Redstones were launched.

In the Soviet Union, development of the R-3 stalled and was terminated in 1952. Valentin Glushko was unable to increase engine performance enough to lift the Soviet Union's five-ton atomic bomb. While Sergei Korolev was preoccupied with cruise missiles, von Braun worked on the Jupiter long-range ballistic missile. Its Rocketdyne engine burned kerosene and oxygen, and instead of the double-walled combustion chamber and nozzle, it had a system of parallel-shaped tubes—called a spaghetti-type engine. Control was achieved by swiveling the whole engine instead of using vanes.

Reentry heating was the biggest challenge facing ballistic missiles. There were two options: heat sink and ablation. Heat sink uses a massive layer of a good conductor such as copper in the outer wall of the warhead/capsule. It heats up but does not reach unacceptable temperatures.

The ablation method has the warhead made of a thin, low-conductivity material with a melting temperature that is slightly below what it will encounter. The hot air that melts the ablative material blows it away before the heat soaks through the wall. The air force chose the heat-sink method for its *Atlas* rocket, and von Braun's army group chose the abla-tion method for the Jupiter-C (composite) in 1952.

That same year, Korolev designed the Soviet Union's first intercon-tinental ballistic missile (ICBM), the R-7. Glushko overcame severe vibration problems with the engines by having four chambers share one turbopump. The R-7 provided more than twice the thrust of the American Atlas. It had four RD-107 Glushko engines, each with four thrust chambers around the circumference of the vehicle and one four-chamber RD-108 Glushko core engine at the center. These engines were much more efficient than the old V-2 engines and weighed about a third as much. The four RD-107s burned for 107 seconds and dropped off. Then the RD-108 would fire for a total of 320 seconds. This allowed the vehicle to reach any city in the United States.

The first American Jupiter-C (minus its nose cone) was launched September 20, 1956, with two upper stages of solid-propellant rockets developed by JPL. It reached 682 miles (1,090 km) and a distance of 3,400 miles (5,440 km), a world record at that time. The second rocket, a first test of the nose cone and the ablation system, was lost in the ocean. On August 8, 1957, the nose cone of the third rocket was recovered after a trip of 1,200 miles (1,920 km). The ablation method had worked, solv-ing the reentry heating problem. President Eisenhower showed the nose cone in a press conference and erroneously gave credit to the air force instead of the army.

The first Soviet R-7 was launched on May 15, 1957, and exploded in flight. The next four also failed, three because of a problem with a nitrogen valve. The August 21, 1957; flight went the entire range. This was more than 15 months before the American Atlas achieved a similar range. The Atlas was more sophisticated though, using advanced materials and miniaturized electronics. It had two booster engines and a sustainer engine that provided about 200 metric tons of thrust. It was much lighter and had a stainless steel skin so thin that it needed pres-surization to keep from collapsing. In contrast, it was possible to walk on the R-7's hull. The R-7 weighed 23 tons and the Atlas only 7.7, includ-ing the warhead.

The R-7's liquid propellants boiled off quickly, so it could not be launched on short notice. The American Atlas used storable propel-lants and required about 15 minutes to load the liquid oxygen before launch. Korolev avoided storable propellants because they were toxic and expensive. The head of another Soviet design group that competed with Korolev's bureau for funds, Mikhail Kuzmich Yangel (1911–71), embraced the use of storable propellants. Korolev worked on automating prelaunch operations for the R-9, but the military in both countries chose storable propellant rockets for their ICBMs. Yangel's R-12 was the rocket of the Cuban missile crisis in 1962.

Secretary of Defense Charles E. Wilson (1890–1961) had the air force develop Thor, a missile almost identical to the Redstone. In November 1956, two months after the first successful Jupiter-C flight, Wilson ordered Army general John Bruce Medaris (1902–90) to stop work on long-range ballistic missiles at Redstone.

Satellites for Politics and Science

In 1950, geophysicist Dr. Lloyd V. Berkner (1905–67) proposed an international study of the Earth's environment to the International Council of Scientific Unions. This led to the creation of the International Geophysical Year (IGY). The IGY was not a calendar year but the period from July 1957 to December 1958 when the Sun was at the peak of its 11-year cycle. In 1954, the IGY committee urged the participating nations to launch small satellites.

In May 1954, Sergei Korolev proposed to Minister of Armaments Dmitri Ustinov that they launch a satellite using his R-7 rocket. No action was taken until President Eisenhower announced on July 29, 1955, that the United States intended to launch a satellite during the IGY. The Soviets soon issued a similar statement, though the project was not officially authorized until January 30, 1956. Once approved, Korolev arranged for Mikhail Klavdiyevich Tikhonoravov (1900–74) and his satellite science team to become part of his organization. The program was given priority after the chief theoretician of the Soviet missile program, Minister Mstislav Vsevolodovich Keldysh (1911–78), made a case for beating the Americans to the Soviet Academy of Sciences in September 1956.

In September 1955, the American Department of Defense chose the navy's Vanguard over the army's Jupiter for the satellite launch vehicle. (The Atlas was not yet operational.) Though the Jupiter was ahead in development, the Navy Research Lab proposal by Milton W. Rosen (1915–) was more politically acceptable because it utilized a research organization rather than a weapons developer. The army satellite program was cancelled, but Wernher von Braun and Dr. William H. Pickering (1910–2004), head of JPL, set aside some rockets in "long-term storage" tests in case the government changed its mind.

The American Vanguard program was soon mired in delays while Korolev's R-7 had its first successful flight in August 1957. The rocket was ready, but unfortunately, the satellite was not (it would become *Sputnik 3*). Korolev had his team create a simple satellite in a month. Called *Sputnik* for "fellow traveler," the highly-polished 23-inch (58-cm) aluminum sphere had four antennas and weighed 184 pounds (83.6 kg) (see photo on page 124). On October 4, 1957, *Sputnik 1* became the world's first artificial satellite. Everybody with a radio receiver heard its beep-beep

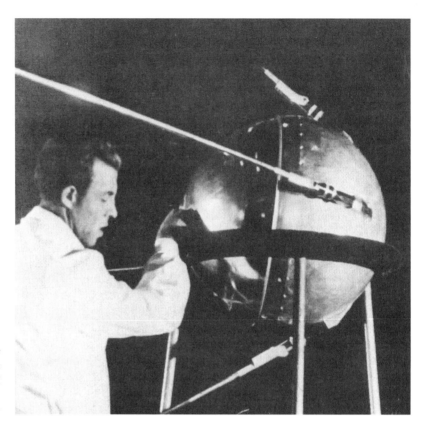

On October 4, 1957, the "space race" began when the Soviet Union put the first artificial satellite into orbit, Sputnik 1. (NASA)

every 96 minutes. The sphere was filled with nitrogen, so it offered the first chance to check for meteoroid detection, though no penetrations were reported. The transmitters operated for three weeks until the batteries failed.

The *New York Times* announced "SOVIET FIRES EARTH SATELLITE INTO SPACE" in half-inch capital letters across the front page. The flight was such a success that the Soviet leader Nikita Khrushchev (1894–1971) asked Korolev to launch something else in time for the anniversary of the revolution—in just one month!

So on November 3, 1957, *Sputnik 2* was launched with a capsule of 1,120 pounds (504 kg) and a female dog Laika ("Barker") onboard. A television camera sent photos of Laika at 10 frames/second. With no way to recover her, the Soviets planned automatic euthanasia, but Laika died from heat exposure after a few days because insulation tore off during launch. The capsule stayed up for 162 days and was eventually recovered.

With Vanguard still not done, Khrushchev needled the Americans during a speech on November 6 at the 40th anniversary of the Revolution. "It appears that the name Vanguard reflected the confidence of the Americans that their satellite would be the first in the world. But . . . it was the Soviet satellites which proved to be ahead, to be in the vanguard."

In response, President Eisenhower revived the army satellite project. Von Braun's Jupiter-C rocket was taken out of storage. Pickering got the Sergeant upper stages out of storage too, and JPL prepared the satellite payload and tracking system. Dr. James Van Allen (1914–2006) provided a Geiger counter to measure cosmic rays.

On December 6, 1957, the media was invited to witness the first launch of Vanguard. The booster stage ignited and erupted into one big fireball. The *London Daily Herald* headline read, "OH, WHAT A FLOPNIK!"

The Jupiter-C was mated with its three upper stages and called Juno 1. It was much smaller than the Soviet R-7 (see figure on page 126). It was transported to Cape Canaveral in Florida and launched on January 31, 1958. The satellite was six inches (15 cm) in diameter and about four feet (1.2 m) long. President Eisenhower named it *Explorer 1* (see photo at right). Its altitude was 223 miles (357 km) at perigee and 1,580 miles (2,528 km) apogee with a period of 113.2 minutes. Von Braun, Pickering, and Van Allen monitored it from the Pentagon in Washington, D.C. Von

Explorer 1 *was the first U.S. satellite, launched on a Jupiter-C rocket in January 1958.* (NASA)

Braun told reporters, "We have firmly established our foothold in space. We will never give it up again." *Explorer 1* was a mere 10.83 pounds (4.0 kg) and yet made a major scientific discovery—the high-intensity radiation belts around the Earth that were subsequently named Van Allen belts (see figure on page 127). The rocket stayed in orbit 12.3 years.

The second Vanguard attempt exploded on February 5, 1958. *Explorer 2* was launched March 5, but it crashed in the ocean. *Explorer 3* on March 26 was successful. *Vanguard 1* finally launched on March 17, 1958, with a satellite weighing 3.25 pounds (1.5 kg). Precision tracking of the satellite determined that the Earth was pear shaped.

On April 27, 1958, a failed Sputnik attempt was kept so secret that not even the search crews knew what they were looking for. *Sputnik 3* launched successfully on May 15, 1958. Its instruments could have mapped the outer Van Allen belt, but the tape recorder failed. Instead, *Explorer 4* on July 26 and *Vanguard 2* in February 1959 provided

COMPARISON OF FIRST SATELLITE LAUNCHERS

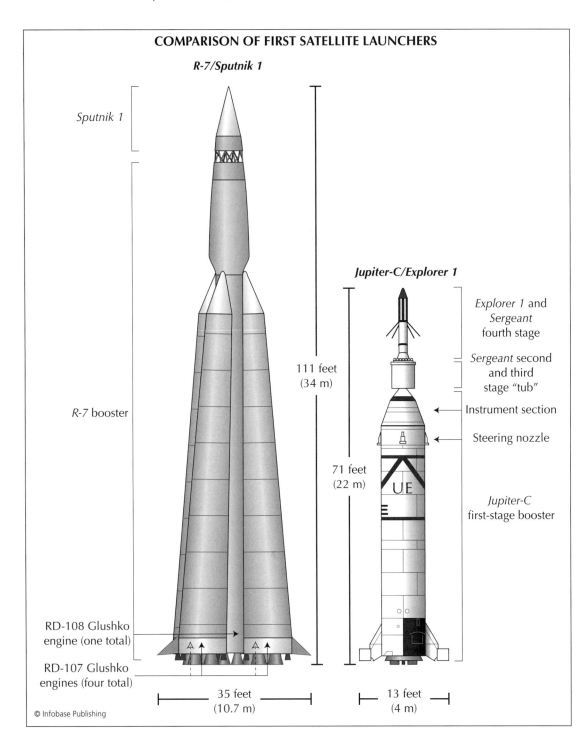

R-7/Sputnik 1

Sputnik 1

R-7 booster

RD-108 Glushko engine (one total)

RD-107 Glushko engines (four total)

111 feet (34 m)

35 feet (10.7 m)

Jupiter-C/Explorer 1

Explorer 1 and Sergeant fourth stage

Sergeant second and third stage "tub"

Instrument section

Steering nozzle

Jupiter-C first-stage booster

71 feet (22 m)

UE

13 feet (4 m)

© Infobase Publishing

that data. However, the mammoth 1.3 ton *Sputnik 3* removed any doubt that the Russians had the capability to send an ICBM to the United States.

In response to *Sputnik*, Eisenhower proposed the formation of a civilian space agency. Senate Majority Leader Lyndon Baines Johnson (1908–73) pushed the legislation (see Further Reading), and the National Aeronautics and Space Administration (NASA) was created, effective October 1, 1958. NASA absorbed 8,000 NACA employees plus three research centers: Langley, Ames, and Lewis (later Glenn). In December, the army's JPL was also transferred to NASA. Eisenhower appointed T. Keith Glennan (1905–95) NASA administrator, and Hugh L. Dryden (1898–1965), former director of NACA, became deputy.

Emphasizing the "missile gap" with the Soviets, John F. Kennedy (1917–63) was elected President in 1960. Vice President Johnson took charge of the space race that he would one day have to end.

(Opposite page) The Russian R-7 rocket designed by Sergei Korolev that took Sputnik 1 *into space contained four RD–107 engines around the outside and one RD-108 in the core. The Jupiter-C designed for the Americans by Wernher von Braun that took* Explorer 1 *into space had one A-7 engine and a second stage containing 11 modified Sergeant rockets, a third stage with three, and a fourth stage with one. The R-7 had 10 times the thrust of the Jupiter-C.*

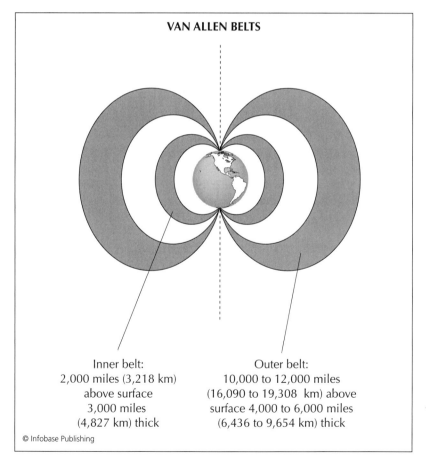

VAN ALLEN BELTS

Inner belt:
2,000 miles (3,218 km) above surface
3,000 miles (4,827 km) thick

Outer belt:
10,000 to 12,000 miles (16,090 to 19,308 km) above surface 4,000 to 6,000 miles (6,436 to 9,654 km) thick

© Infobase Publishing

The inner Van Allen radiation belt was discovered by America's first satellite, Explorer 1, *in 1958. The outer belts were mapped by* Explorer 4 *and* Vanguard 2 *in 1959.*

Flying to the Moon

After the successful Sputniks, Korolev proposed using a three-stage R-7 to send a probe to the Moon. The Americans had similar plans. On August 17, 1958, the United States attempted the first lunar launch. The Thor booster exploded. Three other attempts also failed. The Soviets reached the Moon first with *Luna 1*, launched on January 2, 1959. It passed within 3,700 miles (5,995 km) of the surface, and became the first artificial object to go into orbit around the Sun. It released a cloud of sodium gas when it was 70,625 miles (113,000 km) from Earth, allowing astronomers to track it. The onboard magnetometer showed that the Moon has no magnetic field, and the Geiger counter indicated that the solar wind fills interplanetary space.

The first American success was *Pioneer 4*, which launched on March 3, 1959. It passed within 37,000 miles (60,000 km) of the Moon and provided tracking and radiation information. Later that year, the director of NASA Ames, Harry J. Goett (1910–2000), chaired a committee that set a manned lunar mission as NASA's next goal. But when Eisenhower saw the cost estimates in 1960, he said that he was "not about to hock my jewels," in reference to Queen Isabella of Spain's financing of Columbus. Still, NASA adopted the lunar goal and received support from Congress, especially from Johnson who chaired the Senate committee that oversaw NASA.

With a lunar goal, it made sense to transfer Project Vanguard and its lunar programs from the navy to NASA. This was done in 1960 with the creation of the Goddard Spaceflight Center in Maryland. NASA needed a big booster to reach the Moon. Von Braun's team had started work on a big rocket called *Saturn* in 1958. The military did not need it, so Congress transferred the army's 4,500-member rocket team to NASA, creating the George C. Marshall Space Flight Center (MSFC) with von Braun as director.

The Soviets continued their lunar "firsts" with *Luna 2*. Launched September 12, 1959, it sent back the first clear images of the lunar surface and then impacted on it. *Luna 3* launched three weeks later, on the second anniversary of *Sputnik 1*. This impressive satellite returned the first photos of the Moon's far side. It demonstrated solar cell power, photoelectric cells to orient the spacecraft with respect to the Sun, gas-jet stabilization, and onboard film processing.

There were seven straight U.S. Moon-shot failures through 1960. NASA administrator Glennan said, "we are not going to attempt to compete with the Russians on a shot-for-shot basis in attempts to achieve space spectaculars." Still, the success of *Pioneer 5*, launched on March 1, 1960, was welcome. It gathered the first solar flare data and established a communications record distance of 22.5 million miles (36.2 million km). Then NASA launched *Tiros 1* in April 1960, leading to a series of weather satellites that changed weather forecasting throughout the world. In

August 1960, NASA successfully tested the bouncing of radio beams off a satellite, a concept suggested by Arthur C. Clarke in 1945 and one that would lead to a global communications network that would be used by the world to watch the first Moon landing.

Project Mercury

NASA's first assignment was Project *Mercury*, with the goal of putting a man into orbit. The rockets were the responsibility of von Braun's team at MSFC. The Space Task Group (STG) under Robert R. Gilruth (1913–2000) at Langley was in charge of everything else.

Based on work by chief engineer Maxime A. Faget (1921–2004), STG recommended a conical Mercury capsule with ablative material on the blunt end. It would parachute into the ocean. In February 1959, McDonnell Aircraft Company was contracted to build it. The Soviets chose a spherical shape for the *Vostok* capsule (see figure below) because it did not require sophisticated attitude control.

President Eisenhower directed NASA to choose pilots from the military. The men would be called astronauts and had to be under 5 feet 11 inches (180 cm) tall, between the ages of 25 and 40, and have at least 1,500 hours of flying time. An initial list of 508 pilots were screened and narrowed down to 31 candidates who underwent extensive scrutiny. Seven were chosen. On April 9, 1959, Glennan introduced the men to

The Mercury and Vostok capsules are shown to scale. NASA chose a conical shape that required attitude control and an escape tower to pull it free during an abort. The Soviets chose a spherical shape for entry simplicity and an ejection seat in case of an abort.

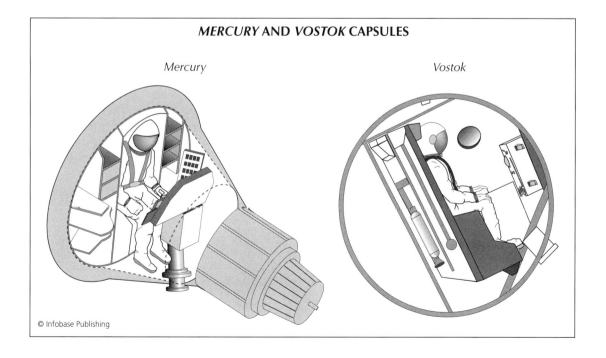

MERCURY AND VOSTOK CAPSULES

Mercury

Vostok

© Infobase Publishing

The Mercury 7 *astronauts were introduced to the public in April 1959. Shown here with a model of the Mercury rocket are from the left, front row, Virgil "Gus" Grissom, Scott Carpenter, Donald "Deke" Slayton, and Gordon Cooper; back row: Alan Shepard, Walter Schirra, and John Glenn.* (NASA–LaRC)

an adoring public. The "seven" were: John H. Glenn (1921–), Walter "Wally" M. Schirra (1923–), Alan B. Shepard (1923–98), M. Scott Carpenter (1925–), L. Gordon Cooper (1927–2004), Virgil "Gus" Grissom (1926–67), and Donald "Deke" Slayton (1924–93).

The astronauts were followed everywhere and inundated with media requests. To relieve the constant barrage, and also to provide the families with life insurance, NASA allowed the men to sell their personal stories to *Life* (later *Time–Life*) magazine for $500,000. The money was divided among their families regardless of who was chosen to fly first.

In contrast, the Soviet Union went about selecting its cosmonauts in secret. The Soviets also chose from among test pilots, but their health was more important than their experience. Consequently, the physicians selected 20 men who were about 10 years younger on average than their American counterparts. The men could not be taller than 5 feet 6 inches (167 cm) and not weigh more than 143 pounds (65 kg). The Americans were about three inches taller on average and more than 20 pounds heavier. The 20 were narrowed down to six: Yuri Alexeevich Gagarin, Gherman Stepanovich Titov (1935–2000), Andrian Grigoryevich Nikolayev (1929–2004), Pavel Ramanovich Popovich (1930–), Valery

Fedorovich Bykovsky (1934–), and Grigori Grigoyevich Nelyubov (1934–66). Nelyubov was fired for drinking in 1963 and committed suicide three years later. The final choice of who would fly first was made by Korolev just days before the historic flight in 1961.

Women were also evaluated as potential American astronauts. In 1960 Geraldyne M. "Jerrie" Cobb (1931–), who had twice as many flight hours as John Glenn, underwent the same tests as the men. Her results were so good that 25 other female pilots were also tested. The studies showed that the women were less prone to heart attacks and less vulnerable to loneliness, cold, heat, pain, and noise. They also weighed less, saving at least $1,000 per pound to orbit. However, the president restricted astronaut selection to military test pilots, and women were not eligible for those programs. Evaluation stopped in 1961.

The astronauts joined the STG at Langley and trained at facilities across the nation. They trained for high accelerations on centrifuges and for weightlessness via short, parabolic airplane hops. They experienced reduced pressures in decompression chambers, were conditioned for high heat loads by being toasted in giant ovens, and had vertigo induced via rotating rooms and devices. Based on their experiences, the astronauts recommended changes in the Mercury controls and procedures. Recognizing their limits was also important in determining what spacecraft systems to automate.

The Soviets automated all their systems. As a result, the cosmonauts had a passive role and only required physical training.

On August 21, 1959, the first Mercury test flight with two rhesus monkeys launched atop a cluster of solid-fueled rockets from Wallops Island, Virginia. In September, a capsule was placed atop an Atlas missile, a combination called Big Joe. The Atlas malfunctioned, but the Mercury capsule performed well and was recovered. On July 29, 1960, the Atlas ruptured and the rocket exploded. A "belly band" joining the Mercury to the Atlas solved this problem in 1961.

The first unmanned test of *Vostok* was May 15, 1960. It made 64 orbits but was lost in space. The next *Vostok* test exploded on July 28, 1960, killing two dogs. On August 19, 1960, dogs Belka and Strelka became the first animals to be recovered from orbit. They parachuted down after 18 orbits.

The media was invited to watch the first Mercury–Redstone launch on November 21, 1960. The rocket ignited, lifted up about four inches, and settled back down on the launch pad. A too-short cable had unplugged too soon after liftoff and signaled the engine to shut down. This triggered the escape sequence. Red-faced controllers watched as the escape tower shot skyward, followed by the parachute package, the main chute, and the reserve parachute. The press ridiculed NASA's performance.

The Soviets had planned to launch a human in December, but plans were delayed after an R-16 ICBM launch-pad disaster on October 24 killed 165 people. Then two dogs died during reentry on December 1.

Scientist of the Decade: Sergei Pavlovich Korolev (1907–1966)

Sergei Pavlovich Korolev was the secret mastermind of the Soviet space program who beat the Americans into space with the flights of *Sputnik* and Yuri Gagarin.

Korolev was born in Zhitomir, in the Ukraine, on January 12, 1907. His mother Maria Nikolaevna Moskalendo left his father Pavel Yakovlevich Korolev when Sergei was three. She went to Kiev, and Sergei lived with her parents in Nezhin. His mother married Grigory Mikhailovich Balanin when Sergei was nine. They moved to Odessa in 1917. Korolev's vocational school trained him to be a roofer.

Teenage Korolev charged down school corridors on his hands and swam over to watch military seaplane operations at the port. He helped the mechanics and joined them on flights. During a wing walk in 1923, he plunged about 300 feet (91 m) into the sea. But he kept flying and built his own glider when he was 17.

Inspired by Konstantin Tsiolkovsky, Korolev planned a career in aviation. He finished a two-year program in mechanical engineering at Kiev Polytechnical Institute. In 1925, he joined a course on glider construction. On one flight via catapult, he crashed into a water pipe and cracked his ribs. In July 1926, Korolev attended Moscow Higher Technical School to study aeronautical engineering.

Korolev soloed in a biplane in 1928. In 1929, he flew a glider that he built in a competition. He wrote to his mother, "I feel a colossal sense of satisfaction and want to shout something into the wind that kisses my face, and makes my red bird tremble, with its gusts."

Korolev, with a degree in aeromechanical engineering, in 1929 went to work at an aircraft factory. In 1930, he earned his pilot's license. He built a glider and entered it in a competition. A veteran pilot performed three loops with it, the

Sergei Pavolovich Korolev was the secret chief designer of the Soviet space program that put the first satellite, the first dog, and the first human into space. (RKK Energia)

first time anyone had done this outside America. Korolev was not present to enjoy the praise. He was hospitalized with typhoid fever, followed by surgery for a severe ear infection. He did not fully recover until March 1931.

Korolev worked on a heavy bomber for Andrei Tupolev (1888–1972), and after hours, he worked on rockets with Fridrikh Tsander at GIRD. When GDL and GIRD merged into the Reaction Propulsion Institute in 1933, Korolev became deputy chief engineer.

He married Xenia (Lyalya) Vincentini on August 6, 1931, in Moscow. On April 10, 1935, they named their daughter Natasha Rostov from *War and Peace.*

As part of the Stalin purges, Valentin Glushko was arrested. He accused Korolev of collaborating with the Germans. Korolev was thus taken in the middle of the night in June 1938. He was beaten (his jaw broken), forced to confess, and sent to Kolyma gulag in far eastern Siberia.

His teacher Tupolev put Korolev's name on a list of engineers who could help with the war effort, so he was released after five months of torturous labor. In subzero temperatures with six feet (2 m) of snow on the ground, travel to Moscow was impossible. So the future chief designer worked as a laborer to stay alive until spring. He nearly died of scurvy before finally reaching Moscow in September 1940. He was transferred from one prison to another, working on bombers and jet engines with his accuser, Glushko, until his release in 1944.

He was finally freed and flew to Germany as a new colonel in the Red Army in September 1945. In October, a bull-necked Korolev arrived at the British V-2 launch demonstration disguised as a captain. He was not allowed in and supposedly saw the launch from outside the gate.

Back in Russia, Korolev divorced Xenia in 1948 and married Nina Ivanona, greatly upsetting his daughter, who was a lung surgeon. Their relationship was reconciled after she had Andrei, Korolev's first grandson. She then had Sergei, who became an engineer, and Maria.

Korolev worked on R-1, R-2, and R-3 rocket programs in the late 1940s and early 1950s. In April 1950, Korolev was named head of his own design bureau. When Stalin died in March 1953, Korolev immediately impressed the Soviet Union's new leader, Nikita Khrushchev. Korolev obtained funding to build the R-7 rocket that became Russia's first ICBM and also was used for *Sputnik.*

After the successful launch of the world's first satellite, Korolev said, "I've been waiting all my life for this day!"

Yet, the man who put the first satellite and the first man into orbit was forbidden to share the glory. His name was kept secret. He could not greet adoring crowds with Yuri Gagarin and Khrushchev. He was not even allowed to wear the medals indicating that he was twice a "Hero of the Socialist Labor." The all-powerful Communist Party that Korolev had joined in 1952 despite being a former prisoner feared that American spies might assassinate their space mastermind.

Nevertheless Korolev delivered the first spacewalk, the first flight of a woman into space, the first photos of the Moon's far side, and the first impact on the Moon and on Venus. He launched the first Soviet spy satellites in 1962 and *Molniya* communications satellite in 1965. Under pressure to provide a steady stream of propaganda, Korolev often lost his temper. One engineer recalled him shouting at an army general that, "If you don't fix this in ten minutes I will make you a soldier." Many workers feared his wrath, but those who knew him best said that he was quick to forgive and also provided generous bonuses for good work.

Khrushchev was removed from power in 1964, and Korolev lost his top-seated connection. Still, the chief designer rushed ahead with the N-1 rocket and plans to land a man on the Moon. Those plans were cut short when Korolev died at age 59. During a routine polyp removal, a large tumor was discovered that would have killed him in a few months even if he had survived the operation. He died on January 14, 1966. The next day, the public heard his name for the first time. He was given a Soviet hero's funeral, and the cosmonauts whom he trained and put into space placed his remains in the Kremlin wall of heroes.

Mercury Facts

Launch Height: 93 feet (28 m), including 16-foot (5-m) escape tower.
Capsule Height: 9.5 feet (2.9 m)
Weight: 4,200 pounds (1,909 kg) including escape tower at launch, 2,400 pounds (1,090 kg) at splashdown
Width: 6 feet (1.8 m) across the base
Cost: $400 million. Built by McDonnell Aircraft for NASA.

Control: 18 thrusters using superheated steam
Equipment: 16-mm camera, periscope with magnification
Environment: 100 percent oxygen
Data: 100 items downloaded to Mission Control at 1,000 bits/second
Parachutes: 6-foot (1.8-m) diameter drogue opened at 21,000 feet (6.4 km), and main opened at 10,000 feet (3 km)

Two other dogs were recovered from an aborted flight on December 22. Final approval for a human launch attempt would wait until after two more dog flights in 1961.

NASA corrected its cable and signal problems and had a successful flight on December 19. The decade ended with hope that the United States could still be first to put a man into space.

Further Reading

Books and Periodicals

Harford, James. *Korolev.* New York: John Wiley & Sons, 1997. This book includes details about the life and work of the chief Russian rocket scientist.

Hoyle, Fred. *Home Is Where the Wind Blows: Chapters from a Cosmologist's Life.* Mill Valley, Calif.: University Science Books, 1994. This book is an autobiography of British astronomer Sir Fred Hoyle who discovered how stars forge all the elements and also proposed the steady-state theory as an alternative to the big bang theory to describe the universe.

———. "On Nuclear Reactions Occurring in Very Hot STARS. I. the Synthesis of Elements from Carbon to Nickel." *Astrophysical Journal Supplement* 1 (1954): 121. Available online. URL: http://articles.adsabs. harvard.edu//full/seri/ApJS./0001//0000123.000.html. Accessed on March 9, 2006. This is Hoyle's original paper describing the synthesis of the elements and includes the diagram shown on page 117.

———, and Martin Schwarzschild. "On the Evolution of Type II Stars." *Astrophysical Journal Supplement* 2 (June 1955): 1. Available online. URL: http://articles.adsabs.harvard.edu/cgi-bin/nph-iarticle_ query?1955ApJS....2....1H. Accessed on March 9, 2006. This scholarly paper describes the discovery and provides the detailed data that shows that main-sequence stars evolve into red giants.

————, W. A. Fowler, G. R. Burbidge, and E. M. Burbidge. "Origin of the Elements in Stars." *Science* 124 (October 1956): 611–614. This scholarly paper describes the slow and rapid processes involved in the production of the elements in stars.

Kuiper, Gerard P. "On the Origin of the Solar System." *Proceedings of the National Academy of Sciences* 37, no. 1 (January 15, 1951). Available online. URL: http://www.pnas.org/cgi/reprint/37/1/1. Accessed on March 9, 2006. This is the publication of the historical paper where Kuiper presents the first mathematical model to predict accurately the masses and placement of bodies in the solar system.

Launius, Roger. *NASA: A History of the U.S. Civil Space Program.* Malabar, Fla.: Krieger Publishing Co., 1994. Written by NASA chief historian, this book summarizes the first 35 years of the American space program and provides a copy of the bill that created NASA, President Kennedy's famous speech, and other readings from hard-to-find sources.

Swift, David W. *SETI Pioneers.* Tucson: University of Arizona Press, 1990. This book summarizes the first efforts in the search for extraterrestrial intelligence and provides a collection of personal interviews of the scientists involved, including Frank Drake and Iosef Shklovskii.

Web Sites

Mae Mills Link. "Space Medicine in Project Mercury." NASA Special Publication, 4003 in the NASA History Series, 1965. Available online. URL: http://history.nasa.gov/SP-4003/toc.htm. Accessed on January 8, 2007. Site descibes early animal and human tests.

Judy Rumerman. "Joseph Kittinger." U.S. Centennial of Flight Commission. Available online. URL: http://www.centennialofflight. gov/essay/Explorers_Record_Setters_and_Daredevils/Kittinger/EX31. htm. Posted in 2003. This site was created for the Centennial of Flight in 2003 and tells the story and includes photos of the Project Man High program that preceded the manned space program.

Margaret A. Weitekamp. "Lovelace's Women in Space Program." NASA History Division. Available online. URL: http://history.nasa.gov/flats. html. Accessd on August 29, 2006. The article includes the list of women who were evaluated for the astronaut program in the 1950s.

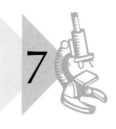

7

1961–1970:
Putting Humans on the Moon

This is the decade when people first left the Earth and walked on the Moon, perhaps the most historic achievement of the 20th century. The main focus of this chapter is the progress and culmination of the space race between the Soviet Union and the United States. The decade started with the Soviets in the lead, placing the first man, Yuri Gagarin (see photo on page 140), and the first woman Valentina Tereshkova (see photo on page 142) in orbit in 1961 and 1962. The American President

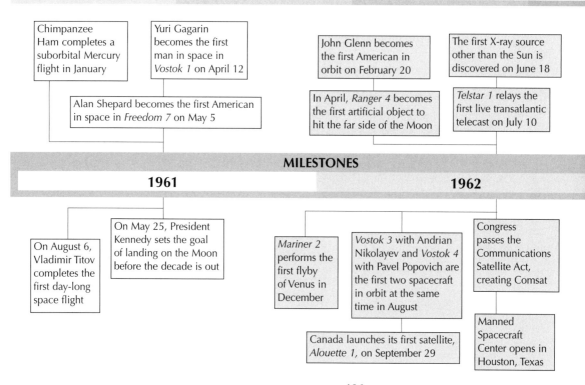

Chimpanzee Ham completes a suborbital Mercury flight in January

Yuri Gagarin becomes the first man in space in *Vostok 1* on April 12

John Glenn becomes the first American in orbit on February 20

The first X-ray source other than the Sun is discovered on June 18

Alan Shepard becomes the first American in space in *Freedom 7* on May 5

In April, *Ranger 4* becomes the first artificial object to hit the far side of the Moon

Telstar 1 relays the first live transatlantic telecast on July 10

MILESTONES

1961

1962

On August 6, Vladimir Titov completes the first day-long space flight

On May 25, President Kennedy sets the goal of landing on the Moon before the decade is out

Mariner 2 performs the first flyby of Venus in December

Vostok 3 with Andrian Nikolayev and *Vostok 4* with Pavel Popovich are the first two spacecraft in orbit at the same time in August

Congress passes the Communications Satellite Act, creating Comsat

Canada launches its first satellite, *Alouette 1,* on September 29

Manned Spacecraft Center opens in Houston, Texas

John F. Kennedy (1917–63) boldly responded by directing NASA to land a man on the Moon and return him before the decade was out. Implementing that goal was the primary responsibility of Robert Gilruth, the scientist of the decade (see sidebar and photo on page 162) who built and headed the Manned Spacecraft Center in Houston, Texas, that designed the vehicles, wrote the procedures, and trained the flight control teams and astronauts. The chapter details the options that NASA considered for reaching the Moon (see figure on page 143) and describes the technical challenges of perfecting rendezvous and space walking during the American Gemini program and the Russian *Vosktok* and *Voskhod* (see figure on page 147) programs.

Tragedy struck both sides in 1967 with the loss of the *Apollo 1* crew in a fire and the crash of *Soyuz 1* during reentry. The Soviet program could not recover and keep up with the massive resources applied by the Americans who triumphed in flying around the Moon in 1968. *Apollo 11* landed Neil Armstrong (1930– ; see photo on page 155) and Buzz Aldrin (1930–) on the Moon in July 1969, ending the space race. Having lost the race, the Soviets pretended not to have been in it, and focused on space stations that are a major topic of the next chapter.

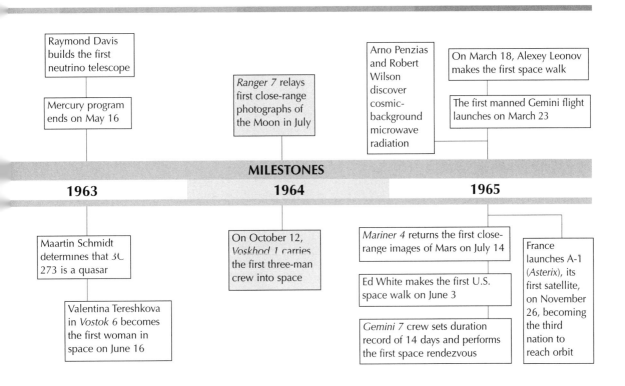

The chapter also covers new advances in astronomy that were achieved as the space race provided the means for making observations outside the Earth's atmosphere (see figure on page 157). Both superpowers explored the Moon with satellites and landers. The Soviets were first to reach Venus in 1962, and the Americans performed the first successful Mars flyby in 1965. That year also marked the discovery of cosmic background radiation by Arno Penzias (1933–   ) and Robert Wilson (1936–   ). This discovery provided strong support for the big bang theory. Improved radio observations led to the discovery of the first pulsar (see figure on page 160) by Jocelyn Bell (1943–   ) in 1967 and its identification as a spinning neutron star. These discoveries provided new insight into the conditions of the early universe, leading to the acceptance of the reality of black holes and dark matter that would become key topics of astronomy in the next decade.

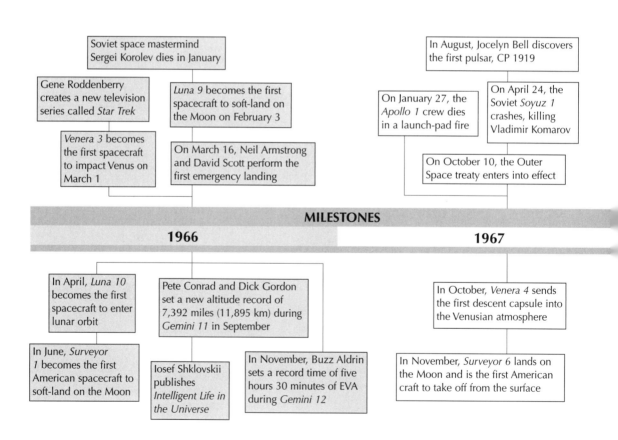

Soviet space mastermind Sergei Korolev dies in January

In August, Jocelyn Bell discovers the first pulsar, CP 1919

Gene Roddenberry creates a new television series called *Star Trek*

Luna 9 becomes the first spacecraft to soft-land on the Moon on February 3

On January 27, the *Apollo 1* crew dies in a launch-pad fire

On April 24, the Soviet *Soyuz 1* crashes, killing Vladimir Komarov

Venera 3 becomes the first spacecraft to impact Venus on March 1

On March 16, Neil Armstrong and David Scott perform the first emergency landing

On October 10, the Outer Space treaty enters into effect

MILESTONES

1966

1967

In April, *Luna 10* becomes the first spacecraft to enter lunar orbit

Pete Conrad and Dick Gordon set a new altitude record of 7,392 miles (11,895 km) during *Gemini 11* in September

In October, *Venera 4* sends the first descent capsule into the Venusian atmosphere

In June, *Surveyor 1* becomes the first American spacecraft to soft-land on the Moon

Iosef Shklovskii publishes *Intelligent Life in the Universe*

In November, Buzz Aldrin sets a record time of five hours 30 minutes of EVA during *Gemini 12*

In November, *Surveyor 6* lands on the Moon and is the first American craft to take off from the surface

The First People in Space

On April 12, 1961 *Vostok 1* roared into space. Blue-eyed 27-year-old Yuri Gagarin (see photo on page 140) shouted, *"Poyekali!"* [Let's go]. As his craft slowly rotated, the first man in space said, "I see the clouds. The landing site. . . . It's beautiful, what beauty!" He had no trouble eating and drinking, but he quit writing in his journal because his pencil floated away. An hour after launch, he reported that the flight was "smooth as silk."

The braking rocket fired on schedule, but the conical equipment section that was supposed to separate from the *Vostok* "ball" remained connected by cables. The vehicle rotated dangerously like a yo-yo. Gagarin recalled later, "It felt as if the g-load was 10 g." Amazingly, he did not pass out. The cables finally burned through and broke. At an altitude of about 22, 960 feet (7,000 m), the hatch blew off as planned. Gagarin was

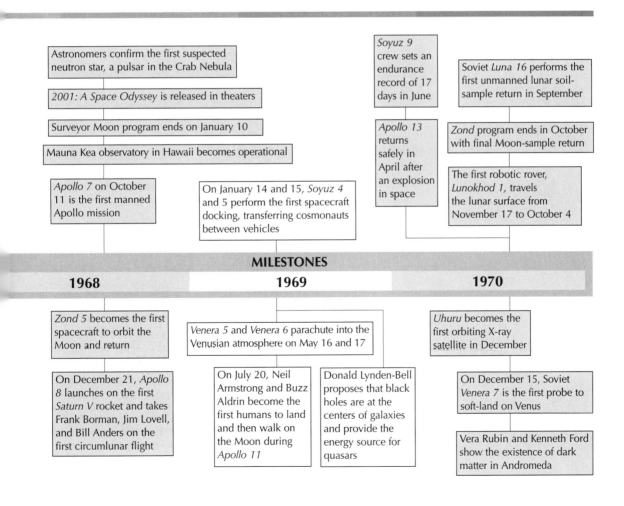

On April 12, 1961, Yuri Gagarin, shown here on his way to the launch pad, became the first man in space. (NASA)

ejected. "I flew out in the seat. Then a cannon fired, and the stabilizing chute deployed," he explained—but not to reporters. His method of landing was kept secret because to qualify for an international record, he needed to land in the same craft in which he took off.

Gagarin parachuted down in farmland near the Volga River. "I saw some women there tending a calf. . . . It feels as if everyone is looking at my pretty orange canopies." He landed in a field. "I went up on a knoll and saw a woman and a little girl coming toward me. . . . I saw the woman slow her pace, and the little girl broke away. . . . I then began to wave my arms and yell, 'I'm one of yours, a Soviet, don't be afraid, don't be scared, come here.'" He then went up to her and told her he had come from space.

Overnight, Soviet leader Khrushchev had a propaganda coup on his hands. The paper *Pravda* [Truth] declared, "GREAT EVENT IN THE HISTORY OF MANKIND." Official Washington had little reaction, but the NASA team was angry. Back in January, Jerome B. Wiesner (1915–94) of MIT had become Presidential Science Advisor. Wiesner was ardently against the manned space program. Robert Gilruth recalled, "Wiesner had these hearings to see whether or not Mercury should be cancelled." The new NASA Administrator, James E. Webb (1906–92), wanted permission to fly Alan Shepard, and

Wiesner would not give permission—not because the rocket might blow up but because, in his opinion, men could not survive weightlessness. Webb was assured by his technical team that men would have no problem in space.

If a chimpanzee named Ham could have testified, he would have told Congress that weightlessness was the least of their worries. He had flown on January 31, 1961. The Redstone shut down early causing the escape tower to yank his Mercury capsule away at a brutal 17 g's. To test Ham's performance in weightlessness, he was trained to press buttons in order. If he did it right, he got a food pellet. If not, he got a shock to the bottom of his foot. As the capsule soared up to 157 miles, the test equipment failed, and Ham got shocked no matter what he did. The capsule overshot the recovery zone by more than 100 miles and struck the water so hard that the cabin was punctured by the heat shield. Ham tossed on the waves for an hour and 45 minutes while water leaked in. Still, he survived the ordeal. The NASA team was confident a man would, too, especially after a March 24 flight proving that they had fixed the early shutdown problem. Only Wiesner stood in the way. Webb cultivated political allies and won approval for Shepard's flight in May.

Meanwhile the Soviets flew two more successful flights with dogs (Chernushka then Zvezdochka) in March. Sergei Korolev received quick approval for a manned flight. At 4 A.M. on April 12, a reporter called NASA public relations chief, John A. "Shorty" Powers (1922–80) on the phone. "The Russians just put a man into space!" the reporter yelled. "Do you have a comment?"

The words did not register in Shorty's mind, and his response would be quoted around the world as NASA's official reaction, "We're all asleep down here," he mumbled, hanging up the phone.

When Alan Shepard flew his suborbital flight on May 5, 1961, the American public was delighted. Shepard was an instant hero who had reached an altitude of 116.5 miles (187.5 km). But now Project Mercury was not enough. Gilruth recalled, "Kennedy came along and said, 'Look, I want to be first. How do we do something?'" Gilruth and others recommended a manned lunar flight.

On May 25, 1961, President Kennedy challenged the U.S. Congress: "[T]his nation should commit itself to achieving the goal, before this decade is out, of landing a man on the Moon and returning him safely to the earth." When reporters asked when the United States might surpass Russia in space, Kennedy remarked that "the news will be worse before it is better." It was.

The second Mercury suborbital flight on July 21, 1961, ended with Gus Grissom almost drowning and the capsule sinking in the ocean. (It was recovered in 1999.) The flight also paled in comparison to Vladimir Titov's (1947–   ) 17-orbit flight in *Vostok 2* on August 6.

Building to orbital flights, NASA switched from the Redstone to the Atlas booster and launched the first unmanned Mercury to orbit on

Russian Valentina Tereshkova was the first woman to reach space. (NASA)

September 13, 1961. Then on November 29, they sent up the chimp Enos for two orbits.

Finally, on February 20, 1962, NASA was ready to send the first American into orbit. Thousands of people parked along the Florida beaches to wait for the launch of John Glenn, creating trailer towns complete with mayors. Hundreds of millions more watched the launch on television. There was real life drama, too. Glenn was forced to take over manual control when one of the jets failed. Then Mission Control discovered that the capsule's heat shield was loose. Without it, the capsule would burn up and Glenn would die. The heat shield was underneath the retropack, three small rockets that slowed the capsule for entry. Mission Control ordered Glenn not to release the retropack after firing but instead to use it to help hold the heat shield in place. As *Friendship 7* plunged through the atmosphere, the retropack caught fire. Glenn reported, "That's a real fireball outside." The heat shield held, and Glenn splashed down after orbiting Earth three times. The nation celebrated with a parade in New York City.

Scott Carpenter's flight on May 24 splashed down 261 miles (420 km) off target because of reentry errors. In comparison, *Vostoks 3* and *4* with Andrian Nikolayev and Pavel Popovich launched a day apart and came within three miles (5 km) of each other in August 1962. On October 3, Walter Schirra completed six orbits and splashed down within five miles (7 km) of the recovery ship. On May 15–16, 1962, Gordon Cooper flew the last Mercury mission, completing 22 orbits and performing a manual reentry.

The Soviets claimed another "first" with *Vostoks 5* and *6* on June 14–19, 1962. Valery Bykovsky did 81 orbits, but he was hardly noticed as Valentina Tereshkova (1937–) (see photo at left) became the first woman in space. She launched in *Vostok 6* on June 16 and completed 48 orbits, passing within three miles (5 km) of Bykovsky's ship. These close passes were the result of precisely timed launches, but it led the Americans to assume that the Vostoks were equipped with rendezvous equipment.

A Rendezvous with the Moon

The American decision to go to the Moon seemed easy compared to the debate on how it should be accomplished. It took a year and a half and more than 1 million man–hours to reach a consensus. Four basic options were considered (see figure on page 143). The option initially favored by Gilruth's Space Task Group was called Direct Ascent. In this option, the first three stages of a five-stage rocket would propel the upper two stages and the capsule into a transfer orbit to the Moon. The fourth stage would slow the vehicle and land it on the Moon. The final stage would launch

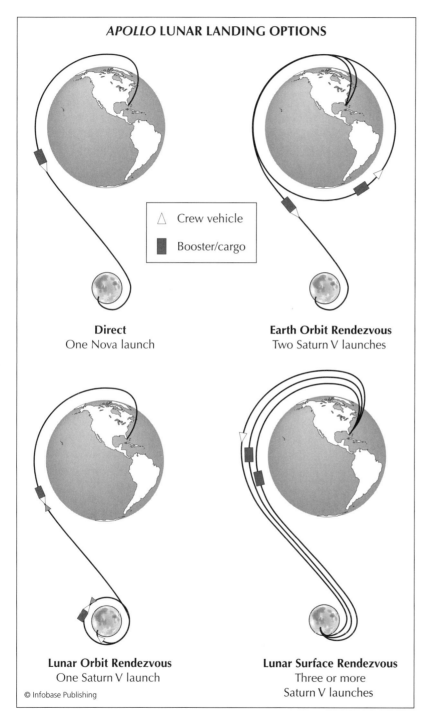

APOLLO LUNAR LANDING OPTIONS

△ Crew vehicle

■ Booster/cargo

Direct
One Nova launch

Earth Orbit Rendezvous
Two Saturn V launches

Lunar Orbit Rendezvous
One Saturn V launch

© Infobase Publishing

Lunar Surface Rendezvous
Three or more
Saturn V launches

The decision of which of four options to use to reach the Moon determined what hardware and facilities to build and what skills must be mastered by astronauts and ground crews. After a long and heated debate, Lunar Orbit Rendezvous was selected.

it from the Moon. This option required a launcher twice as powerful as a Saturn V. This superrocket, called a Nova, only existed on paper.

Wernher von Braun's team suggested the Earth Orbit Rendezvous (EOR) method. This called for launching two Saturn V's that would meet in orbit. One would carry the lunar spacecraft, the other the fuel for it to reach the Moon and return. Von Braun felt that learning to do rendezvous and fuel transfers was useful for future destinations such as Mars.

JPL proposed sending several unmanned Saturn rockets to the Moon, placing a return vehicle and its propellants and equipment near each other. After the return vehicle was assembled, fueled, and checked out automatically, the astronauts would be launched. This Lunar Surface Rendezvous option was rejected because robotic systems were not yet sophisticated enough.

The option finally chosen was Lunar Orbit Rendezvous (LOR). This method required one Saturn V launch. Three stages were used for ascent; then the third stage was restarted, and it sent the vehicle to the Moon. The vehicle had two parts: a Lunar Module (LM) to go to and from the surface and a Command and Service Module (CSM) that waited in lunar orbit and then returned to Earth. This technique had been proposed in 1916 by Russian Yuri Vasilievich Kondratyuk (pseudonym of Oleksandr Ignatyevich Shargei [1897–1942]), a contemporary of Valentin Tsiolkovsky (1857–1935). Von Braun and others proposed versions of the technique in the 1940s, but it did not get serious consideration until John Cornelius Houbolt (1919–) at Langely pushed for it. He discussed the benefits of this option when NASA Associate Administrator Dr. Robert C. Seamans, Jr., (1918–) visited Langley in September 1960. Seamans asked Houbolt to brief the NASA team in December. Houbolt told them that LOR would reduce the launch weight by a factor of 2.0 to 2.5. "His figures lie," lead engineer Max Faget accused. "He doesn't know what he's talking about."

Others were more polite than the fiery Faget, but they declared Houbolt had underestimated the weight that was needed for two sets of spacecraft systems. The main objection was the fear that astronauts would be left in an orbiting coffin 240,000 miles away. A failed rendezvous in Earth orbit would just bring the crew home early. Houbolt countered that the lunar and command modules could be backups for each other, a capability that proved itself during *Apollo 13*.

Seamans created one committee after another to study the options during 1961. They all favored EOR. In November, a frustrated Houbolt wrote to Seamans expressing his concern that LOR was being dismissed as too complex. His letter was passed along to a sympathetic Joseph F. Shea (1926–99) in the office of manned space flight.

Shea found that Faget had changed his mind after studying the problem of landing a big, tall rocket on the Moon. "It was a mess," Faget admitted. "Lunar-orbit rendezvous was the only sensible alternative." So in early 1962, LOR became the front-runner. Robert Gilruth was concerned about the computer-controlled maneuvers that were required on the far side of the Moon, out of contact with Earth. IBM assured him that their new computers were up to the task. To the surprise of many at MSFC, von Braun threw his support behind LOR as well. But Jerome Wiesner was firmly opposed, so NASA Administrator Webb lined up political support before making the decision for LOR final on November 7, 1962.

"It is my opinion to this day," NASA deputy administrator George Low (1926–84) wrote in 1982, "that had the Lunar Orbit Rendezvous Mode not been chosen, Apollo would not have succeeded." Little did anyone imagine that the young president would not live to see that success. Kennedy was killed in Dallas on November 22, 1963.

The Russians also had a difficult time reaching a decision and split scarce funding among competing designs. In 1961, Vladimir Chelomei (1914–84) was given a contract to develop a rocket and spacecraft for a circumlunar trip by a solo cosmonaut. Chelomei designed the UR-500K, a three-stage rocket that could lift 20 tons. The first stage used six RD-253 Glushko engines. His spacecraft was the *LK-1*. Chelomei was described as a genius who was difficult to work with but who had enormous political influence because he had hired Khrushchev's son Sergei (1935–) to head his guidance lab.

The funding of Chelomei's circumlunar mission deeply upset Sergei Korolev. He proposed instead to send two cosmonauts to the Moon using an N-1 booster with an L-3 spacecraft. In 1962, Korolev was given the go-ahead to develop the N-1 for the military. In mid-1963, the N-1 was redesignated for a manned lunar landing mission. In late 1964, Korolev adopted a lunar-orbit-rendezvous mode similar to Apollo. After a single N-1 launch, the L-3 spacecraft would go to the Moon, and one cosmonaut would stay in lunar orbit while the other went to the surface. To do it in one launch, the N-1 had to lift 92 tons. So Korolev added six more NK-33 Kuznetsov oxygen-kerosene engines for a total of 30 to the N-1 first stage. By 1965, the program was in deep trouble: the rocket engines were not powerful enough, and the spacecraft was too heavy.

Korolev pleaded unsuccessfully for more funds to create an N-2 with liquid-oxygen and liquid-hydrogen upper stages like the American Saturn. With no money, no large stands were built to test the clustered engines. This decision doomed the program.

As late as 1965, Chelomei was still proposing alternatives to Korolev's N-1/L-3 plan. Chelomei proposed the UR-700 with nine new Glushko RD-270 engines rather than the 30 NK-33 engines of the N-1. The upper stages of the UR-700 would have been the UR-500 that later became the reliable *Proton* booster. The RD-270 required ground test facilities that did not exist, and there was no time to lose in the race with the United States. Korolev's N-1 kept its assignment.

After Chelomei's UR-500 lifted the heaviest Soviet payload ever (26,840 pounds/12,200 kg) to orbit on July 16, 1965, it was chosen to be the launcher for the circumlunar flight. With no real progress on Chelomei's LK-1 spacecraft, Korolev proposed that the UR-500 lift a lightweight version of the Soyuz. This was approved on December 15, 1965, just a few weeks before Korolev's death in January 1966.

Voskhod and Gemini

Though work progressed on the new *Soyuz* capsule, it lagged behind *Gemini*'s development. Khrushchev demanded that Korolev stay ahead, resulting in the *Voskhod* [sunrise], a *Vostok* modified to carry three cosmonauts. Korolev chose Konstantin Petrovich Feoktistov (1926–) to engineer the capsule to fit three without adding much weight and then to fly the hazardous mission himself. With no room for spacesuits or escape systems, the capsule had to be leak-proof. Life support cleaned the air, but did not replace any losses. Feoktistov designed a soft-landing system using small retrorockets with help from Gai Severin (1926–).

After one unmanned test, *Kosmos 47*, *Voskhod* was launched on October 12, 1964, with Feoktistov, Vladimir Mikhailovich Komarov (1927–67), and the first doctor to go into space, Boris Borisovich Yegorov (1937–94) on board. They completed 16 orbits. Korolev's deputy, Vassily Mishin (1917–2001), said it was a "circus act" because the men were too cramped to do anything useful. However, the West concluded that the Soviets had a multiseat craft before they did. Khrushchev, who had ordered the flight, was deposed on October 14, the day after it returned.

The second and last *Voskhod* flight included a sensational first extravehicular activity (EVA) or space walk. Instead of having the hatch open and exposing both men to vacuum as *Gemini* did later, Severin designed a collapsible airlock. It was a three-foot (1 m) cylinder that was stove piped at an angle into the *Voskhod*'s side (see figure opposite). Made of a flexible fabric, it folded into the capsule shroud for launch and then opened like an accordion in space. It was tested on an unmanned *Zenit* spacecraft on March 15. The spacesuit was also designed by Severin and required the cosmonaut to breathe oxygen to purge himself of nitrogen (and prevent the bends) before putting it on. The flight test self-destructed by accident, but Severin decided to go ahead with the manned flight. So on March 18, 1965, on *Voskhod 2*, Alexei Leonov performed the first spacewalk or extravehicular activity (EVA) while Pavel Belyayev (1925–70) stayed inside. It lasted 20 minutes and occurred just days before Gus Grissom and John Young (1930–) flew the first *Gemini* on March 23. The spacewalk TV pictures were broadcast all over the world. What the world did not know was that Leonov almost did not make it back inside because his suit ballooned in size.

The *Voskhod 2* history-making crew also had a harrowing entry. Their automatic reentry system failed, and Belyayev had to use an untested manual method. They overshot the landing area by 1,200 miles (2,000 km). The ship fell into a dense forest and stuck between two fir

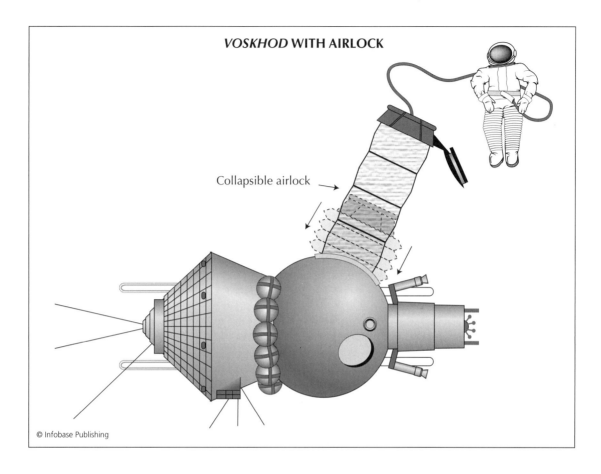

VOSKHOD WITH AIRLOCK

Collapsible airlock →

© Infobase Publishing

trees about 13 feet (4 m) above deep snow. The men spent the night in the bitter cold with wolves howling below. The next day, the cosmonauts skied out with their rescuers.

Voskhod 3 was to be an artificial gravity mission. It proved too difficult to develop, and the project was abandoned.

Unlike the *Voskhod*, the *Gemini* spacecraft was a major step forward in technology. It weighed about three times more than Mercury and had onboard propulsion, guidance, and rendezvous radar. Gemini's main purpose was to learn to do rendezvous. The rendezvous were done between Titan-launched Gemini capsules and Atlas-launched *Agena* spacecraft. Two unmanned flights were followed by 10 manned flights starting in 1965.

Flying with Jim McDivitt (1929–), Ed White (1930–67) topped Leonov's spacewalk by one minute on *Gemini 4* on June 3, 1965. Then Gordon Cooper and Pete Conrad (1930–99) showed on *Gemini 5* that eight days—the length of the Moon mission—of weightlessness were not a problem. On *Gemini 7*, Frank Borman (1928–) and Jim Lovell

The Soviet two-man Voskhod capsule had a collapsible airlock that allowed Alexei Leonov to perform the first spacewalk in 1965.

(1928–   ) set a longevity record that stood for five years: 14 days in space. *Gemini 6* flew after 7 because the *Agena* vehicle blew up six minutes after launch. Wally Schirra and Tom Stafford (1930–   ) performed the first space rendezvous, bringing the two ships within 6.5 feet (2 m) of the Borman–Lovell craft.

Gemini 8 was the first, and almost the last flight, of Neil Armstrong. He and David Scott (1932–   ) launched on March 16, 1966, and successfully docked to an *Agena* booster. Suddenly, they began to flip end over end. Armstrong separated from the booster, but the spinning increased because a Gemini thruster was stuck on. Armstrong remained calm and used the reentry rockets to stop the deadly spin. He and Scott splashed down safely into the ocean. Armstrong's cool handling of this emergency led to his being chosen for the first Moon landing.

Gemini 9 with Tom Stafford and Eugene Cernan (1934–   ) launched June 6, 1966. This flight had a grueling 127-minute spacewalk by Cernan. *Gemini 10* launched July 18, 1966, with John Young and Michael Collins (1930–   ). It docked with the *Agena 10* and used its engines to reach a record altitude of 474 miles (763 km). It also rendezvoused with *Agena 8*, and Collins retrieved a package during a 39-minute EVA. *Gemini 11* with Pete Conrad and Richard Gordon (1929–   ) launched September 12, 1966. They set a new record of 850 miles (1,369 km). During a spacewalk, Gordon connected the Gemini and *Agena* by a tether. Then the vehicles undocked and did a cartwheel motion, a test of artificial gravity. They also completed the first automatic computer-guided entry. *Gemini 12* was the last one. It launched with Jim Lovell and Edwin "Buzz" Aldrin on November 11, 1966. They docked with the *Agena*, and Aldrin did a five-hour-and-30-minute spacewalk, the longest yet.

The Gemini program achieved 2,000 man-hours in orbit and 12 hours of EVA. With the lessons learned, NASA felt ready to tackle the voyage to the Moon.

Probes and Satellites

NASA's budget went from $500 million in 1960 to a high of $5.2 billion in 1965, 5.3 percent of the federal budget. About 50 percent went to human spaceflight. The Saturn cost $9.3 billion to develop. From 1960 to 1966, NASA's workforce expanded to 36,000, and contractor employees grew from 36,500 to 376,700. Administrator Webb fit a lot of science and new technology under this huge Apollo umbrella. Thus radar tracking and communications stations served both manned and unmanned missions. The University of Hawaii's 24-inch (60-cm) telescope, designed to support the Moon landing, became the first major observatory on Mauna Kea in Hawaii in 1968. Webb's Sustaining University Program paid for graduate educations of more than 5,000 scientists and engineers. Apollo "support" missions included the *Ranger, Lunar Orbiter,* and *Surveyor* series.

A total of nine Rangers were launched between 1961 and 1965. All but the last three failed, though *Ranger 4* did become the first artificial object to impact the Moon's far side. *Ranger 7* relayed the first close-range lunar photos in July 1964. *Ranger 8* provided more coverage, and *Ranger 9* in March 1965 sent images shown live in the first television spectacular about the Moon.

The first Surveyor soft-landed on the Moon in June 1966. Also that summer, the first of five Lunar Orbiters was launched to take photos and test ground tracking systems. *Surveyor 2* crashed in September, but *Surveyor 3* landed in April 1967. The *Apollo 12* crew landed nearby in 1969 and retrieved a piece of it. *Surveyor 4* crashed, and *5* landed in the Sea of Tranquility. *Surveyor 6* landed and took off from the surface, the first American spacecraft to do that. The last Surveyor reached the Moon on January 10, 1968. It landed in the crater Tycho that was featured as the location of an alien obelisk in the popular 1968 movie, *2001: A Space Odyssey.*

The *Mariner* series focused on Venus and Mars. Built by JPL, the first success was in 1962 when *Mariner 2* reached Venus in December. It estimated temperatures, measured charged particles, and found no magnetic field. Launched on November 28, 1964, *Mariner 4* passed within 6,117 miles (9,844 km) of Mars on July 14, 1965. *Mariner 4* took the first close-up images of Mars and finally proved that Percival Lowell's canals did not exist. *Mariner 5* visited Venus in 1967. *Mariner 6* and *7* passed Mars in 1969 and laid the groundwork for later landings. They found craters and volcanoes and discovered seasonal polar caps made of carbon dioxide.

The first live transatlantic telecast was on July 10, 1962. It was broadcast by the American satellite, *Telstar 1*, developed by Bell Telephone Labs. Congress passed the Communications Satellite Act of 1962, creating Comsat to manage global satellite communications for the United States. The International Telecommunication Satellite Consortium (INTELSAT) was founded by 19 nations to deal with international issues. It oversaw the development of *INTELSAT 1* in 1965, the first global communications network. Within a few years, telephone circuits increased from 500 to thousands, and live television coverage of events anywhere in the world became commonplace. Taking advantage of the growing audience for television and the public's interest in space, producer Gene Roddenberry (1921–91) launched a show called *Star Trek* in 1966. This show, which included Russian and black female characters on the crew of the starship *Enterprise*, was destined to become one of the most popular series of all time.

The Soviets had three unsuccessful Venus flybys and two unsuccessful Mars missions in 1962, followed by three unsuccessful lunar missions in 1963. Their luck remained bad in 1963 with three more failed Venus flybys, three failed lunar landers, and one failed Mars flyby. After failures in April, May, and June, *Zond 3* was successful in July 1965, sending back pictures of the far side of the Moon. More failures followed in October,

November, and December. But on November 16, 1965, *Venera 3* began its trip to Venus, where it would become the first spacecraft to impact there on March 1, 1966. However, it did not return any data. On February 3, 1966, *Luna 9* became the first spacecraft to soft-land on the Moon, proving that the surface is firm. Though other spacecraft failed just before and after it, on April 3, *Luna 10* became the first spacecraft to enter lunar orbit. *Luna 11* and *12* in August and October added more orbital maps. On December 24, 1966, *Luna 13* landed on the Moon and provided TV panoramas. *Luna 14* was the last of this series and entered orbit on April 10, 1968.

Lunar exploration continued with the Soviet *Zond* [probe] series starting on September 15, 1968, with *Zond 5*. It was the first spacecraft to orbit the Moon and return (with film). *Zond 6* repeated this feat in November, this time snapping stereo pictures. *Zond 7* followed in August 1969.

On October 18, 1967, *Venera 4* descended into the atmosphere of Venus and returned data on its composition. Several other missions failed, but on January 5 and 10, 1969, *Venera 5* and *6* were sent to Venus. *Venera 5* parachuted into the atmosphere on May 16, and *Venera 6* followed on May 17. Both returned data. On December 15, 1970, the Soviets made the first soft-landing on Venus with *Venera 7*. It sent back data for 23 minutes before succumbing to the intense heat.

Other nations were also getting into space. On September 29, 1962, Canada launched its first satellite (using American rockets), *Alouette 1*, to study the aurora. On November 26, 1965, France launched its first satellite, *A-1* (*Asterix*), becoming the third nation to reach orbit.

Interest in space for political, scientific, and military purposes spawned efforts in the United Nations in 1957 to craft a treaty to prevent colonial competition for celestial bodies and placement of weapons of mass destruction in space. On January 27, 1967, the *Treaty on Principles Governing the Activities of States in the Exploration and Use of Outer Space, Including the Moon and Other Celestial Bodies* (see Further Reading) was signed in Washington, Moscow, and London. The U.S. Senate unanimously approved in April, and what became known as the Outer Space Treaty went into force on October 10, 1967. The countries agreed not to place weapons of mass destruction in orbit around Earth or on any celestial body and to use the Moon and other bodies exclusively for peaceful purposes.

Tragedy in 1967

The first launch of the Saturn I was October 27, 1961. Later Saturns had a second stage with a cluster of six liquid hydrogen-oxygen RL-10 engines developed by Pratt & Whitney and NASA Lewis (now Glenn). These launches tested the clustering of engines, the assembly and checkout of large systems, separation techniques, and guidance and communications systems.

The Saturn V's three stages were powered by two new engines, the kerosene-oxygen first stage F-1, and the hydrogen-oxygen upper stage J-2. The Saturn IB was used to test the J-2 engine, the reentry capsule of the Command and Service Module (CSM), and the Lunar Module (LM).

After the success of Saturn IB flights in 1965 and 1966, a test with the command module was planned for February 1967. The Saturn IB was on the pad, and some last-minute checkout of the capsule was done on January 27 with the astronauts Gus Grissom, Ed White, and Roger B. Chaffee (1935–67) onboard. The countdown test was not going well. "How are we going to get to the Moon if we can't talk between three buildings?" Grissom asked.

They were waiting through another hold at 6:31 P.M. when Chaffee shouted, "We've got a fire in the cockpit!" Because of the intense heat, it took several minutes for pad workers to open the hatch. But it was too late. The men were dead. It was determined that an electric short between wires ignited the insulation. The pure oxygen in the capsule caused the equipment to burn violently.

To keep on schedule, President Johnson let NASA remain in charge of the investigation. Administrator Webb assigned his Chief of Manned Space Flight, George Low, the task of rebuilding the Apollo capsule. Low established a Configuration Control Board that considered 1,697 changes and approved 1,341. For 18 months, about 150,000 Americans worked around the clock to make the changes. Manned Spacecraft Center Director Robert Gilruth recalled in an interview (see Further Reading) that "We almost lost the whole program. But [the fire] certainly did galvanize everybody into doing a first-class job from then on. It probably had a lot to do with the success we had in the lunar program."

The Americans' delay offered the Soviets a chance to catch up. Korolev had died in January 1966, and Vassily Mishin became chief designer. He oversaw three programs: the Soyuz spacecraft development (including docking capability); the UR-500K/L-I circumlunar flight (including a recovery capsule); and the N-1/L-3 lunar landing program. He also had to keep up with the *Molniya* communications satellite program that had two successes in 1965 but a failure on March 27, 1966.

To create the L-1 for the circumlunar flight, the Russians needed to reduce the weight of the Soyuz. They removed the living section, the reserve parachute system, a backup maneuvering system, and some solar battery panels. They added extra jets for reentry control and beefed up the thermal shield. The first unmanned test of the L-1 on a UR-500K was *Kosmos 146* on March 10, 1967. It orbited for eight days, and the L-1's engine performed well. The second test on April 8 failed. Two weeks later, disaster struck.

On April 24, 1967, *Soyuz 1* launched with Vladimir Komarov onboard. A solar panel failed, so there was not enough power to stay in orbit for the planned docking with *Soyuz 2*. *Soyuz 2* did not launch, and Komarov was told to come home. The capsule parachute had not been packed properly and failed during reentry. Komarov was killed. Both the American and Soviet manned programs halted flights until 1968.

Resumption of the Race

The Russians were unable to catch up. On September 28, 1967, the Proton launcher first stage failed on the third unmanned test of the UR-500/L-1. Mishin launched two more unmanned Soyuz in October. Designated *Kosmos 186* and *188*, the two craft performed the first automatic docking in space on October 30, 1967. But on November 23, another L-1 failed to reach orbit.

The Apollo program meanwhile had launched the first redesigned capsule on a *Saturn V* on November 9, 1967. The 806,432-pound (36,656-kg) payload was the largest ever. *Apollo 5* launched on January 22, 1968, and placed an unmanned lunar module in orbit.

Zond 4 was launched on March 2 and confused Western observers. Because the Soviets worked in secret, it was not clear who was actually ahead on the race to the Moon. *Zonds 1, 2,* and *3* had been lightweight craft that had failed on missions to Venus and Mars in 1964 and 1965. This new *Zond* was a 7K/L-1, a modified Soyuz weighing more than 11,000 pounds (5,000 kg). Westerners referred to it as a "Heavy Zond." The first two Heavy Zonds were given *Kosmos* designations because they failed to achieve lunar trajectories. *Zond 4* flew (on purpose) to a lunar distance though in the opposite direction of the Moon. It was lost during reentry when a sensor failed.

Apollo 6 on April 4, 1968, was an unmanned flight using a Saturn V. It experienced severe vibrations called pogo that would have aborted a manned mission. After some 31,000 man-hours studying the problem, NASA solved it with a system of shock absorbers. Also troubling were unexpected shutdowns of the second-stage J-2 engines and the single third-stage J-2 that failed to restart. This problem was corrected by strengthening the bellows to prevent fuel-line ruptures.

On April 15, the Soviets had another successful unmanned docking of two Soyuz, *Kosmos 212* and *213*. On April 23, a Heavy Zond that was supposed to fly around the Moon failed to reach orbit. Another Heavy Zond was destroyed on the launch pad on July 14 when an overpressurized oxygen tank exploded, killing three men. *Zond 5* and *6*, launched September 15 and November 10, made it around the Moon. *Zond 5* suffered an attitude control failure and ended up thousands of miles off course after experiencing a g-load that would have killed a crew. *Zond 6* demonstrated a minimal-heating reentry, but the vehicle was depressurized by a failed gasket and the parachute failed. A crew would have died. Fixing these problems put the Russians further behind.

The first manned mission after the fire, *Apollo 7*, was launched on a Saturn 1B on October 11, 1968, with Wally Schirra, Walter Cunningham (1932–), and Donn Eisele (1930–87) onboard. This was the first flight of the CSM and the first American three-man crew. It was such a success that NASA decided to fly *Apollo 8* around the Moon. This decision dashed Soviet hopes of being first to do a circumlunar flight.

On December 21, 1968, the *Apollo 8* crew of Frank Borman, Jim Lovell, and William Anders (1933–) rode the first Saturn V into space. In the first two and a half minutes, the 12-foot-wide engines of the first stage burned 54 railroad cars' worth of liquid oxygen. After reaching orbit, the third stage engine fired again, taking them to the Moon. Three days later, they successfully entered lunar orbit while out of contact with Earth. They were the first humans to see the far side. Borman reported, "The moon is essentially gray. No color. Looks like plaster of Paris. . . ." Four orbits later, they rolled the spacecraft and saw the Earth hovering over the lunar horizon. Many say the resulting "Earthrise" photograph inspired the environmental conservation movement. On Christmas Eve, their reading from the Bible filled millions of listeners with a sense of awe and wonder, lifting spirits after a year darkened by Vietnam war protests, Yuri Gagarin's death in a plane crash, and the assassinations of civil rights activist Martin Luther King, Jr. (1929–68), and presidential candidate Robert Kennedy (1925–68).

The Race Is Won

Even though the Americans had done the first circumlunar mission, the Russian program continued because the craft was already built. On January 14–15, 1969, they completed the first successful docking of two manned vehicles, *Soyuz 4* with Vladimir Shatalov (1927–), and *Soyuz 5* with Yevgeni Khrunov (1933–2000), Alexei S. Yeliseyev (1934–), and Boris V. Volynov (1934–). Khrunov and Yeliseyev spacewalked over to *Soyuz 4* and rode it home. Volynov came down alone in *Soyuz 5*, enduring a dangerous nose-first entry.

This success was followed by a series of failures. On January 20, 1969, the UR-500K second and third stages failed, and the booster was destroyed. On February 21, the first test of the N-1 with a simplified L-1 failed just over a minute after launch. In both cases, the L-1 spacecraft was saved by the rescue system.

Apollo 9 in March was the first manned flight of the lunar module. It launched on March 3, 1969, with James McDivitt, David Scott, and Russell "Rusty" Schweickart (1935–). Schweickart tested the lunar space suit. *Apollo 10* launched May 18, 1969, with Tom Stafford, Gene Cernan, and John Young. It descended to within 8.7 miles (14 km) of the surface and set the century's manned speed record of 6.88 miles/sec (11.08 km/s) at atmospheric entry.

The Soviet's hopes of reaching the Moon ended with the second N-1 launch on July 3, 1969. A bolt was sucked into the oxidizer pump and exploded one of the 30 first-stage engines. A fire erupted, the rocket fell over, and the entire launch complex was destroyed.

The Soviets tried one more time to do something before the Americans, and that was to return a soil sample from the Moon. *Luna 15* launched on July 13. It crashed in the Sea of Crises on July 21. *Pravda* merely reported, "Flight of Automatic Station *Luna 15* Completed" with no mention of the intention to return soil.

On Wednesday, July 16, 1969, *Apollo 11* launched on its historic flight. The LM named *Eagle* and the CSM named *Columbia* flew nose to nose with their airlocks joined on their three-day trip to the Moon. They entered orbit 65 miles (104 km) above the Moon. On July 20, 1969, Michael Collins helped Neil Armstrong and Buzz Aldrin through a tunnel into the tiny *Eagle*. It had no seats, and the hull was so thin, they could put a boot through it. Armstrong and Aldrin dropped to the Moon while Collins remained alone in *Columbia*.

The computer overloaded during the descent. Tense minutes passed until Mission Control decided not to abort. Another alarm caused Mission Control to take over some of the computer's work to keep *Eagle* flying. Armstrong and Aldrin skimmed over boulders and craters. If they landed on a slope or a rock, the *Eagle* might fall over or break a leg and strand them on the Moon. With only 20 seconds of fuel left, Armstrong found a clear spot to land.

"Houston, Tranquility Base here," Armstrong said. "The Eagle has landed!" Aldrin gave thanks and took communion. The men were scheduled to sleep before their Moon walk, but they were too excited. So at about 9:30 P.M. Houston time on July 20, 1969, Armstrong (see photo opposite) wriggled out through a square hole in the *Eagle*. He lowered a small drawbridge that held a TV camera. Six hundred million people around the world watched as he backed down the ladder. He touched the Moon's surface and said, "That's one small step for man . . . one giant leap for mankind." Collins missed those famous words. He was on the far side of the Moon, out of earshot.

Aldrin soon followed. "Beautiful! Beautiful!" he said. "Magnificent desolation." He and Armstrong planted a U.S. flag, gathered 46.2 pounds (21 kg) of rocks, and set up experiments. After about two hours, they crawled back into the *Eagle*. Moon dust stuck to them, smelling like damp ashes. The men shivered with cold in the paper-thin LM and had trouble sleeping.

They spent 21 hours and 36 minutes on the lunar surface. To reduce launch weight, the space-suit backpacks and trash were dumped out the hatch. They also left the lower half of the lander. On the leg was a plaque that read, "We came in peace for all mankind."

As the *Eagle* rose up, the engine plume blew dust everywhere. "I looked up long enough to see the flag fall over," Aldrin recalled. The lunar orbit rendezvous worked as planned. After the men and their lunar samples were transferred across, *Eagle* was released to crash on the Moon. On July 24, the crew splashed down in the Pacific. The race to the Moon was won.

The first man on the Moon was Neil Armstrong, shown here in his official photo taken before his flight on Apollo 11 in July 1969. (NASA)

President Richard Nixon (1913–94) welcomed the crew on board the USS *Hornet* recovery ship. He said, "This is the greatest week in the history of the world since creation." The astronauts listened from quarantine, where they were stuck for 21 days as a precaution against "moon germs." Mission Control filled with cigar smoke. On the big screen, it said, "Mission Accomplished."

The Waning Moon

The race was over, but both sides kept flying a while longer. On August 14, 1969, *Zond* 7 became the first 7K/L-1 to go around the Moon and return without any failures. Then three spacecraft launched on consecutive days: October 11, 12, and 13, putting seven cosmonauts in orbit at one time on *Soyuz 6, 7,* and *8.* The crew did welding and navigation experiments.

This mission just could not compare to *Apollo 12* that launched November 14 on a 10-day mission with Pete Conrad, Alan Bean (1932–), and Dick Gordon. After a precision landing near *Surveyor 3,* the men completed two EVAs and collected 74.8 pounds (34 kg) of samples. They spent 31 hours, 31 minutes on the surface.

The last Apollo of the decade was the ill-fated *Apollo 13.* It launched on April 11, 1970, with the crew of Jim Lovell, Fred Haise (1933–), and Jack Swigert (1931–82). The mission was aborted following the oxygen-tank explosion in the CSM *Odyssey.* The LM *Aquarius* was used as a lifeboat. They swung around the Moon and made a heroic return to Earth.

As the Apollo program wound down in 1968, a task force recommended that NASA focus on a reusable transportation system. NASA's Associate Administrator George Mueller (1918–) gained wide support for a shuttle that he claimed would lower launch costs and allow all other launch vehicles to be retired. Study contracts were let in 1969. Nixon did not want any grandiose projects, so plans for a Mars mission and station were dropped. In the summer of 1970, NASA opted for a large shuttle with two recoverable stages.

The Soviets publicly pretended that they never planned to send men to the Moon. They touted the success of their unmanned robotic missions. *Luna 16* successfully returned lunar samples in September 1970. *Luna 17* deployed a rover, *Lunokhod 1,* in November 1970 that roamed the Moon for 11 months and took more than 20,000 photos. It conducted more than 500 soil tests.

The Soviets focused on space-station development, even while secretly keeping open the option for future lunar missions. Vitaly Sevastyanov (1935–) and Andrian Nikolayev launched June 1, 1970, on an 18-day *Soyuz 9.* To save fuel, the ship flew head over heels and made the crew sick. They endured 17.71 days of this and returned in terrible shape. The flight accomplished its primary goal though, to take the endurance record from the Americans and celebrate Lenin's 100th birthday.

The Soviets just did not have the funds to compete with the American manned lunar program. It is estimated that the Soviets spent about a tenth as much as the Americans. After the unmanned *Zond 8,* launched October 20, 1970, crashed in the Indian Ocean, Chelomei's UR-500/ L-1 program was cancelled. It had not flown a single cosmonaut, and its development had hindered progress on Korolev's N-1/L-3.

A new test of the L-3 spacecraft was promising on November 24, 1970. It was launched on a Soyuz SL-4 instead of an N-1. The engine was throttled as it would be for a lunar landing, the landing platform was ejected, and the main engine restarted as it would for a lunar ascent. Also successful was a December 2, 1970, flight of a prototype lunar orbiter. The flight, called *Kosmos 382*, tested the multiple-start capability of the oxygen-kerosene engines and the use of storable propellant thrusters for lunar maneuvers. The N-1/L-3 story would not end until early in the next decade.

X-ray and Neutrino Astronomy

Access to space meant access to the parts of the electromagnetic spectrum that are blocked by Earth's atmosphere (see figure below). Thus, the first observations of the Sun's X-ray spectrum occurred from space in 1962. On June 18, 1962, the first known and brightest X-ray source in the sky other than the Sun, Scorpius X-1, was discovered by instruments aboard a rocket. The rocket was launched by a team led by Riccardo Giacconi (1931–) at American Science and Engineering in Massachusetts. By 1968, the team had found 30 X-ray sources. Giaconni, who received a Bruce Medal (see page 249) in 1981 and a Nobel Prize in physics in 2002, organized the first Earth-orbiting mission dedicated to X-ray astronomy. It launched from Kenya on December 12, 1970, and operated through March 1973. It was named *Uhura*, the Swahili word for "freedom." The satellite detected 339 X-ray sources and discovered diffuse X-ray emission from galaxy clusters.

Space-based telescopes allowed astronomers to view parts of the spectrum that were blocked by Earth's atmosphere.

Other X-ray data was obtained through spy satellites. Between May 23, 1969, and June 19, 1979, the American *Vela-5B* spy satellite provided

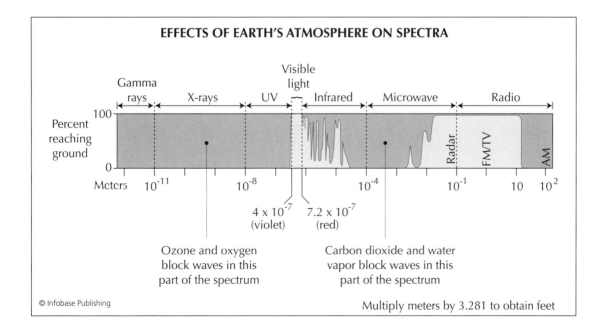

EFFECTS OF EARTH'S ATMOSPHERE ON SPECTRA

Gamma rays | X-rays | UV | Visible light | Infrared | Microwave | Radar | FM/TV | AM | Radio

Percent reaching ground

100

0

Meters 10^{-11} 10^{-8} 10^{-4} 10^{-1} 10 10^2

4×10^{-7} (violet) 7.2×10^{-7} (red)

Ozone and oxygen block waves in this part of the spectrum

Carbon dioxide and water vapor block waves in this part of the spectrum

© Infobase Publishing

Multiply meters by 3.281 to obtain feet

long-term variability data on X-ray binaries and transients. It was also one of the first satellites to detect gamma-ray bursts.

While X-ray telescopes scanned a new part of the spectrum, a new kind of telescope was built to use particles to observe astronomical events indirectly. Hans Bethe had shown that stars produce energy by fusing hydrogen into helium, a reaction that releases positrons and *neutrinos.* The helium and positrons remain in the center of the Sun, and the electromagnetic energy produced takes thousands of years to work its way to the surface. But neutrinos shoot out from the Sun's core at nearly the speed of light and thus provide data on current conditions in the Sun.

The first neutrinos were detected in a nuclear reactor in 1956. Because they are so unlikely to interact with atoms, it is extremely difficult to detect them. A neutrino passing through the entire mass of the Earth has less than one chance in a thousand billion of being stopped. Raymond Davis (1914–) and John N. Bahcall (1934–2005) found a clever way to measure the number of neutrinos coming from the Sun. Bahcall calculated in 1964 that neutrinos coming from the Sun and passing through 100,000 gallons (378,500 l) of cleaning fluid (mostly chlorine) would produce a few atoms a week of argon. Davis then put a tank the size of an Olympic swimming pool about one mile (1.5 km) underground in a gold mine in South Dakota. In 1968 Davis announced his first results. Agreement with the theory and observations provided strong evidence that the Sun does indeed produce its energy through nuclear fusion. The energies of the detected neutrinos also matched predictions. But fewer neutrinos were detected than predicted. Some scientists suggested that a black hole in the center of the Sun was gobbling them up. In about 1969, Russian scientists Bruno Pontecorvo (1913–93) and Vladimir Gribov (1930–97) proposed that the missing neutrinos could be explained if neutrinos produced by the Sun oscillate between states. The chlorine experiment might only detect them in an easier-to-observe state while the ones in the other state pass by. For the next 20 years, evidence supporting this proposal accumulated, but by the close of the century, the mystery of the missing neutrinos had still not been completely solved.

Quasars and Pulsars

New radio telescopes and techniques detected thousands of radio sources with increasing precision during this decade. One of the major new interferometers became operational in 1961 using a 250-foot (76-m) radio telescope at Jodrell Bank Observatory in England and another movable telescope about 100 miles (160 km) away. As the Earth rotated, the interference pattern moved across the positions of the radio sources in the sky. The combined signals gave an output of zero if the source were a point. Wide sources created a smearing effect between adjacent maximum and minimum signals. Using the interferometer, many sources had their sizes determined.

In 1962, Thomas Matthews and Allan Sandage (see Bruce Medalists, page 249) used the Palomar 200-inch (5-m) telescope to identify a radio source called 3C48 with a faint blue starlike object. The object presented a real puzzle. Like Cygnus A, it contained emission lines indicating gas at 10,000 or more degrees. Unlike Cygnus A or any other object they had ever seen, the emission lines did not match those of any known elements.

William Fowler and Hoyle attacked the puzzle in 1962 by considering the idea of a chain of supernovae. They put all the supernovae into one large object with a mass millions of times greater than the Sun. They found that nuclear energy alone was not enough to produce the power of a quasar, and they speculated that the gravitational energy of a massive black hole was required. At this time black holes were still only theoretical.

Working at the University of Sydney, Cyril Hazard realized that the Moon *occulted* some of the radio sources. Because the position of the edge of the Moon is known very accurately for any time, by carefully timing the disappearance and reappearance of the source, he could measure the position and size more accurately than previously possible. In 1963, he used the radio telescope at Parkes, New South Wales, during a lunar *occultation* of 3C273. He found that 3C273 is a double radio source, with one component lying on top of a blue starlike object.

With this accurate position, Maarten Schmidt (1929–   ) of Caltech used the Palomar 200-inch (5-m) telescope to photograph 3C273 and take a spectrum. The photograph showed a starlike object with a jet off to one side. The spectrum showed mysterious, broad emission lines like those seen for 3C48. Schmidt then discovered that the mysterious lines were actually well-known transitions between energy states in a hydrogen atom that were red shifted by about 16 percent. A check of the 3C48 spectrum found an even greater redshift of about 37 percent. These "quasi-stellar" sources, or quasars, were thus billions of light-years away. Yet they were producing as much energy as dozens of the largest and brightest galaxies combined. The discovery of quasars as distant objects was published in the March 16, 1963, issue of *Nature* just two months after Hoyle and Fowler's paper "Nature of Strong Radio Sources" about massive collapsed objects as radio sources (see Further Reading). In 1969, Donald Lynden-Bell (1935–   ) proposed that black holes are at the centers of galaxies and provide the energy sources for quasars. Schmidt and Lynden–Bell both received Bruce Medals (see page 249) for this work.

While doing a survey of quasars in 1967, graduate student Jocelyn Bell made an unexpected discovery. She was studying the "twinkling" of radio sources as a result of the solar wind. For distant radio sources, the solar wind blows pockets of ionized gas past the telescope, causing the radio sources to flicker on a time scale of tenths of seconds. British astronomer Antony Hewish (1924–   ) designed and built the telescope to measure this flickering to find the angular sizes of radio sources (and won a Nobel Prize in physics in 1974). Unlike other telescopes of the time, it recorded the strength of the signal at least 10 times per second.

In August, Jocelyn Bell found that a source designated PSR 1919 flickered in the middle of the night when the solar wind was "calm." On November 28, 1963, she observed the object with a high-speed recorder and found that its period was 1.337 seconds. She had discovered the first *pulsar*. Within a year, more than two dozen more were found.

Some scientists thought pulsars were communications from distant civilizations. In 1961, the first conference to discuss the Search for Extraterrestrial Intelligence (SETI) was held in Green Bank, Wisconsin. Scientists there developed the *Drake equation*, estimating a high probability of other intelligent life in the universe. In 1963, Soviet astronomer Nikolai Kardashev (1932–   ) reported unusual radio signals from CTA–102, and suggested that they might be of artificial origin. These signals were later found to come from a quasar. Iosif Samuilovich Shklovskii (see Bruce Medalists, page 249), who had explained that the Crab nebula's energy was from synchrotron radiation, added to the credibility of these speculations when he published *Intelligent Life in the Universe* in 1966. The book was translated and expanded by Carl Sagan.

In 1968, Tommy Gold published the first speculation that pulsar radio noises were produced by rapidly rotating neutron stars (see figure below). Only neutron stars were dense enough to rotate with such short periods

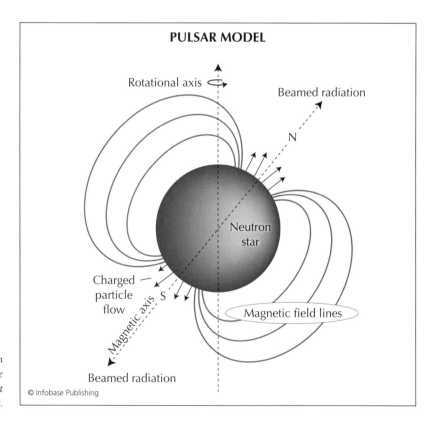

Pulsars were first discovered in 1967 and were confirmed to be rotating neutron stars, the result of supernovae, in 1968.

and not fly apart. Back in 1939, J. Robert Oppenheimer and George Volkoff had calculated that a star made up of neutrons would have a diameter of about 12 miles (20 km). Because of this small size, astronomers never expected to observe one. But in 1968, astronomers at Arecibo radio observatory confirmed Gold's theory when they found a pulsar in the Crab Nebula debris of the great supernova event of 1054.

Abundant Support for the Big Bang Theory

In 1961, the front page of the London papers declared that the steady-state theory was dead. The reporters had been invited by Martin Ryle to witness his presentation of data that he felt dealt a death blow to the theory. In a survey of radio galaxies versus distance, he had found the number of intense radio sources increased with distance, a result consistent with more energetic galaxies in the past than the present. Ryle, still apparently stinging from Hoyle proving him wrong about radio stars, made sure his rival attended this public "flogging" of his theory. Although Hoyle remained a proponent of the steady-state theory, his own work on elemental abundances did far more to undermine his theory than Ryle's radio galaxy survey.

The amount of helium–4 in the universe provides an important test for the big bang theory. The theory predicts that about 25 percent of the matter created in the big bang was helium–4. In 1967, Fred Hoyle, Robert Wagoner (1938–   ) and Willy Fowler computed the abundances of the elements in the primordial universe and found agreement with the big bang theory's prediction for helium–4.

The fusion of hydrogen to helium requires an intermediate step, and that is the creation of deuterium (a proton plus a neutron). Helium–4 is very stable, and deuterium is very unstable. Inside stars, two deuterium nuclei quickly combine and form helium–4. The only way to have "free" deuterium is to have the temperature or density drop suddenly and prevent the deuterium from fusing, as would happen in the expansion after the big bang. So the observation of a significant amount of deuterium supports the big bang theory.

But the amount of deuterium observed required that the early universe be very massive. Only a huge mass would have enough gravitational energy to create the high temperature and density conditions that are required to make that much deuterium. Astrophysicists searched but could not find another process to account for the deuterium. They gradually realized that their assumption about the dense early universe being made of protons and neutrons could be in error. The universe could instead be made largely of unseen dark matter. Vera Rubin (1928–   ) and Kenneth William Ford (1926–   ) published a paper (see Further Reading) on the rotation of the Andromeda Galaxy in 1970 that supported this view. They showed that Andromeda would fly apart unless the gravity of unseen dark matter held it together.

Scientist of the Decade: Robert Rowe Gilruth (1913–2000)

Dr. Robert Rowe Gilruth led Project Mercury that put the first American into space and into orbit. He convinced President Kennedy to set the Moon goal and directed the Manned Spacecraft (now Johnson Space) Center people and resources to accomplish the feat.

Born on October 8, 1913, in Nashwauk, Minnesota, the Gilruth family moved to Hancock, Michigan, and then to Duluth, Minnesota, by 1922. His parents, Henry Augustus Gilruth and Francis Marian Rowe, were both teachers. His older sister Jean was a straight-A student, but Bob was more interested in model airplanes than books. The budding engineer improved the design of rubber-band-powered airplanes that he flew in competitions.

Gilruth received a degree in aeronautical engineering in 1935 from the University of Minnesota where he met his wife, Jean Barnhill (1912–72). Barnhill was also an engineer and one of the first female commercially licensed pilots. She took Gilruth up on what may have been his first flight. On graduate fellowships of $50 a month, both Barnhill and Gilruth worked on high-altitude gondolas with French balloonist Jean Piccard (1884–1963). Gilruth also helped design an airplane that Roscoe Turner (1895–1970) used to twice win the Thompson Trophy.

In December 1936, Gilruth landed a job with NACA and moved to Virginia. Barnhill joined him after they were married in April 1937. She quit flying but joined her husband in their favorite hobby of building and sailing boats. Daughter Barbara Jean was born in 1938.

In 1937, there was a desperate need for data on the effects of supersonic speeds on aircraft. Gilruth invented the "wingflow test" and showed that thin wings performed best. His top-secret technique was used to shape the Bell X-1 that broke the sound barrier in 1947. During World

Robert Gilruth led the U.S. manned space program from Mercury through Apollo. This photo is from 1965, when he was head of the Manned Spacecraft Center in Houston. (NASA)

War II, he was inducted into the military and assigned to stay at NACA.

In 1945, Gilruth organized and headed the Pilotless Aircraft Research Division at Langley with the responsibility for developing a missile range at Wallops Island, Virginia. Though Gilruth was only 31, he soon mastered the world of budgets, recruiting, and operating with industry. "We flew hundreds of rocket-powered airplane models from Wallops Island," Gilruth recalled in an interview (see Further Reading).

In 1952, Gilruth was appointed assistant director of Langley and worked on high-temperature structures and dynamic loads while continuing research at Wallops. Then *Sputnik* came in 1957. "I can recall watching the sunlight reflect off of *Sputnik* as it passed over my home on the Chesapeake Bay in Virginia," Gilruth said in 1972. "It put a new sense of value and urgency on things we had been doing."

Gilruth became director of the Space Task Group in charge of Project Mercury in 1958. At 45, he was not so sure that it was a wise career move. "I didn't think I wanted to do this space business all my life, but I was fascinated by it," Gilruth said. "I thought it was terribly dangerous and probably I'd end up in jail or something."

He did not end up in jail, but he almost got fired in 1961. The first Mercury–Atlas flight had failed (though the capsule was recovered). To get approval for a proposed "belly band" joining the Mercury and Atlas, Gilruth had to bet his job that he was right. He was. The team celebrated the successful flight in February with a new tradition, the "splashdown" party. But the Soviets soon thwarted America's goal to put man in space first.

Gilruth advised President Kennedy to regain America's world standing by going to the Moon. "If you really want to be first, you've got to take something that is so difficult we'll both have to start from scratch." After Kennedy set the Moon goal, Gilruth faced an enormous engineering challenge. On top of managing the vehicles and crews, he built the Manned Spacecraft Center in Houston that opened in 1962.

Though he directed everything from astronaut selection to spacecraft design, not many people outside NASA ever heard of Gilruth. His successor Chris Kraft (1924–) explained why. "He was a dynamic and innovative engineer and manager. But . . . he wasn't a great public speaker." Gilruth preferred to keep a low profile, puffing on his pipe or a cigar in the background. "He sent his key people out front to deliver the briefings, engage in the debates, and in some cases become the faces and the personalities of American space exploration," Kraft wrote in his book (see Further Reading).

The quality of Gilruth's work was noticed, though. After John Glenn's historic flight in 1962, NASA Administrator Webb told Gilruth, "Look, you're going to go right along with him [to New York], and you're going to get every medal that he gets." Gilruth did not expect medals or begrudge "his" astronauts awards for risking their lives. Still, that New York trip was a cherished memory of his career. Others remember when he received the President's Award for Distinguished Federal Services. The modest Gilruth froze at the podium, unable to address President Kennedy or the press. Among other awards, Gilruth was elected to the National Academy of Sciences and received the Robert J. Collier Trophy in 1972 for the greatest achievement in aeronautics or astronautics. He received four honorary Ph.D.s and was one of the first people installed in the National Space Hall of Fame.

Gilruth oversaw 25 manned flights, from the first Mercury flight in 1961 to *Apollo 15* in 1971. He also paved the way for the Apollo-Soyuz mission by leading the first two NASA delegations to Russia in 1970. He took a position as director of key personnel development in 1972. "I wanted a job that was less demanding," he explained. "[Jean] was ill, and we wanted to have time to do a little traveling." Jean died in December 1972, after the launch of *Apollo 17*. Gilruth retired from NASA in 1973 and married Georgene (Jo) Evans (1919–) in July. He worked as a consultant for NASA for another year.

After a long struggle with Alzheimer's, Gilruth died in Charlottesville, Virginia, on August 17, 2000. A memorial service in Houston included a "missing-man" fly-over by NASA astronauts who continue the manned space program that Gilruth fathered.

When George Gamow and others realized in the 1940s that the early universe had been very hot, they also realized that there should be radiation surviving from that time. They predicted the radiation should have a temperature of between 5 and 50°K (–268 to –223°C/ –450 to –369°F). A team at Princeton headed by Robert Henry Dicke (1916–97) and James Edwin Peebles (1935–) refined the calculations in 1964 and concluded the radiation would have a temperature of about 10°K, later revised to 3°K. They built a radio telescope to look for it. Before they were done, Arno Penzias and Robert Wilson of Bell Telephone in New Jersey found it by accident. They were measuring and matching sources of noise in communications, including the Earth's atmosphere, the Sun and the Milky Way. They were unable to explain microwave noise that came from all directions in the sky. They consulted the Princeton group and realized that the noise was *cosmic background radiation* (CBR). Penzias and Wilson published their result in the *Astrophysical Journal* in 1965 (see Further Reading), and shared a Nobel Prize in physics in 1978. The discovery of CBR established the big bang theory as the leading cosmological model.

Further Reading

Books and Periodicals

Chaikin, Andrew. *A Man on the Moon.* New York: Viking, 1994. This book is an accurate historical account of the challenges and drama of *Apollo*s *8* through *17.*

Hoyle, F., and W. A. Fowler. "Nature of Strong Radio Sources." *Nature* 197. (February 9, 1963): 533–535. This scholarly paper was the first proposal that strong radio sources were the result of gravitational energy of extremely massive objects at the center of galaxies.

Kraft, Chris. *Flight: My Life in Mission Control.* New York: Dutton, 2001. The behind-the-scenes stories of triumph and tragedy of the Mercury, Gemini, and Apollo space programs are told by NASA's first flight director.

Kranz, Gene. *Failure Is Not an Option.* New York: Simon and Schuster, 2000. This book covers the U.S. space program from the first flights through *Apollo 17* with extra detail on *Apollo*s *11* and *13* when the author was flight director.

Murray, Charles, and Catherine Bly Cox. *Apollo: The Race to the Moon.* New York: Simon and Schuster, 1989. This book follows a team of engineers and managers including Max Faget and James Webb from the beginning of NASA through the last Apollo flight.

Penzias, A. A., and R. W. Wilson. "A Measurement of Excess Antenna Temperatures at 4080 Mc/s." *Astrophysical Journal* 142 (July 1965): 419–421. Available online. URL: http://articles.adsabs.harvard.edu/cgi-bin/nph-iarticle_query?1965ApJ...142..419P. This is the historic paper that proved the existence of cosmic background radiation that was predicted by the big bang theory.

Rubin, Vera C., and Kent W. Ford, Jr. "Rotation of the Andromeda Nebula from a Spectroscopic Survey of Emission Regions." *Astrophysical Journal* 159 (February 1970): 379–404. Available online. URL: http://articles. adsabs.harvard.edu/cgi-bin/nph-iarticle_query?1970ApJ...159..379R. The authors show that the rotation of Andromeda requires the existence of unseen dark matter to explain its rapid rotation rate.

Swanson, Glen E., ed. "Before This Decade Is Out . . . : Personal Reflections on the Apollo Program." *NASA SP-4223*, 1999. Available online. URL: http://history.nasa.gov/SP-4223/sp4223. Accessed on March 10, 2006. This collection includes interviews with James Webb, Wernher von Braun, Robert Gilruth, George Low, Max Faget, and other leaders of the American space program.

Web Sites

David DeVorkin. "Interviewee: Dr. Robert Gilruth." National Air and Space Museum. http://www.nasm.si.edu/research/dsh/TRANSCPT/ GILRUTH1.HTM. Accessed on August 30, 2006. The site contains unedited transcripts of six interviews with Dr. Gilruth and his wife in which he discusses his life and association with the manned space program, conducted between March 21, 1986, and March 2, 1987.

Marika Griehsel. "Arno Penzias—Interview." Nobelprize.org. Available online. URL: http://nobelprize.org/physics/laureates/1978/penzias-interview.html. Accessed on August 30, 2006. Dr. Penzias talks about how he discovered the cosmic background radiation. A brief autobiography, his 1978 Nobel lecture, and banquet speech are linked to this Web site.

Harvard–Smithsonian Center for Astrophysics. "Cygnus A, Quasars, and Quandaries." SAO for NASA. Available online. URL: http://chandra. harvard.edu/chronicle/0101/cyga2.html. Accessed on August 30, 2006. The article describes the discovery that radio source Cygnus A is a distant quasar.

Per Olof Hulth. "High Energy Neutrinos from the Cosmos." Nobelprize. org. Available online. URL: http://nobelprize.org/physics/articles/hulth/ index.html. Accessed on August 30, 2006. The article explains what neutrinos are and how they are detected.

Christopher C. Kraft, Jr. "Robert Gilruth Biographical Memoir." National Academy of Sciences. Available online. URL: http://www.nap.edu/html/ biomems/rgilruth.html. Accessed on March 10, 2006. This is a detailed biography of Robert Gilruth, based on personal interviews, and written by his successor at Johnson Space Center.

Lunar and Planetary Institute. "Exploring the Moon." Lunar and Planetary Institute. Available online. URL: http://www.lpi.usra.edu/expmoon/ lunar_missions.html. Accessed on March 10, 2006. This site links to descriptions and more resource materials on all lunar programs, including

Apollo, Luna, Lunar Orbiter, Ranger, Surveyor, Zond, and future missions.

NASA. "Enchanted Rendezvous." NASA History. Available online. URL: http://history.nasa.gov/monograph4/intro.htm. Accessed on March 10, 2006. This series of articles covers all the arguments for and against lunar orbit rendezvous and how the choice was made.

National Radio Astronomy Observatory. "Pulsar Bursts Coming from Beachball-Sized Structures." National Radio Astronomy Observatory. Available online. URL: http://www.nrao.edu/pr/2003/pulsaremission/. Accessed on August 30, 2006. This press release includes an image of the Crab Nebula and a diagram and history of its pulsar.

U.S. Department of State. "Treaty on Principles Governing the Activities of States in the Exploration and Use of Outer Space, Including the Moon and Other Celestial Bodies." FirstGov. Available online. URL: http://www.state.gov/t/ac/trt/5181.htm. Accessed on March 10, 2006. This is the text of the Outer Space Treaty signed by the United States, the Soviet Union, and 89 other nations, agreeing not to claim the Moon or place weapons of mass destruction in space.

David Williams. "Lunar Exploration Timeline." National Space Science Data Center, NASA Goddard Space Flight Center. Available online. URL: http://nssdc.gsfc.nasa.gov/planetary/lunar/lunartimeline.html. Accessed on January 10, 2007. This time line lists unmanned missions to the Moon from all countries, starting with 1959 and including planned missions up to 2008. Links lead to photos or diagrams of the spacecraft and list their accomplishments and failures.

Anatoly Zak. "Chronology: the Moon Race." Russian Space Web. Available online. URL: http://www.russianspaceweb.com/chronology_moon_race.html. Accessed on March 10, 2006. A time line from 1957 to 1976 is provided with dates of key events in the Russian and U.S. space programs side by side.

8

1971–1980:
From the Moon to Jupiter

Space exploration gradually changed through this decade from a focus on spectacular "firsts" to practical basic research that was done from stations in Earth orbit or by unmanned planetary probes and telescopes. The chapter opens with a description of the final Apollo missions that ended with *Apollo 17* in 1972, followed by the first American space station, *Skylab* (see figure on page 172) in 1973. The Soviet space-station program is also covered, starting with the world's first space station, *Salyut 1*, in 1971. After a record-setting stay in space, its first crew died during reentry. This tragedy solidified efforts to create an international space-rescue capability that resulted in the *Apollo-Soyuz* mission in 1975. This mission is covered in the chapter as well as the Soviet improvements in space stations that lead to *Salyut 6* (see photo on page 176). Through the use of automated supply ships, the Soviets increased the time that was spent in space to a record of 185 days by the end of the decade.

Planetary exploration, beginning with *Mariner 9* in 1971 that revealed the solar system's largest volcano (see figure on page 179), is the main focus of the astronomy sections of this chapter. The controversial results from tests for life that were conducted by the Viking landers in 1976 are described. Also covered is the exploration of Venus (see photo on page 181) and the debate about its age and origin between Immanuel Velikovsky and Carl Sagan who is the featured scientist of the decade (see sidebar and photo on page 186). Sagan spearheaded the plaque (see photo on page 182) that announced Earth's location to aliens who may one day encounter *Pioneer 10* or *Pioneer 11*, the first spacecraft to reach Jupiter and head out of the solar system. These spacecraft were followed by the two Voyagers at the end of the decade.

This decade also includes the discovery of the first gravitational lens (see figure on page 185) and the first binary pulsar. These discoveries and new methods of determining distances in space led to a refinement of the big bang theory and the development of new space-born telescopes that would be launched in the next decade by the new American space shuttle.

Roving around the Moon

The new decade began with the roar of *Apollo 14* toward the Moon on January 31, 1971. Onboard was America's first man in space, Alan Shepard, with crew members Edgar Mitchell (1930–   ) and Stuart Roosa (1933–94). Tension was high after the failure of *Apollo 13* nine months earlier. Shepard and Mitchell landed near the lunar equator on February 5. During two Moon walks totaling nine hours, they collected 92 pounds of rocks and gathered soil samples by driving core tubes into the ground. They also deployed a nuclear-powered science station. Most memorable to the public was Shepard's one-handed golf shot that he said went "miles and miles." The return flight was routine and restored confidence in America's manned space program.

The Russians also began the decade with a successful launch on February 26, 1971. *Kosmos 398* was officially an investigation of the

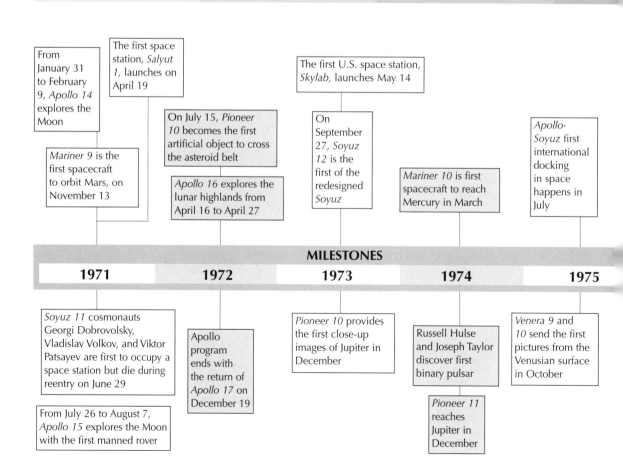

From January 31 to February 9, *Apollo 14* explores the Moon

The first space station, *Salyut 1,* launches on April 19

Mariner 9 is the first spacecraft to orbit Mars, on November 13

On July 15, *Pioneer 10* becomes the first artificial object to cross the asteroid belt

Apollo 16 explores the lunar highlands from April 16 to April 27

The first U.S. space station, *Skylab,* launches May 14

On September 27, *Soyuz 12* is the first of the redesigned *Soyuz*

Mariner 10 is first spacecraft to reach Mercury in March

Apollo-Soyuz first international docking in space happens in July

MILESTONES

1971   **1972**   **1973**   **1974**   **1975**

Soyuz 11 cosmonauts Georgi Dobrovolsky, Vladislav Volkov, and Viktor Patsayev are first to occupy a space station but die during reentry on June 29

Apollo program ends with the return of *Apollo 17* on December 19

Pioneer 10 provides the first close-up images of Jupiter in December

Russell Hulse and Joseph Taylor discover first binary pulsar

Venera 9 and *10* send the first pictures from the Venusian surface in October

From July 26 to August 7, *Apollo 15* explores the Moon with the first manned rover

Pioneer 11 reaches Jupiter in December

upper atmosphere, but it was actually the second unmanned test of the T2K lunar lander. Unlike Apollo's LM that used separate systems for descent and ascent, the T2K used the same two engines for both phases. Clamshell doors prevented contamination from blowing lunar dust. The T2K used regular air at 0.74 atmospheres instead of the 100-percent-oxygen Apollo system.

The lunar rover made its debut on *Apollo 15* that launched on July 26, 1971. Commander David Scott and James Irwin (1930–91) used it to explore a valley between the 15,000-foot (4,600-m) Apennine Mountains and the mile-wide (1.6 km) canyon called Hadley Rille. Thanks to improved backpacks, the men performed three Moon walks and collected 171 pounds of samples. Scott demonstrated Newton's third law by dropping a feather and a hammer. On the airless Moon, both reached the ground at the same time. The two moonwalkers joined Alfred Worden (1932–   ) in lunar orbit where they ejected a 78-pound (35-kg) satellite

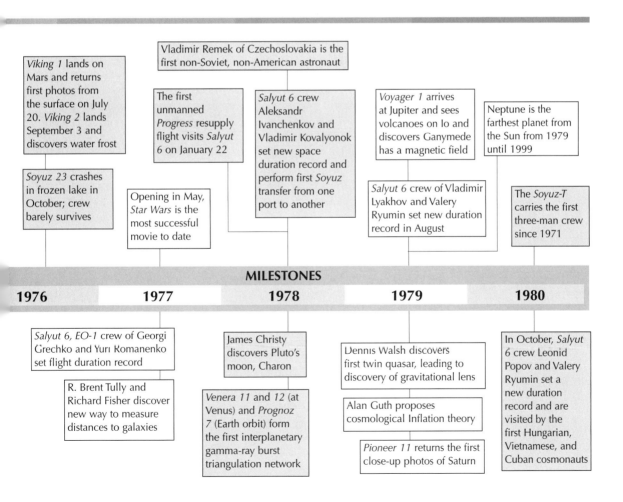

Vladimir Remek of Czechoslovakia is the first non-Soviet, non-American astronaut

Viking 1 lands on Mars and returns first photos from the surface on July 20. *Viking 2* lands September 3 and discovers water frost

The first unmanned *Progress* resupply flight visits *Salyut 6* on January 22

Salyut 6 crew Aleksandr Ivanchenkov and Vladimir Kovalyonok set new space duration record and perform first *Soyuz* transfer from one port to another

Voyager 1 arrives at Jupiter and sees volcanoes on Io and discovers Ganymede has a magnetic field

Neptune is the farthest planet from the Sun from 1979 until 1999

Soyuz 23 crashes in frozen lake in October; crew barely survives

Opening in May, *Star Wars* is the most successful movie to date

Salyut 6 crew of Vladimir Lyakhov and Valery Ryumin set new duration record in August

The *Soyuz-T* carries the first three-man crew since 1971

MILESTONES

1976   **1977**   **1978**   **1979**   **1980**

Salyut 6, EO-1 crew of Georgi Grechko and Yuri Romanenko set flight duration record

R. Brent Tully and Richard Fisher discover new way to measure distances to galaxies

James Christy discovers Pluto's moon, Charon

Venera 11 and *12* (at Venus) and *Prognoz 7* (Earth orbit) form the first interplanetary gamma-ray burst triangulation network

Dennis Walsh discovers first twin quasar, leading to discovery of gravitational lens

Alan Guth proposes cosmological Inflation theory

Pioneer 11 returns the first close-up photos of Saturn

In October, *Salyut 6* crew Leonid Popov and Valery Ryumin set a new duration record and are visited by the first Hungarian, Vietnamese, and Cuban cosmonauts that provided lunar data for a year. While 200,000 miles (320,000 km) from Earth, Worden performed the most distant spacewalk to date. *Apollo 15* splashed down on August 7 with two parachutes after one failed during reentry.

On August 12, 1971, *Kosmos 434* successfully completed the final test of the Soviet T2K. The engine designer, Mikhail Yangel, died content shortly after this test. But the N-1 booster that was to take it to the Moon had blown up spectacularly on June 27. Though the program continued for another year, the political motivation for it was gone, and Soviet leader Leonid Brezhnev (1906–82) cancelled the program in 1974. He replaced Vasily Mishin with Sergei Korolev's old accuser, Valentin Glushko. The existence of the N-1 program costing about 6 billion rubles in its 17-year existence was revealed to the public in 1989, the year that Glushko died.

While the manned program languished, Soviet robots explored the Moon. *Luna 18* crashed during landing in September, but *Luna 19* studied the Moon from orbit in October. On February 21, 1972, *Luna 20* landed on the Moon, retrieved a sample, and returned to Earth on the 25th.

The *Apollo 16* crew of John Young, Ken Mattingly (1936–) and Charlie Duke (1935–) launched on April 16, 1972 on the only mission to the lunar highlands. Young and Duke explored the rugged Descartes Mountains south of the equator. They collected 213 pounds of rocks during three excursions. The astronauts operated a portable magnetometer and recorded the first evidence of weak magnetism on the Moon. This implied that the Moon once had a molten interior and had spun faster on its axis. They landed on April 27.

A half-million people watched darkness become daylight when *Apollo 17* launched on December 7, 1972, at 12:33 A.M. Eugene Cernan and Ron Evans (1933–90) were joined by the first American scientist astronaut, geologist Harrison Schmitt (1935–). Cernan and Schmitt landed in a mountain-ringed valley named Taurus-Littrow. During three days of exploration using their rover (see photo opposite), they collected 243 pounds of rocks, including some dating back to the origin of the solar system. They splashed down on December 19, the last Moon mission of the 20th century.

A month later on January 15, 1973, Soviet *Luna 21* landed near the *Apollo 17* site. It deployed the solar-powered *Lunokhod 2* rover. The rover hibernated at night, heated by a radioactive source. *Lunokhod 2* operated until June 4, covering 23 miles (37 km) and returning 86 panoramic images and more than 80,000 TV pictures.

Luna 22 entered orbit on June 3, 1974, and operated for 18 months. *Luna 23* arrived on the Moon in October, but the sample collection failed. *Luna 24* landed in view of it in the Sea of Crises on August 18, 1976. *Luna 24* was the last of the series and the third Soviet mission to return a sample.

U.S. and Soviet lunar programs pushed the maturation of miniaturized electronics, high-strength, heat-resistant, low-weight materials,

The lunar rovers used on Apollo 15, 16, and 17 (shown here) allowed the astronauts to explore a lot more territory than earlier crews. (NASA)

and rocket engines. The first spin-offs of space technology reached the marketplace as pocket calculators, medical instrumentation, supermarket barcodes, and home computers. These practical applications were further investigated in the coming era of Earth-orbiting stations and spacecraft.

The First Space Stations

The Soviets launched the world's first space station, *Salyut 1*, on April 19, 1971. Four days later, *Soyuz 10* carrying Vladimir Shatalov, Alexei Yeliseyev, and Nikolai Rukavishnikov (1932–2002) achieved an incomplete "soft" dock with it. A problem with their hatch prevented entering the station.

On June 3, 1971, fear of tuberculosis caused doctors to disqualify Valeri Kubasov (1935–) from the upcoming *Soyuz 11* flight. Despite a protest from the mission commander, Alexei Leonov, the entire crew was replaced with their backups: Georgi Dobrovolsky (1928–71), Vladislav Volkov (1935–71), and Viktor Patsayev (1933–71).

Soyuz 11 launched three days later and used a new mechanism to achieve hard dock with *Salyut 1*. The crew busied themselves with experiments

The U.S.'s first space station, Skylab, lost a solar panel and part of the thermal shield during launch in May 1973. The first crew deployed a sunshade to cover the damaged area and released the solar panel that had been trapped next to the lab. The solar observatory and lab facilities provided the first long-duration data on the Sun and the effects of freefall on humans and materials.

and photography. Mission control cut short the planned 30-day mission after a fire and other problems. After 23.77 days in space, the history-making crew boarded their Soyuz for the trip home. The ship landed on June 29, 1971. The three men were found dead. A pressure-release valve had prematurely vented the cabin. The men were not wearing space suits and suffocated instantly.

Despite failure and tragedy, the Soviets continued to explore space. In April 1973, they launched their second space station. *Salyut 2* had been in space less than two weeks when the engine exploded. A military spy station called *Cosmos 557* met a similar fate in May.

On May 14, 1973, the United States launched its first space station. Made from leftover Saturn V boosters, *Skylab* (see figure below) was three and a half times bigger than *Salyut 1*. During launch, the combina-

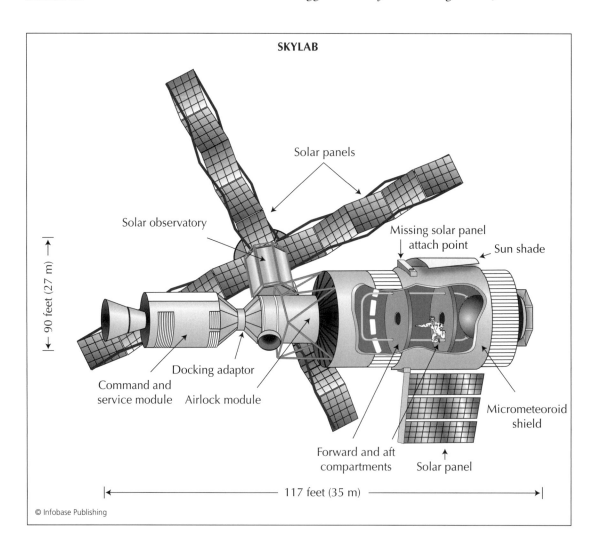

SKYLAB

Solar panels

Solar observatory

Missing solar panel attach point

Sun shade

90 feet (27 m)

Command and service module

Docking adaptor

Airlock module

Forward and aft compartments

Solar panel

Micrometeoroid shield

117 feet (35 m)

© Infobase Publishing

tion heat/meteoroid shield ripped off, taking a solar panel with it and jamming the other against the lab. The launch of the first crew, Charles "Pete" Conrad, medical doctor Joseph Kerwin (1932–   ), and Paul Weitz (1932–   ) was postponed while Mission Control considered what to do.

Without the heat shield, the temperature inside *Skylab* rose to 165°F (73°C). Food, film and medicine would quickly spoil at this temperature. If it remained high, the lab would become permanently uninhabitable as instruments failed and insulation emitted poisonous gases. Mission Control altered *Skylab*'s orientation to reduce sunshine on the damaged area. The temperature dropped but not enough.

A NASA technician designed a collapsible nylon umbrella using fishing poles. The crew and the "parasol" launched on May 25. The sun shade was pushed out a small scientific airlock and unfolded to cover the damaged area. The station cooled, and the men moved in. They studied the Sun, performed medical experiments, and showed off their 12,250 cubic-foot (347 cu-m) lab to the public. To free the trapped solar wing, Pete Conrad and Joe Kerwin did a daring space-walk through the maze of trusses outside *Skylab*. They assembled a 25-foot (7.6-m) pole out of tubing and attached a cutting tool to the end. They used the pole to cut the trapped wing free, doubling the power previously available. The crew returned on June 22, 1973, after 28 days in space.

The *Skylab 2* crew of Alan Bean, Jack Lousma (1936–   ), and solar physicist Owen Garriott (1930–   ) launched on July 28, 1973. Five days later, a master alarm blared from their Apollo module. One of four sets of steering rockets had lost pressure. Another set had already been shut down because of a leak. At least one set was required for entry. A thousand engineers worked around the clock analyzing the options. NASA prepared for an emergency rescue using an Apollo capsule modified to fit five men. It was not needed. Analysis showed that the two failures were not connected, and the crew resumed their mission. Garriott and Lousma set a new spacewalk record of six hours and 31 minutes. They erected a new sun shade to replace the deteriorated parasol. The entry on two rockets went smoothly, and the crew returned after a record of 59 days in space. Despite increased exercise, the men lost weight, red blood cells, and calcium. These changes would be further examined in future decades.

The Soviets launched a redesigned *Soyuz 12* on September 27, 1973, the first flight since the accident. The crew was reduced from three to two to accommodate space suits. A second test flight (*Soyuz 13*) on December 18 included a large ultraviolet camera.

The last of the *Skylab* missions launched on November 16, 1973. Gerald Carr (1932–   ), William Pogue (1930–   ), and Edward G. Gibson (1936–   ) observed comet Kohoutek during its closest approach to the Sun on December 28. "I tell you it's one of the most beautiful creations I've seen," Gibson said. The tail was more than 8 million miles

(13 million km) long. Their observations were coordinated with those of ground observers, making Kohoutek the most studied comet in history.

After a month in space, tension developed over the crew schedule. Mission Control was used to scheduling experiments tightly on short missions, and the crew wanted flexibility to follow up on discoveries and try new procedures. The planning process was changed, and performance dramatically improved for the rest of the 84-day mission.

On June 25, 1974, the Soviets launched *Salyut 3*, the first space station with solar arrays that were able to track the Sun. *Soyuz 14* visited from July 3 to 19. *Soyuz 15* failed to dock in August. *Salyut 3* reentered the atmosphere in January 1975. *Salyut 4* was launched on December 26, 1974. *Soyuz 17* docked with it on January 11, 1975, and the crew stayed for a month. *Soyuz 18* docked with *Salyut 4* from May 24 to July 26. This crew was in space during the Apollo-Soyuz Test Project (ASTP).

From Apollo-Soyuz to Shuttles

The *Apollo 13* and *Soyuz 11* accidents in 1970 and 1971 spurred efforts to develop an international rescue capability. NASA's Glynn Lunney (1936–   ) and Soviet Professor Konstantin Bushuyev (1914–78) worked out a way to dock the Apollo and Soyuz capsules despite hatches of different sizes and different operating pressures. On May 24, 1972, President Nixon and Premier Aleksei Kosygin (1904–80) authorized the Apollo-Soyuz Test Project (ASTP).

In January 1973, NASA announced the crew of Thomas Stafford, Vance Brand (1931–   ) and Donald (Deke) Slayton, an original Mercury astronaut who was finally cleared to fly after an operation cured his irregular heartbeat. The two-man Russian crew was announced at the Paris Air Show in May. Selected were Alexei Leonov and Valeri Kubasov who had almost flown the ill-fated *Soyuz 11*. More than 400,000 visitors flocked to the Apollo-Soyuz display.

The Soviets conducted two successful unmanned tests, *Cosmos 638* and *672*, of the modified Soyuz in April and August. But when *Soyuz 15* failed to dock with *Salyut 3* in August, the American media and Senator William Proxmire (1915–2005) questioned the safety of Russian hardware. On December 2, 1974, the *Soyuz 16* crew checked the systems to NASA's satisfaction, though Senator Proxmire continued to criticize the mission.

Soyuz 19 and *Apollo 18* launched from their separate countries on July 15, 1975. The historic docking took place on July 17. The two crews conducted joint operations for 47 hours. *Soyuz 19* landed on July 21. As *Apollo 18* descended on July 24, toxic fumes entered the cabin through an automatic air intake. Brand passed out. Stafford shut down the jets that were creating the fumes and got out gas masks. Brand revived quickly, but doctors said much more exposure would have killed them all.

The reduction in tensions between the two nuclear superpowers as a result of Apollo-Soyuz was welcomed by the scientific community. Carl

Sagan and others had postulated that the reason that the search for extra-terrestrial life had produced null results was that advanced civilizations had destroyed themselves in nuclear wars. It was hoped that cooperation in space would avoid the kind of planet-destroying disaster that was depicted in the blockbuster movie *Star Wars*, which opened in 1977.

Apollo-Soyuz was the last American manned spaceflight of the decade. The original shuttle proposal for a two-stage fully reusable vehicle was modified to cut the cost from $10 to $6 billion in 1971. The smaller orbiter with a separate external fuel tank and partially reusable solid rockets was approved in 1972 and planned to be ready by the end of 1977. The shuttle test vehicle *Enterprise* was flown in a series of five drop tests in 1977. Technical challenges with the engines and thermal tiles delayed final delivery of the first flight shuttle, *Columbia*, into the next decade.

The Soviets thought that the American shuttle was a cloaked military program, especially after approval of a shuttle launch facility at Vandenberg Air Force Base in California. Military payloads launched from Vandenberg could reach the main missile centers in Russia in only 3.5 minutes. Knowing that a first strike would decide a war, the Soviets pursued their own shuttle, *Buran* [blizzard], to launch on a new giant rocket called *Energia*.

Long-Duration Spaceflight

Princeton professor Gerard O'Neill (1927–92) imagined future space stations housing 10,000 people and supplying energy to Earth. His papers, books (see Further Reading), and appearances received front-page media coverage and inspired the creation of the nonprofit L-5 Society (later National Space Society) with the goal of building space settlements.

While Americans dreamed of space colonies, Russians focused on the practical problems of keeping two people in space. They launched *Salyut 5* on June 22, 1976. *Soyuz 21* docked to it from July 6 to August 25. The mission was cut short because Vitali Zholobov (1937–) became sick and psychotic. His poor health and that of his commander were blamed on toxic fumes.

After a successful Earth observation mission in September, the Soviets had a near disaster. *Soyuz 23* failed to dock with *Salyut 5*, so Valeri Rozhdestvensky (1939–) and Vyacheslav Zudov (1942–) began their return. Their Soyuz plunged into the frigid Lake Tengriz during a snow storm. The wet parachute dragged the capsule under water. Amphibious vehicles were unable to reach it. A cable was attached by swimmers, and a helicopter dragged the capsule for miles across the icy sea. The men barely survived overnight in the unheated capsule at below freezing temperatures.

Soyuz 24 docked to *Salyut 5* from February 7 to 25, 1977. No toxins were found in the cabin air. Yuri Gazkov (1939–) and Viktor Gorbatko (1934–) vented the cabin anyway and then returned to Earth.

The Russian Salyut 6 *space station was the first to have more than one docking port. With both an emergency crew escape and a supply ship that was able to dock, cosmonauts set an endurance record of 185 days in space.* (RKK Energia)

Determined to beat the American endurance record, the Soviets designed *Salyut 6* (see photo above) with two docking ports. One was for a return/escape ship, and the other for delivery of supplies and trash removal. No longer would time in space be limited by supplies taken on the initial trip. *Salyut 6* launched on September 29, 1977. *Soyuz 25* failed to dock in October. *Soyuz 26* arrived on December 10 with the first extended operations (EO) crew. Georgi Grechko (1931–) and Yuri Romanenko (1944–) performed the first Russian spacewalk since *Voskhod 2*. During 20 minutes outside, they inspected the port where *Soyuz 25* had failed to dock. It was undamaged and available for supply flights.

Oleg Makarov (1933–2003) and Vladimir Dzhanibekov (1942–) were the first people to visit a resident space-station crew when they arrived at *Salyut 6* on January 10, 1978. They stayed for five days and returned in *Soyuz 26*, leaving their "fresh" *Soyuz 27* for the *EO-1* crew to use for their return. This exchange of capsules was necessary because Soyuz tanks and systems gradually leaked and degraded in the vacuum of space. Replacing them every 90 days became standard procedure and provided opportunities to fly international visitors.

The first unmanned Progress arrived at the station on January 22, 1978. It brought food, air, water, and fuel. The crew unloaded *Progress 1*, filled it with waste, and sent it to burn up in the atmosphere. In March, Vladimir Remek (1946–) of Czechoslovakia became the first non-Soviet, non-American space traveler when he visited *Salyut 6*. The *EO-1* crew left in *Soyuz 27* on March 16, having spent 96 days in space. The Soviets had successfully solved the complicated logistics issues of long duration flight and beat the American endurance record set on *Skylab 4.*

The *EO-2* crew of Aleksandr Ivanchenkov (1940–) and Vladimir Kovalyonok (1942–) flew up in *Soyuz 29* on June 15, 1978, for another record-setting mission. The first Polish cosmonaut Miroslaw Hermaszewski (1941–) visited in June, and the first German cosmonaut, Sigmund Jaehn (1937–), visited in August. The resident crew moved the Soyuz to the forward port in October in the first of what became routine transfers. Only the aft port could be used for refueling, and this move cleared the way for *Progress 4.* The crew left the station on November 2, 1978, setting a record of 139.62 days in space.

The *EO-3* crew that launched on February 25, 1979, added several years of life to *Salyut 6* through a clever repair. A ruptured bellows in a fuel tank had allowed nitrogen to mix with the fuel. Vladimir Lyakhov (1941–) and Valeri Ryumin (1939–) first emptied one tank by putting its fuel in with another. Then the ground commanded the station to spin end over end to separate the fuel and the nitrogen in the damaged tank. The fuel was then pumped into the empty good tank and also into tanks on *Progress 5.* The damaged tank was vented, sealed, and filled with nitrogen. *Salyut 6* was left with two good tanks.

The first Bulgarian cosmonaut, Georgi Ivanov (1940–) had a short flight. An engine problem with *Soyuz 33* brought the ship home on April 12, 1979, without reaching the station. The *EO-3* crew needed a fresh Soyuz because their *Soyuz 32* capsule would exceed its 90-day-stay limit in May. So Mission Control sent *Soyuz 34* unmanned, and the crew sent *Soyuz 32* home unmanned. American systems never achieved this level of automation.

Progress 7 delivered a 770-pound (350-kg) KRT-10 radio telescope in June. After *Progress 7* cleared the port, Ryumin unfurled the antenna to its full 33-foot (10-m) diameter. On August 9, the antenna was supposed to separate from the station but caught on the aft docking target. The antenna blocked the engines and would prevent future supply flights. The crew rocked the station in an attempt to shake it free. This did not work, so they performed a spacewalk. Ryumin cut cables and pushed the antenna away with a barbed pole, clearing the port. They returned on *Soyuz 34* on August 19, 1979, having spent a record of 175 days in space.

The *EO-4* crew of Leonid Popov (1945–) and Valeri Ryumin launched on April 9, 1980. Ryumin had served on the previous long-duration crew and was a last-minute replacement for an injured Valentin Lebedev (1942–). The crew melted materials in furnaces to grow crystals and hosted four visiting crews during their six-month stay. The first Hungarian, Bertalan Farkas (1949–), was part of the first Soyuz "change-out" crew in April. Their Soyuz was in turn replaced by another visiting crew in July that included Pham Tuân (1947–) of Vietnam. In between these visits was a test of a redesigned Soyuz called the T-2 that cleared the way to resume three-man crews. The first Cuban cosmonaut, Arnaldo Tamayo–Méndez (1942–), visited in September. The *EO-4* crew left after 185 days on October 11, 1980, the longest stay time on *Salyut 6*.

Salyut 6's first three-man crew arrived on November 27, 1980. Leonid Kizim (1941–), Oleg Makarov, and Gennadi Strekalov (1940–2004) rode to space in *Soyuz T-3*. They spent most of their time maintaining the aging station and rode home on December 10, 1980, the last spaceflight of the decade.

Deserted Mars

The U.S. and Soviet space programs competed to be first in planetary exploration as well as manned programs. The American *Mariner 9* reached Mars just two weeks ahead of two Soviet ships and became the first spacecraft to enter Mars orbit on November 14, 1971. Soviet *Mars 2* went into orbit on November 27, completing 362 orbits. Its lander crashed. The Soviet *Mars 3* lander was the first to make it intact to the surface but shut down 20 seconds later, a possible victim of a global dust storm. The *Mars 3* orbiter completed only 20 orbits. Images of the battered moons *Phobos* and *Deimos* put to rest I. S. Shklovskii's theory that the satellites were artificial remnants of an extinct Martian civilization.

Mariner 9 operated until October 1972, providing the first global map of Mars. The map revealed the solar system's largest volcano, Olympus Mons (see figure opposite), and the Valles Marineris, a canyon 2,500 miles (4,000 km) long and three times deeper than the Grand Canyon. The map and dust-storm data proved the theory that was postulated by Carl Sagan and Jim Pollack (1939–94) that blowing dust (not vegetation) produce observed color and brightness changes. Sagan and Pollack had speculated that the Martian canals were geological features akin to the midocean ridges of Earth. *Mariner 9* showed no ridges. Percival Lowell's canals were indeed illusions. Left to be determined was whether or not there was life on Mars.

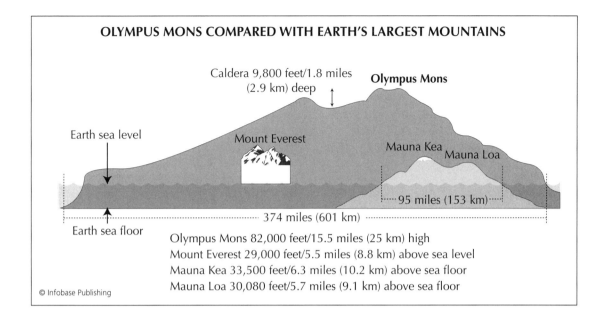

OLYMPUS MONS COMPARED WITH EARTH'S LARGEST MOUNTAINS

Caldera 9,800 feet/1.8 miles (2.9 km) deep

Olympus Mons

Earth sea level

Mount Everest

Mauna Kea   Mauna Loa

95 miles (153 km)

374 miles (601 km)

Earth sea floor

Olympus Mons 82,000 feet/15.5 miles (25 km) high
Mount Everest 29,000 feet/5.5 miles (8.8 km) above sea level
Mauna Kea 33,500 feet/6.3 miles (10.2 km) above sea floor
Mauna Loa 30,080 feet/5.7 miles (9.1 km) above sea floor

© Infobase Publishing

The next batch of Soviet ships arrived in February and March of 1974. *Mars 4* and *7* missed the planet. *Mars 5* failed after a few days in orbit. *Mars 6* provided 224 seconds of data—the first data on the atmosphere—then crashed.

Next up was the $1.1 billion American dual Viking missions. Carl Sagan claimed in the *New York Times* in February 1975 that there was "no reason to exclude from Mars organisms ranging in size from ants to polar bears." He raised public expectations more by parading a snake, a chameleon, and two tortoises past a Viking camera at Great Sand Dunes National Monument.

Viking 1 landed on July 20, 1976, on a barren orange–red desert in Chryse Planitia. No ants or polar bears basked under the pink sky. To check for microscopic life, dirt was scooped into onboard biology experiments.

Biology team leader Harold Klein (1921–2001), considered to be the father of exobiology, reported that the Gas Exchange experiment showed that the soil was "very active" with "some chemical or physical entity." Next was the Labeled Release experiment. A radioactive broth was added to a sample of soil in a closed chamber. Any organisms present would presumably absorb the broth and release gas that contained radioactive carbon. When the broth was added to the soil, a detector in the chamber measured radioactive gas. No gas was released when the soil was heated before broth was added, presumably because heating killed the organisms. Excitement built until the next phase of the experiment. When more broth was added to the unheated soil, there was no new release of gas as there would be for a growing organism. This ambiguous result was

Mariner 9 provided the first global map of Mars in 1971. Olympus Mons was revealed as the solar system's largest mountain, nearly three times taller than Mount Everest (measured from sea level) and two and a half times taller than Mauna Kea (measured from the sea floor to the peak)

interpreted by Klein as a chemical reaction. Team member Gilbert Levin (1924–   ) disagreed. He performed numerous tests and research into the 21st century in support of his conclusion that there is life on Mars.

The Miller–Urey experiment in 1953 had shown how easy it is for organic molecules (the building blocks of life) to form from a "primordial soup" of chemicals. But the Viking Gas Chromatograph–Mass Spectrometer did not detect any organic molecules in the Martian soil. Norman Horowitz (1915–2005), a Nobel-Prize-winning biologist, concluded that Mars was lifeless.

On September 3, 1976, *Viking 2* landed on Mars's Utopia Planitia and repeated the biology experiments. Dr. Levin saw lifelike colors in the pictures. Others could not distinguish the colors from noise in the data. Carl Sagan scrutinized the images for signs of life such as trails or footprints. All he found was a letter *B* on a rock. The team report said, "It is clear that a single letter by itself is not sufficiently improbable to force the hypothesis of intelligent origin." In an appearance on the *Tonight Show*, Sagan remarked how absurd it would be for aliens to carve the letter *B* on a rock.

Picturing Venus

Models of Venus evolved from steamy jungles to dry deserts to global oceans of carbonated water. In 1967, Carl Sagan suggested that "float bladder macro-organisms" might live in the atmosphere. Gerard Kuiper argued in 1969 that dust particles, not ice, caused the clouds to be opaque. Radar studies of the surface in 1970 detected dark, circular regions that were interpreted as giant impact basins. All of these models would be found lacking before the end of the decade.

Soviet *Venera 8* landed on Venus on July 22, 1972. With a new refrigeration system, it survived the intense heat for 50 minutes. Scientists were surprised that *Venera 8* measured light levels that were similar to a cloudy day on Earth. They had not included a camera because they assumed that almost no light would penetrate the thick clouds.

The Americans sent *Mariner 10* past Venus in November 1973 (the first *gravity assist*) and discovered a cometlike tail of particles from the solar wind. *Mariner 10* then flew past Mercury in March of 1974, becoming the only spacecraft to see that cratered world in the 20th century.

Everyone agreed about one aspect of Venus: it was hot. In his 1950 book *Worlds in Collision* (see Further Reading), psychiatrist Immanuel Velikovsky (1895–1979) proposed that Venus was a comet that had been ejected by Jupiter. Velikovsky promoted his mythology-based theories on Canadian and British television in 1972 and 1973. By February 1974, his ideas were so widespread that the American Association for the Advancement of Science sponsored a debate between Velikovsky and Carl Sagan. Sagan showed that Velikovsky's "prediction" of Venus being hot was not a prediction at all because he had not defined how hot it would be. Sagan pointed out that Rupert Wildt (1905–76) had given

BEHEPA-9 22.10.1975   OБPAБOTKA ИППИ AH CCCP 28.2.1976

temperature ranges and suggested the cause as the greenhouse effect back in 1940. Other scientists had calculated that the energy required to eject Venus from Jupiter would not merely heat it up but would vaporize it. Logic and data overcame myth and pseudoscience, and Sagan was declared winner of the debate.

Pseudoscience aside, Venus was still a "hot" topic. In October 1975, *Venera 9* and *10* sent back the first photos (see photo above) from the surface. There was no ocean, only pancake-shaped rocks under a rosy-peach sky. The surface temperature was 890°F (477°C), hotter than anyone had predicted. The clouds were not thick with dust or ice. Instead, the spectra matched that of sulfuric acid. A human who survived the descent to the surface would be crushed by pressures 93 times that of Earth. Under a thick veil of clouds, Venus offered a poisonous hell.

Venera 11 and *12* arrived at Venus in December 1978. The camera covers did not eject, and the soil-collection experiments failed. The *Venera 11* and *12* orbiters operated successfully. In combination with *Prognoz* 7, a Soviet-French satellite launched into a highly elliptical Earth orbit in 1978, they formed the first interplanetary gamma-ray-burst triangulation network through June 1979. The three satellites detected 30 gamma-ray bursts.

Pioneer Venus was the last in this decade. It arrived on December 4, 1978, and provided radar maps and other data until May 1992. A set of four probes arrived on a separate spacecraft (*Pioneer 13*) and entered the atmosphere on December 9. The probes showed evidence of lightning and distinct layers in the atmosphere.

Soviet Venera 9 *sent back this first photo of the surface of Venus in October 1975. The white object at the bottom of the image is part of the lander. Rocks are 12–15 inches (30–40 cm) across, and the horizon is visible in the upper corners, distorted by the imaging system. This photo dispelled any notions of Venus as a wet jungle world.* (NASA)

Exploring the Giants

Crowds gathered on the stormy night of March 2, 1972, to watch the launch of the first spacecraft destined to leave the solar system. *Pioneer 10* would provide the first close look at Jupiter. Then it would sail out, reaching Aldebaran in Taurus in about 2 million years. Attached to an antenna strut was a plaque declaring humanity's existence to any intelligent beings who might pluck it from the vast ocean of space.

Science writer Eric Burgess (1920–) suggested the plaque to Carl Sagan in 1971. Sagan recruited his wife Linda Salzman to do the

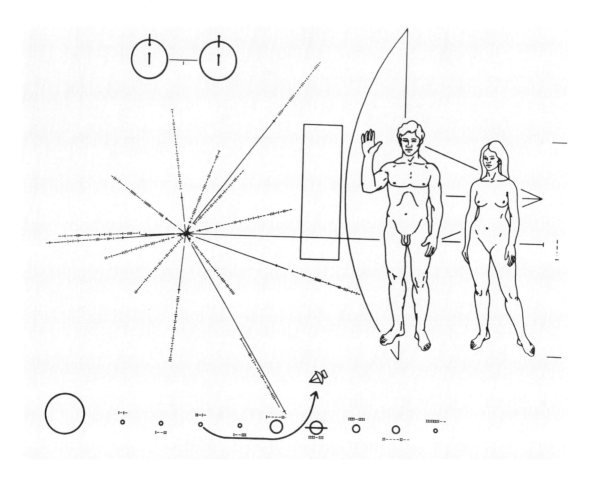

The Pioneer plaque by Carl and Linda Sagan and Frank Drake was etched into a gold, anodized, aluminum plate and mounted on an antenna strut to protect it from interstellar dust. A schematic of a hydrogen atom acts as a universal yardstick and clock. The radial pattern shows the Sun's position relative to 14 pulsars. The spacecraft's origin is shown in a diagram of the solar system. The humans are drawn to scale with the spacecraft. (NASA)

artwork and Frank Drake, his colleague at Cornell, to design an appropriate plaque (see figure above). NASA agreed to include it on *Pioneer 10* and *11*.

On July 15, 1972, *Pioneer 10* became the first spacecraft to enter the *asteroid belt* between Mars and Jupiter. Scientists predicted that the craft had a one in 10 chance of being hit by a particle more than 1/50 of an inch (0.05 cm) in diameter traveling at 15 times the speed of a rifle bullet. When *Pioneer 10* emerged undamaged from the asteroid belt in February 1973, scientists cleared the almost identical *Pioneer 11* for launch in April.

The mission requirements of *Pioneer 10* pushed spacecraft design to new levels. Nuclear radioisotope power generators (RTGs) were developed to provide electrical power for the long mission far from the Sun. To safeguard the experiments from radiation, science instruments were mounted on one of three booms, with two RTGs on each of the other two booms. Multiple blankets of aluminized plastic, electric heaters, and louvers to release excess heat protected the equipment from impacts and extreme temperatures.

Radio signals become weaker with distance because the waves spread out. At Jupiter's distance, an 85-foot (26-m) antenna on Earth would require 16.7 million years to gather enough energy from *Pioneer 10*'s transmitter to light a 7.5-watt nightlight for a thousandth of a second. More-powerful transmitters were too heavy for rockets to accelerate to the speeds necessary to reach Jupiter. But the Deep Space Network (DSN) was able to capture these faint signals even when *Pioneer 10* crossed the orbit of Neptune (that was farther than Pluto from 1979 to 1999). To avoid noise in the data, the rate at which information was transmitted, called the bit rate, was lowered while the duration of the bit itself was increased. The spacecraft was also spin stabilized so the antenna axis, like the tip of a spinning top, remained pointed toward Earth. The signal to Earth was detected until February 7, 2003.

One of *Pioneer 10*'s primary objectives was to determine how close it could reach without damage from Jupiter's radiation. The total dose was a combination of the intensity and duration of exposure. A close approach increased the intensity of the radiation, but it also accelerated the craft's speed so that the exposure duration was less. The scientists opted for a distance of about one and a half Jupiter's diameter.

The DSN received the first close-up pictures of Jupiter on November 26, 1973. The next day, instruments confirmed that Jupiter's magnetic field is upside-down compared to Earth's. The radiation dose saturated several experiments, but none failed. *Pioneer 10* showed that the Great Red Spot, first observed in 1664, is a collection of hurricanes that rise above all other clouds. Early astronomers thought that the spot was a raft or an island because clouds swept around it. Smaller storms appeared as bright white spots.

Pioneer 10 survived its radiation dose, so *Pioneer 11* was directed to approach three times closer. In December 1973, it flew over Jupiter's polar region, seeing blue sky through the cloud tops. The closer approach gave *Pioneer 11* enough gravity assist to head for Saturn.

On September 1, 1979, *Pioneer 11* flew within 13,000 miles (21,000 km) of Saturn. Instruments found an extra ring and two new moons. Titan, with its thick nitrogen-methane atmosphere, was found to be too cold to have liquid water.

After the Pioneers, astronomers hoped to take advantage of a planetary lineup that happens about every 179 years. This "Grand Tour" included four launches to the outer planets between 1977 and 1979. Budget cuts scrubbed the plan to two spacecraft, *Voyager 1* and *2*. The Voyagers were almost three times heavier and had about nine times more power than the Pioneers. *Voyager 2* launched on August 20, 1977. *Voyager 1* launched on September 5, but because of Earth's motion, bypassed *Voyager 2* as it sped through the asteroid belt.

On July 2, 1978, astronomer James Christy (1938–) discovered Pluto's first moon. (Two more were found in 2005.) The discovery of Charon (pronounced SHAR-on) allowed the mass of Pluto to be determined. Prior to this, astronomers thought that Pluto was much larger because the images of Charon and Pluto were blurred together.

Voyager 1 reached Jupiter and its moons on March 5, 1979. It discovered rings around Jupiter, confirmed the prediction of volcanoes on Io, and discovered that Ganymede has a magnetic field and a molten core. *Voyager 2* followed with its closest approach on July 9. Together, the two Voyagers observed nine volcanoes on Io with plumes extending 190 miles (300 km) above the surface. Material from Io was seen swept outward by Jupiter's magnetic field to form a torus of ions around the planet. *Voyager 2*'s images of Europa showed features so flat that one scientist said that they "might have been painted on with a felt marker." They speculated that the moon may have a thin crust of water ice over a deep ocean. Five new moons were found because of Voyager data, bringing the total to 16.

Voyager 1 reached Saturn on November 12, 1980. Small moons were found that "shepherd" material around the rings. The irregular shape of the smallest moons reinforced the theory that the rings are fragments of larger bodies. Spokes in the rings were proposed as the result of electrostatic charging effects. Saturn's magnetic field was found to extend out more than 1 million miles (2 million km) and be perfectly aligned with its rotational axis. The moon Enceladus displayed faults and valleys, and Mimas was scarred with an impact that should have broken it apart. *Voyager 1*'s trajectory sent it past Titan and behind Saturn's rings. This trajectory bent the spacecraft's path northward out of the ecliptic plane—the plane of the Sun's equator—and prevented encounters with Uranus and Neptune. *Voyager 2* would provide the first close-ups of those worlds in the next decade.

Observing Space

New observatories in space provided a wealth of data on the Sun, the galaxies, and other objects and mapped the sky in ultraviolet, gamma-ray, and X-ray wavelengths. This data allowed astronomers to find long-period pulsars, designate Cygnus X-1 as the first black-hole candidate, establish that Seyfert galaxies emit X-rays, and discover X-ray emitting gas in galaxy clusters.

Combining this data with ground observations revealed new correlations. In 1976, Sandra Faber (1944–) and Robert Jackson (1949–) discovered the Faber-Jackson relation that the brightest elliptical galaxies have the biggest spread of stellar velocities. Because stars in massive galaxies orbit faster, the greater the velocity spread, the greater the mass of the galaxy. Assuming a standard distribution of stars, the mass estimate leads to a brightness estimate. Comparing calculated brightness with the observed brightness yields distance. Beatrice Tinsley (1941–81) showed in 1966 that galaxies evolve as they age, and thus brightness changes while size and shape may not. Therefore, distances found using the Faber-Jackson relation are not very accurate.

In 1977, R. Brent Tully (1943–) and Richard J. Fisher (1943–) discovered that the brightness of a spiral galaxy correlates with the rotational speed of its gas disk. This rotation leads to an estimate of the galaxy's mass, true brightness, and distance. The Tully-Fisher relation is the measurement tool of choice for distant spirals because it correlates well with distances that are found by using Cepheid variables.

In 1974, graduate student Russell Hulse (1950–) used a computerized search and the Arecibo radio telescope to find the first binary pulsar, PSR 1913+16. He and his adviser, Joseph H. Taylor (1941–), immediately realized the significance of this discovery. This system "provides a nearly ideal relativity laboratory including an accurate clock in a high-speed, eccentric orbit and a strong gravitational field," Russell Hulse wrote in announcing the discovery in the *Astrophysical Journal* (see Further Reading). The two astrophysicists predicted that effects of general relativity would cause a four-degree rotation of the elliptical orbit per year. This prediction was confirmed and allowed the first measurement of the mass of a neutron star (about 1.4 solar masses). It also proved the theory of general relativity to a new level of accuracy, for which the men shared a Nobel Prize in physics in 1993.

In 1979, British astronomer Dennis Walsh (1933–2005) and collaborators discovered the first twin quasar. The two images in Ursa Major were six seconds of arc apart and are almost identical in their spectra, absorption lines and redshifts. Dennis Walsh proposed that a galaxy between Earth and a distant quasar acted as a gravitational lens (see figure below) and split the light to create two images of one object. This

Dennis Walsh discovered in 1979 that the twin quasar Q0957+561 is actually a double image of a single object whose light is split by a massive elliptical galaxy acting as a gravitational lens.

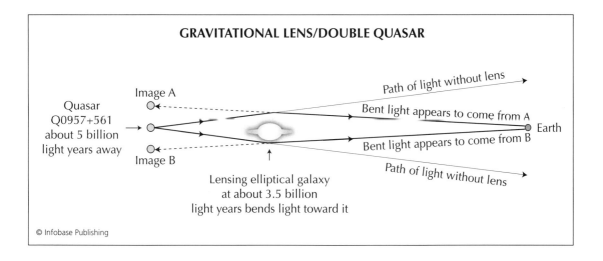

GRAVITATIONAL LENS/DOUBLE QUASAR

Quasar Q0957+561 about 5 billion light years away

Image A

Image B

Path of light without lens

Bent light appears to come from A

Bent light appears to come from B

Path of light without lens

Earth

Lensing elliptical galaxy at about 3.5 billion light years bends light toward it

© Infobase Publishing

Scientist of the Decade: Carl Edward Sagan (1934–1996)

Through television, books, and speeches, Carl Sagan became the most publicly recognized scientist of the 1970s. "The popularization of science . . . the communication not just of the findings but of the methods of science seems to me as natural as breathing," he said at a conference in Seattle in 1994. "After all, when you're in love, you want to tell the world."

Born to Jewish parents in Brooklyn, New York, on November 9, 1934, Carl fell in love with science at an early age. School bored him even after he skipped several grades. *Astounding* (later *Analog*) science-fiction magazine and Edgar Rice Burroughs's novels nurtured his creative imagination. He planned to be an astronomer. His grandfather remarked, "Yes, but how will you make your living?"

In 1947, the Sagans moved to Rahwey, New Jersey, and Carl happily discovered that astronomers actually were paid. He graduated at the age of 16 and enrolled at the University of Chicago.

During summer break, Sagan worked at Indiana University under Nobel Prize–winning biologist Hermann Muller (1890–1967). Hermann Muller shared Sagan's love of science fiction and the belief that there was life on other planets. Sagan got his bachelor's degree in physics in 1955 and his masters' in 1956. He spent the summer at McDonald Observatory under Gerard Kuiper.

Sagan did his thesis work at the University of Chicago's Yerkes Observatory. He organized a lecture series on "The Creation of Life and the Universe" in 1957. Despite standing-room-only crowds, some faculty members disapproved of "Sagan's circus." His interest in aliens and popularizing science did not sit well with conservative scientists.

After Sputnik in 1957, Carl Sagan worked part time for NASA. In his 1960 Ph.D. thesis, he proposed that water vapor contributed to Venus's greenhouse effect. *Mariner 2* flyby data in 1962 supported his conclusions, though other gases later proved to cause the greenhouse.

Sagan and Lynn Alexander (later Margulis, 1938–) met at the University of Chicago and

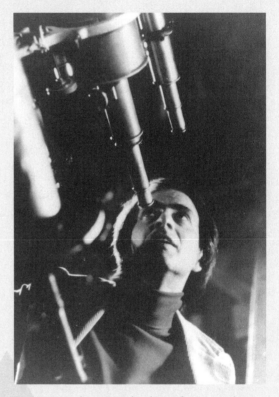

Astronomer Carl Sagan was best known for Cosmos, his popular television series that aired on Public Television in 1980. He is shown here at Lowell Observatory in 1979. (Cornell University; AIP Emilio Segrè Visual Archives)

were married in 1957. The marriage failed as Lynn struggled with graduate school (she became a renowned biologist) and caring for sons Dorion Solomon (1959–) and Jeremy Ethan (1960–) with no help from the self-absorbed Sagan. They divorced in 1963.

Sagan received a fellowship to the University of California at Berkeley in 1960. This led to an appointment with the Smithsonian Astrophysical Observatory and an assistant astronomy professorship at Harvard in 1962. Before moving to Massachusetts, he studied exobiology at Stanford under Nobel winner Joshua Lederberg (1925–   ). During this time, Sagan worked on a secret government program to detonate an atomic bomb on the Moon.

In 1966, Sagan collaborated on *Intelligent Life in the Universe* with I. S. Shklovskii. He also coauthored *The Planets,* speculating that "balloon" animals may live in planetary atmospheres. In 1968, he became editor of the journal *Icarus.*

Sagan was an outstanding teacher at Harvard. But his research was considered too speculative and superficial by traditional scientists. So, in 1968, he was denied tenure. Sagan then took a job with Cornell. He and his new wife, artist Linda Salzman (1940–   ), moved to Ithaca, New York. Nicholas Julian Zapata Sagan was born in 1970.

Sagan thought that microbes were plentiful in the solar system. He advocated NASA's quarantine of astronauts to prevent contamination. He was disappointed in 1969 when Apollo Moon rocks showed no sign of life. In 1971, Sagan was disappointed again when no alien messages were found via the giant Arecibo radio telescope. In 1972, Sagan and Frank Drake designed the famous plaque for *Pioneer 10* that included drawings by Carl Sagan's wife Linda Salzman.

Carl Sagan became a household name in 1973 after the first of many appearances on the *Tonight Show*. His book, *The Cosmic Connection: An Extraterrestrial Perspective,* was a best-seller. Scientists felt that he had sold out to the celebrity machine, but audiences were captivated by the hip and handsome astronomer who debunked UFO sightings, yet spoke of his belief in alien life. In 1977, Carl Sagan published *The Dragons of Eden*. This book about the nature of intelligence won the Pulitzer Prize. This was followed in 1978 by *Murmurs of the Earth: The Voyager Interstellar Record,* that Sagan coauthored with Drake, his current and future wives, and two others.

While working on the *Viking* and *Voyager* programs in 1976, Sagan fell in love with Ann Druyan (1949–   ). After a messy divorce from Linda Salzman, Sagan married Ann Druyan in 1981. Rachel (Sasha) was born in 1982, and Samuel Democritus Druyan in 1991.

Sagan took leave from Cornell in 1978 and moved with Ann Druyan to Los Angeles to work on *Cosmos*. The 13-part PBS series debuted in 1980. He explored the universe in his "spaceship of the mind," walking on a cosmic calendar and sliding down a black hole. *Cosmos* won three Emmys and a Peabody award. Sagan, the "showman of science," adorned the cover of *Time* magazine and founded the Planetary Society in 1980.

Sagan worried that extraterrestrials had not been found because they had blown themselves up in wars. So he used his fame to protest nuclear weapons. He was arrested for civil disobedience, addressed the pope, and wrote a book about nuclear winter. The tensions of the cold war and his own near-death after an operation in 1983 also inspired books. *Shadows of Forgotten Ancestors: A Search for Who We Are,* written with Ann, explored social evolution. *Contact,* a fictional meeting with aliens published in 1985, netted him a $2 million advance.

Controversy followed Carl Sagan. Jealous scientists blocked his admission to the National Academy of Sciences in 1992. But 300 people expressed support for his work at his 60th birthday in 1994. Students said that they had majored in science and decided to study planets because of Sagan. An African student started an astronomy club after reading *Cosmos*. A Russian scientist told how Sagan had influenced President Mikhail Gorbachev (1931–   ) to suggest a joint Mars mission with the United States. Sagan was then informed that asteroids had been named 2709 Sagan and 4973 Druyan.

In 1995, Sagan was diagnosed with bone-marrow disease. Between treatments, he worked on the filming for *Contact* and wrote *Demon-Haunted World: Science as a Candle in the Dark* (1996), and *Billions and Billions: Thoughts on Life and Death at the Brink of the Millennium* (1997). Sagan contracted pneumonia after a last appearance on *Nightline* and died on December 20, 1996. His many television, radio, novel, and spacecraft messages continue to speed out into the cosmos.

interpretation was reinforced with the discovery of a galaxy nearly in front of one of the images.

Other examples of gravitational lensing with triple and quadruple images were later discovered. For objects that are not aligned, the path that the light takes around the lens results in different flight times for the images. The time delay for brightening of a variable quasar can then be used to find its distance.

New observational data led to new questions about galactic distribution and movements. By measuring the peculiar velocities (movement toward mass concentrations) of hundreds of galaxies, astronomers estimated the *density parameter* Ω (omega) of the universe. It was found to be close to one, meaning that space is flat. Even adding in the presence of dark matter in galaxies, confirmed by Vera Rubin through multiple observations in this decade, did not change the conclusion. A more massive universe would be curved and eventually contract. A lower mass universe would expand forever. The big bang theory offered no explanation for how a universe with a uniform cosmic background radiation (CBR) ended up clumped into galaxies or how it ended up so flat.

In 1979, Alan Guth (1947–) proposed the inflation theory to address these problems. Inflation states that 10^{-34} seconds after the big bang, the universe was on the brink of a *phase change*. During inflation, gravity was repulsive, and the universe doubled in size every 10^{-34} seconds. At 10^{-32} seconds, the universe underwent a phase change, and gravity became attractive, ending inflation and beginning the Hubble expansion. With inflation, the universe was small enough long enough for the temperatures to have equalized in all directions, explaining the uniformity of the CBR. Small random fluctuations were magnified during inflation, leading to large-scale clusters. The rapid expansion flattened space similar to the way that an expanding balloon appears flat to an ant on its surface. Many variations of this theory were proposed in the next few decades and tested by new observations and methods.

Further Reading

Books and Periodicals

Davidson, Keay. *Carl Sagan: A Life*. New York: John Wiley & Sons, Inc., 1999. This book provides much detail on the life and times of Carl Sagan.

Ezell, Edward Clinton, and Linda Neuman Ezell. *The Partnership: A History of the Apollo–Soyuz Test Project. NASA SP–4209*. Washington, D.C.: Scientific and Technical Information Office, 1978. This book offers a comprehensive history of the Apollo–Soyuz program with numerous diagrams and photos of the hardware and quotes from original sources.

Fimmel, Richard, William Swindell, and Eric Berger. *Pioneer Odyssey. SP–349/396*. Washington, D.C.: NASA History Office, 1977. Available online. URL: http://history.nasa.gov/SP-349/sp349.htm. Accessed on March 11, 2006. This book includes images and descriptions of the Pioneer spacecraft visit to Jupiter in 1974.

Hulse, R. A., and J. H. Taylor. "Discovery of a Pulsar in a Binary System." *Astrophysical Journal* 195 (January 1975): L51–L53. Available online. URL: http://articles.adsabs.harvard.edu//full/seri/ApJ../0195//L000051.000.html. The paper includes the observations and details of the orbital parameters of the pulsar.

Lundquist, Charles A., ed. *Skylab's Astronomy and Space Sciences. NASA SP–404.* Washington, D.C.: Scientific and Technical Information Office, 1979. Available online. URL: http://history.nasa.gov/SP-404/ch4.htm. Read this book to learn more about the astronomy done from Skylab, including observations of Comet Kohoutek.

O'Neill, Gerard K. *The High Frontier: Human Colonies in Space.* New York: William Morrow and Company, Inc., 1977. This visionary view of what life would be like on a city-sized space station at the distance of the Moon began the space movement and forms the core ideas of the National Space Society.

———. *2081: A Hopeful View of the Human Future.* New York: Simon and Schuster, 1981. The book describes the drivers of change: computers, automation, space colonies, abundant energy, and communications that will lead to an improved human condition.

Velikovsky, Immanuel. *Worlds in Collision.* New York: Pocket Books, 1977. Based on mythology and religious writings, the author postulates that Venus was formed and moved into its current orbit about 4,000 years ago.

Web Sites

Russell Hulse and Joseph Taylor, Jr. "Nobel Prize in Physics 1993." NobelPrize.org. Available online. URL: http://nobelprize.org/physics/laureates/1993/index.html. Accessed on August 31, 2006. The site contains the Nobel lecture describing the discovery and significance of the first binary pulsar.

Kenneth R. Land. "NASA's Cosmos." NASA and Tufts University. Available online. URL: http://ase.tufts.edu/cosmos/index.asp. Accessed on August 31, 2006. This resource provides an overview, tutorial, and images about recent discoveries from space missions to the planets, asteroids, and comets and the search for life, with text and figures excerpted from books written by Professor Land.

David R. Williams. "Chronology of Venus Exploration." NASA Goddard Spaceflight Center. Available online. URL: http://nssdc.gsfc.nasa.gov/planetary/chronology_venus.html. Accessed on August 31, 2006. The time line lists missions to Venus from 1961 through planned missions in 2009 with links to details about the spacecraft and the science data returned.

9

1981–1990:
Laboratories in Space

More people of different backgrounds and nationalities flew in space during this decade than ever before. These people took advantage of the new American space shuttle (see figure on page 194) that made its debut on April 12, 1981, and is a major topic of this chapter. After four test flights, this first reusable spacecraft hauled commercial, military, and science payloads into space with crews of up to eight people. The flights of the first American woman and black scientist (see photo on page 195) in 1983 demonstrated that space was no longer just for military pilots. Scientists from friendly nations flew alongside Americans in the modular *Spacelab* (see figure on page 196) built by the European Space Agency (ESA).

The chapter describes the achievements of the first five years of shuttle flights. The pressure to increase flight rate and reduce costs led to the loss of the space shuttle *Challenger* (see photo on page 204) with a crew of seven in January 1986. The shuttle fleet was grounded until 1988 while NASA implemented technical and management changes. After the accident, the shuttle was restricted to scientific missions, including deployment of the *Magellan*, *Galileo*, *Hubble*, and *Ulysses* spacecraft.

The chapter also describes the Soviet mastering of the logistics of maintaining people in space. Their crews successfully set duration records of 211 and then 237 days on their *Salyut* 7 space station. Because their Soyuz-manned "taxis" had to be replaced more often than the station crews, the Soviets flew many foreign scientists. The second female cosmonaut flew a year before America's first woman and did a spacewalk the next year. Cosmonauts completed impressive repairs and salvage operations on *Salyut* 7. They applied the lessons learned through that program to their new *Mir* space station launched in 1986. Its modular design, multiple docking ports, and automatic systems reduced the number of supply flights needed for extended crew durations. Vladimir Titov (1947–   ) and Musa Manarov (1951–   ) became the first humans to spend more than a year in space at the end of 1988. By the end of the decade, *Mir* had four modules and had hosted six extended-duration crews.

On the planetary front, the chapter focuses on continued exploration of Venus and comets, including Halley's comet that returned in 1986 and *Voyager 2*'s flyby of both Uranus in 1986 and Neptune in 1989. This mission took advantage of the method of gravity assist (see figure on page 206).

In 1987, the first supernova visible to the naked eye from Earth since 1604 exploded into view. The new insights provided by supernova 1987A (see photo on page 213) are covered in the chapter, as well as new observations of the Milky Way and the distribution of galaxies. Astronomers revealed that galaxies lie in thin sheets with large voids between them, with the largest structure called the Great Wall. Local clusters were shown moving toward an invisible mass called the Great Attractor.

While most astronomers studied visible objects, the featured scientist of the decade, Vera Rubin (see sidebar and photo on pages 210–211), asked questions about unseen matter. In the previous decade, she had discovered that Andromeda's rotation required much more mass than what was visible to remain gravitationally bound. In this decade, she and her colleagues generalized that result to other galaxies, proving that humans have much yet to learn about space.

Space Transportation System

The launch of the first space shuttle (see figure on page 194) was picture perfect. On April 12, 1981, a half-million people watched as veteran moonwalker John Young and rookie Robert Crippen (1937–) rode the first reusable spacecraft into orbit. The three main engines efficiently burned liquid hydrogen and oxygen from the large external tank mounted below the orbiter's belly. The two solid rockets added thrust for the first two minutes, separated, and then parachuted into the ocean for recovery. In less than nine minutes, the empty external tank was dropped, and the orbiter *Columbia* was in space.

The payload bay doors had to be opened to expose the radiator panels before the orbiter ran out of water for cooling. When the doors opened, an expanding cloud of assembly debris, shaken loose during launch, floated out into space. Chuckles in Mission Control were quickly replaced with gasps as the tail area came into view. Like a gap-toothed smile, dark squares appeared where white thermal tiles had been on the engine pods. Controllers feared that tiles from the underside may also have fallen off. If so, burn-through during entry could cause the loss of the vehicle (that happened in 2003).

The crew had no cameras with which to check the underside of the orbiter, so NASA secretly asked the air force to use spy satellites. They reported that the underside appeared intact. This was a relief because there was no on-orbit repair or rescue capability. (A spacecraft launched from Russia could not reach the low-inclination orbit.) The ejection seats could not be used above 100,000 feet (30,000 m).

During a period of entry called blackout, direct communications to the ground are blocked by ions in the superheated air. Despite the air force report, flight controllers worried that tiles might come loose during this critical time. A loud cheer went up from Mission Control when Robert Crippen reported that all was well. *Columbia* landed safely at Edwards Air Force Base in California on April 14.

Within days, *Columbia* was bolted to the top of a Boeing 747 and ferried to Kennedy Space Center. A fuel spill delayed the second flight from September until November 12. Space Transportation System flight 2 (STS-2) was planned for five days. It was cut short after one of three fuel cell power plants failed about two hours into flight. Despite this, the crew of Joe Engle (1932–) and Richard Truly (1937–) put the $100 million Canadian robotic arm through its paces. The 50-foot, six-jointed arm passed all its tests. The fuel cell problem was corrected before the next flight in March.

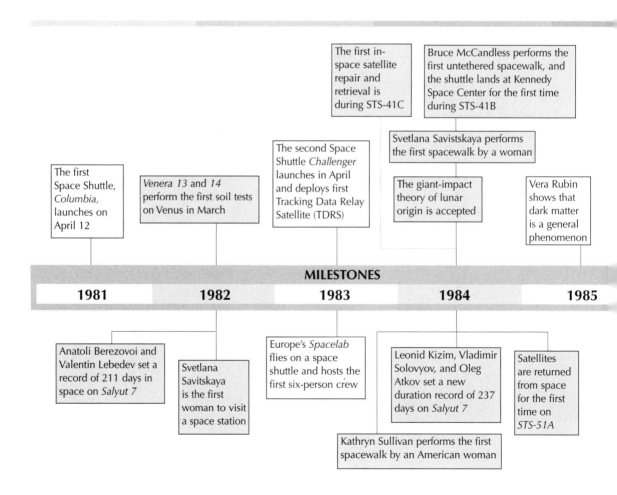

The first in-space satellite repair and retrieval is during STS-41C

Bruce McCandless performs the first untethered spacewalk, and the shuttle lands at Kennedy Space Center for the first time during STS-41B

The second Space Shuttle *Challenger* launches in April and deploys first Tracking Data Relay Satellite (TDRS)

Svetlana Savistskaya performs the first spacewalk by a woman

The first Space Shuttle, *Columbia*, launches on April 12

Venera 13 and *14* perform the first soil tests on Venus in March

The giant-impact theory of lunar origin is accepted

Vera Rubin shows that dark matter is a general phenomenon

MILESTONES

| 1981 | 1982 | 1983 | 1984 | 1985 |

Anatoli Berezovoi and Valentin Lebedev set a record of 211 days in space on *Salyut 7*

Svetlana Savitskaya is the first woman to visit a space station

Europe's *Spacelab* flies on a space shuttle and hosts the first six-person crew

Leonid Kizim, Vladimir Solovyov, and Oleg Atkov set a new duration record of 237 days on *Salyut 7*

Satellites are returned from space for the first time on *STS-51A*

Kathryn Sullivan performs the first spacewalk by an American woman

STS-3 tested the thermal characteristics of the orbiter by pointing the belly and payload bay at the Sun or deep space in turn. The orbiter easily tolerated the extreme temperature changes. The first science experiments also went well. A student experiment on bees showed that they adapt to freefall after an initial period of confusion. A method of separating blood using electrical properties had encouraging results. The crew of Jack Lousma and Gordon Fullerton (1936–) remained in space two extra days. A rainstorm made Edwards too muddy. A dust storm finally cleared at the alternative site of White Sands, New Mexico, on March 30, 1982. STS-3 was the only shuttle ever to land there.

The fourth and final test flight of *Columbia* carried a classified military payload into space on June 27, 1982. President Ronald Reagan (1911–2004) and First Lady Nancy Reagan (1921–) were among a half-million people who greeted the crew on landing. During the ceremonies, the second space shuttle, *Challenger,* flew overhead on top of its Boeing 747 ferry ship.

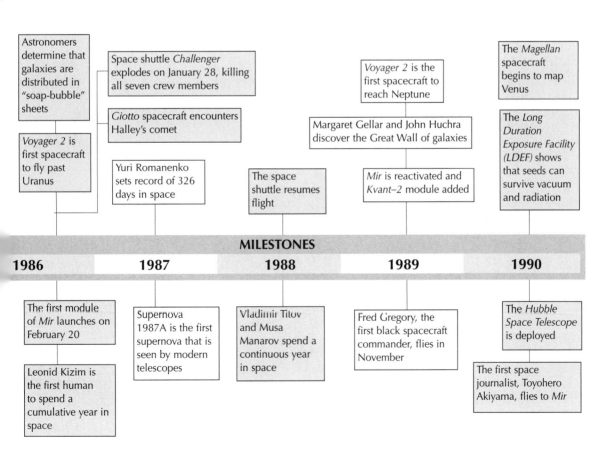

Astronomers determine that galaxies are distributed in "soap-bubble" sheets

Space shuttle *Challenger* explodes on January 28, killing all seven crew members

Voyager 2 is the first spacecraft to reach Neptune

The *Magellan* spacecraft begins to map Venus

Giotto spacecraft encounters Halley's comet

Margaret Gellar and John Huchra discover the Great Wall of galaxies

The *Long Duration Exposure Facility (LDEF)* shows that seeds can survive vacuum and radiation

Voyager 2 is first spacecraft to fly past Uranus

Yuri Romanenko sets record of 326 days in space

The space shuttle resumes flight

Mir is reactivated and *Kvant–2* module added

MILESTONES

| 1986 | 1987 | 1988 | 1989 | 1990 |

The first module of *Mir* launches on February 20

Supernova 1987A is the first supernova that is seen by modern telescopes

Vladimir Titov and Musa Manarov spend a continuous year in space

Fred Gregory, the first black spacecraft commander, flies in November

The *Hubble Space Telescope* is deployed

Leonid Kizim is the first human to spend a cumulative year in space

The first space journalist, Toyohero Akiyama, flies to *Mir*

SHUTTLE FLIGHT SEQUENCE

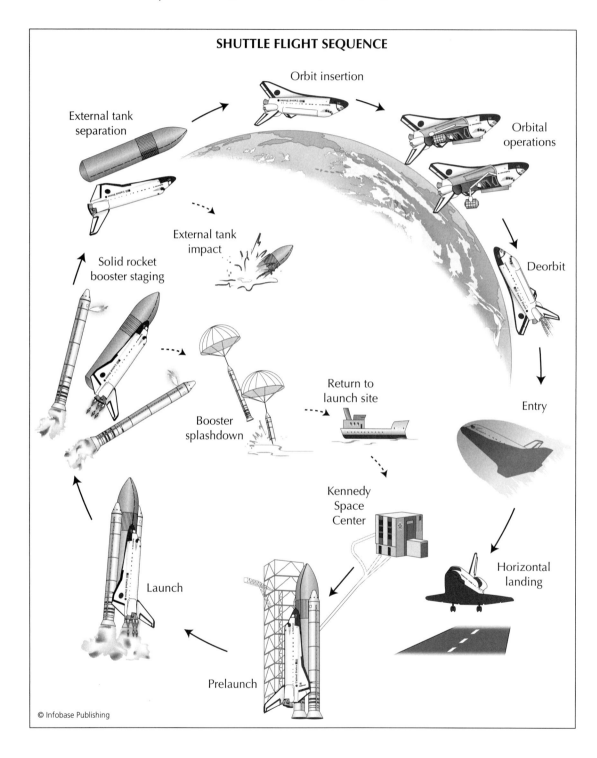

External tank
separation

Orbit insertion

Orbital
operations

External tank
impact

Solid rocket
booster staging

Deorbit

Return to
launch site

Entry

Booster
splashdown

Kennedy
Space
Center

Horizontal
landing

Launch

Prelaunch

With the test program concluded, the two ejection seats were removed from *Columbia*. STS-5 in November then had room for four crew members, including the first two nonpilot mission specialists Joseph Allen (1937–   ) and William Lenoir (1939–   ). They used the robotic arm to deploy two commercial satellites, SBS-3 and Anik-3. NASA expected to recoup operational expenses by collecting fees for launching satellites. The crew got into the spirit by holding up a sign saying "Satellite Deployment by Ace Moving Co. Fast and Courteous Service. 'We Deliver.'"

Challenger made its successful debut on STS-6 on April 4, 1983. The crew deployed the first Tracking Data Relay Satellite (TDRS). Eventually, a series of these satellites would provide a communications network that would eliminate the blackout of entry and allow retirement of expensive ground-tracking facilities. After deployment, mission specialists Story Musgrave (1935–   ) and Donald Peterson (1933–   ) performed the first American spacewalk in nine years.

Sally Ride (1951–   ) became the first American woman in space with the launch of STS-7 on June 19, 1983. She was one of eight women selected as astronauts in 1978 and part of the first five-person crew. Guion Bluford, Jr. (1942–   ; see photo below) made history as the first black astronaut when he flew on STS-8 on August 30. That flight was also the first to launch and land at night.

A refurbished *Columbia* was back in space on November 28, 1983, carrying a crew of six and a European-built pressurized module called

(Opposite page) The reusable space shuttle carried its fuel in a large external tank and launched with the help of two solid rockets. The solids burned for about two minutes and then fell into the ocean, from which they were recovered. The external tank was jettisoned after about nine minutes and burned up in the atmosphere. The payload bay doors opened in space to provide cooling and to allow satellites and other equipment to be deployed using a robotic arm. A deorbit burn slowed the vehicle down for entry, and tiles on the belly provided protection against the intense heat. The shuttle then landed like an airplane.

Guion S. Bluford, Jr., the first black astronaut, is shown here exercising on a treadmill during a shuttle flight in 1983. (NASA)

Spacelab. The crew of STS-9 split into two teams and conducted experiments around the clock.

Five space shuttle missions occurred in 1984. These included the first flight of an EVA jet pack by Bruce McCandless (1937–   ) and the first landing at Kennedy Space Center in February; the first retrieval and repair of a satellite in April; the first flight of the third orbiter, *Discovery*, in August; the first spacewalk by an American woman, Kathryn Sullivan (1951–   ), and a dramatic capture and return of two disabled satellites to Earth in November.

The flight rate ramped up in 1985 in an effort to lower the cost per launch. The record nine flights began with the first dedicated military mission in January. Two flights occurred in April just 10 days apart. One of these was the second Spacelab flight that included U.S. Senator Jake Garn (1932–   ) of Utah. Another shuttle flew in June and the third Spacelab mission flew in July. The July flight almost ended in disaster. A computer shut down one of the main engines. It would have shut down a second and sent the vehicle into the Mediterranean Sea if the crew had not disconnected a faulty sensor. They managed a normal flight at

The European Spacelab program consisted of two sizes of pressurized modules and pallets (one of each shown in the figure) that were designed to carry experiments in the payload bay of the American space shuttle. The first Spacelab mission was flown in 1983.

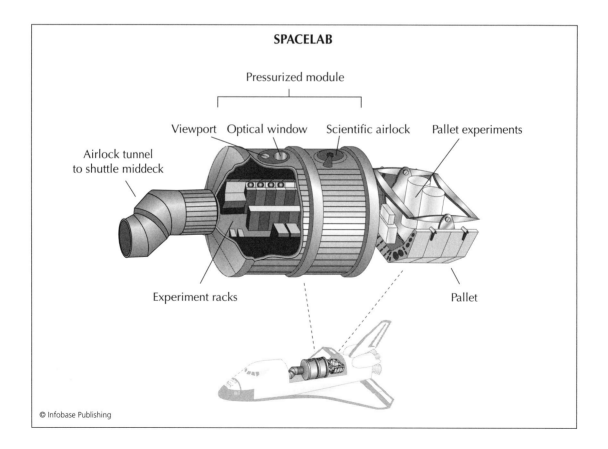

SPACELAB

Pressurized module

Viewport   Optical window   Scientific airlock   Pallet experiments

Airlock tunnel
to shuttle middeck

Experiment racks

Pallet

Shuttle Flight Numbering System

Starting in 1984 with the 10th shuttle flight, NASA adopted an alphanumeric system to designate the year, the launch site, and the order of each shuttle flight. For example, 41B was decoded as follows:

    4 = the last digit of the fiscal year (FY) that runs from October to October, as in 4 for 1984, and 5 for 1985.

    1 = launch site of Kennedy Space Center. The number 2 was reserved for Vandenburg AFB in California but was never used.

    B = the second letter stood for the second flight of the fiscal year.

STS-9 launched in November 1983, so it was the first flight of FY 1984. The 10th flight was then called 41B and launched in February 1984. It was followed by 41C in April and 41D in August. There was no 41E, and 41G launched in October, so it should have been 51A. The real 51A launched in November, followed by 51C and D because 51B was delayed. There was no E or H, but 51G was next, followed by 51F and then 51J in October 1985. 61A launched October 30, 1985, and 61B in November. First up in calendar year 1986 was 61C, but the second flight was 51L that had been postponed from 1985. There was no 51K. After the *Challenger* accident, NASA reverted to a plain numbering system starting with STS-26, though flights continued to fly out of order.

a lower altitude than planned. A flight in August was followed by two flights in October, one featuring the fourth space shuttle, *Atlantis*, and the second a dedicated German Spacelab flight with a record crew of eight. The final shuttle flight of the year was in November. With 15 flights scheduled for 1986, it appeared that NASA's space shuttle was well on its way to achieving reliable and reasonably frequent access to space.

Challenger's Last Flight

The first shuttle flight of 1986 took Florida congressman Bill Nelson (1942–   ) along. As chairman of the House subcommittee on space, he thought the experience would help him monitor NASA's budget. The flight was postponed seven times for technical or weather-related reasons. Once in space, there were so many equipment problems that Mission Control cut the flight short to ease the ambitious spring schedule. But bad weather in Florida delayed the landing three times and finally forced Flight 61B (see sidebar above) to land at Edwards on January 18. The landing added another week to the schedule because it required a ferry back to Florida. Congressman Nelson thus learned firsthand how difficult it was to keep the complex technical shuttle program on schedule.

    Next up was the 25th space-shuttle flight, designated 51L. The crew included teacher Sharon Christa McAuliffe (1948–86). Millions of school children planned to share in the lessons she would teach from space. Another nonastronaut on the crew was Gregory Jarvis (1944–86), an engineer with Hughes Aircraft that built the TDRS that would be deployed by the crew. Commander Francis "Dick" Scobee (1939–86) and Pilot Michael Smith (1941–86) were joined by three mission specialists, all of whom had flown previously. Judy Resnick (1949–86) was the second American woman in space. Ellison Onizuka (1946–86) was the first Asian American to fly, and Ronald McNair (1950–86) was the second African-American astronaut.

A hard freeze swept through Florida in the predawn hours of January 28, 1986. An ice inspection team reported that water from burst pipes had leaked all over the pad, forming icicles up to 18 inches (46 cm) long. When the main engines ignited, the shock might shake this ice loose and hurl it at the shuttle's fragile tiles. This was one reason that the launch criteria required that the temperature be above 31°F (0°C). The forecast called for warming and launch preparations continued. The 51L crew were told at breakfast to expect launch around noon.

Unknown to the crew or ice inspectors, engineers at Morton Thiokol (builders of the solid rockets) had met the night before and recommended against launching until temperatures were above 53°F (11°C). They were concerned that rubber O-rings in the joints between segments of the solid rockets would not seal properly. Data from previous flights showed that the lower the temperature, the greater the escape of hot gas between the seals. Their concern was overruled by managers at NASA's Marshall Spaceflight Center and were not shared with managers at Kennedy.

Shortly before 9 A.M., the crew walked carefully across the icy walkways on pad 39B to climb inside *Challenger*. A member of the closeout crew presented Christa McAuliffe with an apple. By 11 A.M., the temperature had warmed to 36°F (1°C), so the final countdown began.

Liftoff appeared normal. Chunks of ice broke loose but did no serious damage. Unnoticed by anyone but caught by a launch camera, puffs of black smoke issued from the lower joint of the right booster. As the joint rotated, the cold-stiffened puddy in the joint collapsed. Gas of nearly 6,000°F (3,300°C) rushed out. Aluminum oxides from the fuel plugged the leak after 1.5 seconds, and no flame escaped.

Commander Dick Scobee throttled down the engines as planned to 65 percent while the shuttle underwent maximum aerodynamic stress, called max Q. The high winds and pressures of this phase of ascent shook the vehicle, jarring the aluminum oxide plug free. Scobee restored full power, confirming "Go at throttle up."

At 58-seconds after launch, a blowtorch of flame burst through the joint and melted part of the external fuel tank. The strut attaching the booster to the tank broke, and the rocket swiveled on its upper strut. The nose of the rocket pierced the oxygen tank. Liquid oxygen mixed with hydrogen and ignited in an enormous fireball (see photo opposite). Pilot Smith's final words preserved on the data recorder were, "Uh oh!"

The space shuttle Challenger *exploded just after liftoff, killing all seven crew members. The photo shows the space shuttle main engines and solid rocket booster exhaust entwined around a ball of gas from the external tank.* (NASA)

The vehicle exploded. The boosters were destroyed by radio command. The crew cabin shattered when it struck the Atlantic Ocean after falling 8.9 miles (14.3 km). The crew died instantly.

Return to Flight

President Reagan established a commission headed by former Secretary of State William Rogers (1913–2001) to investigate the explosion. Among its members were Neil Armstrong and Sally Ride. In June 1986, the commission cited the rocket booster's O-ring as the direct cause. Engineers spent $2.4 billion incorporating changes to the boosters and adding a bailout system to the orbiter. Another $2.8 billion bought a replacement orbiter.

The commission also faulted NASA's management for treating the booster problem as an acceptable risk instead of fixing it. The directors of Marshall and the Kennedy and Johnson Space Centers were replaced. Astronaut Richard Truly became NASA administrator.

The pressure to meet a high flight rate was cited as another factor in the accident. To relieve this pressure, NASA and the military returned to using expendable boosters to carry astronomical and military payloads. NASA would no longer launch commercial satellites. The shuttle launch site at Vandenburg was mothballed.

The shuttle *Discovery* returned NASA to flight with STS-26 on September 29, 1988. The crew deployed a second TDRS, a $100 million replacement for the one destroyed in the *Challenger* explosion. STS-27 in December, two shuttle flights in 1989 (including the first commanded by a black astronaut, Fred Gregory [1941–   ]), and two more in 1990 carried a backlog of military payloads that were not designed for expendable rockets. All other shuttle flights in this decade were dedicated to science.

In October 1989, STS-34 launched *Galileo* on a six-year mission to Jupiter that required one gravity assist from Venus and two from Earth. This roundabout trajectory was a direct result of a post-*Challenger* decision not to fly a potentially explosive *Centaur* upper-stage rocket in the shuttle payload bay. *Galileo* was then outfitted with a less-powerful *Inertial Upper Stage* and redirected to use gravity assist. The Venus flyby occurred in February 1990.

Four important science missions flew on the shuttle in 1990. STS-32 in January retrieved the *Long Duration Exposure Facility* (LDEF) that had been left in space while the shuttles were grounded. LDEF data showed that seeds can survive exposure to vacuum and radiation. In April, STS-31 deployed the *Hubble Space Telescope*. The discovery that its mirror was carefully ground to the wrong shape was a major embarrassment to NASA. Scientists immediately began to plan to repair it on a future shuttle flight. STS-41 launched the *Ulysses* toward a slingshot with Jupiter to put it over the north pole of the sun during solar minimum in 1995. The final shuttle flight of the decade was STS-35, carrying the *ASTRO-1* payload that included the first focusing X-ray telescope.

With the space shuttle barred from commercial and military uses, it could never become the economic launch system originally promised. But its capability to carry crew and manipulate large modules made it essential to plans for building a permanent laboratory in space.

In his State of the Union address in 1984, President Reagan called for the United States to build a space station within a decade. The dual-keel design resembled a picture frame with a crossbeam supporting a cluster of modules. Plans called for 20 shuttle flights starting in 1992 with completion by 1998. In the spring of 1985, the ESA, Japan, and Canada joined the program. By 1987, the cost had grown from $8 to $20 billion, so the station was scrubbed to the crossbeam and modules. While a presidential commission examined how the shuttle and station fit into the nation's future, work began on building space station *Freedom*.

Russian Space—From *Salyut* to *Mir*

The Russian manned space program remained focused on space-station operations throughout this decade. The last extended operations (EO) crew to visit the *Salyut 6* space station launched on March 12, 1981.

Vladimir Kovalyonok and Viktor Savinykh (1940–) spent 75 days in space and hosted the first Mongolian and Romanian visitors.

The new *Salyut 7* launched in April 1982. Anatoli Berezovoi (1942–) and Valentin Lebedev arrived in May. They set another new duration record of 211 days and hosted the first French cosmonaut. The second woman to fly in space, Svetlana Savitskaya (1948–) visited the station in August 1982, almost a year before Sally Ride flew on STS-7.

The *Salyut 7* station hosted a second EO crew from June through November 1983, and a third EO crew from February to October 1984. The EO-3 crew of Leonid. Kizim, Vladimir Solovyov (1946–), and Oleg Atkov (1949–), set yet another record of 237 days. They hosted two visiting crews including the first Indian cosmonaut. The second visiting crew included Savitskaya, who performed the first spacewalk by a woman. This was three months before American Kathy Sullivan. The EO-3 crew had to deal with many equipment problems: the radios broke, the power failed, and the water pipes leaked. New solar panels and chemical batteries were added, and the pipes were fixed. But the Sun offered one problem that they could not solve. Increased solar activity caused the Earth's atmosphere to warm and expand. The Soviets boosted *Salyut 7* to a higher orbit to avoid the atmosphere, but maintaining this altitude cost a lot of fuel.

After being unoccupied for nine months, three cosmonauts went to *Salyut 7* in June 1985 to perform one of the most impressive space repairs in history. Viktor Savinykh, Vladimir Dzhanibekov, and Georgi Grechko managed to dock with the station despite it rolling randomly and being without power. The air inside was breathable but so cold that frost covered the walls. All the batteries were dead. The cosmonauts wore fur-lined hats while they restored power. The water heater had failed, so they used television lights to melt ice for water. Repair of the attitude-control system cleared the way for *Progress 24* to dock at the end of June. It brought a new water heater, batteries, fuel, and spare parts. An August spacewalk added another solar array. By the end of July, *Salyut 7* had been brought back to life. Two of the crew left in September. Savinykh stayed and was joined by Vladimir Vasyutin (1952–2002), and Alexander Volkov (1948–). Vasyutin became ill, so they all left the station in November 1985.

The next space station was *Mir* [peace]. Designed to be expandable, the core module launched on February 20, 1986. On March 13, Leonid Kizim and Vladimir Solovyov docked to *Mir* and then flew it to an orbit compatible with *Salyut 7*. After six weeks on *Mir*, the cosmonauts undocked and flew to *Salyut 7*, the first time one ship had ever visited two stations. Once again, *Salyut 7* was icebound and without power. They spent 51 days restoring power and environmental control and salvaging 20 instruments such as a spectrometer. On June 25, they left the gutted *Salyut 7* behind and docked with *Mir* the next day. They unloaded and installed the salvaged equipment. On July 3, Kizim passed Valeri Ryumin's record and became the first human to spend an accumulated time of a full year in space. He returned to Earth on July 16, 1986. *Salyut* 7 fell to Earth over Argentina in 1991.

In February 1987, the EO-2 crew of Yuri Romanenko and Aleksander Laveykin (1951–) arrived on *Mir*. In April, the new *Kvant–1* module was delivered. The docking was not secure. The cosmonauts did a spacewalk and removed a garbage bag that was in the way. The *Kvant–1* module was the first to carry *gyrodines*, mechanical wheels that maintain attitude in space without the use of thrusters. The gyrodines used electrical power from a solar array. This system plus improved engines kept the growing station from being dragged down like *Salyut* 7. *Kvant–1* also expanded the science capabilities. Its Roentgen Observatory was used to study Supernova 1987A. Plans for the EO-2 crew to break the endurance record faltered when Laveykin had to return to Earth in July for health reasons. Romanenko remained in space with Aleksandr Aleksandrov (1943–) as part of the EO-3 crew. He stayed until the next long-duration crew arrived in December, racking up a record of 326 days in space.

This record would not stand for long. The new crew, Vladimir Titov and Musa Manarov, became the first humans to live in space for a full continous year. The "parking" time for Soyuz escape ships increased to six months. So the resident crew hosted their first visitors, including a Bulgarian, in June. The first Afghan visited in August 1987. The August flight also brought Dr. Valeri Polyakov (1942–) to stay through April of the next year to monitor the record-setting crews.

The return of the second visiting crew nearly proved fatal. The two men performed the standard separation of the habitation module from the deorbit module. This saved fuel because the engine only had to slow down the mass of one module. A failure during the deorbit burn required Vladimir Lyakhov to shut down the engine. An orbit later, he tried again, but the engine shut down and started a countdown that would jettison the engine, stranding the crew in space. He managed to stop the countdown, but they were stuck in orbit for another 24 hours without the water or toilet facilities of the habitation module. They finally landed on September 7, 1988. On future flights, the habitation module was left connected until after a successful burn.

The two-man EO-4 crew arrived in November with Frenchman Jean-Loup Chrétien (1938–) making his second flight. The two-module *Mir* was very crowded with six people onboard except for when Chrétien and Alexander Volkov took a walk outside. Titov and Manarov left *Mir* on December 21, 1988, having spent 365.94 days in space. Their record stood until 1995. The EO-4 crew of Sergei Krikalev (1958–) and Alexander Volkov left in April with Dr. Polyakov.

Mir was unoccupied for more than a year because of delays with the new Soyuz-TM. Finally, on September 5, 1989, the *Mir* EO-5 crew launched. Aleksandr Serebrov (1944–) and Alexander Viktorenko (1947–) attached the new *Kvant-2* module in November. The *Kvant-2* carried more gyrodines and an *Elektron* system to recycle water. The gyrodines and recycling systems saved money by reducing the number of Progress flights needed to service the station. The new module added an incubator unit for life-science experiments and a rotating remotely controlled camera platform.

The EO-6 crew's Soyuz capsule was damaged during launch on February 11, 1990. After docking to *Mir*, they did an exhausting space-walk to repair the torn insulation. Afterward, they could not close the *Kvant-2* airlock hatch. Running out of air, they vented the middle com-partment and used it as an airlock. They got the hatch closed during a second spacewalk. This experience led to a redesign of hatches to open to the inside so that the internal pressure keeps them closed.

The EO-6 crew oversaw the installation of the fourth module in June 1990. The *Kristall* (crystal) module's chief purpose was for biological and materials science. Its docking port was designed for the Russian *Buran* shuttle that had one unmanned test flight in 1988. (*Buran* was mothballed in the early 1990s.) The EO-6 crew returned safely in their repaired Soyuz in August. The EO-7 crew stayed from August through December. The EO-8 crew arrived in December and brought the first space tourist: Japanese TV journalist Toyohiro Akiyama (1942–) who paid $14 million for the privilege. Although he suffered from space sick-ness, he described seeing the Earth from space as a visual feast that many people would enjoy.

The Moon, Venus, Mars, and Comets

After Apollo, most space scientists set aside their lunar research and fol-lowed the money and the opportunities offered through study of less-vis-ited worlds. So in 1976, when two groups proposed a collision model for how the Moon formed, there was no press conference or public debate or much interest at all. Thus, it was not until a group of lunar scientists held a conference on lunar origin in 1984 that astronomers embraced the giant-impact theory. This theory proposes that the early Earth was struck off center by a body half its current size. The impact spun up the Earth, and it splashed mantle and debris into space that formed the Moon. The theory explains the similarity of Earth and Moon rocks; the Moon's lack of water (heat of the collision boiled it away); the movement of the Moon away from the Earth (if it were captured or formed from the same nebula it would move inward); and the Moon's small iron core (that would be larger if formed from the same nebula as Earth).

The acceptance of the giant-impact theory led to impact-based explanations of other planetary phenomena. Mercury's overly large iron core was interpreted to be the result of a collision that stripped it of lighter materials. Impacts were cited as the reason for the slow rotation of Venus (its day is longer than its year) and for Uranus spinning on its side. Based on dating of the largest lunar craters, some scientists suggested that the Moon, and perhaps the entire solar system, underwent an intense period of bombardment called the cataclysm about 3.8 billion years ago. Samples from the Moon's south pole–Aitken basin, perhaps the oldest-surviving impact crater in the solar system, may settle the question in the next century.

While American astronomers focused attention on the outer planets, the Russian exploration of Venus reached new levels of sophistication with *Venera 13* and *14*. These twin spacecraft arrived at Venus on March 1 and 5, 1982, and landed about 590 miles (640 km) apart near Phoebe Regio. They provided panoramas, relayed to Earth by their orbiters, of bedrock outcrops surrounded by dark, fine-grained soil. Mechanical drills deposited samples in sealed, temperature-controlled chambers inside each spacecraft. An X-ray spectrometer showed that *13*'s sample was similar to lava fields in Hawaii, and *14*'s sample was more like lava found on Mount Vesuvius. Despite surface temperatures of more than 850°F (450°C) and pressures up to 94 times that of Earth, *Venera 14* survived for 57 minutes and *Venera 13* for 127 minutes.

The *Venera 15* and *16* orbiters arrived into orbit around Venus in October 1983. During an eight-month period, they returned the first high-resolution images of Venus's polar regions and thermal maps of its northern hemisphere.

Next up were *Vega 1* and *2* that arrived in June 1985. They dropped probes into Venus's atmosphere. The surface experiments failed apparently because high winds activated gravity sensors while the probes were still airborne. Another disappointment was the failure of two probes to the Martian moon Phobos in 1988. Only a few images were returned before contact was lost with first one probe in 1988 and the other in 1989.

The Americans sent only one mission to Venus and none to Mars in this decade. *Magellan* was deployed by the space shuttle *Atlantis* in May 1989 and reached Venus in August 1990. During its first eight months, it produced radar images of 84 percent of the surface with a resolution that was 10 times better than the Soviet Veneras.

When Halley's comet passed by Earth in 1910, people feared it heralded the end of the world. When it returned in 1986, most people did not even notice. Not only had people accepted comets as natural, not supernatural, in origin; the comet was about twice as far away and did not put on much of a show. City dwellers could not even spot it during its closest approach to Earth in November 1986.

In September 1985, NASA's International Cometary Explorer spacecraft became the first to fly through the tail of a comet. It found that comet Giacobini-Zinner's tail was about 15,500 miles (25,000 km) wide and contained water and carbon monoxide. This confirmed Fred Whipple's "dirty snowball" theory.

In November 1985, the Japanese *Sakigake* [forerunner] and *Suisei* [comet] spacecraft took ultraviolet observations of Halley's comet and then encountered it on the sunward side in March 1986. The European Space Agency *Giotto* spacecraft (launched on an *Ariane* rocket in July 1985) flew closest to Halley's comet, obtaining striking images of the comet's nucleus. The two Soviet Vega spacecraft imaged Halley at lower resolution. Contrary to expectations, scientists found the nucleus is darker than coal. Its density is very low, showing it is mostly made of dust. From Earth orbit the *International Ultraviolet Explorer* and *Solar Maximum Observatory* took ultraviolet images of Halley. They found that times of brightening were caused by release of carbon dioxide.

After flying past Halley's comet in 1986, *Giotto* visited comet Grigg–Skjellerup in 1989. Unlike Halley, this is a more typical short-period comet that completes a circuit of the Sun about every five years. The comet's orbit was changed by an encounter with Jupiter in 1964 so that it almost intersects Earth's orbit. Because comet Grigg-Skjellerup has been warmed by the Sun so many times, it releases about 1 percent as much dust and gas as Halley's comet.

Voyage to Uranus and Neptune

In August 1982, *Voyager 2* completed its flyby of Saturn and headed for distant Uranus (see figure on page 206). The trip took six and a half years and the flyby lasted just six hours in January 1986. Uranus is unique among the planets because it is tipped so that its north and south poles alternatively face toward and away from the Sun. *Voyager 2* discovered that Uranus has a magnetic field. Because of its "sideways" spin, the tail of the field is twisted into a long corkscrew shape behind the planet. The field is also tilted at 60° and offset from the planet's center. Astronomers speculate that the orientation of Uranus's spin and magnetic field are the result of an ancient collision.

Voyager 2 showed that the atmosphere of Uranus is mostly hydrogen with about 12 percent helium and small amounts of ammonia, methane, and water vapor. Winds blow from the west instead of the east. Under the thick clouds, *Voyager 2* found evidence of a deep boiling ocean of water and ammonia. Under this ocean is a core not more than 10–15 Earth masses.

Voyager 2 found 10 new moons of Uranus, bringing the total to 15. These half-ice, half-rocky worlds contain mountains, canyons, and cliffs that may have been carved by glaciers. The innermost moon, Miranda,

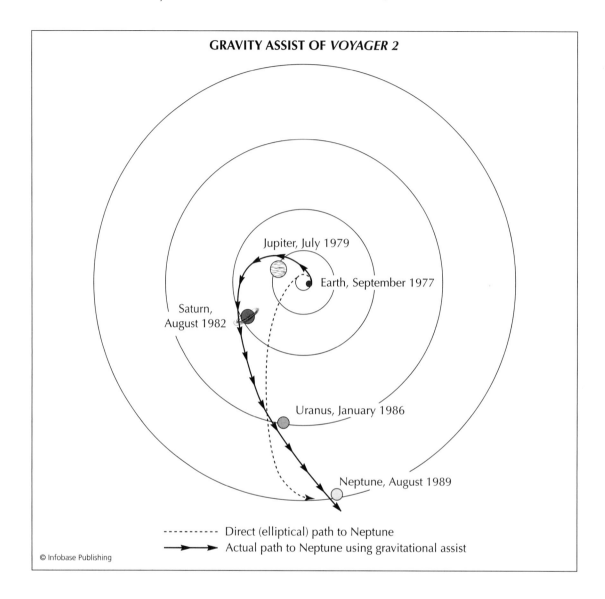

GRAVITY ASSIST OF *VOYAGER 2*

Jupiter, July 1979

Earth, September 1977

Saturn,
August 1982

Uranus, January 1986

Neptune, August 1989

- - - - - - - - -   Direct (elliptical) path to Neptune
————▶   Actual path to Neptune using gravitational assist

© Infobase Publishing

Voyager 2 launched in 1977 and used a gravitational assist (slingshot) from Jupiter in 1979 to bend its path toward Saturn, then from Saturn in 1982 to Uranus, and from Uranus in 1986 to Neptune in 1989. Without gravitational assists, Voyager 2 would have taken about 30 years to reach Neptune instead of 12.

is considered one of the strangest in the solar system. It appears to have been shattered and reassembled in a haphazard way. In addition to the moons, Uranus is circled by a system of 11 rings. Unlike Saturn's fine-grained rings, Uranus's rings consist of dark boulder-sized chunks.

The quick flyby of Uranus was followed by a three-year trip to Neptune, then the most distant planet from the Sun. Arriving in August 1989, *Voyager 2* found a storm about half the size of Earth. This Great Dark Spot generated an ultraviolet aurora and winds up to 1,500 mph (2,400 kph), stronger than on any other planet. High cirrus clouds of natural gas cast shadows on clouds below. One of the most surprising and puzzling discoveries was that Neptune has an internal heat source that drives the winds, whereas Uranus does not. It remains a great mystery why Neptune is the same temperature as Uranus despite being so much farther from the Sun. Neptune's weak magnetic field was found tilted and offset from the planet's center. This suggests that matter is not evenly distributed inside the planet and that the magnetic field derives from a shallow spherical shell, not deep in the core like on Earth.

Voyager 2 found six new moons (Nereid and Triton were previously discovered) and five rings around Neptune. The largest moon, *Triton*, featured calderas about 1,000 feet (300 m) deep and hundreds of miles/kilometers across. Astronomers estimate these "ice volcanoes" produced ocean-sized floods of ice as recently as a half-billion years ago. Other ice volcanoes may have erupted explosively within the last 300 years, ejecting nitrogen ice and gas at speeds of 560 mph (900 kph). Triton's relatively high density and retrograde orbit offer strong evidence that it is a captured object. If true, then tidal forces may have melted Triton and made its surface liquid for as long as a billion years after capture. Triton's surface temperature is now the coldest of any known world in the solar system at –391°F (–199°C).

Voyager 2 was the first spacecraft to visit Uranus and Neptune and answered many questions about these giant worlds. After its encounter with Neptune, the spacecraft dove below the ecliptic plane and headed out of the solar system.

State of the Universe

The center of the Milky Way is shrouded in dust. The infrared astronomical satellite (IRAS) that operated for 10 months in 1983 saw through this dust for the first time. It revealed that the Milky Way has an elongated central barlike bulge from which the spiral arms unwind. IRAS also discovered a disk of dust around the stars Vega and Fomalhaut, a precursor of discoveries in the next decade that would find planets around other stars.

The Milky Way is just one member of the Virgo supercluster of galaxies. The universe is filled with similar clusters each millions of light-years across. As ground and space observatories mapped and measured these clusters, the large scale structure of the universe emerged. Physicists Rashid Sunyaev (1943) and Yakov Zel'dovich (1914–87) of the Moscow Institute of Applied Mathematics realized in 1980 that hot gas in clusters offered a way to find their distance. The Sunyaev-Zel'dovich effect predicts that a small fraction of the cosmic microwave background photons will collide with hot electrons as they pass through a galaxy cluster. The electrons give some of their energy to the photons by reverse *Compton scattering*. The result of this scattering is that the cluster appears less bright in the microwave band and

Supernova 1987A in the Large Magellanic Cloud was the first to be studied by modern telescopes. This composite image was taken by the Hubble Space Telescope *in September 1994.* (NASA)

brighter in higher frequencies. The Sunyaev-Zel'dovich effect was first confirmed in 1983 and added to evidence of the cosmological origin of the cosmic background radiation (found "behind" every cluster). (Both Zel'dovich and Sunyaev received Bruce Medals [see page 249] for their work.) By combining radio data with X-ray observations (provided by European and Japanese X-ray satellites), the distance to clusters is determined. These distances in turn provide a measure of the Hubble constant of expansion. Because the intensity of cosmic background radiation is reduced only about a half percent by galaxy clusters, lots of observing time is required to precisely measure the Sunyaev-Zel'dovich effect.

On February 24, 1987, the light from a blue star about 160,000 light-years away in the Large Magellanic Cloud exploded in the most violent outburst known in nature, a supernova. As bright as Megrez in the Big Dipper, it was the first supernova close enough to be visible to the naked eye since 1604. Designated SN 1987A (see photo opposite), it was perhaps the most intensely studied astronomical event in history. The day before, 19 neutrinos were detected by the deep underground facilities in Japan and Ohio. Because these particles so rarely interact with matter, this meant that more than 1×10^{14} neutrinos passed harmlessly through the Earth.

Prior to SN 1987A, astronomers thought that only red giant stars became supernova. This star was a hot blue star of about 20 solar masses. Since 1987A, astronomers have realized that composition makes a big difference. Unlike most stars in the Milky Way, stars in the LMC are deficient in heavier elements. These stars evolve into red supergiants like other stars, but shortly before they explode, they become hot blue stars again. A shell around the supernova that was lit up by light from the supernova indicated that the star had been a red supergiant about 30,000 years ago. The star brightened a few hours after its explosion and then began to dim. A week later, it unexpectedly began to brighten again, reaching its brightest about three months after the explosion. This event confirmed ideas about core collapse and element production (predicted by Fred Hoyle) and also showed that not all supernovae are alike.

Supernovae vary, galaxies vary, and it seems that even on the largest scale, the universe is not uniform. In 1986, astronomers Margaret Geller (1947–) and John Huchra (1948–) at the Harvard–Smithsonian Center for Astrophysics (CfA) revealed the first of a series of maps (see Further Reading) of the universe showing that galaxies are not evenly distributed in space. The maps described a "soap-bubble universe" with galaxies clustered on the surfaces of thin sheets surrounded by vast voids in space. Some of the voids were as large as 160 million light-years. In 1988 Donald Lynden-Bell and others published data (see Further Reading) that showed that the local clusters of galaxies are streaming toward a large concentration of mass in the direction of the constellation Centaurus. This invisible "Great Attractor" has a mass in excess of 5.4×10^{16} solar masses. Geller and Huchra published a more complete large-scale map set in the November 17, 1989, issue of *Science* magazine (see Further Reading). In "Mapping the Universe," they described the largest structure as the "Great Wall." This filament of galaxies is about 200 million light-years away. It is more than 500 million light-years long, 300 million light-years wide, and 15 million light-years thick, making it the largest known structure in the universe. Some astronomers speculate that this "wall" follows weblike strings of dark matter.

The nature of dark matter and its connection to galactic origins and structure remained one of the most intriguing questions in astronomy throughout the rest of the century. Vera Rubin (see sidebar and photo on pages 210–211) published a study of 16 galaxies in 1985 showing that dark matter is a general phenomena. She explained in an interview with

Scientist of the Decade: Vera Cooper Rubin (1928–   )

Astronomer Vera Rubin proved that galaxies are not evenly distributed in space and that 95 percent of the mass of galaxies is invisible dark matter.

Vera Cooper was the second daughter of Philip and Rose Cooper. She was born in Philadelphia, Pennsylvania, on July 23, 1928. Her father worked as an electrical engineer and moved the family to Washington, D.C. In the new house, 12-year-old Vera often stayed awake to watch the stars through the window above her bed.

In 1945, Vera accepted a scholarship to attend the all-women Vasser College where one of the first American women astronomers, Maria Mitchell (1818–89), had taught. Vera was the sole graduate of the astronomy program in 1948.

After graduation, she married Robert Rubin, who was in graduate school in physical chemistry at Cornell. She worked on her master's degree while he finished his Ph.D. Her work focused on the large-scale motions of galaxies, using data recorded by others because women were not given access to telescopes. She noticed that in addition to the outward expansion motion of galaxies, there was also some sideways motion. She presented her findings at a meeting of the American Astronomical Society in 1950 and quickly left to nurse her three-week-old baby. The next day, her paper was featured on the front page of the *Washington Post*. "It got an enormous amount of publicity, almost all negative, but at least from then on, astronomers knew who I was," Rubin said in an interview in *Discover* magazine in 1990. Rubin got her master's degree in 1951.

She earned her Ph.D. at Georgetown University by taking night classes while her parents watched her first two sons, David and Allan, and her husband waited in the car to drive her home. After the children were in bed, she worked until 2 A.M. "Then I'd get up with the children in the morning and spend the whole day with them. It was hard, but it was harder not doing astronomy," she wrote in *Scientific American* in 1998. Rubin wanted to know if galaxies were distributed randomly as assumed by most astronomers. With no computers available, it took months to do the calculations on a desktop

calculator. The results showed that galaxies were clumped into superclusters. She completed her doctorate work under George Gamow in 1954.

Rubin took a job teaching three days a week at Montgomery County Junior College in 1954. The next year, she began teaching and doing research at Georgetown. She had two more children, Karl and Judy. She is very proud of the fact that all four children earned Ph.D's in science or math.

Most astronomers did not take Rubin's work seriously. That changed in 1963 when she collaborated with astronomers Margaret and Geoffrey Burbidge to study galaxies. "In my mind I had at last become an astronomer," Rubin said in 1990, "for the Burbidges were actually interested in my ideas." She was the first woman to use the telescopes at Mount Palomar Observatory.

In 1965, Rubin took a position at the Department of Terrestrial Magnetism of the Carnegie Institution of Washington. She teamed up with W. Kent Ford, Jr. who invented the image-tube spectrograph to measure the rotation curves of spiral galaxies. The two researchers focused on the question of whether or not galaxies just "go along for the ride" as the universe expands or if they also move around on their own. Results showed that galaxies move separately from the expansion, a phenomena called the Rubin–Ford effect.

Rubin and Ford also studied the question of why spiral galaxies differ in brightness and structure. Some are tightly wound with arms close, and others are loose with arms wide. She thought the spin might explain the pinwheel shape. They measured how fast the stars and gas in Andromeda spin around the center. Astronomers had assumed that most of the mass of a galaxy would be in the center. If so, the stars would go faster around the center than near the edge—like the motion of the planets in the solar system. "What's observed is that the stars far out are going just as fast as the stars near the center or even faster!" she told the author in 2004. "That means that the distribution of matter is not at all related to the distribution of light." This surprising discovery showed that most of the mass of galaxies is not visible and that this

Vera Rubin convinced her fellow astronomers that galaxies are mostly made of dark matter. (Jack Parsons)

dark matter is not concentrated in the center of galaxies. She found that almost all of the mass in the galaxy is in the halo and that the spiral arms do not contribute to the motion. "Probably about 95 percent of the universe is dark," Rubin explained. "When you look at the stars, you are not looking at the universe. When you look at galaxies, you're not looking at the universe. Most of the galaxy is invisible to us, and we don't know what it is."

In 1981, Rubin was elected to the National Academy of Sciences. In 1993, she was awarded the National Medal of Science by President Bill Clinton (1946–), "for her pioneering research programs in observational cosmology which demonstrated that much of the matter in the universe is dark and for significant contributions to the realization that the universe is more complex and more mysterious than had been imagined." She was only the third woman to receive this prize.

At age 75, Vera Rubin was awarded the Bruce Medal for her years of work on the motions of galaxies. She continues to study stars and galaxies to shed light on the nature of dark matter and gravity. A galaxy called NGC4550 with stars revolving in opposite directions over its poles may offer some clues. The theory that it went through a galactic merger does not fit all the data. NGC4550 is flat except for a central bulge. "If two galaxies merge, it tends to puff up the galaxy, and then they don't remain a disk," she noted in an interview with the author.

Inspired by the example of Maria Mitchell, Rubin has become a role model for young astronomers. She advises them not to get discouraged "They'll get lots of reasons why it is impractical to be an astronomer. But if they really think that is what they want to do, they shouldn't listen to those reasons."

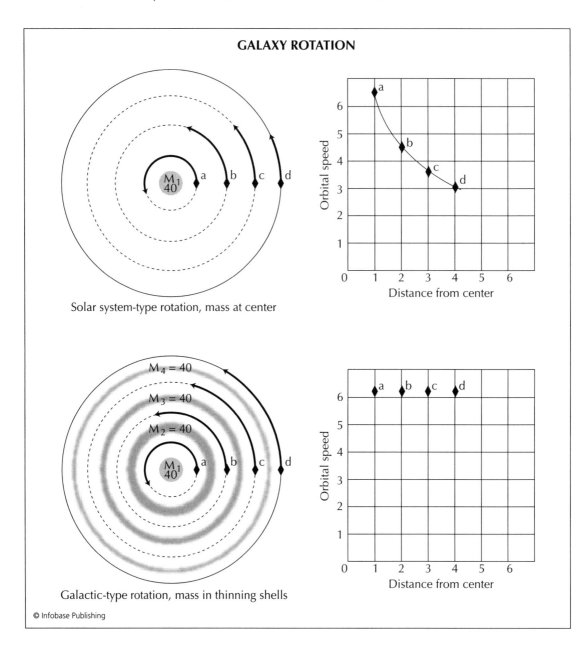

GALAXY ROTATION

Solar system-type rotation, mass at center

Galactic-type rotation, mass in thinning shells

© Infobase Publishing

the author that scientists still have no idea what dark matter is, only what it is not. "If we knew what it was, I don't think we'd call it dark matter," she said. "Dark matter is totally mysterious." Its existence is not debated, though. Its effects are clearly seen in plots of galactic rotation (see figure above) and in the amount of mass required to bend light around gravitational lensing galaxies.

Further Reading

Books and Periodicals

Geller, Margaret J., and John P. Huchra. "Mapping the Universe." *Science* 246. (November 1989): 897–903. The article provides the data and maps showing that galaxies in the nearby universe lay in thin sheets with the "Great Wall" the largest structure.

Geller, Margaret J., John P. Huchra, and Valérie de Lapparent. "Large-Scale Structure: The Center for Astrophysics Redshift Survey." Observational cosmology; *Proceedings of the IAU Symposium, Beijing, People's Republic of China, August 25–30, 1986.* Dordrecht: D. Reidel Publishing Co., 1987, 301–313. Available online. URL: http://articles. adsabs.harvard.edu/cgi-bin/nph-iarticle_query?1987IAUS..124..301G. This paper provides the first maps and data that support the "bubble-like" geometry of the universe.

Godwin, Robert. *Space Shuttle: STS Flights 1–5, The NASA Mission Reports.* Burlington, Ontario, Canada: Apogee Books, 2001. These reports include all the technical and historical details of the first five space-shuttle flights.

Lord, Douglas R. *Spacelab: An International Success Story. NASA SP–487.* Washington, D.C.: NASA, 1987. This is a great resource for the history, diagrams, and missions of the European Spacelab program.

Lynden-Bell, D., S. M. Faber, et al. "Spectroscopy and Photometry of Elliptical Galaxies. V—Galaxy Streaming toward the New Supergalactic Center." *Astrophysical Journal*, part 1, vol. 326 (March 1, 1998): 19–49. This paper analyzes the dynamics of 400 elliptical galaxies and shows that the supergalactic center, later dubbed the "Great Attractor" is in Centaurus.

Trefil, James. Foreword by David H. Levy. *Other Worlds: Images of the Cosmos from Earth and Space.* Washington, D.C.: National Geographic Society, 1999. This book includes photos of Uranus and Neptune from *Voyager 2*.

Web Sites

Bill Arnett. "Comet Halley." Available online. URL: http://www.nineplanets. org/halley.html. Accessed on March 13, 2006. Photos and history of Halley's comet are available on this site.

John Huchra. "John Huchra's Website." Harvard Smithsonian Center for Astrophysics. Available online. URL: http://www.cfa.harvard.edu/ ~huchra/. Accessed on March 13, 2006. Professor Huchra provides maps of the universe and links to original papers and quality Web resources on all topics related to galaxies.

John Logsdon. "Chapter 15: Return to Flight: Richard H. Truly and the Recovery from the *Challenger* Accident." Available online. URL: http:// history.nasa.gov/SP-4219/Chapter15.html. Accessed on March 13, 2006. This footnoted article provides a list of the recommendations of the

(Opposite page) *Vera Rubin found that the orbital speed of stars (proportional to the square root of mass divided by distance) did not decrease with distance (a–d) the way it does for planets in the solar system (top graph). Stars move (bottom graph) as if there are shells (M_{2-4}) of equal (but not visible) mass spaced throughout the galaxy in addition to the visible mass concentrated at the center (M_1).*

Rogers Commission and how NASA responded to them to return to flight after the *Challenger* accident in 1986.

NASA. "Voyager: the Interstellar Mission: Uranus." NASA Jet Propulsion Laboratory and the California Institute of Technology. Available online. URL: http://voyager.jpl.nasa.gov/science/uranus.html. Accessed on March 13, 2006. The site includes links to details about the Voyager spacecraft and discoveries made during its encounter with Uranus in 1986.

David Portree. "Mir Hardware Heritage." NASA. Available online. URL: http://spaceflight.nasa.gov/history/shuttle-mir/references/r-documents-mirhh.htm. Accessed on August 31, 2006. This is a book in English about the Russian *Mir* and *Salyut* space station and Soyuz spacecraft hardware history and development.

Anatoly Zak. "SPACECRAFT: Manned: Mir." The Russian Space Web. Available online. URL: http://www.russianspaceweb.com/mir.html. Accessed on March 13, 2006. The site provides a model of the *Mir* that links to detailed technical data about each module of the station and includes a historical chronology and a review of dangerous close calls.

1991–2000:
Space Telescopes and Stations

The final decade of the 20th century saw a change from competition to cooperation in space, the setting of many new records; new missions to the Moon, Mars, asteroids, and Jupiter; and the discovery of the first extrasolar planets.

The chapter begins with the accomplishments of space-shuttle missions, including the repair and servicing of the *Hubble Space Telescope* in 1993 (see figure on page 219); the 1994 first flight of a cosmonaut on a shuttle; John Glenn's flight at age 77; and Eileen Collins (1956–   ) becoming the first female shuttle commander. Also covered are the early Shuttle–*Mir* missions that resulted from the end of the cold war and the agreement that Russia would join the United States as a partner in building the *International Space Station*. The experiences of the astronauts who stayed on *Mir* (see photo on page 237) are described, including Shannon Lucid's (1943–   ) record-setting six-month stay for a woman in 1996, and the dramatic fire and crippling collision in 1997. The 15-year-old *Mir* was retired in 2000, the same year the first U.S.-Russian crew took up residence on the new *International Space Station*.

Planetary missions got a lot of attention in this decade and are a main topic of the chapter. After problems with large complicated spacecraft, NASA adopted a "smaller, cheaper, faster" philosophy for unmanned missions. The first of these was *Mars Pathfinder* (see photo on page 223) that landed a rover in 1997. Record public interest in this flight was kindled the previous year by the finding of possible bacterial life in a Martian meteorite. On its way to Jupiter, *Galileo* took the first close-up photos of an asteroid (see photo on page 225) in 1991 and covered the impact of Comet Shoemaker-Levy 9 that struck Jupiter in 1994. *Galileo* dropped a probe into Jupiter's atmosphere in 1995, finding that it was drier than expected. Conversely, *Lunar Prospector* found possible water on the Moon, making a future outpost there more feasible. Its impact buried the first human remains on the Moon, those of Eugene Shoemaker (see sidebar on page 221).

One of the most significant discoveries of the decade that is another major topic of this chapter was the detection of the first extrasolar planets using the Doppler shift method (see figure on page 227). The scientist of the decade, Geoffrey Marcy (1954–   ) (see sidebar and photo on pages 236–238), found 70 of the first 100 extrasolar planets.

Many of the discoveries of this decade were the result of new tele-scopes such as the twin Keck optical telescopes (see photo on page 229) and the very-long-base interferometer (see figure on page 230) that are described in the chapter. These new instruments were combined with new distance-measuring methods (see figure on page 232) to find the source of gamma-ray bursts, view galaxies 13.6 billion light-years away, and find evidence that the expansion of the universe is accelerating.

Research and Records

The first shuttle flight of 1991 showed the utility of having human prob-lem solvers in orbit. After a ride to space on the shuttle *Atlantis* in April,

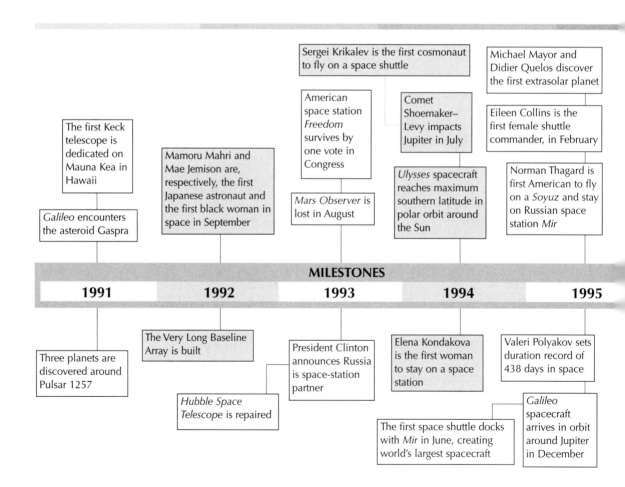

the *Compton Gamma-Ray Observatory*'s (CGRO) high-gain antenna failed to deploy by ground command. Jerry Ross (1948–) and Jerome Apt (1949–) did a spacewalk and manually deployed it. The first flight of the new orbiter *Endeavour* in May 1992 also benefited from human ingenuity. The crew of STS-49 were assigned to repair *Intelsat VI*, but first they had to capture and secure it in the shuttle payload bay. Two spacewalkers with a capture bar tried twice unsuccessfully to nab the satellite. Though the shuttle airlock was designed for two, Richard Hieb (1955–), Pierre Thuot (1955–), and Thomas Akers (1951–) crammed in and did the first three-person spacewalk. The extra pair of hands was what they needed to capture the spacecraft. The men repaired the spacecraft during the longest spacewalk to date at 8 hours, 29 minutes.

The landing of *Endeavour* on May 16, 1992, was the first to use a drag chute. This was one of many upgrades made to the orbiters. The chutes increased the lifetime of the shuttle's brakes and tires. The *Columbia*

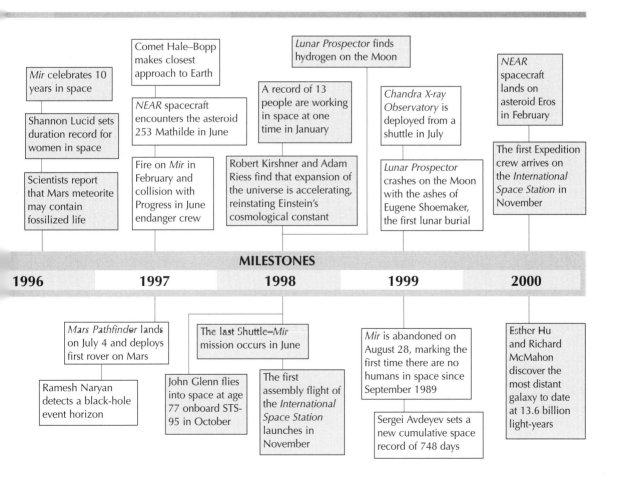

MILESTONES

| 1996 | 1997 | 1998 | 1999 | 2000 |

Mir celebrates 10 years in space

Shannon Lucid sets duration record for women in space

Scientists report that Mars meteorite may contain fossilized life

Comet Hale–Bopp makes closest approach to Earth

NEAR spacecraft encounters the asteroid 253 Mathilde in June

Fire on *Mir* in February and collision with Progress in June endanger crew

Lunar Prospector finds hydrogen on the Moon

A record of 13 people are working in space at one time in January

Robert Kirshner and Adam Riess find that expansion of the universe is accelerating, reinstating Einstein's cosmological constant

Chandra X-ray Observatory is deployed from a shuttle in July

Lunar Prospector crashes on the Moon with the ashes of Eugene Shoemaker, the first lunar burial

NEAR spacecraft lands on asteroid Eros in February

The first Expedition crew arrives on the *International Space Station* in November

Mars Pathfinder lands on July 4 and deploys first rover on Mars

Ramesh Naryan detects a black-hole event horizon

The last Shuttle–*Mir* mission occurs in June

John Glenn flies into space at age 77 onboard STS-95 in October

The first assembly flight of the *International Space Station* launches in November

Mir is abandoned on August 28, marking the first time there are no humans in space since September 1989

Sergei Avdeyev sets a new cumulative space record of 748 days

Esther Hu and Richard McMahon discover the most distant galaxy to date at 13.6 billion light-years orbiter was outfitted with new systems for carbon-dioxide removal and a pallet with extra hydrogen and oxygen tanks for the fuel-cell power plants. These improvements allowed *Columbia* to stay in space for a record 15 days during the STS-50 Spacelab flight in June 1992.

Spacelab flights throughout the decade provided opportunities to fly a diverse group of international scientists. Three women flew together for the first time on a June 1991 Spacelab mission. A Spacelab flight in 1992 included the first Canadian woman, neurologist Roberta Bondar (1945–   ). STS-47 in September 1992 included the first Japanese astronaut, Mamoru Mohri (1948–   ), and the first black woman, Mae Jemison (1956–   ). The first Japanese woman, Chiaki Mukai (1952–   ), flew on a Spacelab flight in July 1994. Spacehab, a small pressurized module first used in 1993, also provided a bridge to the new space station. In October 1998, John Glenn returned to space on a Spacehab mission. At age 77, he was the oldest person ever to fly in space. Twenty Spacelab missions studying everything from the human nervous system to topographical geology of Earth were flown between 1991 and the end of 2000.

Shuttle missions also deployed important satellites and tested new technologies. A third TDRS went up in August 1991, and a fourth in January 1993, completing the satellite tracking network. In July 1992, STS-46 deployed an innovative tethered satellite system developed by NASA and the Italian Space Agency. Scientists planned to study and eventually tap into the electrical potential caused by the movement of the tether through Earth's magnetic field. The tether jammed after extending about 800 feet (250 m). The system flew again on STS-75 in February 1996. The tether extended more than 12 miles (20 km) during five hours. Although the tether snapped and the satellite was lost, the data proved that it is possible to use tethers to generate electricity in space.

The STS-61 *Hubble* repair mission in December 1993 was one of the most memorable of the decade. After *Hubble* was deployed in 1990, astronomers discovered that the primary mirror had been carefully ground to the wrong shape (see figure opposite). Commander Richard Covey (1946–   ) and Pilot Kenneth Bowersox (1956–   ) flew *Endeavour* to an altitude of 358 miles (576 km) to rendezvous with *Hubble*. (The only shuttle flight to go this high previously was the *Hubble* deployment.) ESA astronaut Claude Nicollier (1944–   ) captured and secured the telescope with the robotic arm. A record five spacewalks were required to carry out the servicing. The four spacewalkers, Story Musgrave, Jeffrey Hoffman (1944–   ), Thomas Akers, and Kathryn Thornton (1952–   ) spent hundreds of hours prior to the flight practicing in NASA's underwater training facility. One misplaced tool could have ruined the $1.5 billion telescope.

During the first spacewalk, the crew successfully changed out *Hubble*'s rate-sensing units, electronics control unit, and eight fuse plugs. One solar array was jettisoned and replaced with two new ones during the

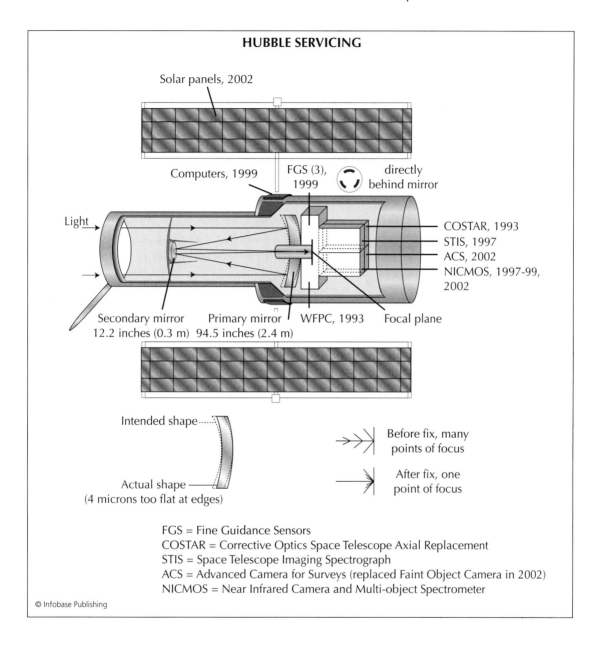

HUBBLE SERVICING

Solar panels, 2002

Computers, 1999

FGS (3), 1999

directly behind mirror

Light

COSTAR, 1993
STIS, 1997
ACS, 2002
NICMOS, 1997-99, 2002

Secondary mirror 12.2 inches (0.3 m)

Primary mirror 94.5 inches (2.4 m)

WFPC, 1993

Focal plane

Intended shape

Actual shape
(4 microns too flat at edges)

Before fix, many points of focus

After fix, one point of focus

FGS = Fine Guidance Sensors
COSTAR = Corrective Optics Space Telescope Axial Replacement
STIS = Space Telescope Imaging Spectrograph
ACS = Advanced Camera for Surveys (replaced Faint Object Camera in 2002)
NICMOS = Near Infrared Camera and Multi-object Spectrometer

© Infobase Publishing

second spacewalk. The third spacewalk provided *Hubble* with a new wide-field camera that compensated for the focusing problem. The "eyeglasses" were officially called the Corrective Optics Space Telescope Axial Replacement (COSTAR). COSTAR was installed on the fourth spacewalk, along with a new computer. During this spacewalk, Thomas

The Hubble Space Telescope was repaired in 1993 and serviced by space-shuttle crews in 1997, 1999, and 2002.

Akers broke the spacewalking record (previously held by moonwalker Eugene Cernan) by accumulating more than 29 hours outside. The final spacewalk replaced electronics and installed a new spectrograph. The *Hubble* was again successfully serviced and upgraded in February 1997, December 1999, and March 2002 (see figure on page 219).

The next shuttle flight marked a new era in space as Russian cosmonaut Sergei Krikalev joined the crew of STS-60 in February 1994. This flight had its roots in a 1992 agreement between U.S. President George H. W. Bush (1924–) and Russian President Boris Yeltsin (1931–). The two presidents had agreed that an American astronaut would visit *Mir* and two Russian cosmonauts would ride the shuttle. This agreement expanded in scope in 1993 after Bill Clinton became president. A scaled-down space station *Freedom* had survived being terminated by just one vote in Congress in 1993. To build political support and also discourage the Russians from selling ballistic-missile technology, the new administration invited the Russians to join with the United States to build the *International Space Station*. In December 1993, the United States agreed to pay $472 million for Americans to visit *Mir* through 1999 and for the Russians to provide a propulsion module for the new station. The Russians agreed to supply a crew habitat similar to the core module of *Mir*. Their three-man Soyuz would serve as escape ships, and shuttles and Progress rockets would both provide supplies.

Prior to his assignment to fly on a space shuttle, Sergei Krikalev had spent 312 days on *Mir*. He had launched to *Mir* on May 18, 1991, with his commander Anatoly Artsebarsky (1956–) and visiting British researcher Helen Sharman (1963–). The EO-8 crew and Dr. Sharman departed eight days later. During the summer, the political situation in the Soviet Union deteriorated as union members declared themselves independent. With funding uncertain, the next two planned flights to *Mir* were reduced to one. The October flight that should have brought a replacement crew instead brought only a replacement commander and two visitors, one from the newly independent Kazakhstan and one from Austria. Sergei Krikalev agreed to stay as the flight engineer for EO-10 commander Alexander Volkov. The communist Soviet Union that sent them into space ceased to exist on December 31, 1991. The two men returned to a democratic Russia in March 1992.

Sergei Krikalev and his five American crew mates launched on the space shuttle on February 3, 1994. The flight also included a test of the 12-foot (3.6-m) diameter Wake Shield Facility (WSF). Problems with the WSF's control system prevented its planned deployment. It successfully grew some thin films while attached to the end of the robotic arm.

A year later, in February 1995, Russian Vladimir Titov became the second Russian to fly on an American shuttle. It was also the first flight of a female pilot, Eileen Collins. STS-63 came within 37 feet (11.2 m) of

Mir, practicing procedures for a flight in June that would physically bring the two nations' space programs together.

New Life in Moon/Mars Research

Thirteen years after the last spacecraft landed on the Moon (*Luna 24* in 1976), Japan became the third nation to send spacecraft there. *Hiten* [celestial maiden] entered lunar orbit on January 24, 1990. After three years of mapping, it impacted the near side in 1993. The U.S. *Galileo* (see Further Reading) spacecraft flew past the Moon twice, in December 1990 and December 1992. *Galileo* provided unique photos of the Moon's far side and also a stunning "family portrait" of the Earth and Moon. The American *Clementine* probe, launched in January 1994, mapped the Moon in new detail for several months and found hints of hydrogen near the poles. Unlike Earth rocks, none of the Apollo or Russian lunar samples showed any water or hydrogen. Because humans need water and water is extremely heavy to lift into space, having a source of hydrogen on the Moon greatly reduces the expense of establishing an outpost there. So when *Clementine*'s data hinted that hydrogen may be present, scientists were anxious to send another instrument. *Lunar Prospector* entered lunar orbit in November 1997. It provided strong evidence of hydrogen in permanently shadowed craters near the lunar poles. After completing is mapping mission, *Lunar Prospector* was purposefully crashed on July 31, 1999, near the lunar south pole (see Further Reading) to see if it would kick up any dusty ice. None was observed. This crash resulted in the first burial on the Moon because the ashes of geologist Eugene Shoemaker (see sidebar below) were on board.

Lunar Burial of Eugene Shoemaker

The crash of *Lunar Prospector* in 1999 resulted in the first burial of human remains on the Moon. A lipstick-sized canister of ashes of geologist Eugene Shoemaker was strapped inside the spacecraft. As the first head of the United States Geological Survey's Center of Astrogeology (founded in 1965), Eugene Shoemaker is considered the father of *astrogeology,* the geologic study of celestial bodies such as the Moon, asteroids, and Mars. He headed the Apollo lunar geology efforts and trained the astronauts. Separately or with his wife Carolyn Spellman (1929–), he discovered 32 comets and 1,125 asteroids, including *Shoemaker–Levy 9* that impacted Jupiter in 1992. He was well known for his conviction that comets and asteroids pose a threat to life on Earth. He supported the theory of Luis (1911–88) and his son Walter (1940–) Alvarez that an impact was responsible for the Cretaceous–Tertiary extinction of the dinosaurs 65 millions ago. Eugene Shoemaker died (see Further Reading) in a violent car collision while studying impact craters in Australia in July 1997 at age 69.

No Little Green Men

Publication of scientific papers does not often generate headlines. But when news leaked that the August 16, 1996, issue of the prestigious journal *Science* would contain a paper (see Further Reading) offering proof of life on Mars, NASA Administrator Dan Goldin (1940–   ) had to schedule a press conference to stop wild speculations by the media. "I want everyone to understand that we are not talking about 'little green men,'" he said in announcing the press conference. "These are extremely small single-cell structures that somewhat resemble bacteria on Earth." Journalists packed the room on August 7 to hear from Johnson Space Center scientists David McKay (1936–   ), Everett Gibson (1940–   ), and Kathie Thomas-Keprta (1957–   ). Millions listened in as they described their two-year study of a 4.5-billion-year-old meteorite from Mars, designated ALH84001. They claimed that complex organic molecules, carbonate globules, and tiny structures similar to fossilized remains of organisms on Earth were evidence that microscopic bacteria once lived on Mars.

Though some scientists argued for nonbiological explanations of the evidence, they did not dispute that the meteorite came from Mars. Its chemistry matched that measured by the Viking spacecraft in 1976. The rock was apparently knocked free of Mars by an impact about 15 million years ago. It fell to Antarctica about 13,000 years ago and was found in 1984. The new technology of a scanning electron microscope and a special laser mass spectrometer had made the discovery of the previously hidden tiny structures possible. President Clinton said, "Today, rock 84001 speaks to us across all those billions of years and millions of miles. It speaks of the possibility of life. If this discovery is confirmed, it will surely be one of the most stunning insights into our universe that science has ever uncovered."

This discovery intensified public interest in the next mission to Mars. The last American mission to Mars was an $813-million-dollar failure. *Mars Observer* was lost just three days short of reaching Mars in August 1993, most likely the result of a propulsion leak. In 1992, NASA adopted a "faster, better, cheaper" philosophy of sending multiple less-expensive missions. The first of these was *Mars Pathfinder*, developed in three years with a budget of $265 million compared to $3.9 billion for Viking. On July 4, 1997, it literally bounced its way to the surface of Mars. After streaking through the Martian night, explosive bolts ejected a parachute that slowed the craft. Three small rockets fired and brought the ship 50 feet (15 m) above the ground. Then, in just one second, four giant airbags made of a bullet-proof-vest material inflated around the spacecraft. The ball dropped, bounced, and tumbled to rest on the rocky terrain of Ares Vallis. The *Carl Sagan Memorial Station* opened like a flower, and the small *Sojourner* rover rolled free to examine nearby rocks.

The Mars Pathfinder mission included the Sagan Memorial Station, *shown in the foreground in this mosaic, and the* Sojourner *rover, shown examining a rock dubbed "Moe." The view shows the South Twin Peak on the horizon about 0.6 miles (1 km) away.* (NASA–JPL)

The Mars Pathfinder Web site (see Further Reading) exploded with activity, setting an Internet record of 47 million hits on July 8. Within a month, more than 500 million people had visited the Web site and viewed rocks that the team affectionately named after cartoon characters such as Barnacle Bill and Yogi. Hot Wheel toy versions of the rover sold out. Some rocks were found to resemble Earth conglomerates formed by running water. This implied that Mars had water for a long period of time in its past. The mission ended when the station's batteries failed on September 27, 1997.

While *Sojourner* explored Mars, the *Mars Global Surveyor (MGS)* team worked to save its mission. One of the spacecraft's solar panels had jammed after launch. Controllers worried that this panel might break off when the spacecraft dipped into the Martian atmosphere to slow itself down, a technique known as aerobraking. Aerobraking reduced the amount of fuel that it had to carry, thus reducing cost by allowing it to launch on a smaller, cheaper rocket. On September 11, 1997, MGS entered orbit successfully. Aerobraking maneuvers over the next few orbits showed that the atmosphere was thicker than expected. The spacecraft was flown "backward" to protect the damaged panel and slowly eased from an elliptical to a circular orbit over several years. This strategy had the unexpected benefit of bringing the spacecraft closer to the surface than originally planned. MGS captured images of canyons and possible water-deposited sediments.

The next set of "faster, better, cheaper" Mars missions were as much a failure as *Pathfinder* was a success. In September 1999, NASA became the butt of jokes as the *Mars Climate Orbiter* crashed because a navigation program failed to convert English units to metric units. The spacecraft was ordered into an orbit that impacted the planet. Then the twin *Mars Polar Landers* were lost on December 3 as they descended to the Martian south pole. A software defect caused the braking rockets to shut off 130 feet (40 m) above the surface.

The Japanese also failed to reach Mars. *Nozomi* [Planet B] was supposed to arrive in October, but a faulty valve left the spacecraft short of fuel. It went into solar orbit with a plan to use an Earth swing-by to send it back to Mars in 2003. Continued thruster problems caused *Nozomi* to fly past Mars in December 2003.

Asteroids, Comets, and Extrasolar Planets

The silver-white element iridium is very rare on Earth but not in asteroids. So when scientists found a layer of it in formations dating to the Cretaceous–Tertiary boundary 65 million years ago, they wondered if it might be the remains of an asteroid impact. In 1980, Nobel-prize winner Luis Alvarez and his son Walter proposed that the level of iridium deposited was consistent with an asteroid about six miles (10 km) in diameter, creating a crater 100 miles (160 km) wide. They theorized that its impact likely caused tsunami, fires, and ejected dust (including iridium) that blocked sunlight for a long period of time. Temperatures dropped, plants died, and oxygen levels fell. About 70 percent of all species died by the end of the Cretaceous, and dinosaurs became extinct. Their theory was supported by the discovery and dating of the Chicxulub crater on the Mexican east coast in 1992.

The realization that a relatively small asteroid could cause the extinction of a species that had ruled the Earth for more than 160 million years spurred efforts to find and study celestial threats to Earth. The *Galileo* spacecraft provided the first close-up view of an asteroid when it flew past Gaspra (see photo opposite) in 1991. In 1993, *Galileo* discovered that the asteroid Ida has a satellite, Dactyl. In March of that year, Eugene Shoemaker and David Levy (1948–   ) discovered a most unusual comet: Shoemaker–Levy 9 had been torn to pieces by a close encounter with Jupiter in 1992 and was doomed to impact Jupiter in 1994.

For four days starting on July 16, 1994, observatories around the world and in space watched as fragments crashed into Jupiter. *Galileo*, on its way to the giant planet, captured images of fireballs hotter than the surface of the Sun. Astronomers saw dark-ringed bruises twice the diameter of Earth that persisted for more than a year. The energy released by each fragment was more than that of all the Earth's nuclear bombs combined. If comet Shoemaker-Levy 9 had hit Earth, humanity may have gone the way of the dinosaurs.

The Galileo spacecraft provided the first close-up photo of an asteroid in 1991. Gaspra is about 12 × 7.5 × 7 miles (19 × 12 × 11 km) in size. (NASA)

It may be that giant planets spare their smaller siblings by attracting and absorbing impacts. Jupiter absorbed its first artificial manmade impact in December 1995 when *Galileo* dropped a probe into the atmosphere. The atmosphere was much drier than predicted, but the winds were much greater, up to 330 mph (206 kph). Jupiter's gravity helps clear the solar system of asteroids and comets, and its gravity may also facilitate life on its moons. *Galileo* found evidence that Ganymede, Callisto, and Europa may have subsurface saltwater oceans. Europa is the most promising for life because its gravitational tug-of-war with Jupiter heats the moon.

The study of dangerous solar system bodies continued with the *Near Earth Asteroid Rendezvous* (NEAR) spacecraft launch in 1996. Named *NEAR-Shoemaker* in 1997, the spacecraft took close-up photos of the asteroid 253 Mathilde in June 1997. The coal-dark "rubble pile" was found to be about 37 miles (60 km) wide and pocked with craters. *NEAR* became the first spacecraft to land on an asteroid—Eros—on February 12, 2000. The 21-mile- (34-km-) long potential planet killer, named after the god of love, puzzled scientists with its large number of boulders and sharp boundaries. They had expected the surface to be worn down from eons of "sand blasting" by dust impacts.

Comets spend most of their time lurking in the dark too far from the Sun to form a tail, so it was unusual when comet Hale–Bopp was found while still outside Jupiter's orbit in 1995. A thousand times brighter than comet Halley, Hale–Bopp was visible without a telescope during its closest approach in March 1997. With a period of about 2,400 years, it is one of an estimated trillion long-period comets that are thought to reside in the distant Oort cloud. A nudge by a passing star could send one of them heading toward Earth. To learn more about comets, NASA launched *Stardust* in 1999. It returned to Earth with a sample in 2004. Though the parachute failed, some data was recovered.

As destructive as asteroids and comets may be to planets, prior to this decade, astronomers assumed that no planet could survive a supernova, so they were very surprised in 1991 when Polish astronomer Alexander Wolszczan (1946–) reported evidence that Pulsar 1257+12 in Virgo had three planets. More detailed analysis supported his conclusion. Astronomers speculate that either distant giant planets survived the supernova that created the pulsar or the supernova destroyed a stellar companion and planets formed from the debris.

The pulsar's planets were found through radio observations of changes in the spacing of the pulsar's pulses. Normal stars do not pulse, so finding planets around them is more difficult. One way to look for stellar companions is to watch for Doppler shifts in the velocity of nearby stars. This stellar-wobble method (see figure opposite) requires taking enough spectra of the star to see a pattern repeat.

In 1995, Swiss astronomer Michael Mayor (1942–) and his student Didier Queloz (1966–) at the University of Geneva were using a 76-inch (1.9 m) telescope and the Doppler shift method to hunt for failed stars called *brown dwarfs*. After only a week of data, the team found a wobble in the motion of the sunlike star 51 Pegasi. The size of the wobble indicated that the mass of the companion was only about half that of Jupiter. Too small to be a brown dwarf, they announced finding the first extrasolar planet in October 1995. The puzzling thing was that the period was only four days. Up to this time, astronomers assumed that giant planets like Jupiter formed far from their parent star and had long orbital periods.

The first planet was found before the first brown dwarf. Called Gliese 229B, the brown dwarf was discovered in November 1995, using a combination of an image from the Palomar 60-inch (1.5 m) telescope and a spectrum from the 200-inch (5-m) telescope. The *Hubble Space Telescope* confirmed the discovery. Gliese 229B is a companion of a red dwarf star that is 19 light-years away in Lepus. Estimated to be 20–50 times the mass of Jupiter, Gliese 229B is at least 100,000 times dimmer than the Sun.

After the announcement of the first extrasolar planet having such a short period, astronomer Geoffrey Marcy (see sidebar and photo on pages 236–238) reexamined data that he had collected since the early 1980s. He quickly confirmed Michael Mayor's finding, and in January 1996, he and Paul R. Butler announced the discovery of planets around two more stars. One was another "hot Jupiter," zipping around 70 Virginis at close range. The planet around 47 Ursae Majoris was at a distance comparable to that of Mars from the Sun. It was later found to have a sibling at about Earth's distance from the Sun. Astronomers speculate that one of these planets could have habitable moons.

Marcy's team found the first multiplanet system around a normal star in 1999. The star Upsilon Andromeda has three planets. The previous year, astronomers found a disk of dust similar to the Kuiper belt around 55 Cancri, a sunlike star about 40 light-years away. This star was later shown to also have four planets.

In November 1999, the first extrasolar planet was found using the transit method. As the planet passed in front of a star about 150 light-

(Opposite page) The Doppler shift of a star's radial velocity "wobbles" if a star has a planet.

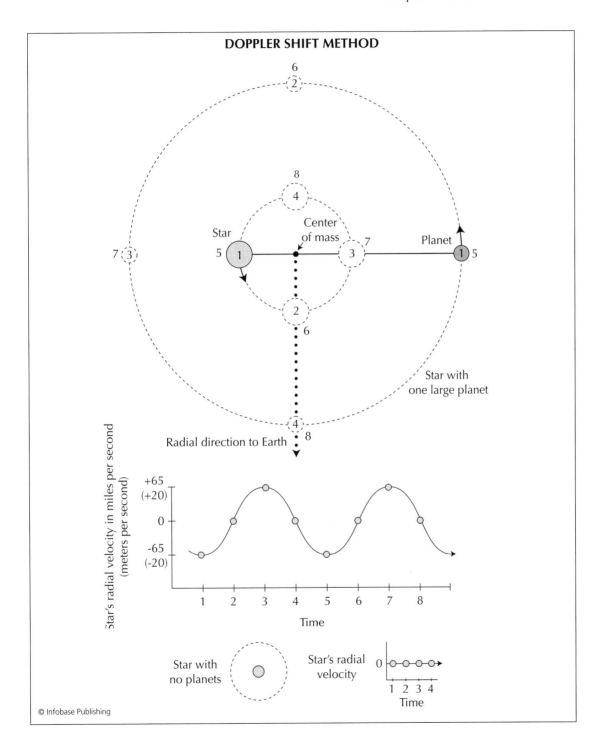

DOPPLER SHIFT METHOD

Star

Center of mass

Planet

Star with one large planet

Radial direction to Earth

Star's radial velocity in miles per second (meters per second)

+65 (+20)

0

-65 (-20)

1 2 3 4 5 6 7 8

Time

Star with no planets

Star's radial velocity

0

1 2 3 4

Time

years away in Pegasus, it dimmed the light by 1.7 percent. This showed the planet has a diameter about 35 percent larger than Jupiter. The *Hubble Space Telescope* detected sodium in its atmosphere and a hydrogen tail that is 124,000 miles (200,000 km) long.

Based on early findings, astronomers estimate that at least 10 percent of stars have planets. Even some binary stars (such as 16 Cygni) have planets. Stars with high-metal content (like the Sun) that are made from recycled supernovae are most likely to have planets. About three-fourths of the planets are in elliptical orbits. Whether or not life can survive the intense radiation and violent impacts that seem to go along with planetary systems is a question that remains for the next century's astronomers.

Space Observatories

The difficulty in producing large single mirrors and supporting them against their weight led to new telescope designs. In 1991, the Hale 200-inch (5-m) telescope lost its title of world's largest to the 394-inch (10-m) Keck I telescope on Mauna Kea in Hawaii. The Keck's mirror is made of 36 hexagonal segments that work as a single piece of glass. Computer-controlled sensors and actuators can realign the segments up to 670 times a second to account for temperature changes and atmospheric distortion. A second Keck telescope on Mauna Kea was dedicated in 1996, and the two telescopes began to work together as an interferometer in 2001. The adaptive optics of these two giant telescopes allow them to obtain images that rival those taken in space.

The largest radio dish at the end of the century was the Arecibo radio observatory in Puerto Rico, built in 1963. Rather than build a larger dish, better resolution than Arecibo was achieved by combining signals of separate telescopes into an interferometer (see figure on page 235). This was accomplished on a new scale with the dedication of the Very Long Base Array (VLBA) in 1993. Ten telescopes spread across 5,000 miles (8,000 km) provide resolution enough to read a newspaper in Los Angeles while standing in New York City. The VLBA was combined with the orbiting Japanese HALCA satellite in 1997 to produce an array with a baseline of 13,000 miles (21,000 km) and 100 times the detail of the *Hubble Space Telescope*.

Adaptive optics and interferometers have greatly improved visual and radio studies of the universe. But even in these wavelengths, space telescopes have the advantage of being able to stare at the same point without having to deal with day and night or bad weather. The *Hubble Space Telescope* stared at a "blank" spot near the Big Dipper for 10 days in December 1995, producing the Hubble Deep Field North image. This feat was repeated for a spot near Tucana in the south for 10 days in October 1998. Using these two "core samples," astronomers determined

The 385-inch (9.8-m) Keck I and II on Mauna Kea in Hawaii are the largest optical and infrared telescopes in the world. They began operations in 1993 and 1996. On the left is the 326-inch (8.3-m) Subaru telescope built in 1999 and operated by the National Astronomical Observatory of Japan. (Thomas Matheson)

that galaxies formed quickly after the big bang and that the early universe appears the same in at least two directions.

The *Chandra* X-ray telescope imaged the same area as both the Hubble Deep Field North and South. Bright X-ray sources showed likely supermassive black holes. An X-ray quasar was found 12 billion light-years away.

The Japanese *Advanced Satellite for Cosmology and Astrophysics* (ASCA) was launched in 1993. In 1997, three astronomers (see Further Reading) at the Harvard–Smithsonian Center for Astrophysics used ASCA to detect the *event horizon* of a black hole. They compared the energy radiated from binary stars. Binaries containing black holes are dimmer in X-rays than binaries with neutron stars because energy disappears once it crosses the black hole's event horizon.

Gamma-ray photons are a million times more energetic than visible light and cannot be focused but merely counted. Gamma rays are so rare that the *Compton Gamma Ray Observatory* measured bursts of less than two minutes about every other day. Launched by the space shuttle in 1991, *Compton* collected data on these mysterious events until June 2000. *Compton* allowed astronomers to locate visible counterparts to bursts and determine that they originate outside the galaxy in all directions. By 1999, the consensus was that gamma-ray bursts signal the creation of black holes or the merger of neutron stars. In the next century, a new space telescope (*Swift*) would reveal that long bursts are black holes forming in young galaxies and that short bursts are from neutron star or black-hole mergers in older galaxies.

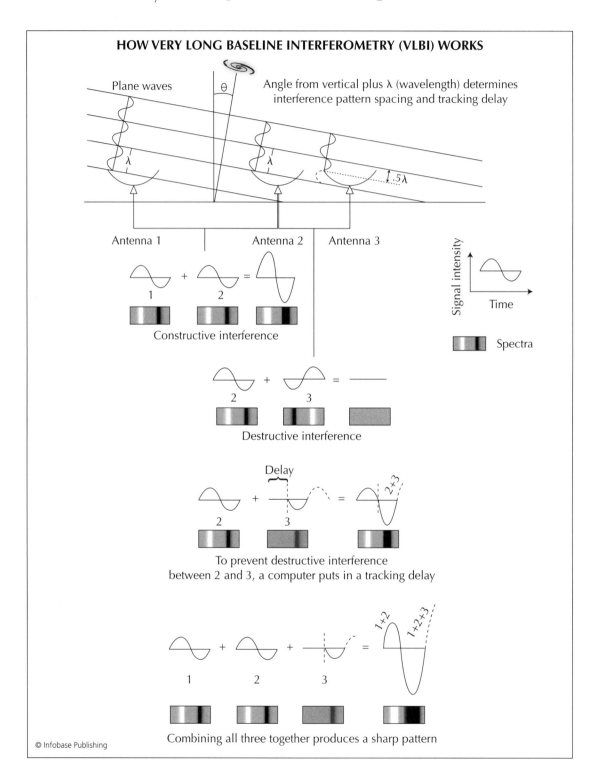

HOW VERY LONG BASELINE INTERFEROMETRY (VLBI) WORKS

Plane waves

θ

Angle from vertical plus λ (wavelength) determines interference pattern spacing and tracking delay

λ

λ

.5λ

Antenna 1   Antenna 2   Antenna 3

1 + 2 =

Constructive interference

Signal intensity

Time

Spectra

2 + 3 =

Destructive interference

Delay

2 + 3 = 2+3

To prevent destructive interference between 2 and 3, a computer puts in a tracking delay

1 + 2 + 3 = 1+2   1+2+3

Combining all three together produces a sharp pattern

© Infobase Publishing

Using data from space and ground-based telescopes, teams led independently by Adam Riess (1969–   ) and Saul Perlmutter (1959–   ) stunned the astronomical community in 1998 with the announcement that the expansion of the universe may be accelerating. The astronomers found that distant supernovae were moving away at a faster rate than nearer ones. They speculated that Albert Einstein's cosmological constant, representing a repulsive force, may need to be reinstated into the equations of general relativity. Data from *Chandra* and other telescopes in the early years of the next century supported the conclusion that some "dark energy" is causing the universe to expand at a faster rate than it did in its first 6 billion years.

To further examine the question of dark energy, gamma-ray bursts, and detect habitable worlds in other solar systems, astronomers depend on distance-measuring tools (see figure on page 232) developed throughout the 20th century. For many years, quasars held the record as the most distant detectable objects because of their brightness. But thanks to the magnifying effect of gravitational lenses, by 2000, the most distant object was a galaxy 13.6 billion light-years away.

(Opposite page) The Very Long Baseline Array (VLBA) of telescopes uses the interference of radio waves from distant objects to create very precise images and distance measurements.

International Space

Life onboard the *Mir* station was pretty routine from the time Sergei Krikalev left in March 1992 until March 1995 when the first American arrived. The EO-11, 12, 13, and 14 crews each served onboard about six months and only hosted visitors at the beginning and end of their stays. The EO-13 crew were treated to the first solar sail deployment a month into their tour. The idea to reflect sunlight as a means of propulsion was first proposed by Konstantin Tsiolkovsky in 1924. The experiment in February 1993 had a less-ambitious goal—to reflect sunlight to Earth. It worked perfectly. A Progress cargo ship deployed a 66-foot (20-m) foil reflector near the station. During its five-hour operation, people in Canada, Europe, and Russia reported seeing the mirror. A follow-up mission in 1999 failed when the much larger sail sadly tangled on an antenna.

The EO-14 crew observed a potentially dangerous display when the Perseid meteor shower peaked on August 12–13, 1993. The "storm" of high-speed pellets caused NASA to delay a space-shuttle launch, and the Russians to put rescue helicopters on standby in case *Mir* were hit. The crew saw more than 200 meteroids burn up in the atmosphere below them and counted 10 hits to the station windows. No serious damage was suffered.

A member of the three-person EO-15 crew that launched in January 1994 set a new endurance record. Valeri Polyakov returned to Earth in March 1995 after 438 continuous days in space. He was on *Mir* to greet American Norman Thagard (1943–   ) in March 1995.

Thagard was the first American to ride in a Soyuz capsule. During his *TM–21* flight to *Mir* where three cosmonauts waited, the space shuttle

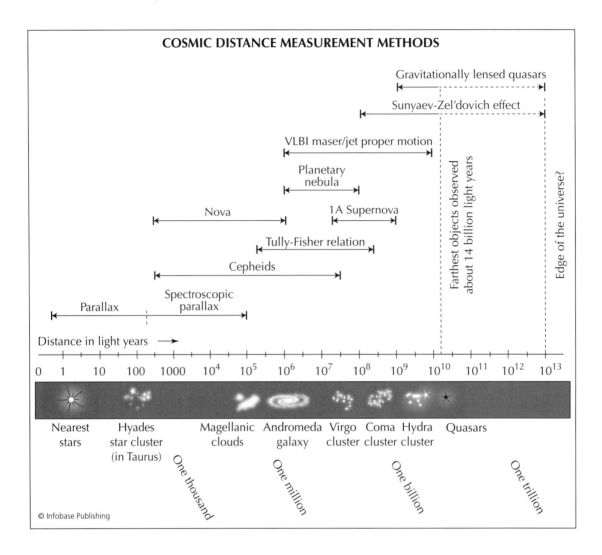

COSMIC DISTANCE MEASUREMENT METHODS

Gravitationally lensed quasars

Sunyaev-Zel'dovich effect

VLBI maser/jet proper motion

Planetary nebula

Nova

1A Supernova

Tully-Fisher relation

Cepheids

Spectroscopic parallax

Parallax

Distance in light years →

0   1   10   100   1000 10^4 10^5 10^6 10^7 10^8 10^9 10^{10} 10^{11} 10^{12} 10^{13}

Farthest objects observed about 14 billion light years

Edge of the universe?

Nearest stars

Hyades star cluster (in Taurus)

Magellanic clouds

Andromeda galaxy

Virgo cluster

Coma cluster

Hydra cluster

Quasars

One thousand

One million

One billion

One trillion

© Infobase Publishing

During the 20th century, astronomers went from simple parallax to many new ways to measure the distance to stars and galaxies.

Endeavour was in the midst of a Spacelab mission with seven crew members. The three spaceships hosted a record total of 13 people (including two women) in space at once in March 1995.

Thagard spent three months with two Russian cosmonauts as a member of the *Mir-18* crew. The bulk of his science experiments were in the new *Spektr* module. When its launch was delayed until June 1, 1995, Thagard did not have much to do. His life-sciences work required blood samples. First his freezer failed, and then he lost too much weight to be a good test subject. All people lose weight in space, but Thagard lost more than 17 pounds because of a diet limited mostly to foods that he disliked. Communications with the ground were sporadic. He relied on ham radio operators to transmit messages to his wife.

The three-man Russian *Mir-19* crew rode to space on the shuttle *Atlantis* in June 1995. The planned historic first shuttle docking was almost canceled because of a leaking shuttle thruster. The Russians feared the horizon sensor on their parked Soyuz return ship might be contaminated. Once the thruster was clear, STS-71 docked with *Mir*. The shuttle exchanged the crew and delivered more than 1,000 pounds of water.

In November, *Atlantis* visited *Mir* again. STS-74 delivered solar arrays and a docking module to attach to the *Kristall* module. This module provided extended clearance between the shuttle and *Mir*'s solar arrays.

February 1996 marked the 10th anniversary of the *Mir* space station. The two Russian members of the *Mir-21* crew arrived that month. In March, *Atlantis* brought American Shannon Lucid, who set a duration record of 188 days for a woman in space. In April, a sixth and final module was added. *Priroda* [Nature] was focused on Earth remote sensing and included a large antenna. In May, Yuri Onufrienko (1961–) and Yury Usachev (1957–) did a commercial for Pepsi outside *Mir*. The ad proved controversial in the United States. Whereas some felt it made good sense for cash-strapped Russia to accept commercial funds for their space program, others felt it demeaning and inappropriate to use cosmonauts this way. This issue came up again in 2001 with the Russian flight of a rich American tourist to the *International Space Station*.

John Blaha (1942–) rode to *Mir* on the shuttle that brought Shannon Lucid home in September 1996. A former shuttle commander and military man, Blaha was very frustrated by a lack of communications with the ground. The situation got worse for medical doctor Jerry Linenger (1955–) who took his place in January 1997.

On February 12, the *Mir* EO-23 crew of Vasili Tsibliyev (1954–) and Alexander Lazutkin (1957–) arrived via Soyuz to replace the EO-22 crew and brought along a visiting German, Reinhold Ewald (1956–). EO-23 Commander Tsibliyev had to do a manual docking because the automatic Kurs docking system failed. The Russians were anxious to replace Kurs because the Ukrainian supplier charged exorbitant prices and delivered incomplete units. Tsibliyev earned a $1,000 bonus for the manual docking. All cosmonauts were paid by contracts that specified bonuses for extra duties such as spacewalks and penalties for disobeying orders. Many Americans felt that this system encouraged risk taking and the cover-up of problems with *Mir*. Their fears were supported by a series of events (see Further Reading) that started during crew handover.

With an extra three people onboard during the EO-22 to 23 handover, the Elektron oxygen generation system was supplemented with a solid-fuel oxygen generator (SFOG). On February 23, Alexander Lazutkin routinely inserted a new cassette or "candle" into the SFOG in the *Kvant* module. Instead of releasing oxygen by a chemical reaction, the unit blazed into a blowtorch, shooting flame about two-feet (0.6-m) long. Thick black smoke filled *Kvant* and the core module. The men donned oxygen masks and prepared for emergency evacuation. EO-22 commander Valery Korzun (1953–) used three extinguishers to put out the fire that was hot enough to melt the metal casing of the SFOG. Though one Soyuz was prepared to evacuate three of the men, the other was attached to *Kvant* and unreachable. They decided not to evacuate.

NASA officials were not told about the fire until 12 hours later. Linenger was furious. He pleaded with the Russians to tell him what chemicals were in the smoke so he could treat the crew. They would not let him use the radio. He accused the Russians of downplaying the severity of the fire to protect the market for *Mir*. His view was reinforced the next month when a near miss of the station during a manual docking test was treated as insignificant. Frustrated with the way his time was wasted by poor communications, and feeling that his complaints were not taken seriously, Linenger quit talking to the ground on March 7.

While Linenger focused on his experiments, Tsibliyev and Lazutkin were overwhelmed with maintenance. The Elektron system failed on March 8, forcing them to use the SFOG again. One crew member stood by with a fire extinguisher each time a new candle was inserted. Comet Hale–Bopp was visible out the window. The crew wondered if it were a bad omen. On March 19, it must have seemed so because a rate sensor failed, causing *Mir* to lose attitude control. With the solar arrays not pointed at the Sun, the *Spektr* module lost power for several days. This further frustrated Linenger, whose experiments were in *Spektr*. In April, the cooling system had to be shut down because of leaks. The temperatures in the core module quickly rose. On April 4, the carbon dioxide system had to be shut down. With the temperature near 100°F (37°C) and carbon dioxide levels near the limit, crew exercise was banned. Linenger exercised anyway, angering his Russian crew mates. Russian Mission Control almost canceled the spacewalk of Tsibliyev with Linenger because of the tension between them. The commander overcame his anger to earn his $1,000 bonus for the spacewalk on April 29, 1997. Linenger cited the airlock hatch from *Kvant 2*, held on with C-clamps, as another example of why *Mir* was no longer safe. Despite his concerns, NASA sent his replacement, Michael Foale (1957–), up on a shuttle flight in May.

Foale was destined to endure even worse conditions than Linenger. On June 5, Tsibliyev rammed headfirst into a basketball-sized ball of leaked antifreeze. He suffered blurred vision and nausea for several days. Lazutkin finally found and repaired the last of the coolant leaks a week later. But there was no rest, literally, for the Russians. Part of their contract required participation in a sleep study that kept them awake for most of two weeks.

On June 25, 1997, the barely recovered and exhausted Tsibliyev nevertheless had to do another manual docking test with a Progress supply ship like the one that caused a near-miss in March. To prevent interference with camera data, the ground turned off the range and rate data. The crew had to rely on looking out the windows to tell how far away the Progress was. Their view of Progress was blocked by a solar array until it was too late. It crashed into an array on *Spektr* and then punctured that module.

With alarms blaring, Lazutkin disconnected 18 cables that ran through the *Sepktr* hatch while Foale prepared the Soyuz for evacuation. The *Spektr* hatch opened into the module and could not be pulled shut against the air rushing out. The crew capped it from the node side. The pressure in *Mir* dropped from 15 psi (780 mm) to 12.9 psi (668 mm) in the three minutes it took to cap the hatch. Tsibliyev activated oxygen canisters that restored some of the pressure. Power was a bigger issue. The arrays on *Spectr* provided 42 percent of *Mir*'s power. The cable carrying that power had been disconnected to seal the hatch. The collision left the station spinning so the remaining arrays did not provide enough power to charge the batteries. Within five hours of the accident, *Mir* plunged into total darkness. An eerie silence descended as the gyrodines wound down.

The station's thrusters normally stop any spin and orient the arrays. But there was not enough power to run the thrusters. Foale suggested using the Soyuz engines instead. This worked. Through their quick actions, the crew had saved themselves and the *Mir* space station from disaster.

A Progress was sent in July with supplies for the crew to do an "internal" EVA to restore power. The crew needed to depressurize the node and enter *Spektr* to reattach cables from the arrays. Tsibliyev was disqualified from the spacewalk because of an irregular heartbeat that was blamed on the stress of dealing with the accident while already in an exhausted state. The spacewalk was then postponed until August when Anatoli Solovyov (1948–) and Pavel Vinogradov (1953–) arrived. After a harrowing close call with a leaking glove, the cosmonauts reconnected the power. A follow-up spacewalk with Foale and Solovyov in September was unable to find and patch the hole in *Spektr*.

The need for spacewalks necessitated a change in the next crew. Wendy Lawrence (1959–) was too short to wear a Russian spacesuit, so she was replaced by her backup, David Wolf (1956–). Lawrence was then assigned to the STS-86 crew that took Wolf to *Mir* in late September and to the STS-91 crew that brought his replacement, Andrew Thomas (1951–), home from *Mir* in June 1998 (see photo on page 237). Wolf did one spacewalk on *Mir* in January. It was Anatoli Solovyov's 16th EVA, giving him a record of more than 80 hours spacewalking. STS-91 was the last flight of the Shuttle–Mir program. Seven Americans had spent 907 days on *Mir*.

The first piece of the *International Space Station* (*ISS*), *Zarya* [Sunrise], was launched unmanned from Kazakstan in November 1998. A few weeks later, the crew of space-shuttle flight STS-88 arrived to connect the American-made node, *Unity*. Because of financial woes in Russia, the critical third module, *Zvezda* [Star], was delayed for more than a year until July 2000. Several space-shuttle flights quickly followed to provide equipment. The first Expedition crew rode a Soyuz rocket to their new home in November 2000. American Bill Shepard (1949–   ) and Russians Yuri Gidzenko (1962–   ) and Sergei Krikalev christened the new station, *Alpha*, though its official name remained *International Space Station*. Later that month, STS-97 brought up the first solar array. The first crew remained until March 2001. The STS-92 flight to deliver a truss to the *ISS* in October 2000 was the 100th of the shuttle program. In 19 years, 260 people and 3 million pounds (1.3 million kg) had been delivered, and 60 satellites had been deployed by the shuttle.

Meanwhile, time ran out for *Mir*. The EO-25 crew with whom Andy Thomas had been in space was replaced in August 1998. These men too replaced by the EO-26 crew in February 1999. The Russians sold two of the seats on the next flight, so Sergei Avdeyev (1956–   ) stayed up and came home with the EO-27 crew in August 1999, setting a new cumulative time-in-space record of 748 days. Their return marked the first time in 10 years that there were no humans in space. Efforts to raise enough money to maintain *Mir* failed. Sergei Zalyotin (1962–   ) and Alexander Kaleri (1956–   ) were the last to live on *Mir*, from April 4 to June 16, 2000. After 15 years in orbit, the abandoned *Mir* met a fiery end over the Pacific Ocean on March 23, 2001.

Scientist of the Decade: Geoffrey Marcy (1954–   )

Astronomer Geoffrey Marcy set out to do the impossible—to find planets around other stars. In 1983, when his quest began, "Everybody knew that planets didn't emit their own light. They were too little. There was no way to detect planets," he said in a 2004 interview with the author. "I thought, well, maybe I'll try it." Marcy eventually succeeded in finding 70 of the first 100 extrasolar planets.

Geoffrey Marcy was born in Detroit on September 29, 1954, and moved with his parents, Robert Marcy (1928–   ) and Gloria Isaacs (1932–   ) and two sisters to Los Angeles when he was four. At age 13, his parents bought him a solar system poster. "I remember lying on my bed as a kid and staring up at that poster, and letting the planets sort of diffuse into me," he recalled. His parents bought him a four-inch (10-cm) telescope the next year. "I'd spend the night out on the roof in the summers and watch the planets and stars. My favorite was definitely Saturn. . . . This big bright dot orbited around Saturn that I learned was called Titan . . . and you could come back the next night and see Titan orbit Saturn."

Marcy assumed that he would become a scientist like his parents, who had degrees in anthropology and mechanical engineering. He took physics and chemistry in high school and went to the

This view of the Russian Mir space station was taken by the STS-91 shuttle crew as they left in June 1998. STS-91 was the last shuttle to visit the Mir that was deorbited in 2001. (NASA)

University of California (UC) at Los Angeles. He graduated summa cum laude, Phi Beta Kappa, in 1976 with a double major in physics and astronomy. He then attended UC Santa Cruz and earned his Ph.D. in astronomy and astrophysics in 1982.

Marcy received a postdoctoral fellowship from the Carnegie Institute of Washington. He was busy taking magnetic field measurements of stars using the 100-inch (2.5-m) telescope on Mount Wilson when he received some devastating news. A well-respected astronomer had challenged Marcy's thesis on magnetic fields as not only uncertain but wrong. "It was one of those kind of critiques that had a grain of truth to it, but on the other hand, was probably overblown." This critique caused

Marcy to lose confidence in himself and his work. Thinking his career was over and that he had nothing to lose, he decided to attempt the impossible: to look for planets.

A solar physicist cautioned Marcy against this research project. "He said, 'you know it is not possible to measure Doppler shifts that precisely.'" He noted that turbulence in the atmospheres of stars can be hundreds of feet (meters) per second. The effect of a planet on a star's velocity toward or away from Earth would be only tens of feet (meters) per second. But Marcy was determined to try. He used the Mount Wilson 100-inch (2.5-m) telescope to measure Doppler shifts.

(continued on next page)

(continued from previous page)

After two years, he had found nothing. The discouraged young astronomer decided to give up on research. He took a job as a professor at San Francisco State University (SFSU) and focused on teaching. A graduate student convinced him to resume the search for planets, even though SFSU did not have a telescope.

Marcy arranged to use a 24-inch (0.6-m) telescope at Lick Observatory. The telescope was small, but it used a world-class spectrometer built by Steven Vogt (1949–). Then Marcy and Paul Butler adapted an idea of Canadian astronomer Bruce Campbell to use a cell of gas to create a static spectral line against which to compare a star's spectral lines. This technique allowed measurement of Doppler shifts more precisely than ever before.

Years went by with no planets found. Marcy taught classes and married chemist Susan Kegley (1957–). He continued gathering data under the assumption that large planets form far from stars and cause shifts that require many years to show up. The October 1995 discovery of a planet with half the mass of Jupiter orbiting 51 Pegasi with a period of only four days took him by surprise.

After this discovery, Marcy worked with Butler to reexamine the data for wobbles of shorter periods. In December 1995, they announced the discovery of planets around 70 Virginis and 47 Ursae Majoris. Both had orbits at about the distance of Mars and periods under three years. Marcy appeared on television talk shows and was the January 26, 1996, *ABC News* "Person of the Week."

In 1999, Marcy's team found the first multiplanet system around a normal star. After this discovery, his wife told a reporter that her husband was truly happy. "He has kept that childlike wonder of his science—the curiosity that put him on the roof at the age of fourteen with his little telescope. He just loves it."

Gone are the days of begging time on small telescopes for an impossible task. Marcy, a professor at both SFSU and UC Berkeley, has been rec-

Geoffrey Marcy discovered 70 of the first 100 extrasolar planets. This photo was taken during a visit to Rice University in Houston in 2004. (Marianne Dyson)

ognized with numerous awards, including election to the National Academy of Sciences in 2002 and the million-dollar Shaw Prize in 2005 (split with Michael Mayor). Marcy's planet quest continues with no less than the largest telescope in the world, the Keck in Hawaii. Lick Observatory built a new 94-inch (2.4-meter) telescope dedicated to planet hunting. With it, Marcy, Debra A. Fischer (1953–), and colleagues hope to discover every detectable planet within 50 parsecs. Marcy said, "I think it is a glorious exploration. It reminds me of the transoceanic journeys of the 1500s when people went off in their little tiny ships knowing they might find islands or continents never before discovered."

After locating the planets, Marcy hopes that humans will visit them with robots and then in person. But he worries that this great exploration may stall unless humans find a way to live in harmony with one another. "We've done well scientifically, but our real challenges are social and cultural," he said. Living together without conflict? Sounds impossible, but maybe someone will decide to give it a try.

Further Reading

Books and Periodicals

Burrough, Bryan. *Dragonfly: NASA and the Crisis aboard* Mir. New York: HarperCollins, 1998. This meticulously researched book details the history of *Mir* from 1992 through 1997.

Esin, Ann A., Jeffrey E. McClintock, and Ramesh Narayan. "Advection-Dominated Accretion and the Spectral States of Black Hole X-Ray Binaries: Application to Nova Muscae 1991." *Astrophysical Journal* 489, part 1 (1999): 865–889. Available online. URL: http://www.journals.uchicago.edu/ApJ/journal/issues/ApJ/v489n2/36538/36538.html. This technical paper describes how the scientists detected the event horizon of a black hole.

Perlmutter, Saul, et al. "Measurement of Omega and Lambda from 42 High-Redshigt Supernovae." *Astrophysical Journal* 517 (June 1, 1999): 565–586. This technical paper is about the expansion of the universe (measured by Lambda).

Reiss, Adam, et al. "Observational Evidence from Supernovae for an Accelerating Universe and Cosmological Constant." *Astronomical Journal* 116 (May 15, 1998): 1,009–1,038. Available online. URL: http://www.journals.uchicago.edu/AJ/journal/issues/v116n3/980111/980111.web.pdf. This technical paper is about the discovery of the acceleration of the expansion of the universe.

Shirley, Donna, with Danelle Morton. *Managing Martians.* New York: Broadway Books, 1998. The author was the program manager of the Mars Pathfinder program and provides a personal behind-the-scenes story of the program's challenges and success.

Villard, Ray, and Lynette R. Cook. *Infinite Worlds: An Illustrated Voyage to Planets beyond Our Sun.* Berkeley: University of California Press, 2005. A perfect addition to the library of those who wonder what strange planets inhabit the galaxy.

Web Sites

John A. Gowan. "Spacetime Map of the Universe." Available online. URL: http://www.people.cornell.edu/pages/jag8/spacetxt.html. Accessed on August 31, 2006. This Cornell astronomer explains the meaning of maps of the universe in layman's terms and clears up the apparent cosmological "horizon" problem.

Jet Propulsion Laboratory. "Mars Meteorite—News Archives." NASA JPL. 1996 to 2002. Available online. URL: http://www2.jpl.nasa.gov/snc/news_archives.html. Accessed on March 14, 2006. The site includes links to hundreds of articles about the Mars meteorite, starting with the original announcement in 1996 and continuing through 2002.

Jet Propulsion Laboratory. "Comet Hale–Bopp." NASA. Available online. URL: http://www2.jpl.nasa.gov/comet/. Accessed on March 14, 2006.

This site contains links to thousands of images of this bright comet that had its closest approach to Earth on March 22, 1997.

John Hopkins University Applied Physics Lab. "Near Earth Asteroid Rendezvous (NEAR)." Available online. URL: http://near.jhuapl.edu/index.html. Accessed on March 14, 2006. This is the official Web site of the NEAR mission and includes photos and instrument data of the asteroid Eros.

Lunar and Planetary Institute. "The Lunar Prospector Mission." Lunar and Planetary Institute. Available online. URL: http://www.lpi.usra.edu/expmoon/prospector/prospector.html. Accessed on August 31, 2006. This site includes the mission trajectory, description of the instruments, and links to data archives.

Mars Pathfinder Project Information. NASA. Available online. URL: http://nssdc.gsfc.nasa.gov/planetary/mesur.html. Accessed March 14, 2006. Check here for photos and data about the Mars Pathfinder program.

Marsden, Brian. "Eugene Shoemaker." NASA JPL. Available online. URL: http://www2.jpl.nasa.gov/sl9/news81.html. Accessed on March 14, 2006. This obituary provides more information on the life and contributions of Eugene Shoemaker.

NASA. "Galileo Legacy." NASA. Available online. URL: http://galileo.jpl.nasa.gov/. Accessed on March 14, 2006. This site includes mission highlights and images of Jupiter and its moons.

National Radio Astronomy Observatory. "Welcome to the Very Long Baseline Array!" National Radio Astronomy Observatory. Available online. URL: http://www.vlba.nrao.edu/. Accessed on August 31, 2006. This site includes a map of all the radio telescopes that are part of the array and has links to the latest results.

University of California. "California & Carnegie Planet Search." University of California. Available online. URL: http://exoplanets.org/. Accessed on March 14, 2006. An almanac of extrasolar planets, links to journal articles on planet discoveries, and links to team members are provided on this site.

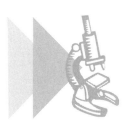

Conclusion

The science of astronomy and the knowledge of space changed dramatically during the hundred years of the 20th century. Astronomy evolved from an observational and mathematical activity to an investigation of the physical properties, chemistry, and underlying structure and dynamics of celestial objects and space itself. Scientists harnessed the power of rockets and overcame the challenges of guidance, control, and human tragedies to learn how to work and live in the harsh environment beyond the safety of Earth's protective atmosphere. Astronomers and engineers combined their talents to build telescopes to see to the very edges of the universe and to probe the mysteries of space and time.

As the 21st century opened, former World War and cold war enemies joined together as partners in building the *International Space Station* (see photo on page 242), combining their hard-won knowledge and experience. Photos of visionary Konstantin Tsiolkovsky and first-man-in-space Yuri Gagarin adorned the wall in the Russian core module. With the addition of the American laboratory named *Destiny* in February 2001, the four-room *ISS* was more massive than *Mir* (that was deorbited in March).

Tsiolkovsky, Werner von Braun, and Gerard O'Neill had foreseen space stations as more than government laboratories. They imagined hotels and factories and whole cities in space. By the end of the 20th century, private aerospace companies were already spending more on space activities than governments, mostly in the area of communication satellites and remote sensing. With the World War II "baby boomers" controlling a large fraction of the economy in the new century, demand for private spaceflight opportunities emerged. New companies such as Space Adventures (see Further Reading), founded in 1998, began to market trips to space on Russian Soyuz "taxi" flights. The first seat was sold to American Dennis Tito (1940–   ) for $20 million. Since the *Challenger* disaster, NASA had been forbidden to use the shuttle for commercial purposes. They objected to using the *ISS* as a tourist destination and forbade Tito access to the American modules. The Russians proceeded to fly Tito in April 2001. NASA then agreed to train future *ISS* visitors,

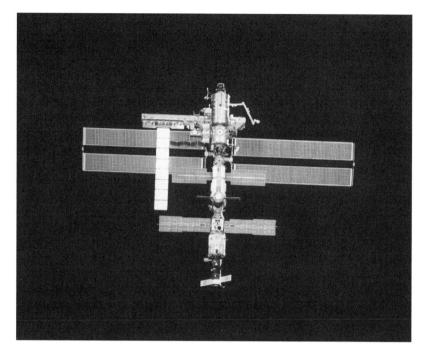

The International Space Station *was photographed by the space shuttle* Endeavor *in November 2002. Its final assembly was interrupted, and its crew reduced from three to two by the* Columbia *disaster in 2003.* (NASA)

and a second tourist, South African Mark Shuttleworth (1973–) was allowed access to the full *ISS* in April 2002. Though still banned from flying paying customers on the shuttle, NASA expanded its mission specialist definition to include teachers. The "educator-astronaut" program was announced in 2003, and the first group was selected in 2004.

Plans for opening the space frontier to more people were postponed by another space tragedy that reminded everyone that spaceflight remains a dangerous endeavor. After a 16-day science mission, the 22-year-old first space shuttle, *Columbia*, broke apart during reentry on February 1, 2003. Commander Rick Husband (1957–2003), Pilot William (Willie) McCool (1961–2003), Mission Specialists Kalpana Chawla (1961–2003), Laurel Clark (1961–2003), David Brown (1956–2003), Michael Anderson (1959–2003) and Israel's first astronaut, Ilan Ramon (1954–2003) were killed. The *Columbia* Accident Investigation Board (see Further Reading), blamed launch debris striking the left wing as the direct cause and management failures as contributing to the accident.

As a result of the *Columbia* tragedy, the remaining three shuttles were grounded, and the *ISS* assembly was put on hold. Russian Progress vehicles delivered supplies, and Soyuz "taxis" took over all crew exchanges. Because the Progress ships could not make up for the shuttle supplies (especially water), the crew was reduced from three to two.

The accident led to a new direction for NASA. In January 2004, President George W. Bush (1946–) unveiled the Vision for Space

Exploration, directing NASA to finish the *ISS*, retire the shuttle by 2010, and send crews to explore the Moon and Mars (see Further Reading). NASA immediately began work on a 4–6 person crew exploration vehicle and more robotic missions to support the new vision. The early designs echoed the Apollo program with capsules on top of rockets to avoid the debris problem that had destroyed *Columbia*. LOR was still favored as the method to reach the Moon, but with sophisticated computers, no astronaut would need to remain in lunar orbit to tend the return ship.

To sustain an exploration program, NASA realized the need to utilize space resources such as oxygen from lunar rocks and water on Mars. Resource mapping and robotic sampling missions therefore took on new priority. American rovers *Spirit* and *Opportunity* (see Further Reading) landed on opposite sides of Mars near the equator in January 2004 and provided some promising results. *Opportunity* found evidence that a body of salty water once flowed over its landing area near Eagle Crater. *Spirit* explored a dry plain of volcanic rocks inside Gusev Crater and found mineral fingerprints of ancient water on nearby hills. Maps provided by *Mars Global Surveyor* (orbiting Mars since 1997) also confirmed that Mars had water in the past. Scientists proposed that at least some of this water may be trapped in the soil. In 2001, *Mars Odyssey* supported this theory with evidence of vast amounts of water ice just below the surface at the poles.

Other nations also joined in the study of the Moon and Mars in the new century. Europe's *SMART1* spacecraft gathered lunar data from 2004 to 2006. Their *Mars Express* entered orbit in 2004 and confirmed water at the south pole. India prepared *Chandryn1* ("Voyage to the Moon"); and Japan prepared two missions, *Lunar-A*, including an orbiter and a penetrator, and a large orbiter, *SELENE*, expected to launch by 2010. China also announced plans for its first lunar orbiter mission, *Chang'e 1*. Western nations were especially interested in this development after China became the third nation to send a man into orbit. *Shenzhou 5* launched Yáng Lìwěi (1965–) on October 15, 2003. A more ambitious two-man flight followed on October 12, 2005, showing the world that China would not be left behind in the new century of space exploration.

Private companies also reached space for the first time at the beginning of the new century. Designed by Burt Rutan (1943–) of Scaled Composites and flown by Mike Melvill (1941–), *SpaceShipOne* (see photo on page 244) exceeded 62 miles (100 km) in altitude on June 21, 2004. Unlike Alan Shepard's suborbital flight in 1961 that parachuted into the ocean, *SpaceShipOne* landed like an airplane on a dry lake bed in California. A flight on September 29 followed by another on October 4 satisfied the criteria for the team to win the $10-million Ansari X-prize. A company called Virgin Galactic teamed with Scaled Composites to offer future suborbital flights for $200,000 each.

The space shuttle returned to flight with Eileen Collins commanding on July 26, 2005. Despite two years of effort, the debris problem was not

SpaceShipOne was the first privately financed vehicle to reach space. The suborbital flight of the ship designed by Burt Rutan occurred in October 2004. (Mojave Aerospace Ventures LLC, 2004. Photo by Scaled Composites. SpaceShipOne is a Paul Allen project.)

solved. The flight landed safely, but the shuttle fleet was again grounded. Space-station operations continued with two-man crews. EO-11 crew member Sergei Krikalev, who had been in space to greet Collins, became the world's most experienced space man. When he returned to Earth in October, he had accumulated 803 days, 9 hours, and 39 minutes in space. He rode home with the third *ISS* tourist, American Gregory Olsen (1945–).

In the summer of 2006, NASA Administrator Michael Griffin (1949–) approved the shuttle *Discovery* for the second return-to-flight mission, STS-121. No major debris was seen during launch on July 4 or found via inspection after *Discovery* docked with the *ISS*. With the shuttle fleet no longer grounded and able to provide supplies again, STS-121 crew member and European astronaut, Thomas Reiter (1958–), was cleared to remain on the *ISS* as the third member of the *ISS–13* crew. When the *ISS* assembly is complete in 2010, the *ISS* will host a crew of six and be the size of a five-bedroom house.

The first 40 years of human spaceflight saw 12 men walk on the Moon and about 400 men and three dozen women reach Earth orbit. Tsiolkovsky said, "Earth is the cradle of humanity, but one cannot live in the cradle forever." As the new century dawned and engineers designed new vehicles to carry humans safely out of their cradle, astronomers mapped and cataloged the resources of the solar system that could be used to support life, located planets around other stars, and sought to understand the forces that create, support, and threaten worlds.

New Worlds

The existence of life beyond Earth loomed as the biggest unanswered question of astronomy in the new century. At the turn of the previous century, Percival Lowell had predicted that life would arise wherever and whenever conditions allowed. Though his belief in canal-building Martians was proven wrong, many scientists at the turn of the 21st century still believed that simple life might be found on Mars or anywhere else that had liquid water. This belief motivated special interest in Saturn's moon Titan that the Voyagers had shown to resemble a primordial Earth. The *Cassini* mission launched in 1997 arrived at Saturn in 2004 and parachuted a probe to the surface of Titan in 2005. The images returned showed a methane-carved shoreline under thick clouds. The moon Enceladus was found to have water vapor in its atmosphere fed by icy eruptions. These worlds are sure to be visited by more probes and possibly by humans in the new century.

Smaller solar-system bodies continued to be of keen interest in the new century as sources of resources for space settlers and as threats to be diverted from future devastating impacts on the Earth. By 2002, more than 11 million asteroids had been found and catalogued. The discovery of a "tenth planet" in 2003 that is larger than Pluto led to a new definition of planet and the reclassification of Pluto. At a meeting of the International Astronomical Union in 2006, planet was redefined as a body that orbits a star and is large enough to assume a nearly round shape and to clear the neighborhood around its orbit. Pluto's orbit over-laps Neptune's, so it was demoted to the new category of dwarf planet, leaving the solar system with 8 planets for the first time since 1930. The large asteroid Ceres and the new world 2003 UB_{313}, dubbed Xena by its discoverer Michael Brown (1966–   ) of Caltech, were also classified as dwarf planets.

In 10 years of operation starting in 1995, the American *Solar and Heliospheric Observatory* satellite discovered 1,000 comets. About 85 percent of these were Sun-grazing comets that passed within 500,000 miles (800,000 km) of the Sun. Many of these are fragments the size of houses and cannot be seen from Earth. *Stardust*, launched in 1999, obtained a sample of comet Wild2 in 2004 and safely returned the first sample of a comet to Earth in 2006. A Japanese sample-return mission to asteroid Itokawa launched in 2003. *Hayabusa* was damaged by a solar flare but landed on Itokawa twice in 2005. In 2005, an asteroid was discovered to have two moons, and *Hubble* found that Ceres (the largest asteroid) might be up to one-fourth frozen water. The American *Deep Impact* bored into comet Tempel 1 in 2005. Imaged by the *Spitzer Space Telescope* launched in 2003, analysis of the impact cast doubt on Fred Whipple's "dirty snowball" model of comets. Tempel 1 was shown to be more fragile than a soufflé and to be layered like an onion rather than a mix of rock and ice. Too porous to be made of ice, calculations suggest that the comet formed at low pressure and temperature and has no liquid water binding it together. This data also cast doubt on the Panspermia theory that ancient comets delivered the seeds of life to Earth.

While spacecraft designers worked on ships to return humans to the Moon, an idea that was science fiction in 1901, visionaries continued to dream of trips to planets around other stars. The list of possible destinations continued to grow in the new century. Polish astronomer Maciej Konacki (1972–   ) found the first planet in a triple star system. Named Tattooine after the home of *Star Wars* movie-hero Luke Skywalker, the planet revolves around three stars that are as close to each other as Saturn is to the Sun. Though planets were found around multiple-star systems, astronomers continued to believe that single stars like the Sun are more likely to form stable planetary systems. Sky surveys in the 20th century indicated that less than half of all stars were singles, but new data released in 2006 showed that the likelihood of being a multiple star depends on the star's brightness. Bright stars have an 80 percent chance of being part of a multiple system, whereas only about a third of red dwarfs are in multiples. Because red dwarfs account for about 85 percent of all stars and are more likely to be singles, extrasolar planets may be more common as well.

Two planets were found in 2003, using the new method of *microlensing*. Microlensing involves looking for a planet when its star passes in front of a background star, causing the light of the background star to flicker. This technique is useful out to thousands of light-years and works best in the direction of the Milky Way, where there are many background stars. Using microlensing in 2006, astronomers announced the discovery of a planet only 5.5 times the size of Earth. At 2.5 AU from its red dwarf star, the planet is thought to be as cold as Pluto.

The *Hubble Space Telescope* surveyed 100,000 stars looking for transits. Candidate stars were then observed by the *Very Large Telescope* in Chile. Preliminary results showed that hot Jupiters are relatively common. Debate continued on whether or not hot Jupiters form far from their stars and spiral in through impacts or hot Jupiters form near the star in gaps in their dust rings. A survey of 754 stars in 2003 found that stars with high metal content had a higher chance of hosting such planets. No stars with less than a third of the metal found in the Sun had planets. Some astronomers proposed that stars with hot Jupiters have more dust in their disks to start with, while others proposed that previous hot Jupiters had spiraled into the stars and added their heavier elements. It was discovered in 2004 that hot Jupiters have strong magnetic fields. One was found at a distance of 5 million miles from its star with a field that drags its star's surface around like a dog on a leash every three days.

Future space-based telescopes are designed to continue and expand the search for new worlds, especially Earthlike planets. Though astronomers continue to listen for messages from extraterrestrial life, some share Carl Sagan's cold-war fear that species with the technology to communicate used it instead to destroy themselves in wars. Impacts from asteroids and comets are another likely cause of destruction. Yet, the biggest factor in the Drake equation (that calculates the probability of encountering intelligent life) may simply be the vast distances and time spans involved.

Supernova data further confirmed that the distances between galaxies are increasing at an accelerating rate. Supernovae serve as markers for cosmic expansion because each has roughly the same intrinsic brightness, allowing their distance to be calculated. The SuperNova Legacy Survey began in 2003, with the first results published in 2005. One surprising finding was that unlike regular matter that is "diluted" with expansion, dark energy remains roughly constant.

Long-held theories of galaxy formation came under increasing challenge in the new century. New data showed that galaxies formed much earlier than what would be expected if only gravity pulled them together. One giant galaxy six times more massive than the Milky Way was found at a distance of 13 billion light-years—meaning that it existed just 800 million years after the proposed big bang. Distant galaxies are typically the same brightness in visible and near infrared but faint in shorter wavelengths because hydrogen in the intergalactic medium absorbs shorter wavelengths. The most distant galaxies therefore drop out of *Hubble* images in blue light and show up in *Spitzer* images at other wavelengths. By comparing data from the two telescopes collected from two ultra-deep fields taken in 2003 and 2004, galaxies were revealed that had formed a mere 500 million years after the big bang. The question remains as to when the first stars and galaxies formed. New computer models such as the Millennium Simulation, released in 2005, showed that dark-matter halos which formed earlier become more tightly bunched than ones which formed later. This implies that galaxies clumped more tightly in the past. In 2004, the *Chandra* X-ray observatory detected an extensive envelope of dark matter around an isolated elliptical galaxy. This discovery raised questions about how galaxies acquire and keep such dark-matter halos.

Future humans will continue to scan the sky and chart the movement of celestial bodies as they have done for thousands of years. But their sky may soon include Earth as a point of light as seen from the surface of Mars or may include the Sun as just another star that is viewed in the "rearview mirror" of their starship. The 20th century developed sophisticated new tools that changed the way humans see their universe. They discovered that the Milky Way is not the only galaxy, that the universe is expanding, that stars produce all the elements of life, that planets are common, that the universe is made of unseen dark matter, and that humans can fly to the Moon and survive in space for years at a time. The possibilities for future discoveries in astronomy and space promise to enrich the lives of all who look to the sky and dream of tomorrow.

Further Reading

Books

Chien, Phillip. *Columbia—Final Voyage*. New York: Copernicus Books, 2006. This book contains the detailed story of the crew and science experiments of the STS–107 mission that ended in tragedy.

Columbia Accident Investigation Board. *Report Volume 1*. Washington, D.C.: Government Printing Office, 2003. This official technical record includes the detailed circumstances that led to the loss of the *Columbia* and her crew and the board's recommendations and findings.

Web Sites

Ed Grayeck. "Upcoming Planetary Events and Missions." NASA. Available online. URL: http://nssdc.gsfc.nasa.gov/planetary/upcoming.html. Accessed on August 31, 2006. This chronology of international missions from the current year to 4,000,000 (when *Pioneer 11* reaches Lambda Aquila) contains links to missions that have been planned and are already in progress.

Michael May. "International Space Station Modules & Elements." Spacenet. Available online. URL: http://www.ag-99.de/spacenet/elements/elements. html. Accessed on March 26, 2006. The site includes descriptions, videos, images, and other information on the modules and crews and cargo of the *ISS*.

S. P. Korolev RSC Energia. "International Space Station." RSC Energia. Available online. URL: http://www.energia.ru/english/energia/iss/iss. html. Accessed on August 12, 2006. This is the official Russian site for information on *ISS* and Soyuz missions. Links to each expedition provide a list of tasks and science experiments accomplished.

Space Adventures. "Space Adventures." Space Adventures. Available online. URL: http://www.spaceadventures.com. Accessed on March 23, 2006. This is the company that offers cosmonaut training experiences and private spaceflights to the International Space Station.

Susan Watanabe. "Jet Propulsion Laboratory: JPL Missions." Jet Propulsion Laboratory, California Institute of Technology. Available online. URL: http://www.jpl.nasa.gov/missions/. Accessed on March 26, 2006. Check this site for the latest on robotic missions to Mars and other planets.

Bruce Medalists

This is a list, in chronological order, of all the Bruce Medalists from 1901 through 2000. The Bruce Medal is awarded by the Astronomical Society of the Pacific, a worldwide organization that includes research scientists, teachers, and amateur astronomers with the goal to advance the science of astronomy. The Catherine Wolfe Bruce gold medal was first awarded in 1898 and is given for lifetime contributions to astronomy. Each year, the directors of six observatories—three in the United States and three abroad—nominate candidates for the medal. For each year, the name of the medalist is given, with dates of birth and death, nationality (at the time of the award), and a description of the accomplishment(s) for which the medal was awarded.

1901

No medal was awarded.

1902

Giovanni Virginio Schiaparelli (1835–1910), Italy, "for observations of solar system objects, including comets and the *canali*, mistranslated as *canals* on Mars that stimulated Percival Lowell to search for life on Mars."

1903

No medal was awarded.

1904

William Huggins (1824–1910), England, "for work in the 19th century, including identifying the spectra of nebulae as gaseous or stellar."

1905

No medal was awarded.

1906

Hermann Carl Vogel (1841–1907), Germany, for work in measuring the Doppler shifts of stars to determine their radial velocities and the first measurement of the Sun's rotation, stellar diameters, and masses.

1907

No medal was awarded.

1908

Edward C. Pickering (1846–1919), United States, for leadership of the Harvard College Observatory for 42 years, including the hiring of Williamina Fleming, Annie Cannon, Antonio Maury, and Henrietta Leavitt, and production of numerous star catalogs and the first all-sky photographic map.

1909

George W. Hill (1838–1914), United States, for detailed mathematical computations of all solar system orbits.

1910

No medal was awarded.

1911

Henri Poincaré (1854–1912), France, for revolutionary work in celestial mechanics and development of chaos theory.

1912

No medal was awarded.

1913

Jacobus C. Kapteyn (1851–1922), Netherlands, for compiling tables of distances to stars by magnitude and motions, the discovery of star streaming, and the founding of the Dutch school of astronomers.

1914

J. Oskar Backlund (1846–1916), Sweden/Russia, for study of the orbit of comet Encke and leadership of Russia's national observatory at Pulkovo.

1915

William Wallace Campbell (1862–1938), United States, for leadership of Lick Observatory, design of the Mills spectrographs, leadership of eclipse expeditions, and studies of Mars, hot stars, nebulae, and Nova Aurigae.

1916

George Ellery Hale (1868–1938), United States, for invention of the spectroheliograph, the founding of Yerkes, Mount Wilson, and Palomar Observatories, and founding the American Astronomical Society and the *Astrophysical Journal.*

1917

Edward E. Barnard (1857–1923), United States, for his discovery of comets, Amalthea (fifth moon of Jupiter), and dark clouds and his introduction of wide-field photographic methods that were used to study the structure of the Milky Way.

1918

No medal was awarded.

1919

No medal was awarded.

1920

Ernest W. Brown (1866–1938), England, for his detailed study of the Moon's motion.

1921

Henri A. Deslandres (1853–1948), France, for study of molecular spectra, planetary rotations, and the Sun.

1922

Frank W. Dyson (1868–1939), England, for leadership of the Royal Greenwich Observatory where he initiated the radio broadcast of time, participated in the international sky survey, and directed the 1919 eclipse expedition that confirmed Einstein's general theory of relativity.

1923

Benjamin Baillaud (1848–1934), France, for leadership of the Toulouse and Paris Observatories where he supported the international sky survey and arranged to transmit time signals from the Eiffel Tower during World War I, and as the first president of the International Astronomical Union.

1924

Arthur Stanley Eddington (1882–1944), England, for extensive work on stellar dynamics and energy transfer and for leadership of a 1919 eclipse expedition to prove Einstein's general theory of relativity.

1925

Henry Norris Russell (1877–1957), United States, for work on the correlation between spectral types and magnitude that led to the Hertzsprung–Russell diagram and for his work on binary stars and stellar composition.

1926

Robert G. Aitken (1864–1951), United States, for work and publications on binary stars and as director of Lick Observatory.

1927

Herbert Hall Turner (1861–1930), England, for leadership of the worldwide effort to create a complete map of the sky and the development of methods to obtain positions and magnitude data from photographic plates.

1928

Walter S. Adams (1876–1956), United States, for leadership of Mount Wilson Observatory, spectroscopic studies of the Sun, and the identification of Sirius B as the first white dwarf star.

1929

Frank Schlesinger (1871–1943), United States, for work on stellar parallax and the first two *Bright Star Catalogues.*

1930

Max Wolf (1863–1932), Germany, for study of the Milky Way and nebulae, the discovery of hundreds of asteroids including the first Trojan asteroid, and development of the stereo-comparator and the first planetarium.

1931

Willem de Sitter (1872–1934), Netherlands, for work on the moons of Jupiter, stellar motions, and solutions to Einstein's equations predicting an expanding universe.

1932

John S. Plaskett (1865–1941), Canada, for leadership of Canadian astronomy, work on radial velocities and spectroscopic binaries, and confirmation of galactic rotation.

1933

Carl V. L. Charlier (1862–1934), Sweden, for statistical studies of the motions of stars, showing hot stars and clusters that form flattened systems.

1934

Alfred Fowler (1868–1940), England, for work in solar physics, including six eclipse expeditions.

1935

Vesto M. Slipher (1875–1969), United States, for work on planetary atmospheres and radial velocities of nebulae.

1936

Armin O. Leuschner (1868–1953), United States, for leadership of the Berkeley Astronomical Department that produced more than 60 Ph.D.'s in astronomy.

1937

Ejnar Hertzsprung (1873–1967), Denmark, for his discovery that giant stars are low density, the first color-magnitude diagram now called the Hertzsprung–Russell diagram, calibration of Cepheid variables, and measurements of binary stars.

1938

Edwin P. Hubble (1889–1953), United States, for his work on nebulae, including his classification system, proof of other galaxies, and the discovery of the velocity–distance relation that provided evidence of an expanding universe.

1939

Harlow Shapley (1885–1972), United States, for his discovery that globular clusters outline the galaxy, showing that it is far larger than previously thought, and for his leadership of the Harvard College Observatory.

1940

Frederick H. Seares (1873–1964), United States, for work on comets and variable stars, standardizing and extending the stellar magnitude system, and service as assistant director of Mount Wilson Observatory.

1941

Joel Stebbins (1878–1966), United States, for his development of photoelectric photometry.

1942

Jan H. Oort (1900–92), Netherlands, for confirming Lindblad's hypothesis of galactic rotation; founding a mathematical theory of galactic structure, the theory on the origin of comets; confirmation of the Crab Nebula's synchrotron radiation; and leadership of European astronomy.

1943

No medal was awarded.

1944

No medal was awarded.

1945

E. Arthur Milne (1896–1950), England, for work on radiative equilibrium and stellar atmospheres.

1946

Paul W. Merrill (1887–1961), United States, for work on peculiar stars, especially long-period variables, and on spectroscopic evidence of the s-process of nucleosynthesis in stars.

1947

Bernard Lyot (1897–1952), France, for study of dust on the Moon and Mars, invention of the coronograph, and the first motion pictures of solar prominences.

1948

Otto Struve (1897–1963), United States, for leadership of four observatories and the *Astrophysical Journal* and for spectroscopic studies.

1949

Harold Spencer Jones (1890–1960), England, for contributions to positional astronomy including more than 1,200 observations of Eros.

1950

Alfred H. Joy (1882–1973), United States, for work on radial velocities of thousands of stars and the study of T Tauri stars.

1951

Marcel Minnaert (1893–1970), Netherlands, for quantitative analysis, an atlas of the solar spectrum, and studies of the Moon.

1952

Subrahmanyan Chandrasekhar (1910–95), United States, for theoretical studies of stellar structure and evolution, energy transfer, and the mathematical theory of black holes.

1953

Harold D. Babcock (1882–1968), United States, for studies of atomic spectra and precise measurements of the Sun's magnetic fields.

1954

Bertil Lindblad (1895–1965), Sweden, for work on galactic rotation and confirmation of the distance to the galactic center.

1955

Walter Baade (1893–1960), United States, for studies of the Crab Nebula, discovery of two types of Cepheid variables that doubled the estimated size of the universe, and first identification of optical counterparts of radio sources.

1956

Albrecht Unsöld (1905–95), Germany, for his work on stellar atmospheres.

1957

Ira S. Bowen (1898–1973), United States, for identification of "nebulium" as ionized oxygen and nitrogen and for leadership of Mount Wilson and Palomar Observatories.

1958

William W. Morgan (1906–94), United States, for work in classifying stars and galaxies and for service as editor of the *Astrophysical Journal.*

1959

Bengt Strömgren (1908–87), Denmark, for work on stellar structure, the theory of ionized gas clouds around hot stars, and the development of photoelectric photometry.

1960

Viktor A. Ambartsumian (1908–96), Russia, for work in theoretical astrophysics, T Tauri stars, and galactic evolution and as president of the International Astronomical Union.

1961

Rudolph Minkowski (1895–1976), United States, for work on planetary nebulae, novae, dividing supernovae into types I and II and for his leadership of the National Geographic–Palomar Sky Survey.

1962

Grote Reber (1911–2002), United States, for building the first radio telescope and developing radio astronomy.

1963

Seth Nicholson (1891–1963), United States, for discovery of four moons of Jupiter, a Trojan asteroid, and decades worth of reports on sunspot activity.

1964

Otto Heckmann (1901–83), Germany, for leadership of the European Southern Observatory in Chile and solutions to Einstein's equations that introduced the possibility of a rotating universe.

1965

Martin Schwarzschild (1912–97), United States, for work on stellar structure and evolution, confirmation of solar convection, and dynamics of elliptical galaxies.

1966

Dirk Brouwer (1902–66), United States, for astronomical calculations, leadership of the Yale University Observatory, and service as editor of the *Astronomical Journal*.

1967

Ludwig Biermann (1907–86), Germany, for work on stellar convection theory, comets, and the prediction of the solar wind.

1968

Willem J. Luyten (1899–94), Netherlands, for work on proper motions of stars, invention of an automated computerized plate scanner and measuring machine that was used in sky surveys, and determination of the density of stars in space as a function of luminosity.

1969

Horace W. Babcock (1912–2003), United States, for work showing the existence of dark matter, the invention of the solar magnetograph and other instruments used to discover magnetic fields on other stars, the proposal for adaptive optics, and leadership of Mount Wilson and Palomar Observatories.

1970

Fred Hoyle (1915–2001), England, for work on stellar evolution and nucleosynthesis of the elements by stars (with Fowler and the Burbidges), development of the Steady State and Panspermia theories, and popularizing science.

1971

Jesse Greenstein (1909–2002), United States, for work on globular clusters showing that stars in the halo are older than the Sun, for detailed studies of white dwarfs, and for discovery of quasars (with Maarten Schmidt).

1972

Iosif S. Shklovskii (1916–85), Russia, for study of the solar corona, cosmic rays from supernovae, synchrotron radiation from the Crab Nebula, and serious examination of the possibility of extraterrestrial life.

1973

Lyman Spitzer, Jr. (1914–97), United States, for study of the physics of the interstellar medium and magnetic fields, ultraviolet astronomy, and the proposal for in-space telescopes.

1974

Martin Ryle (1918–84), England, for pioneering research in radio astrophysics, observations and inventions, and development of the aperture synthesis technique.

1975

Allan R. Sandage (1926–   ), United States, for work on globular clusters, measurements of the most distant objects and the Hubble constant, and the identification of the first optical counterpart of a quasar.

1976

Ernst J. Öpik (1893–1985), Australia, for the physical theory and statistical studies of meteors, comets and asteroids, and stellar structure and extragalactic nebulae.

1977

Bart J. Bok (1906–83), United States, for study of star clusters, mapping of the Milky Way, and investigation of dark nebulae.

1978

Hendrik C. van de Hulst (1918–2000), Netherlands, for his prediction of the 21-cm line of hydrogen in interstellar clouds that led to mapping the spiral structure of the Milky Way.

1979

William Alfred Fowler (1911–95), United States, for theoretical and experimental studies of nuclear reactions of importance in the formation of the chemical elements in the universe (with Hoyle and the Burbidges).

1980

George H. Herbig (1920–   ), United States, for spectroscopic studies of young stars, star formation, and interstellar medium.

1981

Riccardo Giacconi (1931–   ), United States, for the discovery of the first cosmic X-ray sources, leadership of the first X-ray observatories, service as the first director of the Space Telescope Science Institute, and development of the Very Large Telescope and Atacama Large Millimeter Array in Chile.

1982

E. Margaret Burbidge (1919–   ), United States, for her work (with Hoyle and Fowler and G. Burbidge) on the synthesis of the elements by stars, spectroscopic studies of quasars, and development of instruments for the *Hubble Space Telescope*.

1983

Yakov B. Zel'dovich (1914–87), Russia, for work in astrophysics and cosmology, including the discovery of the Sunyaev–Zel'dovich effect used for determining the Hubble constant, and development of a quantum theory of gravity.

1984

Olin C. Wilson (1909–94), United States, for spectroscopic studies of stars and stellar activity cycles.

1985

Thomas G. Cowling (1906–90), England, for the Cowling model of convection and radiation in stars and for work on stellar magnetic fields and magnetospheres.

1986

Fred L. Whipple (1906–2004), United States, for discovery that meteors are mostly comet fragments, six comets, and the "dirty snowball" model of comet nuclei.

1987

Edwin E. Salpeter (1924–   ), United States, for studies on relativistic atomic physics that is applied to stellar evolution.

1988

John G. Bolton (1922–93), Australia, for identification of the first radio sources, correlation of solar flares with aurora, and leadership as first director of the Australian National Radio Astronomy Observatory.

1989

Adriaan Blaauw (1914–   ), Netherlands, for work on "runaway stars," star formation, and cosmic distances.

1990

Charlotte E. Moore Sitterly (1898–1990), United States, for work on stellar spectra, and definitive books on solar spectrum and spectral line multiplets.

1991

Donald E. Osterbrock (1924–   ), United States, for leadership of Lick Observatory, models of red dwarfs, studies of planetary and emission nebulae, and contributions to the history of astronomy through books and articles.

1992

Maarten Schmidt (1929–   ), United States, for identification of the first quasar and for studies of X-ray and gamma ray sources.

1993

Martin Rees (1942–   ), England, for the proposal that black holes power quasars and for theories of galaxy formation.

1994

Wallace Sargent (1935–   ), United States, for studies of stars, galaxies, and quasars and for leadership of sky surveys.

1995

P. James E. Peebles (1935–   ), United States, for his prediction of the cosmic background radiation and for studies of galaxy clusters and dark matter.

1996

Albert E. Whitford (1905–2002), United States, for improving photoelectric photometry and using it to measure stellar brightness and galaxies and for leadership of Lick Observatory.

1997

Eugene N. Parker (1927–   ), United States, for extensive work on the solar wind and magnetic fields in the heliosphere of the Sun.

1998

Donald Lynden-Bell (1935–   ), England, for contributions to theories of stellar motions, formation of the galaxy, evolution and structure and distribution of galaxies, and the proposal of the "Great Attractor."

1999

Geoffrey R. Burbidge (1925–   ), United States, for work on the nucleosynthesis of the elements (with Hoyle and Fowler and M. Burbidge) and for service as editor of the *Annual Reviews of Astronomy and Astrophysics*.

2000

Rashid A. Sunyaev (1943–   ), Russia, for service as editor of *Astronomy Letters* and *Astrophysics and Space Physics Reviews*, leadership of the Max Planck Institute for Astrophysics, the Sunyaev-Zel'dovich effect, and leadership of orbiting X-ray observatories.

Glossary

absolute brightness the actual or intrinsic brightness of a celestial object

accelerometer an instrument that senses deviations from an established trajectory and feeds corrective signals to mechanical systems

active galactic nuclei (AGN) centers of galaxies that shine brightly with ionized atoms (instead of stars) and are thought to be powered by supermassive black holes

adaptive optics a technique that allows computers to move telescope mirrors to account for atmospheric turbulence

apparent brightness the observed brightness of a celestial object

asteroid belt a doughnut-shaped area between 2.1 and 3.3 astronomical units from the Sun where the majority of asteroids are found

astronomical units (AU) the average distance between the Earth and the Sun, equal to about 93 million miles (150 million km)

astrophysics the study of the properties, constitution, and evolution of celestial bodies and the intervening regions of space

barograph a recording barometer used to measure atmospheric pressure for determining altitude

big bang the cosmic explosion that marked the beginning of the universe according to the big bang theory

black dwarf see WHITE DWARF

black hole a region of space from which no matter or radiation can escape that is the result of the extreme curvature of space by a massive compact body

brown dwarf a star with too low a mass for nuclear fusion to begin in its core

Cepheid variable a class of yellow pulsating stars that vary in brightness as they expand and contract, with a period related to their brightness that is used to measure distance

Compton scattering when charged particles such as electrons reradiate photons at a lower frequency, increasing the particle's energy. Reverse Compton scattering is when photons of low frequency are scattered by moving particles and reradiated at higher frequency

cosmic background radiation (CBR)   radiation from all parts of the sky that in the microwave range is highly redshifted and interpreted as leftover radiation from the big bang

cosmic rays   energetic ions and electrons that travel though space at almost the speed of light and are thought to originate from super-novae and pulsars

Cygnus A   a strong radio and X-ray source discovered in the 1950s and later identified as the first black-hole candidate

dark matter   matter than cannot be detected by radiation but is known to exist through its gravitational effects

degenerate gas   a state in which atoms are compressed so that electrons collapse from their orbits and the gas acts like a liquid

density parameter   represented by the Greek symbol Ω (omega), is proportional to the gravitational constant and mass density divided by the square of the Hubble constant

event horizon   the boundary of a black hole beyond which no matter or radiation can escape

gravity assist   when a spacecraft takes up a tiny fraction of the orbital energy of a planet as it is flying past, allowing the spacecraft to change direction and speed

gyroscope   a spinning wheel or a disk or a set of wheels or disks per-pendicular to each other and used to offer resistance to changes in angular momentum

helioseismology   study of the surface oscillations of the Sun

hypergolic   propellants that ignite on contact

interferometer   an instrument or set of telescopes that direct and com-bine electromagnetic waves to produce an interference pattern

ionization potential   the minimum energy required to remove an elec-tron from an atom or a molecule

ionized   an atom that has lost one or more electrons

island universe   nebulae that were later called galaxies

magnitude   a number based on a logarithmic scale that is used to describe the brightness of a star or other luminous body

nebulae   a cloud of interstellar gas and dust, and a term that was also applied to galaxies before they were proven to lie outside the Milky Way

neutrino   a subatomic particle produced in nuclear reactions that only weakly interacts with matter

neutron star   an extremely dense compact star that has undergone gravitational collapse so that most of its material has been com-pressed into neutrons

Newton's law of gravity   states that the force of attraction between two bodies is proportional to the product of their masses and inversely proportional to the square of their distance apart

nova   an explosion on the surface of a white dwarf star in which hydrogen is abruptly converted into helium, causing the star to shine brightly (like "new")

occultation   complete or partial obscuration of one celestial object by another

opposition   when a planet or other body appears opposite the Sun in the sky

phase change   a change in the physical state of a substance

planetary nebula   a luminous shell surrounding a hot star

proper motion   the rate at which a star appears to move across the celestial sphere with respect to very distant stars

quasar   short for a quasi-stellar object that is a compact object or galaxy with a small luminous nucleus

red dwarf   main sequence star that is cooler and less massive than the Sun

spherical aberration   a condition in which light rays converge to a series of points instead of a single point after passing through a lens or being reflected by a mirror

variable star   a star whose physical properties such as brightness change over time

white dwarf   a small dense star that is supported against gravity by the degenerate pressure of its electrons, is white in color/temperature, and will eventually cool to a black dwarf

Further Resources

Books

Bartusiak, Marcia. *Archives of the Universe: A Treasury of Astronomy's Historic Works of Discovery.* New York: Pantheon, 2004. A clear and concise history of astronomy in eight periods from Ptolemy to modern times including excerpts from the original work of famous astronomers.

Chaisson, Eric, and Steve McMillan. *Astronomy Today: Fifth Edition.* Upper Saddle River, N.J.: Prentice Hall, 2004. A comprehensive astronomy text for non-science majors that covers the history, the planets, stellar evolution, galaxies and cosmology, and space-based astronomy with lots of helpful diagrams and appendices for references.

Fix, John D. *Astronomy: Journey to the Cosmic Frontier, Second Edition.* New York: McGraw-Hill, 1999. A heavily illustrated and very readable astronomy textbook that includes detailed explanations of astronomical concepts and discoveries up through the late 1990s.

Goldsmith, Donald. *The Astronomers.* New York. St. Martin's Press, 1993. Published in conjunction with the PBS television series of the same name, this book includes profiles of scientists and their work in cosmology, stellar evolution, dark matter, quasars, and extrasolar planets.

Illingworth, Valerie, and John O. E. Clark, eds. *The Facts On File Dictionary of Astronomy: Fourth Edition.* New York: Facts On File, 2000. A useful dictionary of terms, theories, astronomers, telescopes, satellites, and instruments with diagrams, graphs, and tables to aid understanding.

Morgan, Tom, ed. *Jane's Space Directory: Fourteenth Edition 1998–99.* Alexandria, Va.: Jane's Information Group, Inc., 1998. A comprehensive reference of military, civilian, international, commercial, and government space vehicles, missions, flight logs, and satellite programs including history, photos, diagrams, and tables.

Internet Sources

William A. Arnett. "The Nine Planets." URL: http://seds.lpl.arizona.edu/nineplanets/nineplanets/. Accessed on August 31, 2006. This site has images and physical data on all objects in the solar system.

AstroWeb Consortium. "Full-Texts of Astronomical Publications." URL: http://www.cv.nrao.edu/fits/www/yp_full_text.html. Accessed on August 31, 2006. The site links to astronomical magazine and journal Web sites where copies are available via archives or for order.

Jeananda Col. "Astronomy Dictionary. Hall of Astronomers." Enchanted Learning. URL: http://www.enchantedlearning.com/subjects/astronomy/glossary/Astronomers.shtml. Accessed on March 26, 2006. This site contains an alphabetical list of astronomers with brief biographical profiles.

Hartmut Frommert. "The Messier Catalog." SEDS. URL: http://seds.lpl.arizona.edu/messier/. Accessed on August 31, 2006. This site provides historical and physical information for all objects in the Messier catalog.

National Aeronautics and Space Administration. "NASA History Division." NASA. URL: http://history.nasa.gov/tindex.html. Accessed on March 28, 2006. Historical information is listed alphabetically by program names and by subjects.

Robert Nemiroff and Jerry Bonnell. "Astronomy Picture of the Day." URL: http://antwrp.gsfc.nasa.gov/apod/astropix.html. Archive URL: http://antwrp.gsfc.nasa.gov/apod/archivepix.html. Accessed on August 31, 2006. Images of almost all astronomical objects and phenomena are available here.

Joe Tenn. "The Bruce Medalists." The Astronomical Society of the Pacific. URL: http://www.phys-astro.sonoma.edu/brucemedalists/. Accessed on August 31, 2006. A list of the winners of the Bruce Medal for Astronomy from 1898 to the present with a description of their contributions and references to their works, obituaries, photos, and other awards.

University of Tennessee. "Astronomy 161: The Solar System." URL: http://csep10.phys.utk.edu/astr161/lect/index.html. "Astronomy 162: Stars, Galaxies, and Cosmology." URL: http://csep10.phys.utk.edu/astr162/lect/index.html. Accessed on February 4, 2006. Material designed for astronomy students provides a technical explanation of all topics in astronomy.

Mark Wade. "Encyclopedia Astronautica." URL: http://www.astronautix.com/. Accessed on March 28, 2006. A comprehensive encyclopedia of civilian and military space history including text and photo entries about satellite, robotic, and human programs listed by people's names, missions, vehicles, programs, and places. For a chronological list of all manned flights, go to www.astronautix.com/flights/mangical.htm.

Anatoly Zak. "RussianSpaceWeb.com: News & History of Astronautics in the Former USSR." Russian Space Web. URL: http://www.russianspaceweb.com/index.html. Accessed on August 31, 2006. This site has great detail and photos of Russian rockets, spacecraft, centers, people, and a chronology of flights including current programs.

▶ Index

Note: *Italic* page numbers refer to
   illustrations. Prior to the alphabetical
   listing is a listing by number of
   asteroids, planets, and stars.

1 Ceres (asteroid) 18, 245
47 Ursae Majoris (star) 226, 238
51 Pegasi (star) 226, 238
55 Cancri (star) 226
70 Virginis (star) 226, 238
243 Ida (asteroid) 224
253 Mathilde (asteroid) 225
433 Eros (asteroid) 225
951 Gaspra (asteroid) 224, *225*
2003 UB$_{313}$ (planet) 245

Abell, George O. 116
ablation 121–122
absolute brightness 27, 31
absolute magnitude 38–39
accelerometers 82
active galactic nuclei (AGNs) 102
Adams, Walter Sydney *20*, 30–31, 252
adaptive optics 119, 228
*Advanced Satellite for Cosmology and
   Astrophysics* (ASCA) 229
aerobraking 223–224
aerospace industry 98
Agena spacecraft 147–148
AGNs. *See* active galactic nuclei
aircraft 90–91, 162
Aitken, Robert G. 252
Akers, Thomas 217, 218–220
Akiyama, Toyohiro *193*, 203
Albert, Project 100
Aldrin, Buzz 137, *138*, *139*, 148, 154
Aleksandrov, Aleksandr 202
Alfvén, Hannes 116
Algol (star) 14
ALH84001 (meteorite) 222

Allen, Joseph 195
Alpher, Ralph A. *91*, 103
Alvarez, Luis 224
Alvarez, Walter 224
Ambartsumian, Viktor A. 256
American Association for the
   Advancement of Science 65, 180
American Astronomical Society 12, 46,
   210
American Physical Society 73
Anders, William *139*, 153
Anderson, Michael 242
Andromeda 33, 34, 45–46, 49, 101,
   108, 161
aniline 87
aperture-synthesis technique 108, 119
Apollo program 137, 151–156, 168–170
Apollo-Soyuz Test Project (ASTP) 167,
   174–175
apparent brightness 27, 31, 46
Apt, Jerome 217
Aquarius module 156
Arcturus (star) 25
Arecibo Observatory 228
Armament, Ministry of 98, 123
Armstrong, Neil 137, *138*, *139*, 148,
   154, *155*, 199
Army, U.S. 123, 125
Army Air Corps, U.S. 86
Artsebarsky, Anatoly 220
ASCA. *See Advanced Satellite for
   Cosmology and Astrophysics*
A series rockets (German) 80, 82–83,
   95–96. *See also* V–2 rocket
A series rockets (U.S.) 70, 80–82, *81*
asteroid(s). *See also* specific asteroids
   discovery of 18
   missions to 224–225, *225*, 245
asteroid belt 182
Aston, Francis W. 54

ASTP. *See* Apollo-Soyuz Test Project
astrogeology 221
astronauts. *See* specific people
astronomical units (AU) 58
Astronomishche Nachrichten 25
Astrophysical Journal 12, 25, 46, 54, 164, 185
astrophysics 11–15
Atkov, Oleg *192*, 201
Atlantic Monthly 4, 16
Atlantis space shuttle 197, 204, 216–217, 233
Atlas rocket 98, 122, 123, 131, 141
atmosphere
      of Earth 5, 55–56, *157*, 157–158
      of Mars 5–6
      of stars 51–54, 55
      of Titan 109
      of Venus 186
atomic mass 54
atoms, planetary model of 30
AU. *See* astronomical units
Avdeyev, Sergei *217*, 236
Aviation, Ministry of 98
aviation industry 98

Baade, Walter *68*, *90*, *101*, *112*
      awards to 101, 256
      on cosmic ray sources 56, 103
      on galactic collisions 115
      on radio wave sources 114–115
      on Schmidt telescopes 51
      on stars 49, 73, 89, 100–101
      on supernovae 55, 73, 74
      on universe, expansion of 101–102
      during World War II 100–102
Babcock, Harold 119–120, 255
Babcock, Horace 119–120, 257
Backlund, J. Oskar 251
bacteria 222
Bahcall, John N. 158
Baillaud, Benjamin 252
ballistic missiles 98, 121–123
Barnard, Edward *21*, 33, 251
barographs 82
Bauersfeld, Walter *44*, 45
Bean, Alan 156, 173
Beljawsky (comet) 20
Bell, Jocelyn 138, *138*, 159–160
Bell Laboratories 70
Bell Telephone Labs 149, 164
Belyayev, Pavel 146
Berezovoi, Anatoli *192*, 201
Berkner, Lloyd V. 123
Betelgeuse (star) 27
Bethe, Hans 69, *69*, 76, *91*, 103

Biermann, Ludwig *90*, 109, 257
big bang theory 76–77
      CBR in 103, 164, 188
      development of 103–105
      elements in 103, 118, 161
      expansion of universe in 49–51
      Hubble constant in 49
      inflation theory in 188
      v. steady-state theory 90, 104–105
      support for 161–164
Big Dipper 13, 228
binary pulsars 185
binary stars xviii, 12–14, 25, 26, 38, 229
biology 120, 179–180
bit rate 183
Blaauw, Adriaan 260
black dwarf stars 55
black holes 41, 74, 159, 229
blackout 192, 195
Blaha, John 233
blinking 56–57
blue stars 21, 24–27, 208–209
Blue Streak missile 98
Bluford, Guion S., Jr. 195, *195*
Bohr, Niels *20*, 30, 54
Bok, Bart 65, 258
Bolton, John *91*, 108, 260
Bondar, Roberta 218
Bondi, Herman *91*, 104
Bonestell, Chesley 120
Borman, Frank *139*, 147–148, 153
Boushey, Homer A., Jr. *90*, 91
Bowen, Ira S. 256
Bowersox, Kenneth 218
Bradbury, Ray 111
Brahe, Tycho xviii, 15, 74
Brand, Vance 174
Brauchitsch, Walther von 92
Braun, Wernher von *90*, *106*, 106–107
      in lunar missions 128, 144–145
      on manned space programs 120
      in Mercury, Project 129
      military rockets developed by 70, 80, 83, 89, 94, 97, 106–107, 121
      in satellite programs 123, 125
      in Society for Space Travel 63, 106
      on space stations 241
      after World War II 96, 97, 100, 107
Brezhnev, Leonid 170
brightness
      galactic 184–185
      stellar
            absolute 27, 31
            apparent 27, 31, 46

mass-luminosity law of 54, 73
    periodicity of 2, 13–14,
      21–22, 31, *32*
    photometry of 14–15
    size and 23–25
Britain 92–93, 96, 97
Brooks (comet) 20
Brouwer, Dirk 257
Brown, David 242
Brown, Ernest W. 251
Brown, Michael 245
Brown, Robert Hanbury *91*, 108
brown dwarf stars 226
Bruce Medals 249–261
Buran space shuttle 175, 203
Burbidge, Eleanor Margaret *113*,
    117–118, 210, 259
Burbidge, Geoffrey R. *113*, 116, 117–
    118, 210, 261
Burgess, Eric 181
Burke, Grace 64
Burroughs, Edgar Rice 17, 186
Bush, George H. W. 220
Bush, George W. 242–243
Bush, Vannevar 105
Bushuyev, Konstantin 174
Butler, Paul R. 226, 238
Bykovsky, Valery Fedorovich 130–131,
    142

calcium 14
calderas 207
California Institute of Technology
    (Caltech) 72, 86, 102
Callisto (moon) 225
Cambridge Catalog 116
Cameron, Alastair G. W. 117
Cameron, G. Harvey *45*, 56
Campbell, Bruce 238
Campbell, William W. 5, 25–26, 27, 251
Canada 150
canals, on Mars xviii, 1, 3–8, *4*, 16–17,
    178
55 Cancri (star) 226
Cannon, Annie Jump 11, *21*, 22, 27, 31
carbon 75–76, 117
Carl Sagan Memorial Station 222–223,
    223
Carnegie Foundation 12
Carpenter, M. Scott 130, *130*, 142
Carr, Gerald 173–174
Cassini spacecraft 245
Cassiopeia 114
Cassiopeia A 108
cataclysm 204
catalogs, star xviii, 31, 116

CBR. *See* cosmic background radiation
Centarus 209
Cepheid variable stars
    brightness of 14, 21–22, 31, *32*,
      101
    cause of variability in 28
    definition of 14
    distance to 31, 45–46, 49, 101
    radiative theory of 22
    types of 89, 101
1 Ceres (asteroid) 18, 245
Cernan, Eugene 148, 153, 170, 220
CGRO. *See* Compton Gamma-Ray
    Observatory
Chadwick, James *68*, 73
Chaffee, Roger B. 151
Challenger space shuttle 190, 195–199,
    199
Chamberlin, Thomas S. *2*, 17
Chandrasekhar, Subrahmanyan 43, *45*,
    55, 73, 255
Chandrasekhar's limit 55, 73
Chandra X-ray telescope 229, 231, 247
Chandryn 1 spacecraft 243
Chang'e 1 spacecraft 243
Charlier, Carl V. L. 253
Charon (moon) 184
Chawla, Kalpana 242
Chelomei, Vladimir 145–146, 156
Chertok, Boris 97–98
China 243
Chrétien, Jean-Loup 202
Christy, James *169*, 184
Churchill, Sir Winston 107
Clark, Laurel 242
Clarke, Sir Arthur C. *90*, 108, 129
Clay, Jacob 55–56
Clementine spacecraft 221
Clinton, Bill 211, *216*, 220, 222
CNO cycle 74–76, *75*
Cobb, Geraldyne M. "Jerrie" 131
Cocconi, Giuseppe 119
Collier's magazine 107, 120
Collins, Eileen *216*, 220, 243–244
Collins, Michael 148, 154
collision model 203
Columbia module 154
Columbia space shuttle 175, 191–196,
    217–218, 242–244
Coma cluster 74
comets. *See also* specific comets
    dirty snowball model of 109, 205,
      245
    formation of 109, 119, 225, 245–246
    missions to 205, 245
    superstitions about 15

comic strips 78
Command and Service Module (CSM) 144, 153, 154
commensurability 56
communications satellites 108, 129, 149
Communist Party 83
Compton Gamma-Ray Observatory (CGRO) 217, 229
Compton scattering 207–208
computers 2, 11–12, 105
Comsat 149
Conrad, Charles "Pete" *138*, 147, 156, 173
constellations 70. *See also* specific constellations
cooling systems 82
Cooper, L. Gordon 130, *130*, 142, 147
Copernicus, Nicholas 46
Corning Glass 71, *72*
coronagraph 54
Corrective Optics Space Telescope Axial Replacement (COSTAR) 219, *219*
cosmic background radiation (CBR) 103, 164, 188, 207–208
cosmic rays 55–56, 73, 103
cosmological constant 41, 231
cosmology 35–41
cosmonauts. *See* specific people
Cosmopolitan (magazine) 5
Cosmos spacecraft 172, 174
Cosmos television series 187
COSTAR 219, *219*
Covey, Richard 218
Cowling, Thomas G. 259
Crabbe, Larry "Buster" 78
Crab Nebula 115, 116
craters, impact 15–18, 118, 221
Crippen, Robert 191–192
Crommelin, Andrew 40
CSM 144, 153, 154
c-stars 25
Cunningham, Walter 152
curtain cooling 82
Curtis, Heber *21*, 22, 32–34, 46
curvature, of space 22, 36–41, *37*, 51
Cygnus A (galaxy) 114–116, 159

Dactyl (moon) 224
dark energy 231, 247
dark matter 74, 161, 188, 209–212, 247
Darwin, George 25, 28, 38
Davis, Raymond *137*, 158
Daylight (comet) 15
Debus, Kurt 121
Deep Impact spacecraft 245
Deep Space Network (DSN) 183

Defense, Department of 123
degenerate gas 55
degenerate matter 55
degenerate stars 55, 73
Delta Cephei (star) 13–14
density parameter 188
Deslandres, Henri A. 251
Destiny module 241
deuterium 161
Dicke, Robert Henry 164
differential analyzers 105
differential rotation 47
dirty snowball model 109, 205, 245
Discover (magazine) 210
Discovery space shuttle 196, 200, 244
Dobrovolsky, Georgi *168*, 171–172
dogs 120, 124, 131–134, 141
Doppler effect xviii–xix, 28, 33, 226, *227*, 237–238
Doppler redshift 40
Dornberger, Walter 79–80, 92, 96, 106–107
Douglass, Andrew 4, 8, 16
Drake, Frank 119, 182, *182*, 187
Drake equation 160, 247
Draper, Henry 25
Druyan, Ann 187
Dryden, Hugh L. 127
DSN. *See* Deep Space Network
Duke, Charlie 170
dwarf planets 119, 245
dwarf stars 21, 39, 55, 226
Dyson, Sir Frank 37–40, 251–252
Dzhanibekov, Vladimir 176–177, 201

Eagle lunar module 154
Earth
    age of xix
    elements on 51, 103
    ionization on 55–56
    in spectrography 5, *157*, 157–158
Earth Orbit Rendezvous (EOR) method *143*, 144
eclipses 14–15, 37–40
Eddington, Arthur *30*
    awards to 30, 252
    on general relativity 37–40
    milestones of *21*, *44*, *68*
    on nebulae 34
    on radiative equilibrium 22, 28–30
    on stars 22, 28, 43, 53, 54, 73
    on universe 49–51, 77
Einstein, Albert *20*
    cosmological constant of 41, 231
    equivalency equation of 29, 54
    on general relativity 22, 36–41

on photoelectric effect 30
on special relativity 35–36
on universe, expansion of 49, 51, 65
Eisele, Donn 152
Eisenhower, Dwight D. 97, *113*, 122, 125, 127, 128, 129
electrons 30
Elektron oxygen generation system 233–234
elements. *See also* specific elements
creation of
in big bang theory 103, 118, 161
in stars 112, 116–118, *117*
in supernovae 89–90, 102–103
on Earth 103
in stellar composition 39, 43–44, 51–54
elliptical galaxies 184–185
Enceladus (moon) 184, 245
encounter theory 25
Endeavor space shuttle 217, 218–220, 232
energy
dark 231, 247
in stars 22, 28–29, 73–77
Engle, Joe 192
ENIAC computer 105
Enterprise spacecraft 175
E.O. *See* extended operations
EOR. *See* Earth Orbit Rendezvous
equivalency equation 29, 54
433 Eros (asteroid) 225
Europa (moon) 184, 225
European Space Agency 205, 243
EVA. *See* spacewalks
Evans, Ron 170
event horizon 229
Evolution of Worlds, The (Lowell) 17
Ewald, Reinhold 233
Ewen, Harold Irving 108, 112, *112*
Excelsior 120–121
exhaust systems 58–60, 84
exobiology 179–180
Explorer satellites 111, *125*, 125–127, *126*
extended operations (EO) crew 176–178, 200–203
extrasolar planets 226–228, 236–238, 246
extravehicular activity (EVA). *See* spacewalks

Faber, Sandra 184–185
Faber-Jackson relation 184–185

Faget, Maxime A. 129, 144
Farkas, Bertalan 178
Feoktistov, Konstantin Petrovich 146
films 63, 78, 120, 175
Firework Nebula 11
Fischer, Debra A. 238
Fisher, Richard J. *169*, 185
fission theory 25, 38
Flammarion, Camille 3
Flash Gordon (comic) 78
Fleming, Williamina 2, 11–12, 22, 27
Flights to Other Planets (Tsander) 79
Foale, Michael 234–235
Ford, Kenneth William *139*, 161
Ford, W. Kent, Jr. 210
Fowler, Alfred 51, 253
Fowler, Ralph Howard 51, 55
Fowler, William "Willy" A. *113*, 117–118, 159, 161, 259
France 150
Freedom space station 200, 220
Friedmann, Alexander *44*, 49–51
Friendship 7 spacecraft 142
From the Earth to the Moon (Verne) xix, 10
Frost, E. B. 13
Fullerton, Gordon 193

Gagarin, Yuri Alexeevich 130, 133, 136, *136*, 139–140, *140*, 153, 241
Gaidukov, Lev Mikhailovich 98
galaxies
active nuclei of 102
brightness of 184–185
catalogs of 116
classification of 46, *47*, 65
clusters of 207–208, 209
collision of 115, 116
dark matter in 209–212
discovery of 43, 44–46, 64–65
distance to 47–49, *48*, 65, 185, 231, *232*
distribution of 46–51, 65, 188, 209, 210
evolution of 46–51
in expansion of universe 49–51, *50*
formation of 247
radio 161
rotation of 46–47, 212, *212*
GALCIT. *See* Guggenheim Aeronautical Lab at Caltech
Galileo Galilei xvii–xviii
Galileo spacecraft 200, 215, 221, 224–225, *225*
gamma rays 229

Gamow, George 74–76, *91*, 103, 118, 164
Ganymede (moon) 184, 225
Gaposchkin, Cecilia Payne. *See* Payne, Cecilia
Garn, Jake 196
Garriott, Owen 173
gas 14, 55
Gas Dynamics Laboratory (GDL) 78–79
951 Gaspra (asteroid) 224, *225*
Gazkov, Yuri 175
Geller, Margaret *193*, 209
Gemini spacecraft 146–148
General Electric 71
general theory of relativity (GTR) 22, 36–41, *37*, 49, 185, 231
Geneva Convention 92
geology 221
geosynchronous satellites 108
German scientists, after World War II 96–100, 107
Germany, military rockets of 70, 79–80, 82–83, 89, 92–96, *95*, 106–107
Gernsback, Hugo 43, *44, 45*
Giacconi, Riccardo 157, 259
Giacobini-Zinner comet 205
giant-impact theory 203–204
giant stars 21, 24–28, 39, 73
Gibson, Edward G. 173–174
Gibson, Everett 222
Gidzenko, Yuri 236
Gilruth, Robert R. *162,* 162–163
  in lunar missions 142, 144–145, 151, 163
  manned spaceflight under 129, 137, 140, 141, 162–163
Giotto spacecraft 205
GIRD. *See* Group for Studying Reaction Propulsion
GIRD-09 rocket 79
Glenn, John H. 130, 131, *136*, 142, 163, *217*, 218
Glennan, T. Keith 127, 129–130
Glenn Research Center 86, 150
Gliese 229B (star) 226
globular clusters *xviii, xix*, 22, 31–32
Glushko, Valentin 78–79, 98, 121, 122, 170
Goddard, Esther 63, 84, 86
Goddard, Robert H. *61*, 84–86, *85*
  milestones of *20, 44, 45, 68, 69*
  rockets developed by 23, 84–86
    exhaust systems of 58–60, 84
    guidance systems of 70, 80, *80*, 85

liquid-fueled 44, 58–63, *59*
  series of 70, 80–82, *81*, 86
  v. Soviet rockets 79
Goddard Spaceflight Center 128
Goett, Harry J. 128
Gold, Thomas *91*, 104, 114, 160–161
Goldin, Dan 222
Gorbachev, Mikhail 187
Gorbatko, Viktor 175
Gordon, Dick *138*, 156
gravitational contraction 25, 28–30, 54–55
gravitational lensing 40, *185*, 185–188
gravitational redshift 40–41
gravity 22, 36–41, 188
gravity assist 180, 191, 200, *206*
Great Comet 15
Great Nebula 33
Grechko, Georgi *169*, 176, 201
Greenstein, Jesse 258
Gregory, Fred *193*, 200
Gribov, Vladimir 158
Griffin, Michael 244
Grigg-Skjellerup comet 205
Grissom, Virgil "Gus" 130, *130*, 141, 146, 151
Grӧttrup, Helmut 98–99, 106
Group for Studying Reaction Propulsion (GIRD) 79
GTR. *See* general theory of relativity
Guggenheim, Harry 82, 86
Guggenheim Aeronautical Lab at Caltech (GALCIT) 86
Guggenheim Foundation 44, 63, 85, 86
guidance systems 70, 80, *80*, 85, 92, 121
gulags 83
Guth, Alan *169*, 188
gyrodines 202, 203
gyroscopes 79, 80, *80*, 82

Haise, Fred 156
HALCA satellite 228
Hale, George Ellery *2, 3*
  awards to 12, 251
  on canals on Mars 8
  at Mount Wilson Observatory 2–3, 12, 64
  at Palomar Observatory 71–72, *72*, 102
  Schmidt telescopes built for 51
  on sunspots 12
  at Yerkes Observatory 2, 12
Hale-Bopp (comet) 225, 234
Hale telescope 71–72, *72*, 102, 228

Halley, Edmund xviii, 15
Halley's comet 1, 14, 15, 109, 204, 205
Hartmann, Johannes 2, 14
Harvard College Observatory 2, 11–12, 27, 31
Hayabusa spacecraft 245
Hazard, Cyril *91*, 108, 159
heat sink 121–122
Heckmann, Otto 257
Heinlein, Robert 111
helioseismology 120
helium 11, 39, 53, 75–76, 118, 161
Henry, James P. 120
Henry Draper Catalog 31
Herbig, George H. 259
Herlofson, Nicolai 116
Herman, Robert C. 103
Hermaszewski, Miroslaw 177
Herschel, William xviii, 12, 13
Hertzsprung, Ejnar *2*, 14, *20*, 21, 23–25, 253
Hertzsprung-Russell (H-R) diagram 21, 22, 27, *29*, 39, 73
Hess, Victor 55
Hewish, Antony 159
Hey, John (James) Stanley *90*, 108
Hieb, Richard 217
Hill, George W. 250
Himmler, Heinrich 106–107
Hipparchus xviii
Hiten spacecraft 221
Hitler, Adolf 70, 74, 83, 92, 106
Hoffman, Jeffrey 218
Hoffmeister, Cuno *90*, 109
Holden, Edward 5
Horowitz, Norman 180
Houbolt, John Cornelius 144
Hoyle, Fred *103*
    awards to 118, 258
    on cosmic ray sources 103
    on elements, creation of 89–90, 102–103, 112–118, *117*, 161
    milestones of *91, 113*
    on radio wave sources 111–112, 114, 116, 159
    steady-state theory of 90, 104–105, 116, 161
    on supernovae chains 159
H-R diagram. *See* Hertzsprung-Russell diagram
Hu, Esther *217*
Hubble, Edwin *64*, 64–65
    awards to 65, 254
    on galaxies 44–51, *47*, *48*, 64–65
    Hale telescope used by 102
    milestones of *44, 45*

on nebulae 33, 44–46, 64, 65, 100
on universe, expansion of 41, 43, 65, 101–102
Hubble constant 49, 208
Hubble Deep Field North 228–229
Hubble's law 47–49, *48*, 65
Hubble Space Telescope 200, 218–220, *219*, 226, 228–229, 245–247
Huchra, John *193*, 209
Huggins, William 249
Hulse, Russell *168*, 185
Hulst, Hendrik Christoffel van de 108, 112, 259
Humason, Milton 47, 65, 102, 116
Husband, Rick 242
Hyades (star cluster) 37
hydrogen
    in CNO cycle 75–76
    on Moon 221
    spin-flip transition in 108, 112
    in stellar composition 11, 39, 44, 51–54, 73
hypergolic propellants 87

IBM 145
ICBM 122–123
243 Ida (asteroid) 224
IGY 123
impacts
    on Earth 15–18, 118, 221, 224–225
    on Jupiter 225
    in planet formation 203–204
India 243
inflation theory 188
infrared astronomical satellite (IRAS) 207
Institut Rabe 97–98
Intelligent Life in the Universe (Shklovskii) 160
INTELSAT 149, 217
intercontinental ballistic missiles (ICBM) 122–123
interferometry 27, 108, 115, 158, 228, *230*
Internal Constitution of Stars, The (Eddington) 43, 54–55
International Astronomical Union 27, 46, 65, 70, 245
International Cometary Explorer spacecraft 205
International Council of Scientific Unions 123
International Geophysical Year (IGY) 123
International Space Station (ISS) 200, 215, 220, 233, 236, 241–242, *242*, 244

International Telecommunication
   Satellite Consortium (INTELSAT)
   149, 217
interstellar dust 33, 49, 207
interstellar gas 14
Io (moon) 184
ionization 55–56
ionization potentials 52–53
IRAS. *See* infrared astronomical satellite
iridium 224
iron 103, 117
Irwin, James 169
island universes 32–34, 46
Is Mars Habitable? (Wallace) 8
ISS. See International Space Station
Italy 218
Itokawa (asteroid) 245
Ivanchenkov, Aleksandr *169*, 177
Ivanov, Georgi 177

Jackson, Robert 184–185
Jaehn, Sigmund 177
Jansky, Karl *68*, 70
Japan 97, 205, 221, 224, 228, 229, 243,
   245
Jarvis, Gregory 197–198
Jeans, James 30, 46
Jemison, Mae *216*, 218
jet-assisted takeoff (JATO) 86, 90–91
jet packs 196
Jet Propulsion Laboratory (JPL) 91–92,
   125, 127, 144
jets, fighter 90–91
Johnson, Lyndon 127, 128, 151
Jones, Harold Spencer 255
Joy, Alfred H. 255
JPL. *See* Jet Propulsion Laboratory
J-2 engines 152
Juno 1 125
Jupiter
   asteroids near 18
   impacts on 225
   missions to 167, 181–184, 200,
      215
   moons of xvii–xviii, 184, 225
Jupiter–C rocket 107, 121–122, 125,
   126

Kaleri, Alexander 236
Kammler, Hans 94, 96
Kaplan, Joe 120
Kapteyn, Jacobus 25–26, 31, 250
Kardashev, Nikolai 160
Kármán, Theodore von *69*, 86, 91
Keck telescopes 228, *229*

Kegley, Susan 238
Keith, Constance Savage 17
Kennedy, John F. 127, *136*, 137, 141,
   145, 163
Kennedy, Robert 153
Kennedy Space Center 121, 196
Kepler's third law 26
Kerwin, Joseph 173
Khrunov, Yevgeni 153
Khrushchev, Nikita 124–125, 133, 140,
   146
Khrushchev, Sergei 145
King, Martin Luther, Jr. 153
Kirshner, Robert *217*
Kittinger, Joseph 120–121
Kizim, Leonid 178, *192*, *193*, 201–202
Klein, Harold 179–180
Kohlschütter, Arnold *20*, 30
Kohoutek (comet) 173–174
Komarov, Vladimir Mikhailovich *138*,
   146, 151–152
Konacki, Maciej 246
Kondakova, Elena *216*
Kondratyuk, Yuri Vasilievich 144
Kopal, Zdenek 105
Korolev, Sergei 11, *132*, 132–133
   death of 146, 151
   imprisonment of 83, 133
   lunar missions under 128, 145–
      146
   manned spaceflight under 131,
      141
   milestones of *69*, *138*
   rockets developed by 70, 79, 98,
      99, 111, 122–123, 133
   satellites under 123–124
Korzun, Valery 234
Kosmos spacecraft 152, 157, 168–170
Kosygin, Aleksei 174
Kovalyonok, Vladimir *169*, 177, 201
Kraft, Chris 163
Krikalev, Sergei 202, *216*, 220, 231,
   236, 244
Kristall module 203, 233
K series rockets 82
Kubasov, Valeri 171, 174
Kuiper, Gerard *90*, *112*
   on H-R diagram 39, 73
   Sagan (Carl) under 186
   on solar system formation 112,
      118–119
   on Titan 109
   on Venus 180
Kuiper belt 119
Kvant modules 202, 203, 234

Lagrange, Joseph-Louis 18
Lampland, Carol Otto 7
Landau, Lev Davidovich *68*, 73
Lane's law 26
Lang, Fritz *45*, 63
Langley Research Center 83, 97, 129, 131, 162–163
Large Magellanic Cloud (LMC) 208–209
Laval, Carl Gustaf de 84
Laveykin, Aleksander 202
Lawrence, Wendy 235
Lazutkin, Alexander 233–235
LDEF. *See* Long Duration Exposure Facility
Leavitt, Henrietta 2, 14, 22, 31, 45, 46
Lebedev, Valentin 178, *192*, 201
Lederberg, Joshua 187
Leighton, Robert B. 119–120
Lemaître, Georges *44*, 49–51, *68*, 76–77
Lenoir, William 195
Leonov, Alexei *137*, 146, 171, 174
Leplace, Pierre-Simon de 41
Leuschner, Armin O. 253
Leverrier, Urbain-Jean-Joseph 36
Levin, Gilbert 180
Levy, David 224–225
Ley, Willy 63, 120
Lick Observatory 5, 7, 238
life
    building blocks of 119, 180
    extraterrestrial 119
        Drake equation on 160, 247
        future research on 245–247
        on Mars xviii, 3–8, *4*, 16–17, 179–180, 222, 245
        nuclear wars and 175
        pulsars as sign of 160
Life magazine 130
light, speed of 36, 40
light curves 32, 74
Lindbergh, Charles 43, 44, 63, 82, 85, 86
Lindblad, Bertil 46–47, 255
line broadening 53
Linenger, Jerry *233–234*
liquid-fueled rockets 44, 58–63, *59*, 79–80, 87
liquid oxygen (LOX) 60, 79, 87
LK-1 spacecraft 145
LM. *See* Lunar Module
LMC. *See* Large Magellanic Cloud
Lockyer, Norman 26
London Daily Herald 125

Long Duration Exposure Facility (LDEF) 200
long-duration spaceflight 175–178, 190, 200–203
LOR. *See* Lunar Orbit Rendezvous
Lousma, Jack 173, 193
Lovell, Jim *139*, 147–148, 153, 156
Low, George 145, 151
Lowell, Percival 1, *3*, 3–8, *4*, *16*, 16–17, 56, 58, 245
Lowell Observatory 1, 3–8, 56–58
LOX. *See* liquid oxygen
L series rockets 82
L series spacecraft 145, 153, 156–157
Lucid, Shannon 215, *217*, 233
luminosity, stellar 54, 73
lunar. *See* Moon
Lunar-A spacecraft 243
Lunar Module (LM) 144, 154
Lunar Orbiter spacecraft 148–149
Lunar Orbit Rendezvous (LOR) method *143*, 144–145
Lunar Prospector spacecraft 215, 221
Lunar Surface Rendezvous method *143*, 144
Luna spacecraft 128, 150, 154, 156, 170, 221
Lundmark, Knut 46
Lunney, Glynn 174
Lunokhod rovers 170
Luyten, Willem J. 257
Lyakhov, Vladimir *169*, 177, 202
Lynden-Bell, Donald *139*, 159, 209, 261
Lyot, Bernard-Ferdinand *45*, 54, 255

Maanen, Adriann van 34, 46
Magellan spacecraft 204
magnetic fields 12, 119–120, 205
magnitude, stellar 27, 38–39
main sequence 21, 27, *29*, 73
Makarov, Oleg 176–177, 178
Malina, Frank *69*, 86–87, 91–92
Manarov, Musa *193*, 202
Manned Spacecraft Center 137, 162–163
Marcy, Geoffrey 226, 236–238, *238*
Margulis, Lynn 186
Mariner spacecraft 149, 178, 180
Mars
    atmosphere of 5–6
    canals on xviii, 1, 3–8, *4*, 16–17, 178
    life on xviii, 1, 3–8, *4*, 16–17, 179–180, 222, 245

meteorite from 222
missions to 149, 178–180, 215,
   222–224, 243
moons of xviii, 178, 204
photos of 7–8
spectrum of 5–6
volcanoes on 178, *179*
water on 5–6, 7–8, 17, 223, 243
Mars (Lowell) 4, 16–17
Mars and Its Canals (Lowell) 7, 16
Mars as the Abode of Life (Lowell) 8, 16
Mars Climate Orbiter spacecraft 224
Mars Express spacecraft 243
Mars Global Surveyor (MGS) 223–224,
   243
Marshall Space Flight Center (MSFC)
   128
Mars Observer spacecraft 222
Mars Odyssey spacecraft 243
Mars Pathfinder spacecraft 215, 222–
   224
Mars Polar Landers 224
Mars spacecraft 178–179
Martian Chronicles (Bradbury) 111
mass, stellar 43, 54–55, 73
Massachusetts Institute of Technology
   (MIT) 105
mass-luminosity law 54, 73
mathematics, in astronomy 11
253 Mathilde (asteroid) 225
Matthews, Thomas 159
Mattingly, Ken 170
Mauna Kea Observatory 148, 228
Maury, Antonia 25
Mayall, Nicholas U. 116
Mayor, Michael *216*, 226, 238
McAuliffe, Sharon Christa 197, 198
McCandless, Bruce *192*, 196
McCauley, George 71–72
McCool, William (Willie) 242
McDivitt, Jim 147, 153
McDonnell Aircraft Company 129
McKay, David 222
McMahon, Richard *217*
McNair, Ronald 198
Medaris, John Bruce 123
M87 (nebula) 115
Melvill, Mike 243
Menzel, Donald 52, 53
Mercury (planet) 36, 204
Mercury, Project 111, *129*, 129–134,
   141–142, 163
Merrill, Paul W. 255
metals 117
meteorites 222
meteoritic hypothesis 26

MGS. See Mars Global Surveyor
mice 120
Michelson, Albert A. *21*, 27
microlensing 246
milestone time lines
   1901–1910 *2–3*
   1911–1920 *20–21*
   1921–1930 *44–45*
   1931–1940 *68–69*
   1941–1950 *90–91*
   1951–1960 *112–113*
   1961–1970 *136–139*
   1971–1980 *168–169*
   1981–1990 *192–193*
   1991–2000 *216–217*
military rockets
   German 70, 78, 79–80, 82–83,
      92–99, *95*, 106–107
   Soviet 70, 78–79, 83, 96–99
   U.S. 83–87, 90–92, 96–97
   after World War II 96–99
Milky Way
   age of 118
   dust in 207
   galaxies outside 43, 44–46, 64–65
   globular clusters in 31
   radio waves from 68, 70–71
   size of xix, 22, 34
   spiral arms of 112, *113*, 207
   structure of 22, 31–34, 46, 207
Millennium Simulation 247
Miller, Stanley L. 119, 180
Millikan, Robert A. *45*, 56
Milne, Edward Arthur 51, 55, 254
Mimas (moon) 184
Minkowski, Rudolph 74, 115, 256
Minnaert, Marcel 255
Miranda (moon) 205–206
Mir space station 190, 201–203, 215,
   220–221, 231–236, *237*
Mishin, Vassily 146, 151, 152, 170
MIT. *See* Massachusetts Institute of
   Technology
Mitchell, Edgar 168
Mitchell, Maria 210, 211
Mizar A (star) 13
Mizar B (star) 13
Mohri, Mamoru *216*, 218
*Monthly Notices of the Royal Astronomical
   Society* (MNRAS) 28, 51, 76
Moon
   eclipse of 14
   formation of 203–204
   hydrogen on 221
   missions to 136–157. *See also* spe-
      cific missions

occultation by 159
    spectrum of 5, *6*
moons, discovery of xvii–xviii. *See also*
    specific moons
Moore, Charlotte E. 53
Morgan, William W. 256
Morrison, Philip 119
Morton Thiokol 198
motion. *See* specific types
Moulton, Forest Ray *2*, 17
Mount Wilson Observatory *2–3*, 8, 12,
    64, 100
movies 63, 78, 120, 175
MSFC. *See* Marshall Space Flight
    Center
Mueller, George 156
Mukai, Chiaki 218
Muller, Hermann 186
Musgrave, Story 195, 218

Naryan, Ramesh *217*
National Advisory Committee on
    Aeronautics (NACA) 83–86, 97, 120,
    127
National Aeronautics and Space
    Administration (NASA) 111, 127,
    148. *See also* specific missions and
    programs
National Defense Research Committee
    (NDRC) 105
National Geographic 86
National Space Society 107, 175
Nature (journal) 77, 159
Navy, U.S. 58, 123
Navy Research Lab 123
Nazi Party 70
NDRC. *See* National Defense Research
    Committee
Near Earth Asteroid Rendezvous (NEAR)
    spacecraft 225
nebulae xix, 32–34. *See also* galaxies
    distance to 32–34, 45–46
    as galaxies 44–51
    as island universes 32–34, 46
    rotation of 33–34, 46–47, 100
    velocity of 33, 64, 65
nebular theory 17
Nelson, Bill 197
Nelyubov, Grigori Grigoyevich 131
Neptune xviii, 119, 205–207
neutrinos 158
neutrons 73
neutron stars 73–74, 103, 160–161
Newton's law of gravity 36–40
New York Times, The 70, 84, 86, 124,
    179

NGC4550 galaxy 211
Nicholson, Seth 257
Nicollier, Claude 218
NII–88 98
Nikolayev, Andrian Grigoryevich 130,
    136, 142, 156
Nixon, Richard 155, 156, 174
Nobel Prizes 30, 76
N-1 rockets 145, 153, 170
North Star 14
novae xviii, 11, 32, 55. *See also*
    supernova(e)
Nozomi spacecraft 224
nuclear chain reactions 69, 74–77
nuclear fusion 25, 54
nuclear war 175, 187
nucleus stars 69, 73

Oberth, Hermann 44, *44*, *62*, 62–63,
    106
observatories, in space 184–188, 228–
    231. *See also* specific observatories
occultation 159
Odyssey module 156
Olsen, Gregory 244
Olympus Mons 178, *179*
O'Neill, Gerard 175, 241
Onizuka, Ellison 198
Onufrienko, Yuri 233
Oort, Jan H. *45*, 47, *91*, 108, 109, 254
Oort cloud 109, 119, 225
Öpik, Ernst J. 258
Oppenheimer, J. Robert 73–74, 161
Opportunity rover 243
opposition 3–4, 8, *9*
optics, adaptive 119, 228
O-rings 198, 199
ORM rocket engines 79
oscillators 84
Osterbrock, Donald E. 260
Outer Space Treaty (1967) 150
Overcast, Operation 97
oxygen 60, 79, 87, 233–234

Pais, Abraham 36
Palomar Observatory 71–72, *72*, 102
Panspermia theory 246
parallaxes 22, 23–24, *24*, 31
Parker, Eugene N. 261
Parsons, John W. 91
Patsayev, Viktor *168*, 171–172
Payne, Cecilia 39, 43–44, *44*, *52*, 52–54
Pease, Francis *21*, 27
Peebles, James Edwin 164, 261
Peenemünde 82–83, 89, 92–96, *94*
51 Pegasi (star) 226, 238

Pennsylvania, University of 105
Penzias, Arno *137*, 138, 164
Perlmutter, Saul 231
Persei (nova) 11
Perseid meteor shower 231
Perseus (constellation) 11
Peterson, Donald 195
Petrone, Rocco 121
phase change 188
Phobos (moon) 204
photoelectric cells 14–15
photoelectric effect 30
photoelectric photometers 105
photography 7–8, 11, 51, 54, 105
photometry 14–15, 105
photons 30
Physical Review 76
Piccard, Jean 162
Pickering, Edward 7, 11, 13, *21*, 25, 27, 250
Pickering, William H. 4, 56, 123, 125
Pictoris (nova) 55
Pioneer spacecraft 128, 167, 181–183, *182*, 187
Pioneer Venus spacecraft 181
Planck, Max 25
Planck's constant 30
planet(s). *See also* specific planets
    discovery of
        Doppler effect in 226, *227*, 237–238
        extrasolar 226–228, 236–238, 246
        microlensing in 246
        predictions of 56
        transit method in 226–228, 246
    formation of
        impacts in 203–204
        model of 112, 118–119
        theories of 17, 109
    new definition of 245
    of pulsars 225–226
planetariums 44–45
planetary model 30
planetismal theory 17
plaque, *Pioneer* 167, 181–182, *182*, 187
Plaskett, John S. 253
Pleiades (star cluster) 14
Pluto 17, 44, 56–58, 119, 184, 245
Pobedonostsev, Yuri 98
pogo 152
Pogue, William 173–174
Poincaré, Henri 250
Polaris (star) 14
Pollack, Jim 178

Polyakov, Valeri 202, *216*, 231
Pontecorvo, Bruno 158
Popov, Leonid *169*, 178
Popovich, Pavel Ramanovich 130, *136*, 142
Popular Astronomy 4
Pound, Robert V. 40
Powers, John A. "Shorty" 141
Pratt & Whitney 150
Pravda (newspaper) 140, 154
primates 100, 120, 131, 141, 142
Princeton University 38–39
Priroda module 233
prisoners of war 92
private space exploration 243
probes 148–150
Progress spacecraft 177, 201, 231, 235, 242
proper motion 26, 27, 30
propulsion systems. *See also* liquid-fueled rockets
        solid-fueled 87, 91
        in Soviet military 78–79
        storable 122–123
protons 76, 77
protoplanets 109
Proxmire, William 174
P series rockets 86
PSR 1257+12 (pulsar) 225–226
PSR 1913+16 (pulsar) 185
pulsars 138, 158–161, *160*, 185, 225–226
Purcell, Edward Mills 108, 112, *112*
Pyrex 71

quasars 116, 158–161, *185*, 185–188
Queloz, Didier *216*, 226

radiation/radioactivity xix
    cosmic 55–56
    cosmic background 103, 164, 188, 207–208
    and stellar classification 25, 27
    synchrotron 116
radiative equilibrium 22, 28–30
radio astronomy 108, 111–116, 119
radio galaxies 161
radio interferometry 115, 158
radioisotope power generators (RTGs) 182–183
radio stars 112–116
radio telescopes xvii, 68–69, 70–71, *71*, 108, 119
radio waves
    from Andromeda 108
    from Cassiopeia 108, 114

debate over sources of 111–116
from extraterrestrial life 119
from Milky Way 68, 70–71
from quasars and pulsars 158–161
from stars 111–112, 114–116
from Sun 108, 119–120
Ramon, Ilan 242
Ranger spacecraft 148–149
Raymond, Alex 78
RD Gushko engines 122, *126*, 145
Reaction Propulsion Institute (RNII)
    79, 83, 132
Reagan, Nancy 193
Reagan, Ronald 193, 199, 200
Realm of the Nebulae, The (Hubble) 46,
    65
Reber, Grote *69*, 70–71, *71*, 115–116,
    256
Rebka, Glen A., Jr. 40
redshift 40–41, *48*, 49, 64, 116
red stars 21, 24–27, 209
Redstone missiles 121, 123, 141
reentry heating 121–122
Rees, Martin 260
reflecting telescopes xvii, 2–3, 8, 12, *13*
refractor telescopes xvii, 2, 12, *13*
Reiter, Thomas 244
relativity. *See* general theory of relativ-
    ity; special theory of relativity
Remek, Vladimir *169*, 177
rescue, space 167, 174
Resnick, Judy 198
retrograde motion 56
Ride, Sally 195, 199, 201
Riedel, Klaus 106
Riess, Adam *217*, 231
Riffolt, Nils 59–60
RNII. *See* Reaction Propulsion Institute
rocket(s). *See also* military rockets; spe-
    cific rockets
    aircraft powered by 90–91
    ballistic missile 121–123
    development of first xix, 23, 44,
        58–63, *59*
    equation for 1, 9–11
    guidance systems for 70, 79, *80*,
        85, 92, 121
    multistage 95–96
    science 99–100
    in World War II 83–87, 89–96
Rocketdyne engines 121
Rocket into Planetary Space, The (Oberth)
    62, 106
Roddenberry, Gene *138*, 149
Rogers, Jean 78
Rogers, William 199

Romanenko, Yuri *169*, 176, *193*, 202
Roosa, Stuart 168
Roosevelt, Franklin Delano 105
Rosen, Milton W. 123
Ross, Jerry 217
Rosseland, Svein 51–52
rotation
    differential 47
    of galaxies 46–47, 212, *212*
    of nebulae 33–34, 46–47, 100
    of planets 5, *6*
Roth, Ludwig 95
rovers 168–171, *171*, 222–223, *223*,
    243
Rozhdestvensky, Valeri 175
RR Lyrae variable stars 31
R series rockets 98, 99, 111, 121, 122–
    123, *126*, 128, 133
RTGs. *See* radioisotope power genera-
    tors
Rubin, Vera *139*, 161, 188, 191, *192*,
    209–212, *211*
Rubin–Ford effect 210
Rukavishnikov, Nikolai 171
Russell, Henry Norris *38*, 38–39
    awards to 21, 39, 252
    H-R diagram of 21, 27, *29*, 39
    milestones of *20*
    on nebulae 34
    on Pluto 58
    on stars 14
        composition of 39, 44, 51–54
        evolution of 25–27, 38–39
        light from 76
        proper motion of 30
    Vogt-Russell theorem of 39, 55
Russell-Saunders coupling 39
Russia 220–221. *See also* Soviet Union;
    specific missions and programs
Rutan, Burt 243, *244*
Ryan, Cornelius 120
Ryle, Martin *91*, 108, 111, 114–116,
    119, 161, 258
Ryumin, Valery *169*, 177–178, 202

Sagan, Carl *186*, 186–187
    on extraterrestrial life 160, 174–
        175, 179, 180, 187, 247
    on Mars 178, 180
    Pioneer plaque by 167, 181–182,
        182, 187
    on Venus 167, 180–181, 186
Sagan, Linda Salzman 181–182, *182*,
    187
Sagittarius 31, 70, 71
Saha, Meghnad 22, 30, 51, 53

Sakigake spacecraft 205
Salpeter, Edwin E. 260
Salyut space stations 167, 171–178, 176, 200–202
Sandage, Allan Rex 116, 159, 258
Sargent, Wallace 261
satellites. *See also* specific satellites
    communications 108, 129, 149
    geosynchronous 108
    scientific 123
    in space race 123–127
    space shuttles launching 195
    weather 128–129
    X-ray astronomy on 157–158
Saturn (planet) xviii, 119, 183, 184, 245
Saturn rockets 106–107, 128, 144, 150–153
Saunders, Frederick A. 39
Savinykh, Viktor 201
Savitskaya, Svetlana *192*, 201
Scaled Composites 243
Schiaparelli, Giovanni 3–4, 17, 249
Schirra, Walter "Wally" M. 130, 142, 148, 152
Schlesinger, Frank 252
Schmidt, Bernhard *45*, 51
Schmidt, Maarten *137*, 159, 260
Schmidt telescopes 51, 72
Schmitt, Harrison 170
Schwarzschild, Karl *21*, 24, 40–41
Schwarzschild, Martin 117, 257
Schwarzschild radius 41
Schweickart, Russell "Rusty" 153
Science and Invention (magazine) 43
Science and Research Development, Office of 105
science fiction 43, 78, 111
Science magazine 209, 222
Science Review, The (magazine) 10
Scientific American 38, 39, 58, 84, 85, 210
Scientific Research Institute–88 98
Scobee, Francis "Dick" 198
Scorpius X-1 157
Scott, David *138*, 148, 153, 169
Seamans, Robert C., Jr. 144
search for extraterrestrial intelligence (SETI) 119, 160
Seares, Frederick H. 254
SELENE spacecraft 243
Serebrov, Aleksandr 203
SETI. *See* search for extraterrestrial intelligence
Sevastyanov, Vitaly 156
Severin, Gai 146
Seyfert, Carl Keenan *90*, 102

Seyfert galaxies 102
SFOG. *See* solid-fuel oxygen generator
Shapley, Harlow *35*
    awards to 254
    on globular clusters 22, 31–32
    Hubble (Edwin) and 65
    milestones of *21*
    on Milky Way 22, 34, 45, 46
    on nebulae 34, 46
    on stars 21–22, 27, 28, 31, 39
Sharman, Helen 220
Shatalov, Vladimir 153, 171
Shea, Joseph F. 144
Shenzhou 5 spacecraft 243
Shepard, Alan B. 130, *136*, 140–141, 168, 243
Shepard, Bill 236
Shklovskii, Iosif Samuilovich *112*, 116, *138*, 160, 178, 187, 258
Shoemaker, Eugene Merle 118, *217*, 221, 224–225
Shoemaker, Walter 221
Shoemaker-Levy 9 (comet) 221, 224–225
Shuttleworth, Mark 242
Siberia 15–18, 83
Sirius B (star) 55
Sitter, Willem de 49, 253
Sitterly, Charlotte Moore 39, 260
Skylab space station *172*, 172–174
Slayton, Donald "Deke" 130, *130*, 174
Slipher, Vesto Melvin 5–6, 8, 14, *20*, 22, 33, 56, 64, 253
Small Magellanic Cloud (SMC) 34, 46
SMART 1 spacecraft 243
SMC. *See* Small Magellanic Cloud
Smith, Francis Graham 114
Smith, Michael 198
Smithsonian Institution 60, 84
Snyder, Hartland S. 73
soap-bubble universe 209
Society for Space Travel 63, 79, 106
soil, of Mars 179–180
Sojourner rover 222–223, *223*
Solar and Heliospheric Observatory satellite 245
solar eclipse 37–40
solar system
    formation of 109, 112, 118–120
    planets outside 226–228, 236–238, 246
solar wind 109, 159
solid-fuel oxygen generator (SFOG) 233–234
Solovyov, Anatoli 235
Solovyov, Vladimir *192*, 201

Soviet Union. *See also* specific missions
and programs
  aviation industry in 98
  military rockets of 70, 78–79, 83,
    96–99, 121–123
  U.S. competition with. *See* space
    race
Soyuz spacecraft 137, 146, 151–153,
156, 171–178
Space, Time, and Gravitation (Eddington)
40
spaceflight. *See also* specific missions,
  programs, and spacecraft
  first manned 139–142
  first successful 89
  long-duration 175–178, 190,
    200–203
  preparation for 120–121
  theoretical foundation for 1, 9–11,
    60–63
Spacelab missions *196*, 196–197, 218
space race xix
  end of 137, 153–155
  to Moon 142–155
  origins of 111, 120
  satellites in 123–127
Space Rocket Trains (Tsiolkovsky) 78
SpaceShipOne spacecraft 243, *244*
space shuttle program
  accidents in 190, 197–199,
    242–244
  commercial use of 195, 241–242
  flight numbering in 197
  flight sequence in *194*
  missions of 191–200, 216–221,
    243–244
  origins of 156, 175
  Russians in 220–221, 232, 233
  space stations and 232, 233, 236,
    244
space stations. *See also* specific stations
  first 167, 171–174
  theoretical foundation for 120
Space Task Group (STG) 129, 131, 142
Space Transportation System (STS)
  191–200, 216–221
spacewalks
  first 146–148
  with jet packs 196
  by women 196, 201
special theory of relativity 35–36, 55
spectra 5–6, *6*, 12. *See also* stellar spectra
spectral lines 5, 12
spectrography 5–6, *6*, *157*, 157–158
spectroheliograph 12
spectroscopic binary stars 13

spectroscopy 11
Speer, Albert 92
Spektr module 232, 234–235
Spellman, Carolyn 221
spherical aberration 51
spin-flip transition 108, 112
spiral nebulae (galaxies) 22, 32–34, 185,
210
Spirit rover 243
Spitzer, Lyman, Jr. 39, 115, 258
Spitzer Space Telescope 245, 247
Sputnik satellites 111, 123–127, *124*,
126
Stafford, Thomas 148, 153, 174
Stalin, Joseph 70, 83, 98
star(s) xviii. *See also* specific types
  age of 118
  atmospheres of 51–55
  brightness of. *See* brightness
  cataloging of xviii, 31, 116
  classification of 2, 11–12, 22, 27
  composition of 11, 39, 43–44,
    51–54
  density of 26–27
  distances to 30–31
  elements created in 112, 116–118,
    117
  energy production in 22, 28–29,
    73–77
  evolution of xviii, 14, 21, 24–27,
    38–39, 54–55
  formation of 25, 38
  mass limits for 43, 55, 73
  meteoritic hypothesis of 26
  radiative theory of 22
  radio waves from 111–112,
    114–116
  size of 21, 23–27
  spectra of. *See* stellar spectra
  structure of 28–31
star clusters 30–31, 73
star counting 33
Stardust spacecraft 225, 245
starlight 25, 74–77
Starship Troopers (Heinlein) 111
Star Trek (TV show) 149
Star Wars (movie) 175, 246
Staver, Robert 97
steady-state theory 90, *104*, 104–105,
  116, 161
Stebbins, Joel 14–15, 254
stellar spectra 2, 11–14, 31, 51–54
stellar thermodynamics 43, 53
stellar-wobble method 226, *227*
Stewart, John Quincy 53
STG. *See* Space Task Group

Strekalov, Gennadi 178
Strömgren, Bengt Georg Daniel *68*, 73, 256
Struve, Otto 255
STS. *See* Space Transportation System
Subaru telescope *229*
Suisei spacecraft 205
Sullivan, Kathryn *192*, 196, 201
Sun
    age of xix
    elements in 39, 43–44, 51–54
    helioseismology of 120
    magnetic fields on 12, 119–120
    position in Milky Way 22, 31–32
    radio waves from 108, 119–120
sunspots 12
Sunyaev, Rashid 207–208, 261
Sunyaev-Zel'dovich effect 207–208
supernova(e) xviii
    cosmic rays from 56, 73
    degeneracy and 55
    discovery of 73–74
    elements in, origin of 89–90, 102–103, 112
    and expansion of universe 247
    planets surviving 225–226
    and stellar evolution xviii, 69
    visible to naked eye 191, 208–209
Supernova 1987A 191, 202, *208*, 208–209
SuperNova Legacy Survey 247
supersonic speeds 162
Surveyor spacecraft 148–149, 156
Swift telescope 229
Swigert, Jack 156
synchrotron radiation 116

Tamayo-Méndez, Arnaldo 178
Tattooine (planet) 246
Taylor, Joseph H. *168*, 185
TDRS. *See* Tracking Data Relay Satellite
telemeters 121
telescopes xvii. *See also* specific types
television 149, 187
Telstar 1 satellite 149
Tempel 1 (comet) 245–246
temperature, stellar *2*, 11, 22, 25, 26, 27
Tereshkova, Valentina 136, *137*, 142, *142*
Thagard, Norman *216*, 231–232
thermodynamics, stellar 43, 53
Thiel, Walter 92, 93
Thiokol 91
Thomas, Andrew 235, 236

Thomas-Keprta, Kathie 222
Thor missile 123, 128
Thornton, Kathryn 218
3C48 (quasar) 159
3C273 (quasar) 159
Thuot, Pierre 217
Tikhomirov, Nikolai 78
Tikhonoravov, Mikhail Klavdiyevich 123
time 36
Tinsley, Beatrice 185
Tiros 1 spacecraft 128
Titan (moon) 109, 183, 184, 245
titanium 52
Tito, Dennis 241
Titov, Gherman Stepanovich 130
Titov, Vladimir *136*, 141, *193*, 202, 220
Toftoy, Holger N. 97
Tolman, Richard 65
Tombaugh, Clyde 44, *45*, 56–58, *57*, 65
tourism, space 203, 233, 241–242, 244
Tracking Data Relay Satellite (TDRS) 195, 198, 200, 218
transistors 121
transit method 226–228, 246
Travel in Outer Space (Ley) 63
triple-alpha process 117
Triton (moon) 207
Trojan asteroids 18
Truly, Richard 192, 199
Trumpler, Robert *45*, 49, 73
Tsander, Fridrikh Arturovich 79, 132
Tsibliyev, Vasili 233–235
Tsiolkovsky, Konstantin *2, 10*
    influence of 11, 132
    rocket equation by 1, 10–11
    rockets designed by 78
    on space exploration 60, 244
    and space stations 231, 241
T2K lunar lander 169–170
Tuân, Pham 178
Tucana (constellation) 228
Tukhachevsky, Mikhail *69*, 79, 83
Tully, R. Brent *169*, 185
Tully-Fisher relation 185
Tunguska River (Siberia) 15–18
"tuning fork" diagram 46, *47*, 65
Tupolev, Andrei 132, 133
Turner, Herbert Hall 252
Turner, Roscoe 162
Twain, Mark 15
twin paradox 36
twin quasars *185*, 185–188

2003 UB$_{313}$ (planet) 245
Uhura satellite 157
Ulysses spacecraft 200

United Nations 150
United States. *See also* specific missions
   and programs
      aviation industry in 98
      military rockets of 83–87, 90–92,
         96–97, 121–123
      science rockets of 99–100
      Soviet competition with. *See* space
         race
Unity module 236
Universal Studios 78
universe. *See also* big bang theory
      cosmology of 35–41
      density parameter of 188
      expansion of *50*
         acceleration of 231, 247
         and age 102
         discovery of xix, 41, 43,
            49–51, 65
         Hubble constant in 49, 202
         prediction of 49–51
      maps of 209
      size of 22, 31–34, 101
      steady-state theory of 90, *104*,
         104–105, 116, 161
      structure of 207–209
Unsöld, Albrecht 53–54, 256
Upsilon Andromeda (star) 226
UR-500K rocket 145, 151, 153
Uranus xviii, 204–207
Urey, Harold C. 119, 180
47 Ursae Majoris (star) 226, 238
Usachev, Yury 233
Ustinov, Dmitri Fedorovich 98, 123

Van Allen, James 125
Van Allen belts 125–127, *127*
Vandenberg Air Force Base 175
Vanguard, Project 97, 123–125, 128
Vanguard satellites 125–127
variable stars. *See also* specific types
      discovery of xix, 12
      Doppler effect in xviii–xix, 28
      period and brightness of 2, 13–14,
         21–22
Vasyutin, Vladimir 201
Vega spacecraft 204, 205
Vela-5B satellite 157–158
Velikovsky, Immanuel 167, 180
velocity-distance relation. *See* Hubble's
   law
velocity-shift method 5, 6
Venera spacecraft 150, 180–181, *181*, 204
Venus
      atmosphere of 186
      length of days on 17, 204

missions to 149–150, 180–181,
   204
origin of 167, 180–181
Verne, Jules xix, 10, 62
Very Large Telescope 246
Very Long Base Array (VLBA) 228, *230*
Very Long Baseline Interferometry
   (VLBI) 228, *230*
Viking research rockets 97
Viking spacecraft 179–180, 222
Viktorenko, Alexander 203
Vinogradov, Pavel 235
Virgin Galactic 243
70 Virginis (star) 226, 238
Virgo nebula 33
Virgo supercluster 207
Viscara (comet) 15
Vision for Space Exploration 242–243
VLBA. *See* Very Long Base Array
VLBI. *See* Very Long Baseline
   Interferometry
Vogel, Hermann Carl 250
Vogt, Heinrich 39, 55
Vogt, Steven 238
Vogt-Russell theorem 39, 55
volcanoes 178, *179*, 184, 207
Volkoff, George M. 73, 161
Volkov, Alexander 201, 202, 220
Volkov, Vladislav *168*, 171–172
Volynov, Boris V. 153
V-1 rocket 96
Voskhod spacecraft 146–147, *147*
Voskresensky, L. A. 99
Vostok spacecraft 111, *129*, 129–134,
   139–140, 141, 142
Voyager spacecraft 183–184, 191, 205–
   207, *206*, 245
V-2 (A4) rocket
      after World War II 97, 98–100
      in World War II 83, 89–96, *93*,
         106–107
Vulcan (theoretical planet) 36

WAC Corporal rocket 92, 100
Wagoner, Robert 161
Wake Shield Facility (WSF) 220
Wallace, Alfred Russel 8
Wallops Flight Center 97
Wall Street Journal, The 8
Walsh, Dennis *169*, 185, *185*
Walther, Erich 93
War of the Worlds (Wells) 78, 84
Washington Post, The 210
water
      on Mars 5–6, 7–8, 17, 223, 243
      on Moon 221

weapons of mass destruction 150
weather satellites 128–129
Webb, James E. 140–141, 145, 148, 151, 163
Weitz, Paul 173
Weizsacker, Carl F. von *69*, 74–76, *90*, 109
Welles, Orson *69*, 78
Wells, H. G. 78, 84
Whipple, Fred *91*, 109, 120, 205, 245, 260
White, Ed *137*, 147, 151
white dwarf stars 21, 55
White Sands Proving Ground 97, 99, 193
Whitford, Albert 15, 261
Wiesner, Jerome B. 140–141, 145
Wild 2 (comet) 245
Wildt, Rupert 180–181
Wilson, Charles E. 123
Wilson, Olin C. 259
Wilson, Robert *137*, 138, 164
wind tunnels 83, 97
wingflow test 162
Winkler, Johannes *68*, 79
Wolf, David 235
Wolf, Max *3*, 18, 253
Wolszczan, Alexander 225
women
    as astronauts/cosmonauts 131, 190, 195, 196, 201
    in astronomy 2
    spacewalks by 196, 201
Worden, Alfred 169–170

Worlds in Collision (Velikovsky) 180
World War II
    computers in 105
    military rockets in 83–87, 89–96
Wren, Christopher 32
Wright, Orville *2*, 10
Wright, Wilbur *2*, 10
WSF. *See* Wake Shield Facility

X-ray astronomy 157–158
X-ray telescopes 158

Yangel, Mikhail Kuzmich 122–123, 170
Yáng Lèwěi 243
Yeager, Chuck *91*, 97
Yegorov, Boris Borisovich 146
Yeliseyev, Alexei S. 153, 171
Yeltsin, Boris 220
Yerkes Observatory xvii, 2, 12, 186
Young, Charles A. 5
Young, John 146, 148, 153, 170, 191

Zalyotin, Sergei 236
Zarya module 236
Zeeman, Pieter 12
Zeeman effect 12
Zel'dovich, Yakov 207–208, 259
Zholobov, Vitali 175
Zond spacecraft 149, 150, 152, 155–156
Zudov, Vyacheslav 175
Zvezda module 236
Zwicky, Fritz 56, *68*, *69*, 73, *73*, 74, 100, 103